PSYCHOLOGY
FROM THE STANDPOINT OF A BEHAVIORIST

PSYCHOLOGY
FROM THE STANDPOINT
OF A BEHAVIORIST

BY

JOHN B. WATSON

FORMERLY PROFESSOR OF PSYCHOLOGY, THE JOHNS HOPKINS UNIVERSITY;
EDITOR, JOURNAL OF EXPERIMENTAL PSYCHOLOGY; LECTURER,
PSYCHOLOGY NEW SCHOOL FOR SOCIAL RESEARCH

SECOND EDITION

PHILADELPHIA AND LONDON
J. B. LIPPINCOTT COMPANY

PRINTED BY J. B. LIPPINCOTT COMPANY
THE WASHINGTON SQUARE PRESS
PHILADELPHIA, U. S. A.

TO

J. McKEEN CATTELL AND ADOLF MEYER

PREFACE TO SECOND EDITION

PRINCIPAL CHANGES IN TEXT

The present volume introduces many changes in text and many additions. The first nine pages are entirely new. The section on Vision, from pages 86 to 128, are entirely new and prepared by a specialist in vision, Professor H. M. Johnson, of the Ohio State University. Considerable new material (pages 208 to 212) is given in the chapter on Glands. The author's Johns Hopkins experiments in the conditioned emotional reaction will be found on pages 233 to 236. The gist of the whole paper on thinking as expressed at the meeting of the International Congress of Philosophy and Psychology will be found on pages 346 to 356.

Since 1919, when this book was first published, behaviorism has been passing through an emotional and logical evaluation. Whether it is to become a dominant *system* of psychology or to remain merely a *methodological* approach is still not decided. The strong reaction for and against behaviorism points to the fact that psychological students are restless. Nor will they lie down and sleep, nor turn to the doings of other things until their trial and error wanderings bring an adjusting formulation.

Most of the younger psychologists realize that some such formulation as behaviorism is the only road leading to science. Functional psychology cannot help. It died of its own half-heartedness before behaviorism was born. Freudianism cannot help. Where it is more than a technique it is an emotional defense of a hero. It can never serve as a support for a scientific formulation. Hence behaviorism must be looked upon as the rough scientific clay which all must shape or else rest content with the deistic idol already fashioned and worshipped by structural psychology.

The form of behaviorism the present author has stood for is now suffering a most serious set-back at the hands of those who are structuralists at heart, yet who profess to be behaviorists—

and since behaviorism has become " respectable " many who
know little of its tenets claim to believe in it. Such half-way
behaviorism and such half-way behaviorists must necessarily
do harm to the movement because, unless its tenets are kept distinct, its terms will become cluttered-up, meaningless and obscure. This is what has happened to functional psychology. If
behaviorism is ever to stand for anything (even a distinct
method), it must make a clean break with the whole concept of
consciousness. Such a clean break is possible because the metaphysical premises of behaviorism are different from those of
structural psychology.

Behaviorism is founded upon natural science; structural
psychology is based upon a crude dualism, the roots of which
extend far back into theological mysticism. Prof. K. S.
Lashley's brilliant formulation (Psychological Review, July,
1923) of behavioristic contentions shows that any student loathe
to give up " consciousness " with all of its past complications
should find happier sailing on some other craft.

Since the origin of behaviorism is now under discussion, the
preface to the 1924 edition may fitly carry a word about the
author's connection with the behavioristic approach. His
researches in animal psychology, stimulated first by Lloyd
Morgan's work and then, more powerfully, by Thorndike led him
to his first conversational formulation in 1903. This formulation was not encouraged. He was told that it would work for
animals, but not for human beings. The author's first public
expression was in the form of a lecture before the Psychology
Department of Yale University in 1908. The sentiment there
likewise was against it. It was called psychology at a descriptive level; and the conviction was expressed that psychology
could never be satisfied with anything short of " explanation "!
How a parallelistic psychology could be explanatory was not
brought out!

The author then let his formulation rest until called upon to
give a course of public lectures at Columbia in the fall of 1912.
The paper published in the Psychological Review in March,

1913—" Psychology from the Standpoint of a Behaviorist "—
gave a part of the first of these lectures. As a result of these
lectures the author was challenged to cope with image and affection. This he attempted to do before the Psychological Semi-
nary of Columbia University in April, 1913. The paper—
" Images and Affection in Behavior "—summarizes the result
of this attempt.

The next systematic attempt at a non-controversial formulation is to be seen in the 1919 edition of this book.

The chapter on thinking became the subject of discussion at the British International Congress of Philosophy and Psychology held at Cambridge in 1920. The
author's paper—" Is Thinking Merely the Action of
Language Mechanism "—published in the October, 1920,
number of the British Journal of Psychology, attempted to
give clearer expression to his views on thinking than was done
in the 1919 book. The only attempt the author has made to
sketch a genetic experimental program which would justify behaviorism as a method, is published in The Scientific Monthly,
December, 1921 (in collaboration with Rosalie Rayner Watson)
—" Studies in Infant Psychology."

Although Professor Knight Dunlap cannot be accused of
favoring a systematic behaviorism, nevertheless his treatment of
the " image " (destructive as it is of the "centrally aroused
sensation ") was a primary factor in the formulation of the
author's paper " Image and Affection in Behavior ".

The author wishes to express his deep obligation to the firm
of J. B. Lippincott Company for long-continued patience in
meeting his wishes as to reprintings, textual changes and the like.

Malba, Long Island, New York,
    January 1, 1924

PREFACE

THROUGHOUT the preparation of this elementary text I have tried to write with the human animal in front of me. I have put down only those things that any properly trained individual can observe—it does not take a psychologist *qua* psychologist to study human activity, but it does take a trained scientist and one trained along special lines. In this conclusion I am in hearty agreement with Cattell's St. Louis address. The young student of behavioristic psychology has to endure no holy vigil before beginning to use psychological material and methods, nor does he at any time have to pass through secret initiation ceremonies before beginning research work. The key which will unlock the door of any other scientific structure will unlock the door of psychology. The differences among the various sciences now are only those necessitated by the division of labor. Until psychology recognizes this and discards everything which cannot be stated in the universal terms of science, she does not deserve her place in the sun. Behavior psychology does make this attempt for the first time. It has been called physiology, muscle-twitch psychology and biology, but if it helps us to throw off the shackles of the present-day conventional psychology and teaches us to face the human being as he is and to deal frankly with him, what name it is given will not be a matter of much consequence. Nor does the author claim behavior psychology as a creation of his own. It has had rapid development and is a direct outgrowth of the work on animal behavior. It is purely an American production and the attempts of Titchener to tie it up with past "revolts" in psychology and of Miss Washburn to link it with the so-called objectivism of Beer, Bethe, von Uexküll, Nuel and other continental writers are based upon an insufficient knowledge of its tenets. Those so-called objectivists, so far as concerns their human psychology,—and this is true of Bechterew as well,—are perfectly orthodox parallelists. While behavior psychology borrows the conditioned reflex methods from Pavlow and Bechterew, and its

courage to face all aspects of human behavior from the psychopathologists, it is neither an objective psychology in Bechterew's
sense nor a modified system of psycho-analysis.

The present volume does some violence to the traditional
classification of psychological topics and to their conventional
treatment. For example, the reader will find no discussion of
consciousness and no reference to such terms as sensation, perception, attention, will, image and the like. These terms are in
good repute, but I have found that I can get along without them
both in carrying out investigations and in presenting psychology
as a system to my students. I frankly do not know what they
mean, nor do I believe that any one else can use them consistently.
I have retained such terms as thinking and memory, but I have
carefully re-defined them in conformity with behavioristic psychology. It is possible to retain attention, to re-define it and
make it serve as a framework for presenting certain aspects both
of the acquisition of any given type of organization and its later
functioning. I have not done so because in an elementary text
the less abstracting of partial functions one can make the better
is the result for the student. Such abstractions are necessary for
pedagogical reasons, but one should strive to get the beginner to
view the organism as a whole as rapidly as possible and to see
in the performance of each and all its acts the working of an
integrated personality. I have tried to do this, but for the sake
of clearness I have clung to the genetic method rather closely
in the hope that if the student could grasp the genesis of the
various types of organization he could put the organism together
for himself. I should like to have had more space to consider the
totally integrated individual in action, but by the time one has
emphasized the necessary part activities, such as instinct, emotions and habits, one has all but exceeded the limits of an elementary text. Another reason which deters me from enlarging upon
this aspect of psychology is that the discussion of total activity
involves a frankness in dealing with human nature which the
American school public is not yet educated to entertain.

While the nervous system, muscles and glands have been given
somewhat detailed treatment in two chapters, it is realized that

only the specially interested student will master them. They can be omitted without injuring the continuity of the text. I have given very few neurological schemes and brain pictures in the remaining parts of the text, because, as a rule, such static pictures interfere with the student's grasp of function. At best, they are lazy substitutes for a more thorough study of the function itself.

THE AUTHOR.

BALTIMORE, MD., September, 1919.

ACKNOWLEDGMENTS

My heaviest obligation is to Dr. Adolf Meyer and to the staff of the Phipps Psychiatric Clinic before whom the manuscript was read as it was prepared. In numerous instances, under the kindly criticism received there, the text has been altered for the better. Captain H. M. Johnson, Dr. K. S. Lashley, Dr. J. L. Ulrich and Dr. N. D. C. Lewis have given generously of their time in reading the manuscript and proof. Each one has made helpful suggestions. I am greatly indebted to Prof. Max Broedel of the Art Department of the Johns Hopkins Medical School and to two of his assistants, Miss G. L. Meakin and Miss A. Motter, who, under his direction, made the excellent drawings of the nervous system after Dr. Florence Sabin had kindly made the dissections. Miss Meakin also made the drawings of the larynx after Dr. Warren Lewis had placed the material at our disposal. Dr. Samuel M. Burka has assisted me greatly in the preparation of the cuts and photographs of the infants.

In 1917, upon recommendation of Dr. J. McK. Cattell, the sum of one hundred dollars was appropriated by the Committee on Grants for Research of the American Association for the Advancement of Science for my assistance in studying the development of reflexes and instincts in infants. The expenses for the genetic work summarized in the text were defrayed in part by the above grant. I wish to make a grateful acknowledgment for this aid.

Finally, I have borrowed generously from many authors. Where the material has been often quoted in the past I have made no reference to the author. Where it is of the research type I have usually put the author's name in parentheses with no further reference. The student hungering for further work cannot be too early trained to use the Psychological Index.

CONTENTS

PSYCHOLOGY
FROM THE STANDPOINT OF A BEHAVIORIST

CHAPTER I

PROBLEMS AND SCOPE OF PSYCHOLOGY

Mediæval Tradition Has Kept Psychology From Becoming a Science.—Psychology, up to very recent times, has been held so rigidly under the dominance both of traditional religion and of philosophy—the two great bulwarks of mediævalism—that it has never been able to free itself and become a natural science. Chemistry and physics have freed themselves. Zoology and physiology are now in the process of becoming emancipated. That they are encountering difficulties is shown by the almost perennial agitation against the teaching of evolution.

In the late sixties an attempt was made to make an experimental science of psychology. The boast was voiced that the psychology growing out of this attempt had become a science without a soul—that is, a natural science. Notwithstanding the establishment of many laboratories both here and abroad, it has never been able to substantiate this claim.

Its Subject Matter Not Objective.—The reason for its failure was largely its limitation of subject matter and choice of method. Psychology limited its subject matter to the so-called states of consciousness—their analysis and synthesis. " States of consciousness," like the so-called phenomena of spiritualism, are not objectively verifiable and for that reason can never become data for science.

In all other sciences the facts of observation are objective, verifiable and can be reproduced and controlled by all trained observers. For example, the physiologist may note an increase in respiration in his animal under certain conditions; the physiological chemist may find that the increased rate is due to the presence of a certain chemical circulating in the blood; the

1

physical chemist can, after proper study, find out the exact constitution of that chemical substance, its weight, structure and ionic relationships. In other words, data of science (verified observation) are common property and the methods of science are the same in principle, however much they may vary in form. There is, however, among the true natural sciences a division of labor and a division of needs. We can illustrate this. Thyroxin—the thyroid hormone—will call out one group of experiments from the animal physiologist, another from the medical specialist in glandular diseases, and still another from the physical chemist. Psychology, on the other hand, as a science of "consciousness," has no such community of data. It cannot share them, nor can other sciences use them. Not only can psychologist A not share his data with physicist A, but also he cannot share them with his brother psychologist B. Even if they existed, they would exist as isolated, unusuable "mental" curiosities.[1]

Introspection a Serious Bar to Progress.—The psychologists' use of "introspection" as its principal method has been another very serious bar to progress. The method of introspection—the looking inward to see what goes on in one's own mind— has been the principal method employed by structural psychologists. One is supposed to need several years' training in a psychological laboratory in the observation of the kaleidoscopic changes that go on every moment in states of consciousness before one's introspection takes on a scientific character. This training supposedly gives one facility to take one's own states of consciousness and subject them to analysis. In other words, the introspectionist claims to become adept in reducing complex states to still simpler states until finally he reaches irreducible data called sensations and affective tones.

So far the psychologist on this basis has never been able to do anything but analyze—and only his own past states at that. Synthesis, the method *sine qua non* of modern science has been found to be impossible in psychology. All that introspective psychology has been able to contribute is the assertion that

---

[1] The behaviorist finds no evidence for " mental existences " or " mental processes " of any kind.

mental states are made up of several thousand irreducible units; for example, the thousands of sensation units like redness, greenness, coldness, warmth, and the like, and their ghosts called images, and the affective irreducibles, pleasantness and unpleasantness (possibly six of the latter if we include strain and relaxation, and excitement and calm).

But the truth or falsity of this assertion is inconsequential, since no other human being can make an introspective observation upon anyone but himself. Whether there are ten irreducible sensations or a hundred thousand (even granting their existence), whether there are two affective tones or fifty, matters not one whit to that organized body of world-wide data we call science.

Introspective Psychology no Longer Serviceable.—The psychology begun by Wundt has thus failed to become a science and has still more deplorably failed in contributing anything of a scientifically usable kind to human nature—in helping people to understand why they behave as they do and how to modify their behavior; and how to bring up the youths in their charge to act in such a way that the youths can live, move and have their being in society, and not have their own individuality swamped and flattened out by society.

Psychology Needs a Re-examination of Its Premises.— One reason why psychology made this false start under Wundt is because it would not bury its past. It tried to hang on to tradition with one hand and to push forward as a science with the other. Before progress could be made in astronomy, it had to bury astrology; neurology had to bury phrenology; and chemistry had to bury alchemy. But the social sciences, psychology, sociology, political science and economics, will not bury their " medicine men." According to the opinion of many scientific men today, psychology even to exist longer, not to speak of becoming a true natural science, must bury subjective subject matter, introspective method and present terminology. Consciousness, with its structural units, the irreducible sensations (and their ghosts, the images) and their affective tones, and its processes, attention, perception, conception, is but an indefinable phrase. Whatever scientific value there is in the colossal number of volumes written in terms of consciousness can

be better defined and expressed when the psychological problems which gave rise to them are solved by genuine objective
scientific methods.

**Behaviorism—the Natural Science Approach to Psychol-
ogy.**—Believing that these arguments against the prevailing
and current presuppositions of psychology were correct,
behaviorism, first showing its head in 1912, attempted to make
a fresh, clean start in psychology, breaking both with current
theories and with traditional concepts and terminology. For
the behaviorist, psychology is that division of natural science
which takes human behavior—the doings and sayings, both
learned and unlearned, of people as its subject matter. It is the
study of what people do from even before birth until death.

Every human being is active throughout the whole of his life.
Activity begins at the beginning of embryological development
and continues without interruption until death. Man's activity
during this period has its high tides and low tides. During sleep,
coma or paralysis it seems reduced to the absolute minimum,
both in amount and in kind. Again both amount and kind of
activity vary from infancy through childhood, adolescence,
adulthood and old age.

Ceaseless Organization and Reorganization of Behavior.—
During the first year of man's existence we find some, but com-
paratively few, highly organized unlearned acts (" instincts ").
We find a multitudinous group of poorly integrated reflexes
consisting of kicking, slashing with the hands and feet, and
wriggling of the whole body, and of movements of the vocal
cords. Two or three years later we find that some of the unlearned
acts have come over intact, others appear in modified form, while
still others have been lost. We find progress too in the coördination or chaining together of the loosely knit acts into what we
call " learnings " or habits. He now reacts definitely and con-
nectedly, with hands, feet, trunk, to a variety of situations. He
reacts definitely with words and groups of words to many different verbal situations.

When we examine him still later we find him possessed of a
still more complex system of habits but almost wholly different
from those he had when he was last under observation. He

dresses himself, speaks conventionally, has established social habits, goes to school, reads, and writes.

If we examine him at maturity, the complexity in his habit organization seems too great for us to measure in any way. He indulges in many acts of skill, has a well developed system of vocational activity, has married and is rearing a family, has become interested in world politics, in schools and the like.

Behaviorism Attempts to Find the Principles Underlying Changes in Behavior.—Behavioristic psychology attempts to formulate, through systematic observation and experimentation, the generalizations, laws and principles which underly man's behavior. When a human being acts—does something with arms, legs or vocal cords—there must be an invariable group of antecedents serving as a " cause " of the act. For this group of antecedents the term situation or stimulus is a convenient term. When an individual is placed face to face with some situation—a fire, a menacing animal or human, a change in fortune—he will do something, even if he only stands still or faints. Psychology is thus confronted immediately with two problems—the one of predicting the probable causal situation or stimulus giving rise to the response; the other, given the situation, of predicting the probable response.

(1) *Observing the Response, to Predict the Probable Situation.*—The first problem is to study man in action, from birth to old age, in such a way that the behaviorist, with reasonable certainty when watching the individual behave can tell what the situation or stimulus is that calls out the act—*i.e.*, can scientifically define the stimulus.

Let use take a very homely illustration: A neighbor sees his friend leaving the house at 7:54 in the morning just in time to catch the Commuters' Special at 8:15. Two blocks from the house the man stops, searches in all his pockets, then suddenly runs back to the house. The neighbor says: " Humph, George forgot his commutation ticket again. He's always doing it." The observer has predicted the stimulus or situation calling forth the act, partly through the present behavior of his friend and partly through the data he has on the past behavior of his friend. This illustration is so common-place that it seems a travesty to use it as an example of scientific but practical procedure. And yet problems similar in kind, but requiring more knowledge to make serviceable answers, are constantly confronting psychologists. Why do men go to war? Why do some men fight evolution? Why did George Smith leave his wife? Why do employees leave my organization after one or two months of service? Why does Henry Doe live in the gutter when he is strong and has a good technical education? Why will a democratic nation every now and then elect a non-entity for a president? All such behavior has just as definable a series of '' causes '' as has a volcanic eruption which engulfs a hundred cities. This side of psychology has been written about and studied in a hit or miss way by sociologists, economists, journalists and many others. These students feel that they have a right (and they have as good a right as, if not better than, the present-day psychologists) to write about this aspect of behavior. Unfortunately the answers returned are rarely serviceable. The explanation is given in terms of some phases of the original nature of man about which we have almost no facts. To answer them correctly we need to have definite reproduceable data concerning man's unlearned behavior; on what various learnings he has annexed; on what traditional factors are influencing his group; on the present social customs he follows; on what effects schools and churches have had upon his development. To answer any of the '' whys '' adequately about human activity we need to study man as the chemist needs to study some new organic compound. Psychologically, man is still a reacting piece of unanalyzed protoplasm.

(2) *Given the Situation, to Predict the Probable Response.*— The other equally important aspect of psychology is so to experiment with man's behavior from infancy to old age that, given the situation or stimulus, we are able to predict the probable response.

Socially we meet many practical problems in this aspect of behavior psychology. Russia has a Soviet form of government following immediately upon hundreds of years of monarchical government of an autocratic kind. What changes in behavior will this situation bring in the lives of the individuals in Russia?

Again in this country a new situation has been set up by the enactment of the Eighteenth Amendment. Before establishing this situation we should have been able to predict the changes in behavior such an amendment would bring. What effect will the recently established liberal divorce laws in Norway and Sweden have upon the sex conduct of individuals?*

On the individual side questions constantly arise. If A's wife, who is constantly ill, should suddenly die, would he become disorganized? What would be the effect of sudden wealth upon B? A man is doing his job poorly; what would be the effect on his conduct if we gave him a severe raking over the coals? Would he improve his work, or would it suffer still more?

Thousands of questions of this practical kind are up before not only psychologists, but also up before the man on the street. Human life goes on. Some kind of prediction has to be made as to what the result of a certain situation will be. But until psychology becomes a science and has amassed data on behavior resulting from situations experimentally set up, prediction of behavior resulting from daily life situations will have to be of the hit or miss kind that it has been since the race of man began.

Control of Human Behavior.—Every scientist feels that he makes progress in his field just to the extent to which he can gain control over the material with which he works—as examples: the harnessing of the tide, protection from lightning by lightning rods, the experimental production of lightning and rain, dissipation of fog.

The psychologist likewise, having chosen human behavior as his material, feels that he makes progress only as he can manipulate or control it. Has this individual within his repertoire of acts gained through general schooling the possibility of being

---

* When far-reaching social situations are set up, is an expert in human behavior called in? No city or corporation would build a dam across a sizeable stream now without consulting experts on agriculture, forestry, etc., to predict what the probable effect would be upon the soil and vegetation of the country above the dam. But here loss of money can be avoided, lawsuits can be saved. If social blunders are made only human sacrifice and unhappiness are involved.

developed into an artist, a singer, a business executive? Could a wonderful golf player be made of this man? If so, what steps should we take, what technique should we employ to establish the necessary habits rapidly and so that they will endure permanently?

Again we find him filled with fears, unduly shy, bashful, stammering. Can we change this behavior? If so, what technique shall we follow? On the other hand, could we put a wholesome fear in this child that plays with snakes, hugs every dog he sees and picks up every strange cat?

In this work there is involved not only ability to predict situation from response, and probable response given the situation, but the experimental manipulation of stimulus and the creation of response—stimuli must be added to or subtracted from until appropriate response is attained and, if the desired or expected response is not in the repertoire of the individual, it must be established if there is raw material of a kind to utilize for building it.

Here, then, we find a true and legitimate field for experimental study of our human material. It must be experimental and we must some time have laboratories. Until we know more about the control of behavior during the tender years of infancy, it seems almost a dangerous experiment to bring up a child. The old argument that a good many millions of children have been successfully reared in the past few millions of years has just about broken down in the light of the now generally recognized lack of success of most people in making satisfactory adjustments to society.

The behaviorist believes that only systematic, long-sustained, genetic studies upon the human species begun in infancy and continued until past adolescence, will ever give us this experimental control over human conduct so badly needed both for general social control and growth and for individual happiness. In our genetic studies on infants in chapters VI and VII, both the need for this work and its possibilities will be more apparent.

This brief summary of the more general phases of psychology should convince us of two things: First, that every human individual needs the data and laws of behaviorism for organizing his own daily life and conduct. Secondly, that since society acting as it has in the past purely upon the basis of mediæval tradition, or at best only on a blundering trial-and-error basis, has made such slow progress in understanding and controlling the phenomena of human behavior, human behavior should be made the object of intense scientific study.

To point out to what extent methods now exist for a thoroughgoing scientific objective study of human behavior will be the principal objective in this volume.

Scientific Procedure.

The Detailed Subject Matter of Scientific Psychology.— As a science phychology puts before herself the task of unraveling the complex factors involved in the development of human behavior from infancy to old age, and of finding the laws for the regulation of behavior. To solve such problems we must necessarily study the simple and complex things which call out action in man; how early in life he can react to the various simple and complex sense stimuli; at what age he usually puts on the various instincts, and what the situations are which call them out. Just what is the pattern of his instinctive acts—that is, does the human being, apart from training, do any complex acts instinctively as do the lower animals? If so, what is man's full equipment of instincts? When does emotional activity manifest itself? and what are the situations which call it out? and what special acts can be observed in emotional behavior? How soon can we observe the beginnings of habits in infants? What special methods can we develop for rapidly and securely implanting and retaining the body and speech habits which society demands?

Stimulus and Response.—This general description of the subject matter of psychology helps us very little as regards the analysis of particular problems in conduct and behavior. In order to plan an experimental attack upon any problem in psychology we must first reduce it to its simplest terms. If we look over the list of problems in human behavior given in the preceding paragraph, and at our practical examples, we shall see that there are common factors running through all forms of human acts. In each adjustment there is always both a *response or act* and a *stimulus or situation* which calls out that response. Without going too far beyond our facts, it seems possible to say that the stimulus is always provided by the environment, external to the body, or by the movements of man's own muscles and the secretions of his glands; finally, that the responses always follow relatively immediately upon the presentation or incidence of the stimulus. These are really assumptions, but they seem to be basal ones for psychology. Before we finally accept or reject them we shall have to examine into both the nature of the stimulus or situation, and of the response. If we provisionally accept them we may say that the goal of psychological study is the *ascertaining of such data and laws that, given the stimulus, psychology can predict what the response will be; or, on the other hand, given the response, it can specify the nature of the effective stimulus.*

Use of the Term Stimulus.—We use the term *stimulus* in psychology as it is used in physiology. Only in psychology we have to extend somewhat the usage of the term. In the psychological laboratory, when we are dealing with relatively simple factors, such as the effect of ether waves of different lengths, the effect of sound waves, etc., and are attempting to isolate their effects upon the adjustments of men, we speak of stimuli. On the other hand, when the factors leading to reactions are more complex, as, for example, in the social world, we speak of *situations*. A situation is, of course, upon final analysis, resolvable into a complex group of stimuli. As examples of stimuli we may name such things as rays of light of different wave lengths; sound waves differing in amplitude, length, phase, and combination; gaseous particles given off in such small diameters that they affect the membrane of the nose; solutions which contain particles of matter of such size that the taste buds are thrown into action; solid objects which affect the skin and mucous membrane; radiant stimuli which call out temperature response; noxious stimuli, such as cutting, pricking, and those injuring tissue generally. Finally, movements of the muscles and activity in the glands themselves serve as stimuli by acting upon the afferent nerve endings in the moving muscles.

It must be emphasized here that only under the rarest experimental conditions can we stimulate the organism with a single stimulus. Life presents stimuli in confusing combinations. As you write you are stimulated by a complex system—perspiration pours from your brow, the pen has a tendency to slip from your grasp; the words you write are focussed upon your retinæ; the chair offers stimulation, and finally the noises from the street constantly impinge upon your ear-drum. But far more important, delicate instruments would show that, though you are not speaking aloud, your vocal mechanisms—tongue, throat and laryngeal muscles—are in constant motion, moving in habitual trains; these laryngeal and throat movements serve largely as the stimuli for releasing the writing movements of the hands. The fact that you are here in the lecture room, facing your instructor and surrounded by your classmates, is another very important element. The world of stimulation is thus seen to be exceedingly complex. It is convenient to speak of a total mass of stimulating factors, which lead man to react as a whole, as a situation. Situations can be of the simplest kind or of the greatest complexity. It should be noted here, finally, that there are many forms of physical energy which do not directly affect our sense organs. As examples we may cite the facts that ether waves longer than $760\mu\mu$ or shorter than $397\mu\mu$ do not lead to visual reactions, and that many of the wave motions in the air are of such length or amplitude that they do not produce auditory stimulation. The inability of the human organism to respond to many possible forms of stimulation will be discussed later.

The General Nature of Response.—In a similar way we employ in psychology the physiological term "response," but again we must slightly extend its use. The movements which result from a tap on the patellar tendon, or from stroking the soles of the feet are "simple" responses which are studied both in physiology and in medicine. In psychology our study, too, is sometimes concerned with simple responses of these types, but more often with several complex responses taking place simultaneously. In the latter case we sometimes use the popular term "act" or adjustment, meaning by that that the whole group of responses

is integrated in such a way (instinct or habit) that the individual
does something which we have a name for, that is, "takes food,"
"builds a house," "swims," "writes a letter," "talks." [2] Psychology is not concerned with the goodness or badness of acts,
or with their successfulness, as judged by occupational or moral
standards. Because a man fails by his separate acts to get his
food, to build his house, to work out his mathematical problem,
or to live in harmony with his wife, is no reason for rejecting him
as a psychological subject. We study him for his *reaction possibilities and without prejudice;* the discovery of the fact that he
will make only abortive attempts to meet and control certain
aspects of his environment is an important part of our task; just
as important as being able to state that he can make certain other
types of adjustment. "Successful" adjustments, "good" acts,
"bad" acts, are terms really which society uses. Every social
age sets up certain standards of action, but these standards
change from cultural epoch to cultural epoch. Hence they are
not psychological standards. Reaction possibilities, however, on
the average probably remain about the same from eon to eon. It
lies well within the bounds of probability that if we were able to
obtain a new-born baby belonging to the dynasty of the Pharaohs,
and were to bring him up along with other lads in Boston, he
would develop into the same kind of college youth that we find
among the other Harvard students. His chances for success in
life would probably not be at all different from those of his
classmates. The results obtained from the scientific analysis of
reaction in the human being should fit any cultural age. It is
part of the function of the psychologist to tell whether a given
individual has the reaction possibilities within him to meet the
standards of that cultural age, and the most rapid way of bringing him to act in accordance with them. The fact that social

[2] But it should be well understood that whatever the man does under
stimulation is a response or adjustment—blushing, increased heart-beat,
change in respiration, etc., are definite part adjustments. We have
names for only a few thousand of the total possible number of such adjustments. The term adjustment is used by most writers to refer to the
doing of one of these *named acts.* In this volume the terms adjustment,
response, and reaction are used almost interchangeably.

values (group *mores*) change puts ever new burdens upon the psychologist, because every change in the *mores* means a different situation, to which man has to respond by a different combination of acts, and any new set of acts must be incorporated into and integrated with the rest of the action systems of the individual. The problems put up to psychology are those of deciding whether the individual can meet the new standards, and for determining and developing methods of instructing him.

Motor and Glandular Indicators of Response.—What is it that the psychologist can observe? *Behavior*, of course. But behavior on analysis is the separate systems of reactions that the individual makes to his environment. When we come to study the mechanics of such adjustments we find that they depend upon the integration of reflexes connecting the receptors with the muscles and glands. It should be emphasized here that objective psychology does not analyze such integrations to the bitter end except where the problem demands it. Concrete, whole activities are as important to the behaviorist as to other psychologists (see page 40).

The unicellular organisms have no separate muscular or nervous systems. Yet a part of their one cell must be specialized in a motor as well as in a sensory way, since these organisms do move in response to stimuli—to light, gravity, heat, cold, electricity, etc. As one passes higher in the animal scale one finds that special sense-organ tissues (receptors) develop, and along with them both motor or effective organs, and neurones connecting receptors and effectors. Action in such cases becomes sharper, more localized, more immediate, and at the same time more sustained. Furthermore, as we pass still further up the scale, glands begin to develop. Glands, like muscles, are responsive organs, and special glandular action takes place whenever motor action takes place. The activity of the glands in turn reacts upon the muscular system and affects its functioning (p. 218). Furthermore, there are two kinds of muscles, striped and unstriped. The striped muscles move the arms, legs, trunk, tongue and larynx. The unstriped muscles control largely the blood-vessels, intestines, the organs of elimination and sex. Usually when we speak of response we mean that the organism goes forward to right or left, or retracts as a whole, that it eats, drinks, fights, builds houses, or engages in trade. But these patent and easily observable changes do not exhaust the term response, as we pointed out on page 12. We should mean by response the total striped and unstriped muscular and glandular changes which follow upon a given stimulus. Our problem of the moment determines which movement shall be studied in relative isolation; in man, though, interest has been largely centered in the integration of separate responses; in getting him to form some habit—that is, to do something with arms or legs or vocal cords. It is important to get at the outset a comprehensive notion of response. A man or animal may stand stock still under stimulation, but we should not say that there was no response. Close observation shows that there are changes in the tension of the muscles, in respiration, in circulation, and in secretion.

The General Classification of Responses.—The various possibilities of reaction are thus seen to be vast; so vast, indeed, that it would seem at first sight as though any classification would be impossible. We can at least find a convenient grouping which will serve both for discussion and for setting experimental problems. Most reactions may be looked upon as falling into one of four main classes:

1. Explicit habit responses: as examples we cite unlocking a door, tennis playing, violin playing, building houses, talking easily to people, staying on good terms with the members of your own and the opposite sex.

2. Implicit habit responses: *"thinking," by which we mean subvocal talking,* general body language habits, bodily sets or attitudes which are not easily observable without instrumentation or experimental aid; the system of conditioned reflexes in the various glands and unstriped muscular mechanisms—for example, conditioned salivary reflexes.

3. Explicit hereditary responses: including man's observable instinctive and emotional reactions as seen, for example, in grasping, sneezing, blinking and dodging, and in fear, rage, love.

4. Implicit hereditary responses: this includes, of course, the whole system of endocrine or ductless gland secretions (p. 181),

changes in circulation, etc., so largely studied by physiology. Here again instrumentation or experimental aid is necessary before observation can be made.

These various types of response will be studied in detail in later chapters. The classification as a whole should be clear, with the possible exception of 2 (implicit habit responses). This group is so important and so generally neglected in discussion that we shall single it out here for brief mention in advance of the chapter in which it is entered into with some care.

What Man is Doing When Not Overtly Acting.—With a highly specialized organism like man, even careful observation often fails to show any overt response. A man may sit motionless at his desk with pen in hand and paper before him. In popular parlance we may say he is idle or "thinking," but our *assumption* is that his muscles are really as active and possibly more active than if he were playing tennis. But what muscles? Those muscles which have been trained to act when he is in such a situation, his laryngeal, tongue, and speech muscles generally.[3] Those muscles are as active and are carrying out as orderly a system of movements as if he were executing a sonata on the piano; they are doing it well or ill, depending upon the training he has had along the particular lines which engage him. While we cannot at present watch the play of this implicit stream of words, there is no reason for hypothecating a mystery about it. Could we bring "thinking" out for observation as readily as we can tennis playing or rowing, the need of "explaining" it would disappear. We shall see later that efforts have been made to bring such responses under experimental control. But entirely apart from our present unreadiness to make observation on implicit habits, we find a certain way of arriving indirectly at the same end: *implicit language habits,* by methods which we shall study, come to issue finally in overt action. By watching the easily observable explicit habits and instincts of an individual keenly enough, and for a sufficient stretch of time, and under varying enough conditions, we can obtain the necessary data for most psychological requirements.

---

[3] Indeed, the whole glandular and muscular systems are contributory.

Scientific Methods Contrasted with Practical Procedure.—
Having now examined at some length into the general nature of
both stimulus and response, we should be prepared to understand the object of a psychological experiment and to contrast
the scientific procedure with the common-sense or practical procedure which we discussed at the beginning of the chapter. We
shall take up almost at random some definite illustrative psychological problems, and the methods of solving them. Our first
problem is *to find out what the reactions of a six-months-old
infant are to living, furry animals.* We first arrange the situation (complex group of stimuli, p. 10). The infant is held by
its mother in a well-lighted room. We observe first that the
infant is smiling, and comfortably disposed. Then, one after
another, we present a white rat, a dog, a cat, a white rabbit,
beetles, and a snake. We next record accurately and separately
the reactions to these objects. The infant, which has only learned
to reach out for objects a short time before, slowly puts out first
one hand and then the other. The smile leaves his face, but no
crying or withdrawing of the hands or external secretions follows. These are only the more easily observed responses. Other
changes take place undoubtedly, in the internal glands, circulation, respiration, etc. It depends upon our immediate problem as
to where the emphasis in observation shall fall in our record of
reaction changes. In this case our problem was to determine
whether there were any overt instinctive tendencies on the baby's
part to react against or withdraw the hands or whole body from
live animals. Our problem might very well have led us into
observing the changes in the eyes, respiration, blood-pressure,
salivation, or in the endocrine glands, or in several of these at
once. Again, it should be noted that our problem is not so simple
as it seems at first sight. Suppose we had found that the baby
did withdraw from the objects, began to cry, void urine, or
attempt to hide behind the mother's clothing—could we have
concluded that there was an instinctive reaction against live
furry animals? *Not without delving into the baby's past.* If
we had had the child under constant observation, and found no
record of previous acquaintanceship with live animals, our

answer would be that the observable responses were probably instinctive. But if, on the other hand, we found that the child had been severely bitten by a cat only two days before our test, our conclusions would have to wait upon more extended observation. Nor can we, from the behavior of this one child, draw any conclusions as to what other children of the same age will do, or what this child might do at a slightly different age or when tested under different conditions. Before generalizations can be made many children should be brought under systematic observation.

As another example of a somewhat more restricted type, let us take the case of a man whose every-day behavior has led us to suspect the normality of his responses to monochromatic (colored) light. Common-sense has nothing to say; it can give no adequate report on him. His mistakes may be due to one or many things. We take him into the laboratory where monochromatic light is under control, and we put him in situations where he has to react to the lights in pairs, and where each one of the lights can be widely varied in energy. In the course of the investigation we find that when there is a certain energy relation obtaining between the red and the green light he can no longer react to them differentially (that is to say, they do not offer different stimulating values). We note further that we can find a white light of a certain intensity to which he reacts as he does to either of the monochromatic lights. But at no energy relation between any other two colors can we break down his differential responses. We conclude after this careful study that the man is red-green blind, that is, that he reacts to red and green as he does to certain intensities of white light.[4] Let us take another example, and this time from the field of vocational psychology. Suppose that the telephone directory of a large city is getting entirely too bulky and complex for men to handle easily. What is the best method for obviating this? The telephone people and the psy-

---

[4] If we find by repeated tests that the anomaly is more than temporary, we are right in advising this man that he will be handicapped if he enters certain occupations, e.g., locomotive and marine engineering, geology, advertising, etc. In other words, the results of psychological experimentation are as immediately practicable as are results in any other scientific field.

2

chologists work together. The psychologist may suggest printing
in smaller type and four columns to the page instead of three.
These and many other possible suggestions may lead to a solution of the problem. But the matter has to be put to severe trial
both at the hands of individuals trained to look up names in a
directory and individuals having no more training than has the
general public. *Systematic* trial and error is the procedure here,
with statistical treatment of the results. In the end it is found
that a four-column page with a certain amount of spacing between
the lines of print makes the directory not only 20 per cent. less
bulky, but also one in which the subscribers can find names 10
per cent. more rapidly (Baird).

THE DIVISIONS OF PSYCHOLOGY AND THE RELATIONS OF PSYCHOL-
OGY TO THE OTHER SCIENCES.

The Various Fields of Psychology.—It is just as difficult to
draw a hard-and-fast line between the different branches of
psychology as between the different branches of biology and
of physics. Practical and theoretical interests determine where a
man will throw the emphasis of his observation. All scientific
psychology is experimental, or is at least carried out under such
conditions that rigid and controlled observation is possible. All
psychology is "genetic" in the sense that we have to go back to
the child and contrast it with animals in order to determine what
native systems of integrations belong peculiarly to man. For
purposes of specialization we speak of human psychology as being
made up of *individual, vocational, child, folk, educational, legal,
pathological* and *social* psychology. We may speak of any of
these special branches as being "applied." For our purposes
we need not enter into a separate characterization of these special
branches. The remaining chapters in this book attempt to deal
generally with the simpler results, problems, and methods in
common use in psychology. We shall not emphasize, except here
and there, the particular branch to which such material belongs.

Relation of Psychology to Physics.—Both physiology and
psychology are dependent (as is every other science at bottom)
upon physics for the control of apparatus and of stimulus. It
is essential for a research student in psychology now to know the

general facts about wave motion; as, for example, heat, sound and light. It is important to know how to install and use simple electrical instruments, galvanometers, thermal couples, and photometers.

Relation to Neurology.—It might be supposed that psychology would lean most heavily upon neurology. Indeed, this has been the general assumption in the past. Gradually we are coming to the point of view that psychology is more dependent upon such subjects as physiology and certain branches of medicine such as hygiene, endocrinology, the chemistry of metabolism, pediatrics and psychiatry, than upon neural anatomy. In the past we have been too content with making brain pictures and mechanical neural schema to always look carefully enough at our behavior facts. We need in psychology all of the available facts that the *neurologists* can give us, but we can very well leave out of consideration those ingenious puzzle pictures that compare the action of the central nervous system with a series of pipes and valves, sponges, electric switchboards, and the like. Some notion of the elementary guiding principles in neurology is certainly essential to the beginner in psychology, such as the way sense organs are connected with the central nervous system, and the central nervous system with the muscular and glandular systems. In Chapter IV we touch upon some of the more elementary features connected with the arrangement and functioning of reflex pathways.

Relation of Psychology to Physiology.—It has been claimed by some that behavior psychology is really physiology. That this is not the case appears from even a casual examination of the respective scopes of the two provinces. Physiology teaches us concerning the functions of the special organs. For purposes of experimentation and exposition, the heart, liver, lungs, circulation, respiration, and other organs are isolated, and they are discussed as though they functioned in an isolated way. Muscle-nerve preparations are taken out and their properties investigated; glands and their action are likewise experimented upon. All of the functions of the bodily organs are gone over from this standpoint. It is not meant to assume that physiologists deal wholly with organs in isolation. Certain combined

processes are studied, such as metabolism, digestion, effects of
poisons, etc., but nowhere in physiology do we get the organism,
as it were, put back together again and tested in relation to its
environment as a whole.

From our discussion of the scope of psychology we are now
prepared to see that when the physiologist has learned all that
he can about the functioning of the separate organs of the body
of man, he has encroached upon our field only in a very slight
degree. Our task begins only when the physiologist puts the
separate organs together again, and turns the whole (man) over
to us. The physiologist *qua* physiologist knows nothing of the
total situations in the daily life of an individual that shape his
action and conduct. He may teach us all there is to know about
the mechanism of stepping, but it is not his task to determine
whether man walks before he crawls, the age at which walking
begins, whether walking begins earlier in boys than in girls, or
whether defective children walk at a later age than normal
children. Again, he may teach us a great deal about the functions of the kidneys, the bladder, and of the sphincter control
of the latter; but of the special situations (outside of disease
entities) which may lead to incontinence in children, his science
teaches him nothing, nor of methods of controlling this mal-
adjustment. In studying psychological functions—for example,
the emotions—it does not help us very much to try to picture
what chemical and neural processes go on in the brain. We get
a very incomplete but a somewhat better view if we consider
what glandular action goes on during emotional states. But
even glandular action is not easily observed by methods which
are known to-day. We can, however, study the reaction states
we popularly call sadness, elation, moroseness, rage, fear and
love, from the standpoint of what the organism can do in these
states, and whether the smooth running of the general system of
organized habits is facilitated or disturbed by the presence of
emotional activity. We can, further, often determine by a study
of the life history of the individual how frequently such disturbances come about, and can trace out the causes or factors
leading to their onset. Physiology has nothing to tell us of the
character and personality of different individuals nor of their

emotional stability or lack of emotional control, nor as to what extent their present place in life is dependent upon their upbringing. Physiology tells us nothing of man's capacity to form and retain habits, nor of the complexity of man's habit organization. Hence, if we wish to predict whether an individual is capable of meeting or rising above the environment to which he is at present but poorly adjusted, we should have to go to psychology and not to physiology for our answer. In thus emphasizing the entire theoretical independence of the two fields, let us not set up a false impression of antagonism. Physiology is psychology's closest friend among the biological sciences. We can hardly move a step in psychology without using physiological data. But in this we are not different from the other biological sciences, or indeed from medicine itself.

Overlapping of the Two Fields.—Occasionally we find physiologists who have dealt with functions which overlap the field of human behavior. As examples, we cite the work of Cannon on the bodily effect of violent emotional disturbances, and of Carlson and others on the question of the reactions which are present in the stomach in the absence of food. Where the two fields overlap most, however, is probably in the study of the conditioned motor secretion reflexes and in the realm of sensory physiology. This latter topic seems no longer to seriously interest the physiologists, and where they have shown interest in it—in this country at least—it has been mainly pedagogical. Most of the work in sensory physiology has been done by psychologists. Until the recent work of Pavlow and Bechterew and their students, physiologists have shown little interest in the study of habit formation, which general topic is one of our central ones. In general it may be said that there is some overlapping in the two fields, but that it does not keep them from being separate disciplines. In cases where there is an overlapping, the methods and points of view of the two sciences in no wise differ.

Relation of Psychology to Medicine.—Up to the present time psychology has been of only slight service to psychiatry and medicine generally. It should form a background for the whole field of medicine. But it has dealt hitherto so largely with specu-

lations and with philosophical considerations that its usefulness
for this purpose has been seriously restricted.

The physician, whether medical specialist or general prac-
titioner, would like to know something about the method of
approaching and handling his patients. He must encounter—
and he must be prepared to encounter—such things as stubborn-
ness and unyieldingness in his human subjects, and he must
learn to study his patients in relation to their present environment, and to go back into their life history for an understanding and explanation of such attitudes. He must learn how to
size up his patients, and to get at the details of their individuality and characteristics. He must be able to tell whether the
patient can do what he is told to do, and whether he has sufficient assets to meet the environment in which he has to live, and
whether he has sufficient assets to rise out of the environment
which is unsuited to him. These facts on character adaptation
cannot be expressed in any other terms than behavior terms.
There are, to be sure, factors which concern every one who has
to deal with his fellow-man, but on account of the intimate relationship existing between the patient and his physician they are
of especial importance to the latter. The psychiatrist has not
neglected these factors; indeed, it has been due to him that they
have been emphasized at all, and it is largely through his efforts
that we have a well-developed and systematic technic for isolating
the factors of importance in the life history of the patient. So
far as psychiatry is concerned, I think we can say that the psychology the psychiatrist uses is not different from the psychology
we are trying to study. The psychiatrist has to be both a physician, with a specially developed therapeutic technic, and a psychologist with special interests in certain divisions of psychology.
Psychiatry has no special need for detailed studies on reactions
to sensory stimuli. Much of the detailed work on habit formation and on the separate analysis of instincts is not of special
use to him. On the other hand, any of the material which the
psychologist may offer on the subjects of attachment and detachment of the emotions, on the genesis of instincts and habits and
their inter-relations, on the effect of age, drugs, etc., on habit

formation and retention, upon false reactions and failures in reactions, on the effect of lesions of the central nervous systems in trained animals, and the resultant success that comes from retraining them, can be utilized by the psychiatrist at once, both in a specific way and by reason of its value in helping him to size up his patients. Most psychiatrists will admit that when the proper kind of psychology is developed they can utilize directly a large part of both its methods and its materials. This appears clearly when we examine the various tests which have been devised by psychologists for evaluating the general behavior levels of individuals. Such tests in one or another form are in common use in every psychiatric clinic. Topics such as ''general behavior,'' ''stream of talk,'' ''attitude,'' ''orientation,'' ''retention'' of recent and past happenings, ''general information,'' the emotional level at which acts are carried out, are discussed in relation to every patient admitted to a psychiatric clinic.

Preparation for Psychology.—In dealing with the native equipment of man, the student will find a background of study of animal behavior a helpful one. As a further preparation for this part of his work, he will find that he needs some equipment in physiology and experimental zoölogy. His work in habit formation leads him again into physiology and pharmacology for such factors as the effect of age, drugs, chemicals and glandular extracts upon the human organism. The consideration of habit and instinct conflicts, abortive reactions and failures of adjustment generally which we see so much emphasized in tics, sympathetic chorea, hysteria, obsessions, etc., leads the psychologist into the psychiatric clinic if he wishes to prepare himself to the fullest extent. Business and law are making ever and ever larger demands upon him. Some familiarity with legal and business problems is almost essential. Finally, in order to handle adequately experimental data some training in the use of statistical methods is needed. If a start is made early enough by the student who is preparing for psychology, he can obtain training in the above related branches before he begins his special study of psychology. While to-day is a day of specialists, it should not be a day of narrow specialists.

CHAPTER II

PSYCHOLOGICAL METHODS

Introduction.—In the preceding chapter we referred several times to psychological methods and procedure. It remains to give a somewhat more extended discussion of objective methods as employed in human psychology. In the end we will find that this preliminary survey of methods will assist us in understanding the results which have been obtained in the field of psychology.[1] Psychological methods in detail are very numerous. When we come to look them over, however, we find that most of them fall within the following general classification:

I. Observation, with and without instrumental control.

II. The conditioned reflex methods.

    (*a*) Methods employed in obtaining conditioned secretion reflexes.

    (*b*) Methods employed in obtaining conditioned motor reflexes.

III. The verbal report method.

IV. Methods of testing.

These various methods are not completely independent, but the reasons for such a classification will appear after a careful consideration of the text.

---

[1] The Instructor is advised at this point to give at least two demonstration lectures on the simple forms of apparatus employed in psychology, and upon the method of treating the results. We suggest some demonstration of the expressive methods, showing how respiration, vasomotor changes, can be recorded and timed; upon the way of administering the word-association test, both with a simple stop-watch and with better timing devices; of the method of recording and timing eye movements by photography as the eye moves in reading, etc. The student should be put through some test such as the Trabue language test, the army alpha test, the range of information test, etc. If time permits, the apparatus and methods used in the study of "memory" and the conditioned reflex should be given. Some familiarity with sense organ experimentation is also advised.

I. Observation With and Without Instrumental Control.

Unaided Observation.—Observation, as the man on the
street uses the term, is, of course, the oldest method known to
science. We make our observations in all natural sciences by
the aid of our sense organs. In one sense instrumentation may
be looked upon merely as a device for increasing the number of
observations which can be made simultaneously. In a normal
individual, vision is the sense most usually employed. When
this sense is denied us, or will not work in a particular problem,
we depend for observation upon the auditory and tactual sense
organs. Under ordinary conditions, smell and taste are not used
as organs of scientific observation. At times, however, their
use is indispensable in chemistry, medicine, etc. Our muscular
sense enables us principally to make observations concerning the
movements and positions of our own bodies, serving at the same
time crudely the purpose of enabling us to react differentially
to the size, weight, and position of objects other than parts of
our own bodies.

Practically all of the results which have been obtained in the
psychology of common-sense have come through the use of unaided observation. By such observation we obtain gross changes
in the activities of the individual or the crowd, the general
behavior of children and animals, and certain aspects of emotional and instinctive activity. *We must not confuse the observation made by a scientist without instrumental control with
the amateurish and muddled observation made by the untrained
individual.* Some of the finest work we have in biology has been
done by scientists without instrumental control. We cite the
behavior work of Fabre, Wheeler, and the Peckhams. Unaided
observation, however, even when employed by the trained man,
becomes a genuine scientific method only when he puts his results
down and begins to note exceptions, to draw tentative conclusions,
and then to gather new observations to check up such conclusions.
In other words, such data must be subjected to statistical methods
before conclusions can be verified. We brought out in the last
chapter that even without the use of instruments we may learn
something about the stimuli which produce responses in human

beings, and something about the nature of the acts themselves. Without instrumentation, however, many of the phenomena of conduct cannot be brought under adequate scientific control. At best the unaided method in our field is only a rough and ready one that enables us to proceed in a provisional way. We may illustrate this by the following example: A person comes into the room; we speak to him in an ordinary conversational tone. He does not respond to our words. We immediately infer that the individual has defective hearing. But from such rough observation, even after watching him for several days, we get little indication of the extent of the defect, and of the types of limitations to which he is subject. Again, in the sphere of learning we may note that a given individual fails to learn quickly, and does not retain his training for any length of time. If we wish to get an accurate picture of his defects, one accurate enough to compare with that obtained from another individual, systematic observation with instrumental control has to be employed.

Observation with the Aid of Instrumentation, and Control of the Subject.—Progress in any science can be measured by the extent to which apparatus and improved methods of observation have been employed. This has been well illustrated in the technical world, and especially in physics, chemistry and engineering. Psychology likewise early felt the necessity of devising special instruments for the study of behavior. These methods are clearly illustrated both in the field of sensory physiology and in that of the more complicated reactions. In general we may say that whatever phenomenon is open to unaided observation can be more accurately studied where instrumentation and control of the subject are employed. If we are testing the rapidity with which an individual can repeat the separate members of a list of common words, we must have some kind of measure of the process. Unaided observation is all but worthless. An ordinary watch gives only a rough indication. A $1/_{5}$-second stop-watch gives an approach towards a scientific instrument; a standard chronoscope, indicating $1/_{100}$ of a second, gives a scientific record which at present is probably a finer measure than we need in psychology.

The extent to which instrumentation is being employed is clearly recognized in the various devices for photographing and timing eye movements, in the devices for measuring the speed and accuracy of hand and finger movements, as in tapping, steadiness and strength of grip. The need of accurate apparatus is clearly recognized in the technic used in determining sensory responses, and in the various psychophysical measurements. Instrumentation is just being introduced into the measuring and timing of secretion responses—for example, in the salivary, sweat and indirectly in the endocrine glands (glandular secretions are discussed on page 181). Certain divisions of psychology have all but resisted the use of instrumentation. There have been few experimental studies upon emotional reactions (page 198), few upon internal muscular reactions, and, until recently, few upon the internal responses connected with hunger, thirst, and the temperature responses to stimulation of the alimentary tract. Few, if any, experiments have succeeded in bringing the sub-vocal mechanisms under control. Indeed, many of the glandular responses have, from a psychological standpoint, not been touched—for example, the possible conditioned reflexes which we may find in the thyroid, adrenal, and sex glands, and in the secretions of the kidneys. At present there is no way of using instrumentation where the individual or group has to be observed for long periods of time, as, for example, in sleep, reaction of crowds to emotion-producing stimuli, and the influence of children upon each other.

The Setting of an Experiment.—In general, in most psychological investigations of the laboratory type, where accuracy and control in observation are demanded, the experimenter makes his observations upon one, or, at best, a few subjects. In addition to the instruments necessary to make observations, we must control certain aspects of the subject's environment—depending upon the nature of the experiment, we place him in a dark room, or in a well-lighted room; we leave him in the room alone, or make him react before other people. Indeed, it is often necessary to control his diet, sleep, and living conditions, as is illustrated by the experiments which have been carried out upon hunger, thirst, and salivary secretions, the effect upon general behavior of fasting and drugs. We may look upon such controls as the experimental setting for an observation. In short, we may say that in order to make accurate psychological observations, we need instruments delicate enough to suit the general purpose of the investigation. Furthermore, we need to be able to control and modify at will the temporary or permanent environment of the subject. Naturally there are many psychological investigations which cannot be conducted in this way. Certain important psychological undertakings probably can never be brought under laboratory control. Reference here, of course, is made to the social problems which psychology sometimes has to study. A youth, for example, is not making good in his school environment: we take him into the laboratory and study his character and temperament as best we can, run him through all the necessary tests, size him up, and then we advise certain changes which the parents and teachers should make in his environment. Time must be given for these recommended changes to have their effect. Dr. Adolf Meyer often speaks of his psychopathic patients as experiments of nature. There are many problems of this character in psychology that yield only little at the hands of a laboratory man. Much of the work now being done in the field of vocational psychology and in educational training is of this type. In such broad psychological problems the environment is not under the immediate control of the observer. In such cases we do the best we can, calling in all the observational, experimental, and statistical aids we can summon.

II. The Conditioned Reflex Methods.

Introduction.—In the various conditioned reflex methods we have a special example of the way instruments are employed in the making of psychological observation. By means of these methods many phenomena of reaction can be brought under control which cannot be observed by the verbal report methods to be described later. It is impossible for us to state by unaided observation whether action in the salivary glands is accelerated or the reverse by the sight of certain kinds of food. These reflex methods have been in common use in the Russian laboratories

for a number of years. The data obtained by such methods are
not entirely new, but the technic of the methods had not been
well established until the work of Pavlow and Bechterew appeared.
The methods can be employed both upon the muscles and upon
the glands. In general they depend upon the following fact:
Every fundamental reflex in the body has an appropriate stimulus
for the calling out of that reflex. On page 233 we discuss some
of the fundamental reflexes. We may anticipate somewhat and
mention a few of them here. If the patellar tendon is touched
with a small percussion hammer, the familiar kick of the leg
appears. If the sole of the foot, or the great toe, is stimulated
by an electric current, the foot will jerk back, or the toe will rise.
If the finger is pricked or burned, the finger will draw back.
In a similar way, if the mouth is stimulated by food, and especially by an acid, the salivary glands will begin to pour out
their secretions more rapidly. Let us call the stimuli that produce native or fundamental reflexes, the normal or adequate
stimuli to the reflexes. The question before us is whether we
can get any other stimulus to touch off such a fundamental or
native reflex—whether we can get a transfer or substitution of
stimulus. Without entering too much into the details of the
method, we find that it is possible to get a stimulus which does not
ordinarily call out one of the fundamental reflexes to call it out,
provided the proper conditions are observed. It is a real question
whether we should call these methods conditioned reflex methods,
or substituted stimulus methods. The term "conditioned reflex"
seems to be fairly well incorporated in the literature, and it is
probably best for us to use that term. In the following paragraphs we shall illustrate this method by taking some simple
laboratory situations.

A. Methods Employed in Obtaining Conditioned Secretion
Reflexes.

Conditioned Salivary Reflex.—The conditioned salivary reflex has been made popular through the work of Pavlow and his
students upon the dog. Not until very recently was it possible
for us to use this method upon man, since an operation was neces-

sary to bring the gland to the surface of the cheek. Recently
Lashley, of the Hopkins laboratory, has used the simple instrument shown below for making the responses of this gland plainly
visible to the eye (Fig. 1). The parotid glands (page 176) of
the two cheeks are easiest to work with, although the submaxillary gland can be used. Each parotid gland has leading out from
it a small duct called Stenson's duct. The instrument shown in
Fig. 1 consists of a metal disc. 18 mm. in diameter, in which two
concentric chambers *A* and *B* are cut. The inner one of these
is 10 mm. in diameter and 3 mm. deep; the outer, in the form of
a circular groove, is 2 mm. wide and 3 mm. deep. The two
chambers open through the back of the disc into two separate
tubes, *C* and *D*, of 2 mm. bore and 15 cm. in length. The tubes
are of silver. The instrument is placed against the inner surface

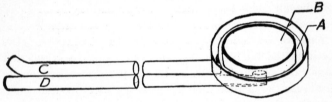

FIG. 1.—Instrument for collecting secretions from parotid gland. Explanation of parts
in text.

of the cheek so that the central chamber covers the mouth of
Stenson's duct, and the air is exhausted from the outer chamber
by a suction pump. The disc then clings tightly to the cheek for
as long a time as one cares to work. In a few moments the saliva
fills the central chamber and begins to flow out through the tube
C to a suitable measuring device. When the jaws are closed
the tube lies between the cheek and the upper molars, and passes
out through the corner of the mouth. The instrument interferes
little with talking or eating, and may be worn for hours. The
drops of saliva may be recorded in various ways. They may be
merely counted and the average number of drops per minute
determined, or the drops may be collected in a calibrated tube.
We next determine in any individual subject the normal rate of
flow at a given interval after food has been eaten. We are then
in a position to tell whether certain forms of stimulation which

we may employ increase or decrease the flow. In this way we may test the effect of chewing hard and soft substances, of hot water, cold water, etc. So far as described, the method is at the service both of the physiologist and of the psychologist. Indeed, we may look upon all such tests as purely physiological tests of the functioning of the glands. We find by employing this instrument the various stimulating factors which affect the gland. The psychological question now comes up: Is the action of the gland connected in any way with the individual's habit systems?

We find by repeated trials that the sight of unaccustomed objects does not have any effect upon the flow of the glands. On the other hand, if we bring the hungry subject into a situation where he has obtained food, and then show him food which he has been in the habit of eating (food positively reacted to), the glands immediately begin to function above normal. In other words, these visual stimuli which ordinarily have no effect upon the functioning of the glands, come by the process of substitution to serve as stimuli for increasing the flow of secretion. This probably can be shown most clearly by actual experiment. After determining the ordinary rate of the flow of the salivary gland, a bar of chocolate almond was handed to the subject. He was allowed to smell it, to bring it to his lips, and to hold it at arm's length. The following table shows the result of this experiment:

Normal rate: about one drop per minute.
Chocolate placed in subject's hand:
        1st minute .... 4 drops
        2nd minute .... 3 drops
        3rd minute .... 4 drops
Subject smelled chocolate .... 5 drops
Brought chocolate to lips but kept mouth closed. 9 drops

Unless this method had been employed, we would not have known that the mere sight and touch of food had such a stimulating effect. The subject's own report is worthless, because the food might have inhibited swallowing, and his mouth would have filled with saliva, even though the fluid came at a normal rate. He probably would have told us that his mouth watered. Some situations as we have experimentally determined do actually in-

hibit swallowing; then the mouth fills with fluid, even though
the stimulus actually produces glandular inhibition. In other
words, it is quite clear that the presentation of the chocolate
produced not only the overt response of reaching out for it and
taking it towards the mouth, but at the same time produced
implicit habit responses, which showed in the glandular reaction. It was only by means of the introduction of instrumentation that we were able to bring this fact out. It is quite
possible that all the glands of the body are subject to stimulus
substitution.

B. Methods Employed in Obtaining Conditioned Motor Reflexes.

Introduction.—In a similar way, Bechterew has shown that
reaction in both striped and smooth muscles can be conditioned.
These conditioned *motor* reflexes are quite common in daily life.
We see them often in moving-picture tragedies; as, for example,
when the villain displays a revolver and pulls the trigger, or
strikes the unfortunate hero over the head with a black-jack, the
mere sight of these acts makes many in the audience jump or
withdraw exactly as though the sound were present, or the blow
had fallen upon their own heads. In the laboratory the technic
of the method is quite simple. Suppose we have our subject sit
with a bare foot resting upon two metal electrodes. When the
faradic stimulus (slight electric shock) is given, the foot is jerked
up from the metal electrodes. We introduce some system for
recording upon smoked paper the jerk of the foot, and for marking on the record the moment the stimulus is given. The electric shock will inevitably and invariably make the foot jump.
The ringing of an electric bell, however, has no such effect. Now,
if we sound the bell and stimulate the foot with the high frequency current simultaneously for a certain number of times
(20 to 70 usually), we will find that the ringing of the bell alone
will produce the upward jerk of the foot. Here, as before, there
has been a substitution of stimulus: a sound which does not
ordinarily call out the reflex soon comes to do so. Probably the
simplest way to carry out conditioned reflex experiments is to
use the finger. In Fig. 2 we show the simple device employed.

The palm of the hand is placed on one electrode, the middle finger upon the other. A little receiving tambour, having a cork saddle attached to it, is placed directly above the finger. At each upward fling of the finger, the tambour, attached to a writing lever, makes a mark upon a smoked drum. A somewhat more complicated recording system than is demanded in the present type of experiment is shown on page 36.

As may readily be seen, the finger can be more conveniently used for general laboratory purposes than the foot. This technic

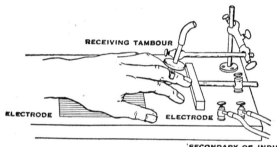

RECEIVING TAMBOUR

ELECTRODE   ELECTRODE

'SECONDARY OF INDUCTORIUM

Fig. 2.—Method of recording finger movement and of giving faradic stimulation. A large electrode is placed under the hand, and a small electrode under the finger. When the key, in the experimenter's room, is pressed down by the operator the secondary current from the inductorium causes the finger to rise from the small electrode. A receiving tambour, to the face of which a saddle-shaped button has been shellacked, enables a graphic record to be made of such movements.

is now in general use, and can be used with children, with defective individuals, as well as with normal adults. Our method for obtaining the reflex is somewhat as follows: In beginning work upon any new subject we first sound the bell alone to see if it will produce the reflex. We have never been able to get the reflex evoked by the bell alone prior to electrical stimulation. We next give the bell and shock simultaneously for about five trials, and then offer the bell alone. If the conditioned reflex does not appear, we next give five more stimulations with the bell and electric current simultaneously, and repeat this routine until the reflex appears. The conditioned reflex makes its appearance at first haltingly—that is, it will appear once and then disappear. Punishment is frequently resorted to. It may next appear twice in succession and again disappear. After a time it begins to appear regularly each time the bell is offered. In the best cases we get a conditioned reflex after about fourteen to thirty combined stimulations. In attempting to use this method one must be prepared to find certain subjects who do not readily show conditioned reflexes. Just what the reasons for this are cannot readily be stated at present. The method is really in its infancy.

So far we have discussed the motor conditioned reflex as it appears in the striped muscles of the hands, feet, legs. The unstriped and mixed striped and unstriped groups show conditioned reflexes as well. If a technic is developed for measuring the width of the pupil, a bright light may be used in place of an electrical stimulation. The bell is sounded at the same instant the bright light is flashed. The light causes the pupil to contract, and after the bell and light have appeared enough times together, the bell alone will produce the contraction. The respiratory mechanism can be very easily and readily made to show conditioned reflexes, as can the heart-beat.

Some General Characteristics of the Conditioned Reflex.— It is interesting at this point to treat of certain characteristics of the reflex.

First, as regards the similarity and difference between the conditioned reflex and the primary reflex upon which it is grafted. However much they may differ so far as the central nervous pathway is concerned, the general and coarser motor features are closely similar. One watching the movements of a subject first beginning to show a conditioned reflex cannot tell whether he is being stimulated by the bell alone or by the bell and punishment combined. The conditioned motor reflex is usually sharp, quick and widespread, the whole body as a rule being brought into the reaction at first. Gradually the reflex becomes more circumscribed.

Second, as regards persistence of the reflex; after the reflex has once been thoroughly established it carries over from one day's experiments to the next for an indefinite period. Sometimes a single punishment at the beginning of a day's work is necessary to cause the reflex to make its appearance. We are not able to state over how long a period of time the unexercised reflex will persist. In one case we trained one subject thoroughly in

May to the bell, then did not test him again until October. The reflex did not appear on the first ringing of the bell, but after the first administration of the combined stimuli (at which the subject disrupted the apparatus although the induction shock was very weak) the conditioned reflex appeared regularly to the bell alone.

Third. We know that the conditioned motor reflex can be made to undergo reinforcement and inhibition by factors such as those described on page 171. A few examples of the rôle such factors play in the control of the reflex may be of interest. Take first the ''fatigue'' of the reflex. A well-trained subject will react regularly for an indefinite period of time to a stimulus given at an interval of four to five seconds. If now we give the stimulus, that is the bell, every two seconds for a short time, he may react for the first three times and then fail. If the interval is then lengthened, or a rest period introduced, the reflex will again appear. It will be seen later that we utilize this principle of fatigue in setting up differential reactions. Oftentimes before the conditioned reflex is thoroughly set up, it will after a time begin to decrease in amplitude. Whether the time is increased is not known. When the reflex is beginning to vanish it can be strengthened in a variety of ways, the most usual way being the introduction of the current, but it can be reinforced also by introducing simultaneously with the bell some other form of stimulation, such as contact or temperature.

Psychological Use of the Conditioned Reflex.—In the cases of the deaf and dumb, of infants and of some pathological subjects, language methods cannot be used. This, of course, is true with respect to the animal world also. Consequently we may say in general that the conditioned reflex method may prove of service wherever language cannot be depended upon (whether due to defect or not). In the second place, the conditioned reflex method may be used as a check upon the verbal report method to be described later. We may briefly illustrate some of the uses of the method as we have so far described it. Suppose we wish to determine the limits of spectral sensitivity in man, that is, how far out into the red and into the violet he can still react visually to ether waves. We start with any intermediate wave length and by use of the electric shock establish a conditioned reflex. Each time the light appears the reflex occurs. We then increase the length of the wave rather sharply and if the reflex appears we again increase the wave length. We finally reach a point where the reflex breaks down, even when punishment is used to restore it—approximately at $760\mu\mu$. This wave length represents the human being's spectral range at the red end. We then follow the same procedure with respect to the violet end ($397\mu\mu$). In this way we determine the individual's range just as surely as if we had stimulated the subject with monochromatic lights varying in wave lengths and asked him if he "saw" them. A use similar to this is possible in all the other sense fields, sound, cutaneous, smell, taste, etc. Even as we have discussed the method, it is also serviceable in the study of fatigue, adaptation and in the investigation of many other problems that lie in the borderland between physiology and psychology.

Use of the Method for Determining Differential Sensitivity.—The method has a much wider range of applicability.

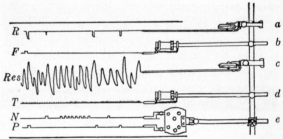

Fig. 3.—Showing system of making records. *a*, Marey tambour, connected with the receiving tambour from the finger (Fig. 2); *b*, electro-magnetic signal marker, connected with the key for giving the electrical shock; *c*, Marey tambour, connected with the pneumograph; *d*, signal marker connected with second's pendulum; *e*, double signal marker; one pointer moves when the negative stimulus (stimulus not to be reacted to) is given; second pointer moves only when the positive stimulus is given. The letters on the left refer as follows: *R*, the record of the finger reaction; *F*, faradic stimulation (punishment); *Res*, respiratory curve; *T*, time; *N*, negative stimulus; *P*, positive stimulus. A short schematic record of the ordinary curves obtained in the laboratory is shown. The eye should begin at the bottom and read up. The first record shows that the positive stimulus bell was given, that punishment was given simultaneously with it, and that the reflex occurred. The second record shows that the negative stimulus (a different bell) was given, that no punishment was given with it, and that the reflex appeared (conditioned, but undifferentiated reflex). Then followed eight stimulations with the negative bell to produce fatigue to the negative stimulus. After fatigue the positive bell was given, but with no punishment; the reflex appeared. The negative bell was next given but no reflex appeared. The positive bell was again sounded and the reflex appeared (differentiation). It will be noticed that respiratory changes occur at every stimulation. There is a deep inspiration each time either of the bells is sounded, and also slowing in rate. When training is continued long enough, differentiation occurs in respiration. (See Fig. 4.) That is, in a short time only the positive bell can produce the changes shown in this drawing.

We may employ it in some cases as a substitute for the verbal report method. In order to use it in the place of the latter method, we have to arrange conditions so that the reflex will appear when, for example, a red light is given, but not when a violet light is given; or when a tone of 256 d.v. is given, and not when one of 264 d.v. is given. By using the method in this way it becomes possible to state what the smallest difference in wave length between two lights must be in order to arouse differential reaction; the smallest vibration difference between two tones; the

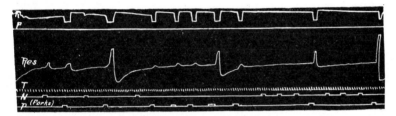

Fig. 4.—Perfect differentiation with one subject when the difference is 6 v.d.

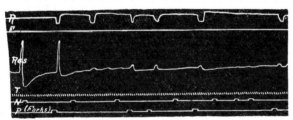

Fig. 5.—Perfect differentiation with another subject when the difference is 3 v.d.

smallest difference in intensity between two tones of the same pitch or two lights of the same wave length. In other words, instead of asking the subject as we do in the verbal report method: *Is this light brighter or dimmer than another light,* or, *Is this tone lower or higher than that tone?*—we use the conditioned reflex method. The technic is as follows: Suppose our problem is to establish a conditioned reflex to a tuning fork of a certain pitch (256 d.v.) and to a second fork of a different pitch (264 d.v.). We will call these two forks F_1 (positive) and F_2 (negative). As in the method already described, we give the electric stimulus with F_1 until the reflex appears. The recording system is shown in Fig. 3. After this is thoroughly established we throw in F_2 and the reflex, of course, will appear. We then continue stimulating with F_2, but never introduce the electric stimulus coincidently with it. After five or ten stimulations in rapid succession with F_2, the reflex to it will disappear. We then suddenly throw in F_1 and if the reflex does not appear we introduce punishment. After this procedure has been continued for some time we finally reach the desired stage where, without any electrical stimulus at all, the reflex will always appear with F_1 but will not with F_2. It now remains to see how fine we can make this difference. In order to test this we gradually decrease the vibration difference between F_1 and F_2. (Figs. 4 and 5 show a difference limen which was developed in a very short time.)

Other Objective Methods.—The conditioned reflex methods have been looked upon as the only objective methods in psychology. This is not true when we consider psychological methods in a broad way. All methods used in reaction time experiments and in experiments on ''memory'' and association are purely objective methods: much of the testing work, the work in experimental pedagogy and in business psychology, has been done with the aid of objective methods.

III. Verbal Report Methods.

Introduction.—The methods so far discussed have dealt with the integrated motor and glandular behavior of individuals other than ourselves. The methods have been largely developed by and have come into prominence through the study of animal behavior and infant human subjects. Indeed, in these fields we must depend largely upon such methods, since the observation of the happenings in their own bodies and the verbal reports of the same are impossible in the case of animals, or very imperfect in the case of abnormal individuals. Man is above all an animal which reacts most often and most complexly with speech reactions. The notion has somehow gained ground that objective psychology does not deal with speech reactions. This, of course, is a mistake. It would be foolish and one-sided to an absurd degree to neglect man's vocal behavior. Often the sole observable reaction in man is speech. In other words, his adjustments to situations are made more frequently by speech than through action of the remaining motor mechanisms. We shall in a later chapter develop our notion of the implicit and explicit language adjustments. We wish here mainly to show the use of speech reactions as a part of general psychological methods. As an illustration of the use of the verbal report method in an actual experiment we may glance for a moment at the tests on sensitivity to warmth and cold on a given area of the skin. We first mark off a small area and go over it with a warm and a cold cylinder: we say to the subject, "Tell us each time the cold cylinder is applied and each time the warm cylinder is applied." If the area touched is sensitive to cold he *responds with the word "cold,"* and similarly when the warm cylinder is applied with the word *"warm."* The verbal report or response is put down in our records of the results of the experiment and is used exactly as the conditioned reflex responses would be used had we adopted that form of experimentation in our test.

Is There a Verbal Report Method Distinct from Other Observable Methods?—Up to the present time psychologists have employed the verbal report method in a somewhat different sense from that used here. Without entering into this bitterly contested and controversial field, we can briefly outline the position of this text in regard to it. The question: Can I make the same observations upon myself that I make on other individuals? brings home the difficulties. The answer is, of course, "yes," but it will be remembered that on page 13 we stated that all we can observe in another individual is his behavior, and we defined behavior as the integrated responses of muscles and glands. The question now becomes simpler: Can I observe the movements of my own muscles and glands and their integration? For example, that I am writing, that my face is flushed, etc.? Who would deny it?

At this point we diverge for a moment to correct a misconception which has arisen with reference to objective psychology. The misconception lies in the fact that a good many psychol-

ogists have misunderstood the behaviorist's position. They insist
that he is only observing the individual movements of the muscles
and glands; that he is interested in the muscles and glands in
exactly the same way the physiologist is interested in them. This
is not the whole statement. *The behaviorist is interested in integrations and total activities of the individual.* At one moment
we ask the question: What is the individual doing? We observe
that he is typewriting, searching for a lost pocket-book or "reacting" to an emotional stimulus. If the latter happens to be true
and we are interested in the way his emotional life as a whole
hangs together, we may go on to show why the individual reacts
in an emotional way to this particular stimulus. We may show
how his fear reactions to certain situations arose in his infancy
and how they have affected his whole personality and more
highly organized habit activities. To illustrate this we may
give a hypothetical example: Through some injury (or other
emotional happening) in youth, occasioned by a rapidly moving
mechanical toy, the individual cannot be induced to enter an
automobile or motor boat or to ride in a train if it can possibly
be avoided. In the occupations and activities of individuals we
do not stop as a rule to reduce the total activity to muscle
twitches. We can do it if necessary and we do do it at times
when it becomes necessary to study the various part reactions.
Surely objective psychology can study brick-laying, house building, playing games, marriage or emotional activity without
being accused of reducing everything to muscle twitch or the
secretion of a gland. It is just as fair to accuse the behaviorist,
or indeed the conventional psychologist as far as that goes,
of reducing everything to the ionic constitution of matter.
All of us believe that matter is constituted as the physicist would
have us believe, but his formulation does not help us very much
in specific psychological problems. On the psychological side,
we can describe a man's behavior in selecting and marrying a
wife. We can show how that event has influenced his whole life
after marriage. In detail, how the increased responsibility
stabilized certain emotional mal-adjustments, how the added
financial burden led him to work longer hours and to study the

details of his profession so that his salary would be increased and his number of business connections enlarged. It would not help us very much in the present state of science to be able to trace the molecular changes in cell constitution—they certainly exist, but are aside from our problem. Our problem is the effect of marriage upon the general behavior of this one individual.

In the psychological laboratory we do find it necessary often to study the details of the total activity we see in daily life. When it becomes necessary to make such observations we find it extremely difficult to observe the part or individual reactions of our own bodies. We pointed out above that observation is often impossible without the use of instrumentation and the control of the experimental setting. Hence the movements which we would have to make in the manipulation of the instruments and the setting would interfere always with the movements we are trying to observe in ourselves. It is perfectly possible for a subject to make observations by the use of his eyes of the number of drops coming from the salivary glands after some one has attached the apparatus for him; but in reaching for acids, water to wash out the mouth, etc., certain variable factors are introduced which disturb the purity and the scientific character of the observation. Physiology has to answer this same question; but who doubts that the physiologist can make observations of a kind upon his own heart, respiration, and movements of the food particles in the intestines? But if the physiologist limited himself to what he could learn from observing and experimenting upon his own organs, he would long ago have given up the science. But now and then the physiologist and the physician, like other human beings, observe that something goes wrong with one of their organs. They immediately put themselves into the hands of a skilled observer who brings all of the technic of modern science to bear upon the observation he is about to make. His report may be that there are adhesions, mitral leaks, or an enlarged spleen. In other words, in physiology and in medicine self-observation is crude and inexact and is discarded just as soon as other methods can be brought to bear. We suffer in psychology to-day greatly because methods for observing what goes on in another individual's internal mechanisms in general are lacking. For this reason we have to depend in part at least upon his own report of what is taking place. We are gradually breaking away from this inexact method; we shall break away very rapidly when the need is more generally recognized. Suppose we have a subject in the laboratory. We record his arm and finger responses to a given experimental situation. During the course of the experiment we may also want to know whether there is an increased tension in the leg muscles. We ask the subject: When you move your hands in this experiment do your leg muscles contract? He may say "yes" or "no" and he may be right. But if we want a scientific answer to depend upon, we immediately attach an instrument which will record any change in the tension of the leg muscles. We discard crude self-observation and turn to instrumentation wherever it is necessary or possible.

But in many spheres of psychology and especially in psychiatry, self-observation, which is usually expressed in words by the subject, is the only kind of observation at our immediate disposal. The patient comes to the psychiatrist and says: "I feel 'sad' and 'gloomy' "; or, "Doctor, I am under a terrible strain —I fear I am going to kill my wife and children." This is a psychological situation which the physician must meet. The physician then by a series of skillful questions begins to take the word responses of the patient. These responses, however, are from the physician's standpoint as objective as would be a moving-picture photograph of the subject's activity in weaving a rug or basket. The responses are a part of the record of the subject's way of adjusting to his world. These responses the physician can in virtue of his past training connect with the remote and immediate situations in the life of the patient which have produced the mal-adjustment. The physician has found that when speech reactions of such and such types are made by the patient, they are to be associated with disturbances of the remaining action systems—the individual's action systems are no longer integrated and no longer function as a unit, as is necessarily the case when the patient is well.   .

IV. Methods of Testing.

Introduction.—Psychological tests of one kind or another have been in use since the founding of psychology. During the early history of psychology, tests were developed largely around sensory reactions. Fairly serviceable tests of keenness of vision, auditory acuity and color defects have been in use for more than fifty years. Sometime later methods of testing accuracy of motor coördination, speed of reacting to simple and complex situations appeared. Until the last two decades such tests were incorporated in the general treatment of psychology. These tests were looked upon as a part of the routine of the laboratory and no particular use was made of them except in the testing of railway and marine engineers. Within the past twenty years there has grown up a veritable school of testers which has abstracted the sensory methods from psychology and added a very much larger number of special tests. Since the time of Binet's early work, tests have gradually taken on a broader character. They have had to do with general abilities, "intelligence level" correlated with age and with occupations, rather than with the special senses. The field of testing is now extensive and even though the value of the results obtained from the various methods is not yet agreed upon, it is generally admitted that this work is in line with common-sense and has wide possibilities of still further extension. In general we may consider the tests under three headings: (1) general behavior tests for determining whether the individual possesses the various functions and the degree of plasticity (capability of forming new habits) demanded by society (so-called intelligence tests); (2) tests of special ability, and (3) research and statistical work in tests.

A good many psychologists are inclined, or were inclined in the beginning, to look upon tests as a development of a purely practical side of psychology, and, hence asserted that they belonged wholly to applied psychology. But by degrees this difference between "pure" and "applied" science has given way in psychology as it has in other fields. Now we look upon tests as we look upon any other group of methods in psychology. When the psychologist has special need of making them he either uses a test already available or else goes about in a systematic way the development of a test to suit his needs. He does this, or he should do this, in the same spirit that he would carry out other psychological investigations. On the whole though this distinction is valid, *viz.*, that psychological experimentation is carried out usually without any reference to the immediate usability or applicability of the results, whereas the tests are used in practical situations and are (or ought to be) scientifically developed in the laboratory in order to meet practical situations.

The tests so far developed have had most to do with the language behavior of individuals and depend largely upon the individual's ability to speak; that is, they have concerned themselves with the ease and complexity of the language response to social and other environmental settings. This is, of course, unfortunate since we have many individuals who are deprived of speech altogether and many others with defective speech (aphasics and bad stammerers, for example), and still others who speak only the most difficult foreign languages. The ability of such individuals to do certain things with their hands, to form certain habits with the remaining musculature of their bodies, has not been disturbed. To meet such cases, and indeed to serve many other purposes as well, very much greater emphasis should be laid upon tests of explicit and overt types of behavior where language is not necessary.[2] Owing to the remarkable but widespread notion that language behavior has some peculiarly great significance, the development of performance tests has been seriously handicapped. We can give only a brief characterization of the various types of tests here.

1. Tests to Determine the General Level of Behavior.— The validity of general behavior tests depends upon the fact that in individuals of approximately the same age and from the same general environment, certain systems of common activities are developed. As has been brought out before, this expected or demanded level of activity is a purely conventional one. Nevertheless, every individual must be possessed of a certain minimal set of assets and activities, such as speed in forming

---

[2] Some of the recent army tests have met this difficulty.

habits, number of habits and a certain level of language attainment; of certain methods of attack upon problems and conventional modes of reacting to parents, teachers and companions. If the individual is lacking in any of these requirements, a properly devised test should bring the matter out. Certain tests have been developed which bring out the completeness or incompleteness of such accomplishment with respect to age. We can, for example, give an individual of eight years all of the tests from six to nine years. It he passes all up to and including the eighth year, we say that his attainments are normal. If his attainments age is near that of a six-year-old child, we say that the individual is two years retarded. The mere fact that the individual may be two years retarded calls for special consideration of his case. Is he two years retarded because he has been ill and has not been able to go to school to the same extent as other children of his age? Has he been in a region where he was not able to go to school? Is there any particular psychosis of a permanent or temporary character which has been instrumental in producing retardation? Or has the youth constitutional defects which make it impossible for him to put on the habits required of the other children in his group? The special consideration of the retarded child thus requires the coöperation of a psychologist, a psychiatrist and oftentimes of a surgeon. Serious damage is often done to individuals who are passed upon by a physician alone or by a psychologist alone.

The scales or special tests used in this practical way are those of Binet-Simon with their various modifications at the hands of Terman, Yerkes, Goddard and others, and the performance tests of Healy, Pintner and many others. The various special tests described below may also be utilized to determine the general behavior level of individuals. By the use of special tests in arithmetic, vocabulary, speed and accuracy of habit formation, we arrive at a much more just estimate of the individual's capabilities than by any of the tests for general behavior. Indeed, few of the modifications of the Binet-Simon and other general testing methods are serviceable beyond the 15th year. In estimating an adult's attainments we usually have to employ many special tests.

2. Tests of Special Ability.—On account of various practical demands upon the psychologist both in the realm of the evaluation of attainment in schools and in the economic world, a number of tests too numerous for special mention have grown up for the determination of special abilities. Tests have already been devised for determining the range of general information of an individual, information along a particular line, his mathematical ability, his vocabulary, English, handwriting, musical ability, ingenuity, the possibility of his attaining success in the fields of railway engineering, telephony, stenography, music and aviation. These special ability tests are sometimes used jointly in abbreviated form for running applicants through who are desirous of entering certain vocations. The tests are gradually becoming wider in their scope so as to include personality factors, for example, whether an individual is arrogant, proud, neat, whether he is friendly, or emotionally unstable. It has indeed been suggested that the psychiatrists might assist the psychologists in determining whether a candidate for the more important positions has the proper characteristics and temperament to make him desirable. In connection with this it may be said that an individual's characteristics are dependent to a large extent upon the various conflicts and stresses and strains against which he has had to contend from infancy through adolescence to his present age. Some further discussion of this is given on page 435.

3. Research and Statistical Work in Tests.—So far in our discussion of tests we have assumed the existence of more or less adequate tests for a given purpose. Such tests now at hand for practical use have been developed by means of actual research work. Suppose, for example, we have to develop a test for determining an individual's qualifications for filling a position in stenography. We first set down the various characteristics and attainments we desire such an individual to have. We then go into any large stenographic office and still further increase our knowledge concerning the speed a successful individual should have in taking dictation, speed in typewriting from written material and copying from stenographic notes, length of time it takes the best individuals to make copies of letters, ability to spell, to write unusual words, to file letters and to find letters in a file. On the basis of this wider knowledge we construct a series of performance tests which take, say, half an hour for any stenographer to go through. We may find that our first test is entirely too complicated and that only three or four of the best individuals in a large typewriting office can pass it. But we are just as likely, on the other hand, to make a test which is too easy, so easy indeed that even the poorest members of the group can pass it. We then work at the method until the average good stenographer can pass the test. Naturally the test must be constructed with reference to the field of general stenographic work. This test would not be suitable for accountants, for newspaper reporters or for any other vocational field. Such work is being done constantly by many business houses in consultation with psychologists. Indeed, many of the larger business houses now employ psychological experts for devising such tests. The construction of the test is a research problem. The use of the test can possibly be left to individuals who are not psychologists, but who may have received special instructions in its use.

A slightly different task it at hand when we have to ask the question: What are the general factors which enter into the make-up of a successful lawyer, statesman, newspaper correspondent, or aviator. We may say in advance that no very serviceable correlations throwing light upon such questions have yet been obtained. To make the problem specific we may take up the study of the make-up of a successful aviator: What factors in the previous life of the aviator make for success in flying? Has the amount and kind of academic education anything to do with it? The stratum of society from which he comes, age, previous occupation and salary obtained in it, marriage, and athletic attainments? To answer the question the necessary data are obtained from successful and unsuccessful pilots. The material so obtained is then subjected to statistical treatment and the co-efficients of correlation obtained.[3]

---

[3] For method see Thorndike's *Mental Measurements*. For the extent to which such correlations have been worked out see Thorndike's article *Science*, 1919.

CHAPTER III

THE RECEPTORS AND THEIR STIMULI

Introduction.—As has already been pointed out, the understanding of the nature of human response depends to a large extent upon a knowledge of the various types of stimuli which affect man; of the places where such stimuli must be applied in order to produce appropriate action; and of the various physical and physiological factors which must be taken into account in the control of both the organism and the stimulus. To make this concrete we need only to mention the fact that if the skin of certain animals is stimulated by light of high intensity an overt response will be produced. In man, light, neglecting its heat value, must fall upon a certain part of the eye if action is to be produced. Furthermore, light necessary to produce an overt response in man must have a wave length not less than $397\mu\mu$ (violet) and not greater than $760\mu\mu$ (red). To bring these factors out, we must to a certain extent "dissect" our human being and find the parts which are sensitive to stimulation (bodily areas which each sense organ comprises) and the adequate stimuli which, when applied upon these sense organ areas, will produce action. It must be borne in mind that this procedure is somewhat artificial and like the one the physiologist uses when he studies the heart action, respiration, etc., to the exclusion of the other bodily functions. In later chapters, however, we will put the organisms together, as it were, and study our creation from the standpoint of its reactions as a whole. We must never lose sight of the fact that when man reacts to even the most minute sensory stimulus, the whole body coöperates in the reaction, even if he only raises a finger or says the word "red."

A General Neuro-Muscular Consideration.—We shall find in Chapter V that in every simple reflex act, such as the withdrawal of the hand from a hot object, there is involved on the structural side a *receptor*, or sense-organ structure, a set of neural conductors and an effector (muscle or gland). When a sense

48

structure, like the eye, ear or nose, is played upon by a stimulus, a chemical process of some kind is started which releases a neural impulse in the system of conductors. This neural impulse passes through the conductors, finally reaching the muscle or gland. Under the action of this impulse, the muscle shortens or the gland begins to secrete. The animal thus moves or acts. In order to have these various mechanisms clearly before us, we shall have to study (1) the sense organ side of man: the eye, the ear, the senses of touch, olfaction, warmth, cold, pain, the organic and the kinæsthetic; (2) the neural or conducting mechanism, i.e., the peripheral and central nervous systems (and the sympathetic nervous system) ; (3) the motor and glandular systems— the effectors, consisting of the striped muscles which are under the control of the peripheral and central nervous systems, and the unstriped muscles and glands which are usually under the control of the sympathetic. The student should formulate his problem somewhat as follows: ''(1) What extra-organic and intra-organic stimuli will cause my subject, man, to act; how can I arrange simple and complex situations which will cause him to act in harmony with environmental demands? (2) From my general reading it would appear that the function of the stimulus is to arouse a neural impulse. I want to know for both practical and theoretical reasons what the course of this neural impulse is, i.e., how it finds a way to the muscle, because if there happens to be a defect, either anatomical or functional in this chain of conductors, I know that any stimulus I may apply will not lead to the usual reaction. (3) In order to understand what can be done with man in the way of establishing integrated systems of response, I must have at least an elementary knowledge of the ways in which muscles, tendons and joints function; and know something about the kinds of glands he has, and the influence of these glands upon the muscles.'' The student who has had no physiology will find it profitable to read straight through the three chapters on the sense organs, the conductors, and the muscles and glands, and then turn back and study in detail the chapters in the order in which they appear. In our study of the sense organs which immediately follows, we shall

4

have to neglect many points of interest. Only the common and more every-day phenomena of sensory physiology are treated here.

I. Sense Organs in the Skin (Cutaneous) and Their Adequate Stimuli.

Area.—The whole surface of the skin, including the red portion of the lips, the conjunctiva and cornea of the eye, the mucous

membrane lining the mouth and other external openings of the body, must be looked upon as the area where cutaneous stimuli may be effectively applied. Fig. 6 shows a cross section of skin of the body with the epidermis, or outer layer of the surface, removed.

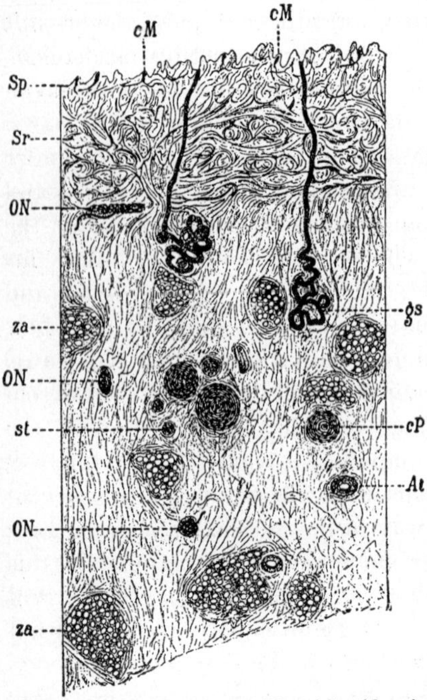

If we investigate this area by either the conditioned reflex method or by the verbal report method (page 38), we shall find that in the skin we are really dealing with four distinct sense organs, each with its proper group of stimuli. They are (1) the cold sense, (2) the warmth sense, (3) the pressure sense and (4) the pain sense. 1 and 2 are known collectively as the temperature sense.

FIG. 6.—Cross-section of skin, with epidermis or outer layer removed (after Ruffini). *At*, cross-section of small artery; *cM*, Meissner corpuscles; *cP*, transverse section of Pacinian corpuscle; *Sp*, papillary layer of the skin; *Sr*, reticular layer of the skin; *ON*, Ruffini cylinders; *za*, adipose tissue; *st*, transverse section of small nerve trunks; *gs*, sweat glands.

1 and 2. The Temperature Sense.—The adequate stimuli for these senses are, from the standpoint of physics, heat radiation. From the practical standpoint, they are objects: metal, wood, fluids and gases (air), being the most common examples. To initiate activity it is not necessary to bring such objects into direct contact with the skin. In general in order to affect the cold sense, their temperature must be lower than the so-called physiological zero, approximately 30° C. The physiological zero is not fixed, but depends upon the state of adaptation of the sense organ. If the temperature of the objects is above this point, the warm sense is called into function. The end organs of temperature can also be stimulated from within by organic changes which occur in fevers, in extreme emotions, either through constricture of the blood-vessels (cold) or by dilatation (warmth). They may also be stimulated mechanically by the action of substances like mustard, pepper, alcohol or menthol, by an electrical current and possibly even by mechanical stimulation—slight tapping, puncturing with a needle, etc. Extremes of temperature tend to destroy the tissue, and hence objects of excessively high temperature stimulate both the warm sense and the pain sense. The essential factor in providing a temperature stimulus is the bringing about of thermal changes in the skin. Unless the temperature of any part of the skin can be changed, fairly rapidly at that, there is no response. This can be illustrated by the old example of immersing the frog and then raising the temperature very gradually. The death of the frog occurs before a temperature (or pain) response is obtained.

Punctiform Type of Stimulation.—In making a systematic and detailed investigation of these senses, one usually marks off on the skin a small, well-defined area and goes over it with a hollow point of metal which can be kept at a constant temperature by passing through it a fluid—water for warmth and moderate degrees of cold, alcohol or other anti-freezing fluids if low temperatures are to be used. For ordinary work the point of metal should be kept at about 12° to 15° C. when the cold sense is being investigated, and 37° to 40° C. when working with the warm sense. If the skin is gone over in a punctiform way, it is found that characteristic responses can be obtained only at certain definite circumscribed spots or points (½ mm. or less in area). Moreover, points which respond to the cold metal point are distinct from those which respond to the warm. Apparently they are permanent: that is, the spots are probably situated immediately above the true sense-organ structure lying within the skin. In general it is found that those regions which are most responsive to pressure stimuli as, *e.g.*, the hands and finger tips, are less responsive to temperature. Parts which are usually covered with clothing are more responsive to temperature than those which are left uncovered, partly because of lack of exposure to changes, but also because they are more generously supplied with temperature organs. The face is exceedingly sensitive, although in most countries it is left uncovered. It is found to be richly supplied with sensory structures.[1] The threshold of stimulation of these spots varies widely.[1] Stimulation of certain warm spots will produce response when the temperature of the object is only slightly above the physiological zero, while the more resistant are not stimulated except by temperatures lying around 40° C. The cold spots show equal variation in the intensity of the threshold stimulus. The number of spots sensitive to these forms of stimuli in any given square centimeter differs widely on the different parts of the body. In general the cold spots are much more numerous than the warm

---

[1] There are two kinds of thresholds. *Liminal thresholds*, abbreviated R. L.: by this is meant merely that any stimulus in any sense field can be made so weak that the work it does upon the sense organ is not sufficient to produce either an explicit or an implicit response. The state of adaptation or the amount of work the sense organ has just done may affect the magnitude of the stimulus necessary to produce a response. The differential threshold (D. L.) always involves two stimuli: a subject may react to a white light of a given photometric value. Suppose we introduce a second white light. By how much must we increase (or decrease) the intensity of this second light in order to have at hand the condition for the subject to react in one way to the first light, and in another way to the second light? Reactions to such stimuli are called in the text differential reactions or responses. There is a separate division of psychology which deals almost exclusively with such relations of stimuli. It is called quantitative psychology. The originators of this type of study were Weber and Fechner. Their studies have been incorporated into so-called laws—the Weber law and the Fechner law, or the Weber-Fechner law. On account of the very narrow application of quantitative psychology and by reason of the technical difficulties in the way of its study, it is neglected in this text, although the subject matter belongs to objective psychology.

spots. On the average the proportion is about 13 cold spots to 2 warm spots. In the matter of the distribution of these spots, attention is called to the fact that the conjunctiva of the eye and the external mucous membrane of the genital organs are insensitive to warmth but sensitive to cold.

Areal Stimulation.—Punctiform stimulation such as we have just described rarely occurs in the daily life of man. It is the cold wind striking all of the exposed surfaces of the body which leads him to put on his overcoat or to go to the coal yards and lay in his winter supply of fuel. It is the warm rays of the sun that make him doff his winter garments and eagerly hunt railway time-tables for summer resorts. Areal stimulation may, apart from daily life, be investigated in the laboratory. A thermal stimulation distributed over a large area of the skin is reacted to more strongly than if the same temperature is applied to a smaller area. A temperature which will just not produce a reflex withdrawal when the finger alone is dipped into a fluid will produce a withdrawal movement if the whole hand or arm is immersed. Most of us have many times tested our bath water with the finger tips, jumping in only to bounce out again when the entire leg or body is suddenly immersed. Objects with different heat conductivities affect markedly the reactions of the subject. Water at 25°C. is a stronger cold stimulus than oil at the same temperature, but less strong than mercury. In addition to the heat-conducting properties, the action (as seen in *R. L.* and *D. L.*) induced by the temperature of an object depends to some extent upon the smoothness or roughness of its surface.

Paradoxical Arousal of Cold Spots.—In areal stimulation another factor enters in when the temperature of the object lies between 45° to 50° C. If we select and mark out on the skin a certain number of cold spots and then stimulate each by a metal point at this temperature, a reaction to cold will be obtained. In other words, temperatures from 45° to 50° C. are ("inadequate") stimuli for the cold spots. This means evidently that when large areas are stimulated with objects possessing such temperatures, both warm and cold spots are functioning. In other words, our general reactions to such temperatures are due to a complex stimulation, *viz.*, the adequate or normal stimulation of the warm spots and the inadequate or paradoxical stimulation of the cold.

3. The Pressure Sense.—The stimulus to the pressure sense is the deformation of the skin surface. In daily life objects such as wood, metal, jets of air or other gases, fluids, mechanical impacts upon the surface of the skin, pulling, wrinkling of the skin, touching a hair, etc., all produce deformation of the skin and hence serve as pressure stimuli. The best method for investigating this sense organ is to stimulate a small area with a series of hairs or bristles of varying length and thickness.[2] If an area is gone over in a uniform way, as was suggested above for the temperature sense, it will be found that spots appear at which reactions may be obtained. It will be noted, further, that these spots are distinct from those of temperature. Distinctions should be made between hairy and non-hairy areas. Movement of the hair itself serves as a pressure stimulation. If the hair is shaved off and the position of each hair is marked and the area then gone over in a punctiform way, it will be found that there is a pressure spot on the skin to the windward of each hair (the hairs enter the skin at an angle). Every part of the skin is supplied with pressure spots with few exceptions. The cornea is said to contain no pressure spots. The parts most richly supplied with pressure spots are the tip of the tongue, the red part of the lips and the finger tips. Not only are the spots more numerous here, but their thresholds are lowest. The average number of spots per square centimeter is about 25, but they may drop to as low as 7 or go as high as 300.

4. The Pain Sense.—Any object which will prick, cut, burn or tear the tissue will serve as a stimulus for calling out pain reactions. It can be aroused by mechanical, thermal, electrical and chemical means. If a very small skin area is moistened thoroughly and gone over with a finely ground needle-point, the

---

[2] Some investigators have used finely spun glass threads, since they are not affected by dampness and are always straight and do not alter their elasticity with use.

pain spots can be located. They are far more numerous than any of the other cutaneous spots. Pain spots do not usually coincide with cold, warmth or pressure spots. The threshold for pain is far greater than that for pressure. Stimulation of small areas shows that sensitivity to pressure is 1000 times greater than that to pain. The cornea is richly supplied with pain spots. Any stimulus applied to the cornea, if above the limen, will produce a strong reflex movement. The posterior portion of the mouth cavity and the back of the tongue are not well supplied with pain spots. In the mucous membrane of the cheeks (opposite lower second molar) pain spots are absent in many subjects.

End Organs Affected by Cutaneous Stimuli.—So far in this work we have not had occasion to study the nervous system in its relation to the sense organs on the one hand and to the muscles on the other. In Chapter IV this relationship will be taken up. All that needs to be said now is that every sense, be it the eye, ear, smell or taste, has within it highly modified sensory structures which are affected by the characteristic stimuli for that sense. One must look upon them as the chemical laboratory in which the energy is liberated that initiates the nerve impulse. These sense-organ structures (cells) are usually not a part of the nervous system, but are highly modified epithelial structures around which the nerve fibers end.

In the outer layer or epidermis of the skin we find the first sense structures. The nerve fiber loses its sheath or covering after passing into the epidermis and splits up into numerous branches which end in between the cells of the skin (the epithelial cells). The endings sometimes pierce these cells or end between any two in small nodules. The epidermis is very richly supplied with nerves ending in this manner. These are the so-called *free nerve endings*. In the upper layer of the true skin we find the complex *corpuscles* of *Meissner* and of *Dogiel* and the *papillary endings* of *Ruffini*, also the *corpuscles* or *end-bulbs* of *Golgi-Mazzoni*. Finally in the deep layers of the skin we find the *Pacini corpuscles* and the *corpuscles* or *cylinders* of *Ruffini*. In addition

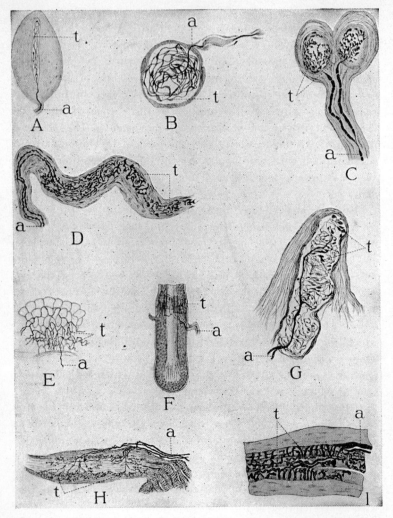

Fig. 7.—Showing some varieties of termination of afferent nerves in skin, muscles, tendons and hairs. A, Pacinian corpuscle (after Dogiel); B, Krause's corpuscle from conjunctiva (after Dogiel); C, two Golgi-Mazzoni corpuscles connected with a single bifurcated nerve fiber. The ramified fibers shown in black present numerous varicosities varying in size and appearance (after Ruffini); D, Ruffini's corpuscle in which the nerve fiber enters at one end of the corpuscle. The nerve endings are extremely complicated (after Ruffini). E, "free terminations" in the epithelium (after Wetzius); F, section through a hair and hair sheath showing the nerve plexus (after Bohm); G, Meissner's corpuscle from the skin. These are exceedingly numerous in non-hairy skin areas (after Dogiel); H, termination upon a tendon sheath (after Huber and DeWitt); I, muscle spindle (after Ruffini). In the drawing "a" refers to the axone, "t" to the terminations of a nerve fiber or axone.

to these principal forms there are many other transitional ones. The *hairs* are also supplied with a highly specialized form of nerve ending and must be looked upon as veritable sense organs. Fig. 7 shows an assemblage of some of the forms of sensory structures most frequently met with in the skin.

Anatomical and physiological researches have not gone far enough for us to assign with certainty definite functions to the various sensory structures we find in the skin. It may be said with some slight probability that the Golgi-Mazzoni end-bulbs or corpuscles and the corpuscles of Dogiel are selective to or thrown into action by cold stimuli; that the deep-lying corpuscles of Pacini and Ruffini are probably thrown into action by warmth stimuli. The evidence for these assignments is slender. It has been found that the conjunctiva of the eye does not initiate responses to warmth stimuli. Anatomical examination shows that the end-bulb type of ending is present but not the Pacini and Ruffini corpuscles. It has been found by experiment that the reaction time (time between application of the stimulus and the subject's reaction) to a warmth stimulus is longer than the reaction time to any other cutaneous stimulus. Since the Pacini and Ruffini corpuscles lie usually in the deepest layers of the skin, their relationship is understandable if those structures are selective to warmth.

The nerve plexuses around the hairs are the pressure sense organs in the hairy areas of the body. On the non-hairy areas, Meissner's corpuscles are probably the pressure organs. Where pressure sensitivity is most highly developed, as on the finger tips, the hand, the tongue and the red area of the lips, the Meissner corpuscles are very numerous. On the hairy areas there are very few of them.

Finally, there is some evidence that the free nerve endings in the epidermis are the sense organs selective to pain stimuli; the evidence for this is mainly one of distribution. The pain spots are very numerous, as we have observed. The only sensory structures in the skin in sufficient quantities to care for this distribution are the free nerve endings.

II. The Kinæsthetic Sense.

Area and Stimuli.—The bodily tissues in which kinæsthetic impulses originate are (1) the muscles, (2) the tendons and (3) the articular surfaces. In all of these tissues lie special sense organ structures which are described on page 59. On account of the location of these organs, few investigations have been made upon them alone. It is impossible to stimulate them, since they lie so deeply imbedded in the tissues of muscles and tendons, without at the same time stimulating the cutaneous organs lying above them. Hence it is with difficulty that we can define the stimulus which affects them. Some success has attended our efforts to more exactly define the stimuli by anæsthetizing (cocaine injection or ether spray) the cutaneous area. It has been found that when the cutaneous organs are thrown out of function, heavy pressure upon the muscle or tendon will still bring out a response. If the pressure is made great enough, pain responses can be obtained. In a similar way it has been found that the sensory structures in the muscles can be stimulated by forcing a contraction of the muscle by means of an electric current.[3] Likewise, the pinching, pulling and forced contractions of the muscles affect the sensory structures both in the tendons and in the surfaces around the joints. Kinæsthetic sense organs are generally stimulated by a movement of the tissues themselves under the influence of normal muscular contraction. This contraction of the muscle stimulates at the same time the structures in the tendons and in the joint surfaces. This occurs most frequently in walking, talking, drinking, eating, etc.; that is, whenever an explicit bodily movement is made. The student cannot grasp too early the fact that while the muscles, tendons and joint surfaces are motor mechanisms, they are at the same time highly important sense organs as well. The muscles usually have a definite tone; that is, they are neither fully contracted nor fully extended. Whenever a muscle either elongates or contracts or

---

[3] Experiments upon animals have shown that the compression of the tendon may set off a reflex in a distant muscle. Pinching the muscle may produce rise of arterial pressure. The knee jerk may be inhibited by pressing or otherwise stimulating one of the leg muscles.

in any way changes its length or diameter under the influence of the motor nerves, the sensory endings in the muscles, in the tendons and in the joint surfaces are stimulated and can, as we shall show later (page 316), arouse new motor impulses, which in turn can arouse new kinæsthetic stimulation, this process being repeated again and again until a series of related acts is executed. From this one will quickly grasp the fact that in the functioning of a perfect habit nearly everything is turned over to the kinæsthetic system (page 317). It is, of course, obvious that the length of the muscle cannot be changed very greatly without at the same time arousing some cutaneous impulses, so that even in executing most habitual acts the cutaneous sense organs are involved. It is well for the student to consider just how an animal, deprived of all of its senses except the kinæsthetic, could execute an act (assuming, of course, that enough organic processes are functioning to keep the animal alive). It would probably be surprising to see how well such an animal could get about, or even thread a complicated maze. In thinking over this it might be well to recall that even an extremely fine singer's voice is little disturbed by anæsthetizing the larynx with cocaine, which throws the cutaneous sense organs in the mucous surfaces out of gear, but does not affect the sense organs in the muscles and tendons.

Types of Kinæsthetic Sense Organ Structures.—In Fig. 7 are shown some of the more characteristic sensory endings serving the kinæsthetic sense as a whole. The most highly specialized sensory nerve ending in the muscle itself is the muscle spindle. In the transitional portions between muscle fibers and tendon fibers, one finds the highly important musculo-tendinous corpuscle of Golgi. In the muscle sheaths, tendinous sheaths and joint capsules one finds numerous structures resembling the Pacini corpuscles already met with in the skin, known as modified Pacini corpuscles. It is well to contrast these sensory endings in the muscles with the motor nerve endings shown on page 177. Nothing further can be said about the special functions of these endings.

III. Equilibrium Sense.

Introduction.—No discussion of the kinæsthetic sense is complete without some reference to the sensory structures in the semicircular canals and in the utricle and saccule. The structure and function of these organs are somewhat complicated, and it must suffice for our present purpose to give only a few central facts. In each ear there are three canals: external, superior and posterior. The canals are set in the ear in approximate conformity with the three dimensions of space. The canals, utricle and saccule are really hollowed out of the petrous bone. Fig. 8 shows a cast of the bony cavities. Inside of the bony cavity will be found a continuous membranous sac, which, in the canals, takes closely the general shape of the bony structure, while in the utricle and saccule the conformity is less close. Inside of this membranous sac is a fluid, the *endolymph*. Between the sac and the bony walls there is the *perilymph*. Each canal is dilated into an ampulla where it joins the utricle. It is in these ampullæ that the vestibular branch of the eighth cranial nerve finds its termination. The ending of the nerve inside the membranous sac together with the epithelial cells or sense structures are called the *crista acustica*. Each cell ends in a long flexible hair jutting out into the endolymph. The hairs are held together by a mucous mass called the *cupula*, so that they are unable to move individually and freely in the endolymph; the nerve fibers end in close connection with these sensory cells. In the utricle and saccule there are similar sensory structures, the structure as a whole being called the *macula acustica*. There is one macula in the utricle and one in the saccule. The sensory cells to be found in the macula are shorter than those in the crista. In the macula the hairs are held together by a denser mass. Lying among the hairs are to be found small carbonate of lime particles called otoliths.

Stimulus to the Sense of Equilibrium.—Variations in the pressure of the endolymph caused by movements of the head serve as the adequate stimuli to the hair cells in the canals of the ear. The movements of the head must be great enough to displace the *cupula*, which as it is displaced stimulates the hair cells.

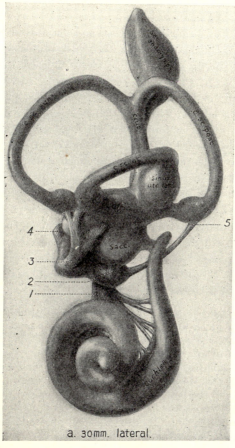

a. 30mm. lateral.

Fig. 8.—Showing the general form of the semicircular canals, utricle, saccule and cochlea, together with their nerve supply (from human embryo). 3, Ganglion of Scarpa containing the cell bodies giving rise to vestibular branch of VIII nerve. Note that three branches are given off near here, two enter the ampullæ of the semicircular canals, the other enters the utricle; 2, branch entering saccule; 5, branch entering posterior canal; 4, vestibular division of the VIII nerve on its way to the brain; 1, the cochlear division of the VIII nerve entering the modiolus. The cell bodies giving rise to this nerve lie in the modiolus. (From the original drawing of Doctor Streeter.)

When these canals are stimulated there occur changes in muscular tone, probably of every muscle of the whole body. If the stimulation is intense the most characteristic reaction to be seen is *nystagmus* of the eyes, a rapid to and fro movement plainly observable without the aid of instruments. If the subject is very sensitive, or the stimulation is made more intense, he may vomit. The easiest way to observe the phenomena of stimulation of the semicircular canals is to hold the head of the subject almost vertical and rotate him with eyes closed and ask him to indicate the direction in which he is being turned. He does this correctly so long as the rate is increasing. If the chair is stopped suddenly, the subject will state that he is rotating in the opposite direction. It will be found that after several rotations there is imparted also the rapid to and fro movement of the eyes mentioned above. If the head is held down during rotation, or to one side, other than the external canals will be stimulated. If after 10 rotations in 20 seconds the subject is asked to straighten up, violent compensatory movements are made. We are thus forced to admit that the semicircular canals contain definite sense organs which are excited by rotary movements of the head in various planes. The sense organ can also be excited electrically and by the introduction of hot and cold water against the ear-drum when the subject is rotated.

Let us take a concrete case: When the head is upright, or better, inclined at an angle of 30°, the external semicircular canals are stimulated when the subject is rotated. If the subject is rotated to the left, there will result in both external canals at first a movement of the endolymph toward the right on account of the inertia of the fluid. This will cause horizontal nystagmus of the eye to the left. When rotation ceases, the endolymph keeps on moving to the left for a short time. This will give rise to a horizontal nystagmus to the right. Usually in rotation experiments the nystagmus during rotation is neglected and only the after-nystagmus observed. If a large number of persons are rotated 10 times in 20 seconds, the after-nystagmus will be found to endure on the average about 26 plus or minus 10 seconds. This test has been much used by the otologists for determining lesions in the central nervous system. Recently the tests have been introduced into the aviation service by a nonscientific group of otologists connected with the War Department as a qualifying test. Unless the nystagmus falls within the range of 26 plus or minus 10 seconds, the candidate is rejected. In view of its highly complex nature, involving both habit and reflex mechanisms, and in view further of the fact that training apparently reduces the time of duration of nystagmus, the test, so far as is known, really has no significance for aviation (it was given up by the British, French and Italian armies after a short time). There is no evidence to show that an individual who has a balanced nystagmus of, say, 15 seconds and below, or one of, say, 37 seconds and above, cannot learn to guide his plane and to manage it as successfully as an individual who shows a nystagmus falling within the 26 plus or minus 10 limit.

In stimulating canals with water, no reaction is obtained if the temperature is at the physiological zero. Above and below this temperature water will serve as a stimulus. The nystagmus is in one direction if the water is cold and in the opposite if the water is hot. Changing the position of the head changes the direction of the nystagmus on any of these caloric tests. In stimulating electrically, the positive pole may be placed over one ear, the negative over the other, or the ears may be stimulated separately by placing one electrode over the ear and the other upon some distant part of the body. When both ears are stimulated simultaneously, a very weak current suffices to bring out nystagmus. If the negative pole is over the ear, the nystagmus is towards that side; if the positive pole, away from that side.

Function of the Utricle and Saccule.—In regard to the stimulation of the utricle and saccule, there are no very sure results. It is supposed that their impulses contribute towards the orienting of the body along the line of gravity. This depends, of course, largely upon the tactual and kinæsthetic impressions, as is shown in the shuffling gait of the patient in locomotor ataxia where kinæsthetic impulses are interfered with. But in swimming when the body is totally immersed, these tactual impulses cannot function differentially; yet the normal subject so immersed can always correctly indicate the position of the body with respect to the vertical. Deaf mutes, whose utricle and saccule are not functional, are said to be unable to do this. The view has been advanced that the saccule and utricle contribute impulses which maintain the head equilibrium when the body is at rest and during progressive (non-rotary) movements of the body. They thus supplement the equilibratory functions of the semicircular canals, which operate mainly in head rotation. The hair cells in the utricle and saccule are supposed to be stimulated by the pressure of the otoliths. When the body is at rest in any position, the otoliths, being heavier than the endolymph, settle down in response to gravity, thus stimulating the hair cells. A change in the position of the head will again change the position of the otoliths, which will again stimulate the hair cells. The semicircular canals, the utricle and the saccule must be looked upon as a vastly important organ connected through the cerebellum with every striped muscle of the body. Any sudden movement of the head will thus initiate impulses which pass through the cerebellum and out to the muscles. It should be mentioned that the speech habits are apparently not connected with the functioning of the vestibular apparatus. The subject can give no verbal report about this operation. After they have functioned and brought about muscular activity, he may report, "I feel dizzy; my eyes jump; vision is blurred; I feel like falling to the right, etc."

IV. THE ORGANIC SENSE.

Area.—The area in which organic impulses originate comprises in general those organs and tissues which lie in the thoracic, abdominal and pelvic cavities. The muscular tissue in which the impulses chiefly originate is largely of the unstriped or smooth variety (heart, diaphragm, etc., excepted), and hence is innervated on the motor side by the autonomic nervous system (page 170); but nearly all of these visceral structures are supplied with afferent or sensory nerves belonging to the spinal cord or brain. These nerves either end free or else in highly specialized structures like the Pacinian corpuscles. When stimulated, they arouse the neural impulses belonging to the organic sense. These impulses, like those from the skin and kinæsthetic sense organ, pass back to the central nervous system and initiate movements of the body as a whole. The organic impulses, as we shall see in a moment, are aroused whenever the body must have food, water, sex outlets, or be freed from waste products and noxious substances (such as calculi, infections, or from the effects of disturbed or torn internal tissue, etc.). Since the very existence of the organism depends upon the adjustment of these conditions, the organic impulses exert a powerful influence upon the striped muscles of the arms, legs, etc., arousing the general reactions necessary to bring about adjustment—such as will bring food, water, companionship of a member of the opposite sex, or make the organism free from substances which irritate it. If the environment is such that the objects which would bring out the adjustment are not at hand, the individual will oftentimes tend to take on the posture or attitude which he would take if he were eating or drinking. Kempf has recently called attention to the great prevalence of these postural attitudes in psychopathological cases, and to their very great variety and complexity.

The sensory endings most frequently stimulated are those lying in the diaphragm and other respiratory mechanisms, the heart and other circulatory mechanisms, the external peritoneum, the stomach and the entrance to the alimentary canal, the soft palate, and finally in those structures connected with sex and with the elimination of body waste. Probably the great majority of the afferent pain endings in the internal structures are never called upon to function in a normal individual.[4] They become functional in disease; for example, the passage of gall stones, infections, etc. It should be mentioned that pain sensitivity seems to be lacking in the heart, the arteries and veins, in the spleen, pancreas, kidneys and lymphatic glands. The functioning of the organic sense organ proceeds oftentimes without involving language. We mean by this merely that if the subject is questioned about what processes are going on, he finds it impossible or next to impossible to make any kind of a serviceable observation. It is true that there is a certain amount of language activity connected with their functioning; for example, people say that they are hungry, thirsty, have pain or colic. But every one must admit that the organic sensory motor processes are but poorly integrated with speech functions. On account of the wide distribution of the sense organ structures and their difficulty of access, detailed experimental work is all but impossible. Some success has been obtained by indirect methods, by the swallow-

---

[4] The pain endings in the periosteum of the bone and in the meninges of the brain and cord are most conveniently classified under the organic sense.

5

ing of rubber balloons which can then be filled with warm or cold water, by the stimulation of structures during operations, and by conditioned reflex methods.

Organic Stimuli.—Notwithstanding the lack of complex language habits connected with organic impulses, one can see the result of their functioning in the clearest manner: in thirst, which is initiated by dryness of the soft palate; in hunger, initiated by the rhythmical muscular contractions of the stomach; in defecation, initiated by the pressure of the fæces upon the muscular walls of the large intestine; in micturition, initiated by the pressure of the urine upon the sphincters of the bladder; in sex activity, initiated, in part at least, by the pressure of the seminal fluid; in the pain reflexes due to internal pressure, infections, etc.; in hiccoughing, vomiting, etc., the stimuli to which are varied. As long as the organic impulses are normally aroused and the vegetative reflexes occur in an orderly way, the individual is said to have a good organic tone.

Many of the activities initiated by organic impulses are rhythmical in function, such as the heart-beat, respiration, hunger, the eliminative functions and sex activity. We see in the organic reflexes a possible basis for a time "sense." In highly complex animal communities one animal will do a definite thing, such as go for food, spell his mate upon the nest, at fairly regular intervals. The same mechanisms are functioning in man when, fairly regularly even in the absence of a watch but guided by the rhythmical contractions of the stomach muscles, he drops his occupation and goes for food. The human being is more dependent upon these rhythms than he usually admits. Students become restless if held over the hour; guests become troublesome and distrait if dinner is delayed too long beyond their customary hour of dining; infants taught to feed at two-hour intervals awaken almost on the moment and cry lustily if food is not forthcoming.

The glands, so far as location is concerned, belong to the area in which organic impulses arise. That afferent or sensory nerves end in the glands is reasonably certain, but what the function of such impulses is does not seem to be known. They are

possibly regulatory of the gland itself. Under the influence of
autonomic motor impulses, the glands secrete, but these secretions have a wide general distribution. Such secretions and
their functions are discussed in detail further on.

V. SENSE OF TASTE.

Area.—The sense of taste as a whole has been very well
worked out, thanks largely to the work of Kiesow. The bodily
areas sensitive to taste are much larger than is generally supposed, and relatively much larger in children than in adults.
The taste buds, which are the organs of taste, are found distributed fairly densely over the tip,
sides and edges of the tongue. The
median part of the dorsum of the
tongue is lacking in taste buds in
adults. The portion of the palate
that lies above the uvula contains
these structures, as do the anterior
pillars of the fauces. Some are
found in a portion of the posterior
wall of the pharynx and in a portion
of the epiglottis and of the larynx.
They are lacking in the lips, hard
palate, uvula, tonsils, cheeks and
lower surface of the tongue, and in
the gums.

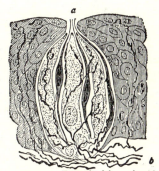

FIG. 9.—Taste bud from the side
wall of the circumvallate papilla of the
tongue: *a*, taste pore; *b*, nerve fiber
entering taste bud. (Herrick, "Introduction to Neurology," W.B. Saunders
Company.)

Organs of Taste.—Each taste bud (Fig. 9) consists of a large
number of modified epithelial cells constituting a pear-shaped
organ 73μ to 81μ in height and about 40μ in width. In addition
to the sensory cells supporting cells are present. Each sensory
cell is supplied with taste hairs. The whole structure is beaker or
barrel shaped. A small pore, opening directly upon the surface,
serves for the reception of the taste solutions. The nerve fibers
are distributed directly to the taste buds. While the buds are the
true organs of taste (corresponding to the hairs and corpuscles
in the skin) one rarely finds them isolated upon the surface of
the tongue, but grouped together around a so-called papilla.

Fig. 10 shows the tongue and its papillæ. With the exception of the 7 to 12 large circumvallate papillæ at the base of the tongue forming the lingual V, the only other form of papilla having a taste function is the fungiform. The latter are extremely numerous as can be verified by drying the tongue with a linen cloth

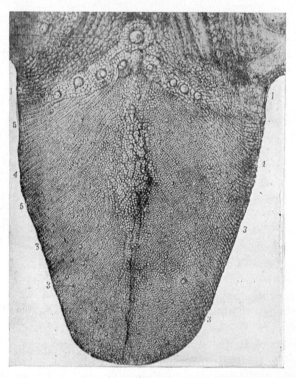

Fig. 10.—Papillary surface of the tongue. 1, Circumvallate papillæ forming the lingual V. 3, the fungiform papillæ; 4, filiform papillæ. (Modified from Sappey.)

and observing them in a mirror. The fine filiform and conical papillæ serve merely to roughen the tongue for the better manipulation of food objects. About 400 taste buds lie in each of the circumvallate papillæ, while a variable but much smaller number are attached to the fungiform.

It must be remembered that the tongue and oral cavity comprise not only a taste organ, but a cutaneous and kinæsthetic area as well. Furthermore, taste as a whole functions in close connection with smell; consequently care must be exerted in making tests upon taste. In general the test fluids must be warmed to body temperature; they must be weak enough to avoid causing reflex tongue movement which would involve kinæsthetic factors; the nose must be tightly plugged up; finally, the individual papilla must be stimulated by the fluid in such a way that the stimulus cannot spread and thereby arouse contact impulses. The fluid can best be applied by the use of a small camel's-hair brush.

When these precautions have been taken it is generally agreed that there are four separate sense organs: one responsive to sweet substances, one to bitter, one to salt and one to acid. Experimenters in the field of taste have used the conditioned reflex method, but more largely the verbal report method.

When the tongue as a whole is investigated it is found that sensitivity to sweet substances is greatest at the tip and least at the base. The maximum sensitivity to bitter substances is in the region of the circumvallate papillæ. Sensitivity to acid is greatest at the median part of the border. Finally, the sensitivity to salt is maximal at the apex and margin and minimal at the base. Apparently the stimuli to the taste buds have to be adequate. The mechanical arousal of the taste bud by electrical, thermal and contact stimuli has not been confirmed. An adequate stimulus is afforded when the underneath portion of the tongue is smartly tapped. The subject reports the presence of the stimulus of salt. This is due to the sudden pressure on the capillaries and the consequent release of small quantities of their contents.

The individual taste bud cannot be stimulated like the cold and warm spots, but if a large group of papillæ is gone over with the four taste stimuli, it is found that not all of them react to the four solutions. Kiesow examined carefully 39 papillæ. Four were insensitive to all four substances, the other 35 reacted as follows:

18 to salt.........3 to salt exclusively;
26 to sweet........7 to sweet exclusively;
18 to acid.........3 to acid exclusively;
13 to bitter.......0 to bitter exclusively.

Certain substances have the power of throwing taste buds out of gear. Gymnenic acid when applied to taste buds abolishes first, sensitivity of organs to sweet, then to bitter and finally to salt. It apparently does not affect the organs sensitive to acid. The gymnenic acid has no effect upon the tactile, temperature or pain sensibility of the tongue. Cocaine affects the cutaneous sensitivity of the tongue and finally gustatory sensitivity.

Some investigation has been undertaken for the purpose of obtaining taste contrasts and compensations. Distilled water apparently affects the organs sensitive to sweet after weak solutions of hydrochloric acid, caustic soda or potassium chloride have been used in the mouth. The use of a solution of sodium chloride and quinine apparently sensitizes the organs responsive to sweet substances to such an extent that a subliminal sugar solution will produce a reaction. There is no good evidence at present for asserting that the presence of one taste solution will neutralize the effects of the others.

Many experiments have been undertaken for the purpose of discovering what peculiar chemical property substances must possess before they can serve as adequate taste stimuli. So far dependable results have not been obtained.

VI. OLFACTORY SENSE.

Area.—The area comprising the olfactory sense proper is very small. It consists of a small saddle-shaped membrane lining the roof and sides of each nasal cavity. The total area (right and left) sensitive to olfactory stimuli is about 5 square centimeters.

Stimuli.—The adequate stimuli to the sense of smell are gaseous particles coming into direct contact with the olfactory membrane. Not all gaseous particles will produce olfactory response. The total number which will is unknown, but is very large. Many objects, such as arsenic, resins and metals, are non-volatile at ordinary temperatures, but they give off particles sufficiently fine to affect the end organs when heated. The question as to whether solutions containing known olfactory stimuli can arouse olfactory reactions when they come into direct contact with the olfactory membrane is not so well settled. According to more recent experimentation, it can be asserted that fluids containing odoriferous substances brought into direct contact with the olfactory membrane can serve as adequate stimuli. In making such experiments great care has to be exerted to keep bubbles of air from excluding the fluid from contact with the membrane. This seems to be in line with studies in comparative psychology, since it has been shown that certain fish even when blind are stimulated by distant food substances.

The membrane can possibly be stimulated inadequately by an electrical current, but there is no general agreement to this. Heat, cold and mechanical irritation seem not to affect it. At present we can say little about the chemical properties which a substance must have in order to affect the olfactory membrane. On the physical side, solubility in liquid and in gaseous air seem to be correlated with the property of arousing the membrane. Ability to arouse the membrane is possibly also to be correlated with the coefficient of absorption of heat rays.

When all has been said we know little about the nature and number of adequate olfactory stimuli. The various odoriferous substances have been classified with reference to the general similarity of response produced by them. This classification, which is given below, has little to recommend it:

Class 1—fruit odors—fruits, wine, ethers, beeswax;
Class 2—aromatic odors—spices, camphor, cloves, ginger, anise;
Class 3—flower odors—flowers, vanilla;
Class 4—musk odors—amber, musk;
Class 5—leek odors—chlorine, iodine, hydrogen carbide, asafœtida;
Class 6—burned odors—roast coffee, tobacco smoke, creosote;
Class 7—hircine odors—caproic acid, cheese, sweat;
Class 8—foul odors—opium, laudanum, bugs;
Class 9—nauseous odors—carrion flowers, fæces.

The phenomena of fatigue and adaptation are most interesting in this field. The student of chemistry or anatomy ceases in a short time to react to the numerous odors surrounding him. Individuals in large audiences housed in poorly ventilated rooms become adapted to the various odors and perfumes. Individuals just coming in react strongly to this situation. In the laboratory it is possible to produce with more or less rapidity adaptation to any particular olfactory substance.

The perfumers have learned the art of combining smell stimuli so as to produce what from a reaction standpoint are entirely new olfactory stimuli. The olfactory organ is undoubtedly peculiar in this respect. The perfumers have worked mainly with the first four classes. Experiments in the laboratory show that combinations of stimuli can be made in a similar way from any of the classes.

Smell compensation or physiological cancellation of stimuli has been sought for in the laboratory. In daily life there seems to be such a principle at work. Carbolic acid is used in the operating room, balsam of Peru is used to offset the effect of iodoform. Creolin is used to counteract the smell in public toilets, tar to offset the odor of ozœna. Just what the cancellations mean physiologically is not known. The fact remains that we constantly use one odor to drown the stimulating value of another odor.

One of the most discussed problems in the recent war was the question as to how to cancel the smell effect of a lethal gas, or to impart to it the smell of a beneficent gas. This was desirable, for if the enemy could be induced to leave off his mask for even a short time, its deadly effect would have been accomplished before the mask could be donned. Zwaardemaker maintains that certain smells can be made to cancel completely; that is, the stimuli can be introduced in such intensities by means of an olfactometer that no smell reaction can be obtained. He maintains that the following cancel when the intensity relations are properly adjusted: cedar wood and rubber; benzoin and rubber; paraffin and rubber; rubber and wax; rubber and balsam of tolu; paraffin and wax. Complete cancellations of these kinds are so infrequently met with in nature that they play little rôle in the normal life of man.

The Smell Sense in Conjunction with Touch and Temperature.—It is well to remember that many taste stimuli are at the same time smell stimuli. All of the delicate differential reactions that the human makes to wines, meats and viands of any kind are made largely on the basis of the olfactory sense. Furthermore, cutaneous nerves are distributed to the nasal cavities and actually to the olfactory membrane itself. Even the anosmic reacts strongly to ammonia, ethers and many other substances when they are placed in the respiratory field. Hence we must consider that in many if not all cases a so-called olfactory stimulus is at the same time a tactual, or even a tactual and kinæsthetic stimulus.

Structure of the Olfactory Organ.—As has been stated above,

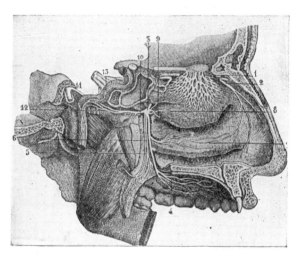

FIG. 11.—Ending of olfactory and other nerves in the outer wall of the nasal cavity. 1, Shows distribution of olfactory nerve (after Sappey).

the olfactory area is quite small. It is situated at the top of the nasal cavity with extension on the sides. It is out of the way of the regular respiratory tract or breathing passages. The streams of inspired and expired air pass just beneath it in both inspiration and expiration. No odoriferous substance will produce an olfactory response if the subject is prevented from breathing it. Or put it another way: in order to produce an olfactory response, the odoriferous substance must be placed in the field from which the air is inspired. It is generally supposed that gaseous particles are given off from the stream of inspired or expired air which by diffusion reach and stimulate the olfactory sense organ.   Fig. 11 shows in a general way the location of the membrane and its relation to the nasal cavity as a whole.

The structure of the individual olfactory elements in the membrane is rather different from that found in the sense organs in the skin.   In the skin we find the nerve fibers ending around highly modified epithelial cells, the sense organ itself being this modified, non-nervous structure.   Fig. 12 shows the olfactory cell or individual sense organ.   The cell body is bipolar and lies in

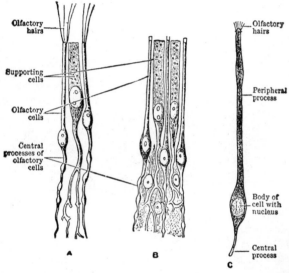

Fig. 12.—Cells from the olfactory mucous membrane. A, From the frog, B and C from man. The olfactory cells which are nerve cells are supplied with hairlets. The cells in between the olfactory cells are non-nervous supporting cells. The central process is really an axone which ends in the olfactory bulb of the brain. (From Herrick's "Introduction to Neurology," W. B. Saunders Co.)

the membrane itself.   The peripheral process of each cell consists of a number of hair-like structures which project into and slightly beyond the membrane.   The other end of the cell gives rise to the nerve fiber (axone, page 130), which can be traced upward through the sponge-like bone to end around cells situated in the olfactory bulb.   The olfactory bulb is shown upon the ventral surface of the brain in Fig. 30. page 143.

VII. Audition.

The Physical Side of Hearing.—Before entering upon the nature of auditory stimulation and the reactions such stimulations call forth, we may profitably glance for a moment at the physical nature of sounding bodies. We find first that some elastic bodies such as steel bars and tuning forks impart to the air when struck a simple pendular or sinusoidal wave motion, equally spaced waves of condensation and rarefaction. Depending upon the length and the structure of such elastic bodies, and the energy with which they are actuated, we may have waves varying in frequency or length and in amplitude through a very wide range. Most elastic bodies, those, for example, used in musical instruments such as the string, vibrate when actuated not only as a whole but in parts as well. The wave motion imparted to the air by such bodies becomes very complex. In such cases we speak usually of the lowest vibration rate given out by the body as its fundamental vibration (or note) and of the other frequencies as its partials. If we have a string vibrating as a whole 100 times per second, experiment will show that it vibrates in one-half its length one-third, one-fourth and one-fifth, etc., at the same time; so that a stretched string when plucked really gives a very complex stimulation. A large bank of resonators arranged so that each unit will signal when its particular frequency appears as a component part of a complex wave enables us to record the total set of vibrations which any given musical instrument will give out when any particular note is struck upon it. By this means it is possible to state with some degree of accuracy the different sets of frequencies set up by two human voices sounding the same musical note. Keyed and fretted instruments differ greatly as regards the complex of vibration rates which they give out. This is the reason why our reactions are different, for example, when middle C is struck on the piano, the flute, the organ or the cornet; they all have the same fundamental vibrations, but they vary enough in their partials for us to learn to react differently to them. We can name the instrument from which it comes, or make one type of reaction to it when it appears on the piano and another type when it appears on the violin.

Such stimuli we call *tonal*. Attention is called to the fact that a simple tonal stimulus, such, for example, as would be offered by a note of 512 d.v. on the tuning fork, could differ in amplitude and in duration, but not in frequency. All tonal stimuli, however, in daily life are complex, and the stimulus as a whole induces the reaction. The farmer drops work and goes to his food when the dinner horn blows; the mother gets up at night when her baby cries. Only in the laboratories and in the science of music are tonal stimuli controlled in the way we treat them below.

A very different type of vibration from those described above is set up by the tearing of paper or by the dragging of a chair along the floor. Here the elastic bodies do not impart an orderly timed disturbance to the air particles, nor do the tonal constituents, which are undoubtedly present, endure oftentimes for more than a fraction of a second. The physical tracings of the air waves set up by such stimuli lack periodicity and regularity. Such bodies are said to give out aperiodic vibrations. We can conveniently group all such stimuli under the general term *noise stimuli*.

The Adequate Stimulus to Auditory Response.—The adequate stimulus for the excitation of the ear is ordinarily the air wave set up by the vibrations of elastic bodies such as a stretched string, a tuning fork or the human voice. In addition to the air waves which produce their effect upon the fluids of the inner ear by means of the chain of ossicles to be described below, the bones of the skull when placed in direct contact with the sounding body can also transmit the vibrations to the fluids and can arouse an auditory reaction. This can be tested by actuating a tuning fork and placing it between the teeth of the subject. We shall for reasons mentioned further on state that it is best to say that the stimulus to an auditory reaction is a wave motion (however produced) in the fluids of the inner ear. In general we may say that such a motion may be imparted to this fluid by (1) air waves generated by the to and fro movement of elastic bodies, (2) by conduction through the bones, (3) by spasmodic or reflex movements of the tensor tympani and by the stapedius muscles— two small muscles belonging to the middle ear structure, and (4) possibly through congestion of any of the membranes of the ear, and (5) possibly through the clicking of the bones of the middle ear as discussed below in Helmholtz's theory of combination tones.

Beats.—Two forks having related frequencies, for example, one of 512 d.v. and the other 511 d.v., when struck simultaneously offer a peculiar type of auditory stimulation. There is first a slow increase in the intensity of the stimulus, then a decrease in the intensity followed once each second by a momentary period of total absence of stimulation (this absence of stimulation is theoretical, since even though the two fundamental notes are in opposite phase and hence cancelled, the upper partials are not cancelled). The ear becomes very sensitive to such fluctuations in intensity. When the beats become very rapid they arouse antagonistic or avoiding reactions which appear when a performer plays a mistuned interval.[5]

Reactions to Tonal Stimuli.—If we investigate the behavior of any individual when stimulated by simple periodic vibrations such as are afforded by a large set of tuning forks, we find that sensitivity to this form of stimulation begins at approximately 40 single vibrations per second and ends at 40,000. We often find this range shortened at one or both ends. With advancing age, the range is almost always shortened at the upper end. We find, furthermore, great sensitivity to even slight differences in vibration frequencies. If one sets up a conditioned reflex (page 35) to the tone 512 d.v., any tone slightly greater or less will set off the reflex; but after training one finds that the tone 515 d.v. will not set it off, nor will one of 509 d.v. arouse it. By decreasing the vibration difference we can approach the differential threshold (D. L.). It has been affirmed that the differential threshold obtained by the conditioned reflex method does not differ markedly from that obtained by the verbal report method (we have not yet confirmed this). By the latter method a difference of less than one-third of a vibration has been reported. This value, however, depends greatly upon what region in the scale we

---

[5] It will be noted that so far as a mathematical calculation is concerned, the formula for determining the frequency of beats is the same as that for determining the difference tones, page 78.

are working with. With musically untrained individuals the
difference is very much greater, and with the so-called tone-deaf
it is very much greater still. Occasionally upon making investigations upon individuals with defective hearing one finds that they
cannot respond to a given tone or group of neighboring tones,
but that they respond normally to vibration rates of greater or
less frequency.

Combination Tones.—One of the remarkable things noticed
when a subject is stimulated by two simple (''pure'') tones simultaneously is the fact that he responds really to three tones (or
more). If the tone of 1328 d.v. and the tone 1024 d.v. are
sounded in the ear of an individual and he is asked to strike
the forks which have been used in the stimulus, he will strike
not only 1328 and 1024 but 304 as well, the ''difference'' tone.
If he is musically trained, he may strike several others, for
example, 720, 416, etc. There is a general law which shows these
relations. If we let u stand for the highest frequency and l
stand for the lowest frequency and D be used to designate the
frequency which is not physically demonstrable, then

D_1 the first   difference tone $u - l = 304$
D_2 the second difference tone $2l - u = 720$
D_3 the third   difference tone $3l - 2u = 416$, etc.

Some investigators have reported another type of tone appearing
in the stimulus complex, namely the so-called summation tone
whose frequency with reference to the two primary or generating
tones is $u + l$. It is doubtful whether this tone is present.

Theory of Origin of Combination Tones.—Just how do these
tones arise? Helmholtz believed that when the middle ear is
forced to respond to two primary tones simultaneously there is an
asymmetrical movement of the ossicles resulting in a click which
can be shown mathematically to have the frequencies called for
in the observed facts. This periodic clicking of the bones becomes a part of the combined wave motion imparted to the fluids
of the inner ear. Thus, although there is no elastic outside body
(or may not be) vibrating with the frequencies corresponding to
the combination tones, nevertheless *such waves are imparted* to
the middle ear. We shall find a similar case when we study the

eye: there the sense organ itself when stimulated in a certain way contributes a part of the stimulus which finally acts upon the sensory nerve endings (simultaneous contrast, page 127).

Reactions to Noise Stimuli.—The various reactions to noise stimuli have not received any great amount of study. Any tonal stimulus interrupted before two complete vibrations have been transmitted to the fluids of the ear is reacted to as a noise. Popular language contains many words characterizing noise stimuli such as *hiss, murmur, sigh, boom, bang, rumble, crash,* etc. It is probable that noise stimuli are more potent arousers of emotional reaction than are tonal stimuli (page 219). Phylogenetically at any rate, sensitivity to differences in vibration frequency comes very late. We know from every-day life that noises have a tremendous significance in human behavior and that complicated reaction systems develop around noise stimuli. This is shown most clearly in the avoiding of automobiles and cars. Echoes and other sound reflections play a part in our responses, especially when vision is cut off. A great many stories have been written around blind detectives, and while the portrayed behavior is exaggerated, it is not without some foundation in fact. A mother has not the slightest difficulty after the first few days in approaching in the dark her own crying infant and picking it out from a large number of other crying children in the nursery. Differential sensitivity as well as liminal sensitivity grow very acute when an individual's occupation demands that he react to a world of noises. We cite the examples of the hunter who can by their cries name the various animals in the forest, and the Indian's delicate attunement and sensitivity to the slightest noise. Noises are the stimuli which are most important in daily life. Tonal stimuli are of significance mainly in the realm of music.

AUDITORY SENSE ORGAN.

Structure of the External Ear.—We have already discussed on page 61 part of the inner ear, namely the vestibular portion consisting of the semicircular canals and of the saccule and utricle. The remaining part of the ear, the cochlea, is devoted to the reception of auditory stimuli.

The structure of a large part of the ear as a whole need not here detain us since several good descriptions are to be found in the various anatomical and physiological text-books. In general, one speaks of (1) the external ear, (2) the middle ear, which consists of the drum membrane attached obliquely at the end of the auditory meatus and of the ossicles with their muscles, (3) the inner ear.

The external ear in man is quite complicated in shape. Its general function in the animal world is to collect and condense the sound waves. In view of its shape in man, of its method of attachment, and the atrophied condition of its muscles, it has little function in hearing. The canal or external meatus which extends from the concha to the middle ear serves as an avenue for the conveyance of air vibrations. It is about 22 mm. in length and its course is somewhat tortuous. The bore varies considerably. The skin which lines it is provided with hairs and wax-secreting glands. The hairs and wax protect the middle and inner ear.

The Middle Ear.—The middle ear, or tympanum, is an irregular chamber in the temporal bone. Its outer wall consists of the membrana tympani, or drum membrane. The drum membrane is ellipsoid in form, tightly stretched, and has a diameter of about 10 mm. It is about 1 mm. thick and is composed of radial and annular fibers. It is stretched over the meatus in such a way that it presents a convex surface towards this opening. In the inner wall of the tympanic cavity which separates the middle ear cavity from the inner ear are situated two openings or windows, the fenestra ovalis and the fenestra rotunda, which are to be described. The tympanic cavity communicates with the buccal cavity by means of the eustachian tube. An irregular chain of bones is stretched between the drum membrane and the membrane covering the fenestra ovalis. The chain of bones consists of the malleus, the incus and the stapes. Fig. 13 shows the method of articulation of the bones as well as their general form. The handle of the malleus is attached to the drum membrane. The head of the malleus (Mcp) articulates with the saddle-shaped depression in the incus. A short process of the incus (Ib) is attached by a ligament to the posterior wall of the tympanum. Its long process (Il) articulates with the stapes. The stapes is attached at its stirrup-like end to the fenestra ovalis.

These bones are under the control of two muscles, (*a*) the tensor tympani, which, when contracted, serves to tighten the drum membrane, and (*b*) the stapedius, which, when contracted, pulls the stapes slightly away from the fenestra ovalis, thus lessening the tension on the whole system (and hence on the drum membrane). The stapedius may thus be looked upon as the antagonist of the tensor tympani. When the air waves impinge upon the drum membrane, it is thrown into a backward and forward motion, forward at the condensation phase, backward upon the rarefaction phase. The frequency is thus the same as that of the elastic or sounding body. This excursion system of the drum membrane is wide but not powerful. The leverage principle upon which the chain of ossicles works is such that the to and fro motion transmitted to the fenestra ovalis is small, but cap-

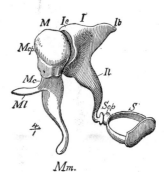

Fig. 13.—The bones of the middle ear. *M*, the malleus; *Mcp*, the head; *Mc*, the neck; *Ml*, the processus gracilis; *Mm*, the manubrium attached to the drum membrane; *Ic*, the incus or anvil bone; *Ib*, its short process; *Il*, its long process; *S*, the stapes or stirrup muscle. (From Howell's Text-Book of Physiology, W. B. Saunders Co.)

able of overcoming strong resistance, which is necessary because of the fact that the wave motion must be transmitted by the stapes to the fluids of the inner ear. While the importance of the middle ear as a transmitting and reinforcing device must be admitted, it should be added that in pathological cases auditory sensitivity is acute in the total absence of the drum membrane and all ossicles.

The Inner Ear, or Cochlea.—The auditory portion of the inner ear, the cochlea, is shown in Fig. 8, together with its relation to the vestibule and to the semicircular canals. The cochlea is a spiral tube divided into two chambers partially by means of a bony shelf, the lamina spiralis, and partly by a membrane, membrana spiralis, which is attached to the shelf at one end and to

6

the inner surface of the bony tube at the other. The upper cham
ber, or scala vestibuli, opens into the vestibule, while the lower
chamber, or scala tympani, communicates with the tympanic
cavity of the middle ear by the fenestra rotunda. At the apex
of the cochlea the two divisions communicate with each other by

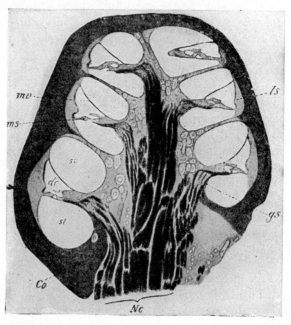

FIG. 14.—Section through cochlea (cat). dc, Ductus cochlearis; gs, ganglion spirale;
Co, bony wall of cochlea; ls ligamentum spirale; ms, membrana spirale or basilar membrane supporting the organ of Corti; mv, Reissner's membrane; Nc, auditory nerve; sv,
scala vestibuli; st, scala tympani (after Sobotta).

a small opening, the heliocotrema. Between the two scalæ is a
small canal, triangular in cross section, called the ductus cochlearis. This is the membranous sac continuous with that of the
vestibule. It contains the endolymph, whereas the scala vestibuli
and the scala tympani are filled with perilymph. The sides of this
triangular sac are made up as follows: the bony shelf and the
membrana spiralis form one side, another is formed by the membrane lining the bony wall, and the third by the delicate membrane of Reissner. These relations are shown clearly in Fig. 14.

It is in this membranous sac throughout its spiral course that we find the true auditory sense organs. These are supported on the membrana spiralis (also called basilar membrane in many of the texts). The center of the cochlea as a whole consists of a spongy bone, the modiolus. The nerve fibers of the VIII, or auditory nerve, pass through the bone and are distributed to the auditory structures lying on the basilar membrane. The auditory apparatus in the narrow sense consists of a group of structures called the organ of Corti (Fig. 15). To understand this organ and the

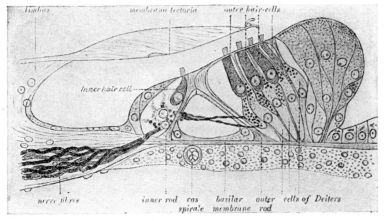

Fig. 15.—Partially diagrammatic representation of the organ of Corti and adjacent structures. The nerve fibers are seen passing to Corti's organ through openings in the bony spiral lamina. (From Bailey's Text-Book of Histology, Wm. Wood & Co.)

Helmholtz resonance theory of auditory stimulation, we must glance for a moment at the structure of the basilar membrane. As may be inferred, this is a spiral membrane about 0.041 mm. across at the base of the cochlea, and about 12 times wider (0.495 mm.) at the apex. If we were to detach the membrane and flatten it out, it would appear something like the stretched string system of the piano in miniature. While there are straight elastic fibers in this membrane, it must be admitted that as a whole it is largely homogeneous and that these elastic fibers are not free to vibrate. On the surface of this membrane superimposed upon the elastic fibers, one finds at close intervals pairs of stiff rod-like cells forming an arch. The upper ends of the cells join, while the lower ends are set wide apart upon the basilar membrane. There is thus formed a continuous row of the so-called arches of Corti. These arches support a series of modified epithelial cells, a single row on the inner side of the inner rod of Corti, and four rows beyond the outer rod of Corti. These cells are supplied with fine, stiff bristles which pierce through a fine cuticular membrane (lamina reticularis) and project out into the endolymph. There are several other supporting cells in the organ of Corti, but they are not important in this connection; since the hair cells are the true sense structures, and it is around them that the fibers of the auditory nerve end. Over the organ of Corti, extending as far out as the last row of outer hair cells one finds the tectorial membrane now looming rather large in the sensory physiology of hearing. One end of this membrane is attached approximately at the junction point between the basilar membrane and the bony shelf, the other end floats freely in the endolymph immediately above the hair cells. It is not generally recognized that owing to the position of the ear as a whole, this membrane works really in a sagittal and not in a vertical plane. Gravity thus has no direct tendency to pull it down upon the hair cells. In our opinion it can have no influence upon the generation of an auditory impulse, except in so far as it may serve as an object against which the hair cells can possibly strike. Even this function is probably not a necessary one.

Theory of Auditory Stimulation.—How is an individual hair cell stimulated? Various theories are advanced. The Helmholtz theory formerly had the most adherents, but it is gradually losing ground. This theory may be stated as follows: When a tuning fork of 500 d.v. sounds, the wave is transmitted to the fluid of the ear. One of the basilar membrane fibers is attuned to that frequency. It begins to vibrate sympathetically. As this fiber vibrates, it forces the hairlets of the hair cells to strike (possibly) against the tectorial membrane. This impact is sufficient to start the chemical processes in the hair cell as a whole, which results in the arousal of a neural impulse in the nerve element connected

with that cell. On purely logical grounds this theory accounts
very well for the various phenomena of hearing as follows: (1)
for the ability of the human being and lower animals to react
differently to different vibration frequencies; (2) for the absence of ability to react to frequencies less than 40 v.s. and
greater than 40,000 v.s. The theory merely assumes that there
are no basilar membrane fibers of sufficient length or shortness
to respond sympathetically to rates of greater or less frequency;
(3) the complete inability to react to auditory stimulation, and
(4) inability to respond to one definite set of frequencies while
having the ability to respond to higher and lower frequencies
(tonal islands).

Objections to the Helmholtz Theory.—Few physicists, however, are willing to admit that the radial fibers of the basilar membrane, forming a part as they do of a homogeneous membrane,
can vibrate as Helmholtz supposed. Ewald has advanced a
theory which seems more plausible upon the physical side. He
assumes that each and every tonal stimulus causes the basilar
membrane to vibrate in its entire length. Since it subdivides
into a series of stationary waves of definite form, he calls the
pattern so impressed upon the membrane the "acoustic image."
Every tone would impress a different acoustic image. These
patterns can be observed if a suitable rubber membrane about
the size of the basilar membrane is stretched over a frame and
made to shine with oil. A pattern of stationary waves appears
on this membrane when viewed under a microscope whenever
a tuning fork or other elastic body is actuated. Theoretically
these pressure patterns can account for the phenomena of hearing
which we have just enumerated if we grant that such patterns
bear sufficient energy to arouse the auditory hair cells. Luciani
suggests replacing the basilar membrane of this theory by the
tectorial membrane. The tectorial membrane under the influence of a given pattern would be pressed downward upon a definite set of hair cells. We have already called attention to the
fact that the tectorial membrane does not work in a plane which
would easily permit this.

There are many other so-called auditory theories which we

cannot enter into here. No one theory is accepted by all investigators, but all admit that there must be some mechanism in the inner ear capable of performing very complex functions, since destruction of the organ of Corti brings in its train the inability to respond to noise and tonal stimuli.

VIII. The Sense of Vision [6]

Visual responses are made possible by electro-chemical changes in the rods and cones (P. 119) of the retina. While

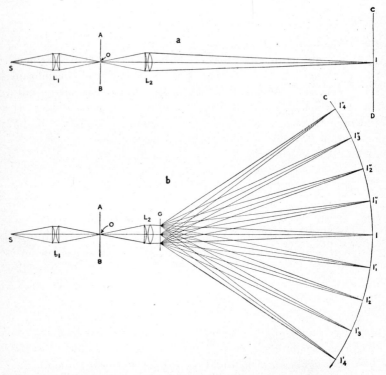

Fig. 15 A.—Showing the formation of a spectrum by the use of a transparent grating

[6] The material on pp. 86–115 was written by Professor H. M. Johnson, of the psychology department of the Ohio State University.

such changes may be excited by mechanical irritation, as in the case of pressure applied to the eyeball, by an electrical current, by an alternating magnetic field about the head, or by direct chemical irritation of substances carried in the blood, they are ordinarily excited by ether wave motion whose wave-lengths and frequencies lie within a restricted range.

If, as in Fig. 15 A-a, we cause the radiation emitted by the lamp S to fall upon a suitable lens L_1 the latter will form an image of the filament of the lamp on the screen AB at O. If we place a narrow, slit-like window at O, the rays which are not concentrated on the slit will be intercepted by the screen while the rest will pass through the slit. If we place a second lens, L_2 and a second screen, CD at suitable distances from O the lens L_2 will form an image I of O on the screen CD. If as in Fig. 15 A-b we place a transparent grating G in the path, a part of the radiation will pass through unimpeded to the original image *I*. The remainder will suffer *interference* by the lines on the grating and will be diverted or diffracted, some to the right and some to the left, in unequal degree, according to their wave-length, the greater wave-lengths being diffracted more than the shorter ones. As a result, on either side of *I* will be formed a spectrum, which is a *series of images* ($I'_{\lambda1}$, $I'_{\lambda2}$, $I'_{\lambda3}$, $I''_{\lambda1}$, $I''_{\lambda2}$, $I''_{\lambda3}$, etc.) *of O, arranged according to the wavelengths of the lights which compose them.*

The shortest wave-lengths,[7] whose images lie nearest the axis of the system, do not excite the visual receptors at all. They will affect a photographic plate, and they are capable of causing certain salts and sugars in the bodily tissues to interact with the protein of the latter and cause it to coagulate. Sunburn on the skin is due to this cause and similar injuries to the cornea of the eye may be likewise produced under extraordinary conditions, as by exposure to electric welding-arcs. These wave-lengths form what is called the *ultra-violet spectrum.*

Passing through this region from the axis of the system one

---

[7] This section presupposes acquaintance with such treatment of light as may be found in a good high school textbook of physics. Edser's " Light for Students " is a more detailed but yet simple and excellent reference text.

next finds a series of colored images of the slit, beginning with violet and extending through blue, green, yellow and orange to red. This portion is called the *visible spectrum.* The radiation within this range of wave-lengths is called "light."

Beyond the red is another series of images in still greater wave-lengths which have no effect on the retina. Their sole importance for vision lies in the fact that if their intensity is very great they may cause the tears which bathe the eyeball to evaporate too rapidly. This region is called the infrared spectrum.

The shortest wave-lengths which excite the retina are in the neighborhood of 400 mμ and the longest near 760 to 800 mμ.[8]

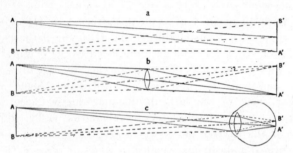

Fig. 15 B.—Showing diagrammatically some of the physical conditions which make vision possible.

Some of the physical conditions which make vision possible may be better understood from reference to Fig. 15 B-a. In this

---

[8] The wave-lengths of the portion of the spectrum which concerns us are very small. The conventional unit of measurement is the millimicron (m μ) equal to $0.001 \mu = 0.000001$ millimeter $= \dfrac{1}{25{,}400{,}000}$ inch.

A given light might as well be designated by its frequency of vibration as by its wave-length, though custom favors the latter mode. Certain relations between light stimuli are more readily exhibited when the latter are designated by their frequencies. The relationship between wave-length and frequency is very simple:

If λ = wave-length in millimicrons,
and f = frequency in trillions (10^{12}) per second,
then $\lambda f = 300{,}000$; $\lambda = \dfrac{300{,}000}{f}$; and $f = \dfrac{300{,}000}{\lambda}$.

figure AB represents a visible object. Each point on the object, such as A or B, may be regarded as *a source of light* in that it may emit light of itself or may reflect or transmit light which passes to it from other light-sources. The radiation from any one point, such as A, travels in straight lines in all directions, and it has a wave-length composition and an intensity determined, other factors being constant, by the physical characteristics of A. A limited part of this radiation may be intercepted by a surface $A'B'$. If we imagine the surface $A'B'$ to represent a portion of the light-sensitive retina of the eye we can see that it would be *stimulated* by the radiation from A, if the following conditions were fulfilled:

(1) Some of the intercepted radiation must lie within the wave-length range between 400 mμ and 800 mμ.

(2) The intensity within this range must exceed a certain minimum.

(3) The duration of the illumination must exceed a certain minimum.

(4) The area on which the radiation falls must exceed a certain minimum.

The receiving surface $A'B'$ being directly exposed to the radiation from AB, it can be seen that light from A passes not only to A' but also to B' and to all the intervening points. Within certain limits of dimensions of AB and $A'B'$ and of their separation from each other, each point between A' and B' receives practically equal illumination from A.

Similarly every point between B' and A' also receives light from B, and the total illumination upon it is the sum of that received from A, and from B and from the intervening points on AB. Subject to the limitation mentioned above every point between A' and B' would receive equal illumination.

Now, if the retina of the eye were directly exposed, as is the *receiving surface $A'B'$* (and as is the rudimentary eye in some simpler organisms) every part of it would receive equal stimulation. In such a case responses could conceivably be made (1) to temporal changes in wave-length of the light; (2) to temporal changes in intensity of the light; (3) to temporal

changes in duration of the light; and possibly (4) to changes
in direction of the light. It would be impossible, however, for
the organism to respond to differences in the spatial distribution
of wave-lengths and intensities among the various parts of the
surface AB since such differences could not be made to exist
without an additional mechanism.

Let us suppose, however, that as in Fig. 15 B-b a suitable lens
is placed between AB and $A'B'$ at suitable distances from each.
This lens serves to refract the rays coming from A so that they
meet at the point A' thus forming an *image* of the point A.
A similar image would be formed of B at the point B' and
likewise images of the points between A and B would be formed
between B' and A', and in corresponding points. If these
images were perfect the light at every point in the image $B'A'$
would have exactly the same wave-length composition and the
same relative intensity as when it left the corresponding point
in the object.

Such a condition is approximated in the eye. (Fig. 15 B-c.)
The anterior chamber, filled with water, and bounded in front
by the transparent curved surface of the cornea; the crystalline lens; and finally the posterior chamber filled with water,
together form a compound lens system which produces more or
less accurate images of visible objects on the light-sensitive
retina and thus subjects the latter to a pattern of stimulation
corresponding to the lightgiving characteristics of the various
points of the surfaces which send the light to the eye. In order
that two adjacent portions of a visible object be distinguish-
able it is necessary (1) that their images lie on different light-
sensitive elements (cf. p. 119) in the retina; and (2) that the
lights composing their images shall differ to a certain degree
in wave-length composition, in intensity or in both; or, if condition (2) be not fulfilled that the retinal elements on which
the images fall shall be unequally sensitive.

Inspection of Fig 15 A-b will make it clear that if one place
in either of the spectra an opaque slide containing a slit-window
which is parallel to the slit O, a limited range of wave-lengths,
depending on the widths of the slits, can be allowed to pass.

If the wave-length range of the selected beam is sufficiently small the light is said to be *homogeneous*. It is an easy matter to *calibrate* the instrument so that given the position of the selecting slit on an arbitrary scale the wave-length selected is known. The instrument is then called a *spectrometer*. If the light selected at the second slit is allowed to fall on a receiving surface, which is to be compared with other surfaces, the instrument becomes a *monochromatic illuminator*.

The selected light will not, in fact, be strictly homogeneous, owing to multiple reflection and scattering in the lens L_2, and the grating; but if it is passed through a second system similar to the first the stray light can be excluded. This is necessary in precise work.

Dependence of Stimulation on Wave-Length.—The energy of ether wave motion varies as the product of the squares of the amplitude and frequency of vibration. One of the most striking facts in vision is that a given amount of radiant power produces a degree of stimulation which depends on the wave-length of the beam. The manner of determining the dependence of stimulating value on wave-length may be readily understood by reference to Fig. 15C. In this figure, the square $ABCD$ represents a plaster cube whose sides AB and BC are viewed with the observer's eye at E. The side AB is illuminated by homogeneous light selected at a slit placed in the spectrum formed by the optical arrangement shown in Fig. 15A. The side BC (Fig. 15C) is illuminated by a lamp L_1 whose distance from BC is varied by moving it along a track on which its carriage rests. The intensity and wave-length composition of the light emitted from L_1 are kept constant and the illumination which it produces on BC varies inversely as the square of the distance between L_1 and BC. (The lamp L_2 and the clear glass mirror M are for mixing white light with the homogeneous beam and are not used in this experiment.)

A homogeneous beam is allowed to fall on AB and its energy is made equal to a certain predetermined value which is kept constant whatever the wave-length of the beam may be. (The energy may be measured directly, with any one of several types

of radiometer, or it may be calculated from the known characteristics of the light source and known losses in passing through
the spectrometer system.) The position of the lamp L_1 (Fig.
15 C) is now adjusted until the subject is unable to decide whether
AB or BC is the brighter. At this point lights forming the
images of AB and BC on the retina have equal stimulating
value. A second homogeneous beam is now substituted for the
first and the procedure is repeated. The relative stimulating
values of the various wave-lengths may then be computed from
the different positions of L_1, since they determined the energy
concentration which produced a stimulating effect equivalent
to that of the several homogeneous bands.

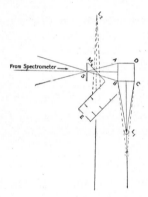

From Spectrometer

FIG. 15 C.—Apparatus for showing the dependence of stimulating value upon the wave-
length of the beam.

An alternative and better method is to keep the lamp L_1
constant as to position and energy-output, etc., and vary the
energy in the homogeneous beam required to produce a brightness match between AB and BC. The relative stimulating values of the different wave-lengths would then be proportional to
the reciprocals of their energies.

If the stimulating values are plotted against wave-length,
the result is called a *luminosity curve;* and each point on it is
regarded as expressing the relative *visibility* of the corresponding wave-length. It is customary to express the visibility of the

most effective wave-length as unity and of the others as fractions thereof.

Fig. 15 D shows two such curves obtained by a more sensitive method than the simple ones described above. The curve AA shows the average results obtained in light adaptation by a large number of experimenters on a large number of observers and it is used as a standard by the illuminating engineering society. The curve BB shows a representative result in dark adaptation. The

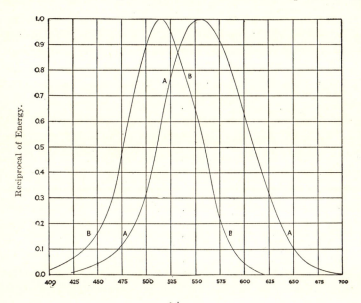

λ in mμ.

FIG. 15 D.—Luminosity curves: AA, standard photopic visibility curve; BB, representative scotopic visibility curve.

differences between the two sets of values are due mainly to Purkinje's effect.

If we express the energy delivered on a unit on retinal area by a homogeneous beam by the symbol E and its " visibility factor " (derived from the luminosity curve) by the symbol v, then its effectiveness as a stimulus is expressed by the product Ev. If the light is not homogeneous, but composed of various wave-lengths, λ_1, λ_2, λ_3, etc., effectiveness of a given wave-length is $E_\lambda v_\lambda$ and the total effectiveness of the beam is the sum of the effectivenesses of each of the wave-lengths or $E_{\lambda_1} v_{\lambda_1} + E_{\lambda_2} v_{\lambda_2} + E_{\lambda_3} v_{\lambda_3}$, etc. This summation is expressed by the common term *brightness*.

If two lights have proportional values of E for every value of λ throughout the spectrum they are said to be *similar*.

Certain important facts follow from what has been said: (1) the energies per unit area in two equally bright images are equal if the lights composing the images are similar. (2) If two images on the retina in similar lights, are unequally bright, their energy contents are unequal; and may be compared by determining the reduction in energy content which the brighter image must suffer to equal the brightness of the other image. (3) Conversely, if two equally bright images are formed in dissimilar lights the energies per unit area delivered at the retina may be unequal; and furthermore (4) the brightness of two images formed in dissimilar lights delivering equal energies per unit area may be unequal.[9]

The "visibility factor" for a given wave-length is greatly influenced by the intensity and duration of previous stimulation of the retina. (Some of these effects will be discussed below, under the heading "adaptation.")

The "visibility factor" also depends on the absolute energy concentration in the image. If the brightness on the retinal image in the middle part of the spectrum is as high as

[9] The validity of the use of photometry in physics as a method of determining energy-outputs and comparing the efficiencies of light-sources, and of the use of optical pyrometry in the measurement of high temperatures (as of steel furnaces) which must be accurately controlled, depends on the precision with which the "visibility factors" have been determined for the particular different observer and on the maintenance of the conditions of observation under which they were determined.

That this condition requires extreme care should be immediately evident: that it is possible of control is apparent from the close agreement found between photometric and radiometric determinations in the hands of skilled technicians.

one or two millilamberts [10] the most effective wave-length lies in the region of 556 mμ (" yellow "). If the absolute brightness is reduced to 0.001 of the original value, the most effective wave-length will be found to lie near 518 mμ (" green "). This increase in the relative effectiveness of the shorter wave-lengths in feeble illumination is called " Purkinje's phenomenon " after its discoverer. It is due to this shift that moonlight, which is physically similar to sunlight, appears greenish.

Differential Responses to Differences in Wave-Length.— A normal barnyard fowl can learn to go to a plaster surface illuminated with homogeneous light whose wave-lengths lie in the neighborhood of 670 mμ and avoid it if it is illuminated with light of say 520 mμ even if the physiological intensities (brightnesses) are made equal for that fowl. A normal human subject could respond by naming the first patch " red " and the second one " green." Obviously the mere naming of a wave-length region is not a highly differentiated response.

Suppose we take a plaster cube, such as the one shown in Fig. 15C and illuminate one side, *AB*, with homogeneous light of approximately 670 mμ ("red"). If the side *BC*, is illuminated by homogeneous light of longer wave-length he cannot make a differential response to the two lights (except on the basis of location) as long as their brightnesses are kept equal. If however, we illuminate *BC* with homogeneous light of about 640 mμ still keeping the two brightnesses equal, the subject may declare a difference, and call *AD* a more yellowish red than *AB*. If we change the illumination on *AD* to light of 650 mμ the subject may say that *AD* is not more yellowish than *AB* half as often as he says it is. This difference of 20 mμ in wave-length (*i.e.*, 670 mμ − 650 mμ) represents the minimal effective decrement, or " lower differential threshold " (DL), for wave-length with a standard of 670 mμ.

As we choose other wave-lengths for the illumination on *AB*

---

[10] A light-source of one candle-power one foot distant from a perfectly diffusing surface whose reflection coefficient is 1.0, lends to the surface a brightness of 1.077 millilambert.

and *BC* we find that the magnitude of the minimal effective difference is by no means constant. For example, if *AB* is illuminated with light of 589.6 mμ and *BC* with 589.0 mμ, an unusually sensitive subject will probably report *BC* to be " less reddish " than *AB* in about 75 per cent. of his judgments. In this region his DL for wave-length is approximately 0.6 mμ.

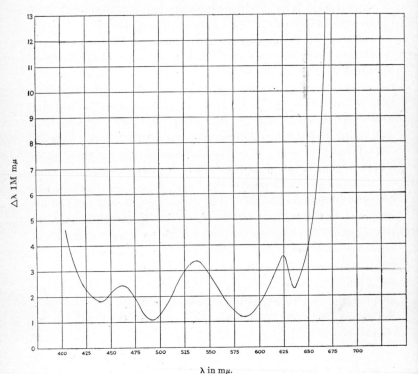

λ in mμ.

FIG. 15 E.—The DL for wave-length plotted against the wave-length of the standard field.
(After Jones.)

In Fig. 15 E is shown the DL for wave-length plotted against the wave-length of the standard field. These data were obtained by a better method than the simple one just described. Between 400 mμ and 660 mμ Jones found some 128 threshold differences in wave-length.

In " total color-blindness " the subject cannot distinguish

between any two homogeneous lights which have been equated in brightness for his eye. There is evidence which tends to show that the white rat and the rabbit, the cat and the dog are totally color-blind, although Smith, who studied the dog's responses, is inclined to draw a different conclusion from her data.

In other forms of " color-blindness " the subject can make differential responses to differences in wave-length but the thresholds are much larger than for the normal observer.

Differential Responses to Differences in Intensity.—If two retinal images in " similar " lights have equal brightnesses the energy delivered on a unit area of the retina is the same in the two cases. Consequently the least perceptible difference in brightness is determined by the least effective difference in energy concentration. If we wish to find the least difference in energy concentration which is effective for an animal or human subject whose visibility curve is undetermined it is essential that the two stimulus lights be " similar." This can be accomplished, within negligibly small limits, by careful choice of reflecting surfaces and by proper calibration and control of the lamps which illuminate them.

It is often important to measure the differential threshold for brightness in the human subject, in order to establish his discriminative ability as compared with other individuals in the same test, or to study the effect of fatigue, adaptation, quality of light, or of drugs on his own visual performance.

A simple means of making such a test is shown in Fig. 15 F. A small piece of white blotting paper, AB, is illuminated by a lamp L_1 at a fixed distance from it and viewed by the observer at E. A second lamp L_2 is arranged to slide on a track placed at right angles to that occupied by L_1. A piece of thin clear plate glass, M, is placed in the path of light so as to reflect a part of the radiation from L_2 on to AB. A vertical rod R (normal to the plane of the paper) is placed in the path so as to shade a part of AB from L_2. (It is desirable that the luminous surface of L_2 be very small, so as to render the shadow as sharp as possible. For this purpose automobile lamps are

7

convenient.)   The shadow of R therefore receives illumination
from L_1 only, while the remainder of AB receives light from
both L_1 and L_2. If L_2 is made sufficiently remote from AB the
brightness which it adds to AB will be ineffective and the shadow
of R will be invisible. If L_2 is brought sufficiently near to AB
its added brightness is effective and the shadow of R is visible.
The minimal effective addition of brightness ΔB, can be found
by noting the position of L_2 at which the shadow can be seen
in 75 per cent. of the total number of trials. The value of ΔB is
usually expressed as a fraction of B, the total brightness of the
screen.   The ratio $\Delta B/B$ expresses the *relative difference threshold* for brightness.

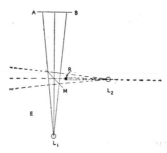

Fig. 15 F.   Apparatus for determining differential threshold for brightness. L_1, L_2, lamps;
AB, white screen; M, partially reflecting mirror; R, opaque rod; E, eye of observer.

If the absolute value of B is varied between limits of 1 millilambert and 1000 millilamberts the ratio $\Delta B/B$ is nearly constant.   The fact thus summarized is a special application of
Weber's law.   For an experienced observer, under favorable
conditions of vision the differential threshold is of the order of
0.5 per cent. to 0.8 per cent. within the region within which
Weber's law is applicable.   As this is about half the whole range
of uncertainty in making a brightness match it will be seen that
the uncertainty of a photometric determination under the
favorable conditions is between 1 per cent. and 2 per cent. in
the average.

As will be seen from Fig. 15G the differential threshold $\Delta B/B$
increases rapidly as the absolute brightness of the screen is

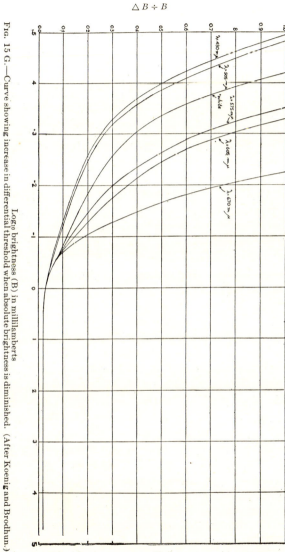

Fig. 15 G.—Curve showing increase in differential threshold when absolute brightness is diminished. (After Koenig and Brodhun.)

diminished below a critical value, near 1 millilambert. Purkinje's effect is manifested in the different rates of change of
$\Delta B/B$ for the longer and the shorter wave-length.

The magnitude of the differential threshold for brightness
$\Delta B/B$ is a very good index of visual performance in general,
as any factors that tend to lessen the sensitivity of the eye in
other respects tend also to increase the threshold. Consequently
its measurement is often used to test the effects of many variable
factors on visual performance.[11]

If the two compared lights are not " similar," the brightnesses of their images on the retina are not directly proportional
to their energy concentration. Consequently two individuals
with different visibility factors (cf. p. 92) may disagree widely
in their attempts to equate them. It is almost impossible for
a single observer to make a satisfactory brightness-match by
direct comparison of two homogeneous lights differing widely in
wave-length and indirect methods are necessary in the photometry of lights of different colors.

**Effects of Mixing Homogeneous Lights—Complementary
Lights.**—If two lights of appropriate wave-lengths, such as 656
mμ (red) and 492 mμ (" blue-green ") are mixed in different
proportions an observer will match the mixture with a mixture of (a) homogeneous light having the wave-length of the
stronger of the two components and (b) " white " light (cf.
p. 97). As the proportions of the red and blue-green are
varied a value can be found which the subject will match perfectly with " white " light without the addition of either the
red or the blue-green. (If the match is not always perfect at
this critical value the subject will select a little red to add to
it as often as he selects the blue-green.) These two lights are

---

[11] It is commonly supposed that the higher the brightness the better
one can see. Inspection of Fig. 15-G shows instantly that this law is not
general. On the contrary, huge increases of the absolute illumination
beyond a certain critical point have practically no effect on vision if the
distribution of lighting is unchanged. This fact is often ignored by engineers in the lighting of offices and factories at considerable monetary cost
to the employer and great inconvenience to the worker.

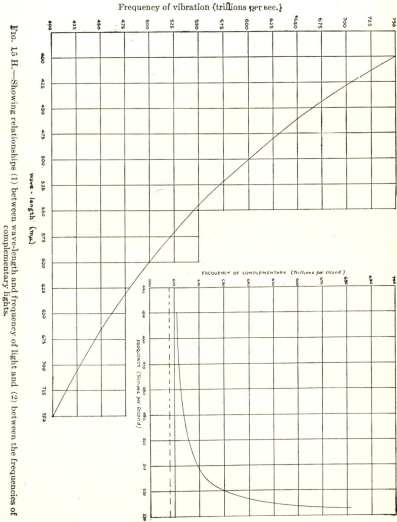

Fig. 15 H.—Showing relationships (1) between wave-length and frequency of light and (2) between the frequencies of complementary lights.

said to be " complementary." Other pairs can similarly be
found, but the wave-length of one component must always
exceed a value near 566 mμ and the wave-length of the other
must fall short of a value near 493 mμ. Priest has shown that
for the average eye the frequencies of vibration of complementary lights are simply related, as is shown in the formula

$$(530 - f_1) (f_2 - 608) = 220,$$

in which f_1 and f_2 represent the frequencies of vibration of the
two complementary lights in trillions per second. This relationship is shown in Fig 15-H. It will be noted that lights in the
" green " region, whose wave-lengths lie between 566 mμ and
493 mμ (and whose respective frequencies lie between 530 and
608 vibrations per trillionth of a second) have no complementary lights in the spectrum. They may be complemented however by mixtures of "red" and "blue" in varying proportions.

Definition of " White " Light.—If the brightness of the
standard " white " surface be kept constant the mixture of any
two complementary lights which match it cannot be distinguished from the mixture of any other two complementaries
which match it. Owing however to Purkinje's effect, a match
made at a moderate intensity will not hold when the intensity
is greatly diminished, or *vice versa*. Also, if the eye is subjected to stimulation from a particular monocromatic beam in
excessive intensity or for an excessively long time, a match
made under normal conditions ceases to be valid until the disturbing effect has been overcome.

In such industries as the manufacture of paints, artists'
supplies, dyes and textiles, and in the arts of painting, lithog-
raphy, advertising, stage lighting and camouflage the ability to
reproduce a dye or paint with accuracy has extreme importance.
It can be readily seen that since any colored surface can be
completely matched by a mixture of white light with one or two
lights taken from the spectrum, it can be adequately reproduced
if the following data are given: (1) The wave-lengths of the
homogeneous lights; (2) the proportion of " white " light which
has to be added; and (3) the brightness of the material as

compared with that of a non-selective reflecting surface when
the two receive equal illumination from a " white " light source.

If the unmodified radiation from an incandescent source is
to be a satisfactory standard of " white," it must be reacted to
at moderate brightnesses and by the most representative
observers as neutral between " yellowish " and " bluish," or
at least be reacted to as " yellowish " not significantly more
often or more seldom than it is reacted to as " bluish." Direct
noon sunlight under favorable conditions almost meets this
requirement but due to selective losses in passage through the
earth's atmosphere, which is continually changing, sunlight
cannot be used as a constant standard. As everyone. has
observed, the cooler an incandescent solid is the more deficient
will its radiation be in the shorter wave-lengths. Years ago,
H. E. Ives, working from known laws of radiation and from
assumed standards of " visibility " calculated that the above
standard of " white " could be obtained from the radiation
from the interior of a furnace at a temperature of approximately
5000° absolute. This standard was then impracticable because
a furnace can hardly be maintained long or controlled accurately
at so high a temperature. Since ordinary incandescent sources,
such as heated tungsten wires, carbon cores, etc., melt at temperatures between 3000° and 3800° absolute, they are reacted to
as " yellowish " and would not suffice alone. Various attempts
have been made to construct filters for use with such sources
but the filters were sometimes short-lived and could not be
reproduced from year to year. Recently Priest has found it
possible, by passing the radiation from an ordinary source
through an arrangement of Nicoll prisms and quartz plates, to
alter the energy wave-length distribution of the transmitted
light so as to correspond to that of a source whose temperature
is higher or lower than the one actually used, and to vary this
distribution at will. By means of such a system he has shown
that the light which best approximates " white " or " neutral "
light is such as would be emitted from a furnace heated to 5200°
absolute. This temperature value may require some slight
correction but it is probable that the future standard of
" white " for color-specification will be determined in this way.

Effects of Mixing of Non-Complementary Homogeneous Lights.—Let us suppose that a, b, c and d represent the wave-lengths of any homogeneous lights either increasing or diminishing in the order given; a and c, however, being complementaries. In general, if a and b are mixed the mixture will be matched by a light whose wave-length lies between a and b. The exact wave-length of the intermediate light will depend on the relative intensities of a and b. In some cases, depending on the proximity of b to c some white light must be added to b to complete the match. If both a and b exceed 540 mμ the addition of white light will be unnecessary.

If a and d are mixed their mixture cannot be matched by a single homogeneous light but can be matched by a mixture of two lights taken from near the extremes of the spectrum to which a certain proportion of white light may need to be added. The proportion will be greater the closer the proximity of d to c.

In colorimetry the response made to a given light is often described in terms of the proportions in which three " primary " lights must be mixed in order to produce an identical response (match). Several triads of primary lights are possible. An essential characteristic, however, is that no one of the three can be matched by a mixture of the other two. A convenient triad consists of (1) a light whose shortest wave-lengths do not exceed 655 mμ; (2) a light whose wave-length range lies between 518 and 527 mμ; and (3) a light whose wave-length range lies near 460 mμ. These primaries may be designated as R, C [12] and B respectively. If the three are mixed in suitable proportions the mixture is indistinguishable from a " neutral " or " white " light. Any homogeneous light whose wave-length lies between R and C can be matched by a definite proportion of R and C, provided a definite amount of B light be added to the homogeneous light to complete the match. Any light whose wave-length range lies between C and B can likewise be matched by mixtures of C and B in definite proportion but a definite amount of R may need to be added to the homogeneous light to complete the match.

---

[12] The symbol C is used as an abbreviation for " Chlor."

A light whose wave-length is shorter than B can be matched by a mixture of R and B with the addition of C to the homogeneous light. Lights which complement those between 493 and 566 mμ are matched by mixtures of R and B.

Differential Responses to Saturation and Purity.—If one half of a field, such as the cube in Fig. 15-C is filled with homogeneous light taken from the spectrum and the other half with a mixture of the same homogeneous light and " white " light, the brightnesses of the two fields being kept equal, the subject can make a differential response when the white light comprises somewhat less than 5 per cent. of the mixture. Jones has found some twenty just discriminable steps between spectral purity and white, the test-field being of medium brightness and the duration of exposure only moderately long.

In general, if the brightness of a monochromatic field is very high or very low the subject reacts nearly, and sometimes quite, as if the stimulus were neutral or white.

Similarly as to the effects of duration of exposure. Probably every student who has worked in a photographic dark-room has observed the effects of continued exposure to light from the " ruby " lamp. The glass bulb of this lamp transmits only wavelengths longer than about 630 mμ and the total radiation transmitted would be fairly matched by a homogeneous band of (say) 660 mμ. When the subject first enters the room he may describe the various surfaces as "reds" differing only in brightness. After a half-hour however, he reacts as if they were all non-selective reflectors, illuminated by neutral or white light.

Let us illuminate the two visible surfaces of the cube in Fig. 15 F with homogeneous lights of the same wave-length and brightness, and then temporarily shade the side BC and require the subject to fixate the edge B for 30 sec. to 60 sec. If now we restore the original illumination on BC the original match will at first be invalid and a considerable amount of " white " light will need to be added to the homogeneous light on BC to restore the match. That is, after prolonged exposure the subject reacts as though, the condition of the eye remaining constant, the homogeneous light had been gradually diluted with white.

If we now fill the side AB with homogeneous light leaving the side BC dark and require the subject to fixate the edge B for 30 sec. to 60 sec. and then suddenly remove the original light and in the same instant fill *both* sides with homogeneous light which is complementary to the first, a still more striking effect may be noted. The subject will declare the side BC to be " paler " than AB and a very considerable amount of white light will have to be added to the homogeneous light on AB to effect a match at the moment of exposure. In other words the subject will respond to the homogeneous light on AB as if it were *more highly saturated* than the light from the spectrum.

Effects of Simultaneous Contrast.—If we should illuminate one side AB of our little cube with homogeneous light and the side BC with " white " light the subject will describe BC as if it were filled with the complementary to the light on AB. If the relative brightnesses of the two sides are properly adjusted the subject will describe the light on BC which is physically " white " as being as fully saturated as the homogeneous light on AB. This response to BC will disappear instantly the homogeneous light on AB is removed.

If AB is illuminated by a mixture of homogeneous light and white light and BC with a mixture of white light with the complementary light to that on AB the subject will describe both lights as being highly, if not fully, saturated. This effect of contrast is very marked even when the homogeneous component in either mixture is imperceptible when the mixture is presented by itself.

If a surface is illuminated by light from a vacuum tungsten lamp and also by sunlight, a shadow cast by the lamp will be reacted to as if it were illuminated by light of wave-length of approximately 484 mμ (" blue "), provided the shadow is cast at a point where the relative illuminations in the two lights are appropriate. The reason is that tungsten light, being deficient in the shorter wave-lengths, has the stimulating effect of a mixture of about two parts of light of wave-length 588 mμ with one part of " white." Since the shadow receives only " white " light, it is reacted to as the complementary of the " dominant wave-length " (588 mμ) in the tungsten light.

A piece of " gray " paper laid on a colored surface will be reacted to as if it reflected an excess of the complementary to the " dominant " wave-length reflected by its background. These facts have to be observed in painting. An asphalt road depicted as alongside a grassy field must be painted in purple.

If two pieces of the same gray paper are laid on papers of higher and lower reflectivity respectively and subjected to equal illumination they will be reacted to as if they had very different brightnesses, that of the first being the lower.

In general, if two lights differing in intensity or in wave-length stimulate adjacent portions of the retina they tend to exert complementary effects. The greater the separation of the stimulated areas the less will be the effect. This fact is called the law of contrast (literally *contra* + *stare*). Different explanations are offered in different hypotheses of vision but none does more than restate the fact in different terms. The effect of contrast is universal though often unobserved by the subject. Striking demonstrations can be easily arranged with ordinary lamps and colored filters.

Effects of Stimulation of the Peripheral Retina with Homogeneous Lights.—If the eye is held in fixation and an image of a small surface is formed in homogeneous light on the peripheral retina the subject will react as if the light were " white." As the image is moved toward the fovea (cf. p. 119) a critical zone will be found within which the subject will usually describe the light, no longer as " white " but as " yellow " or " blue " according as the dominant wave-length is longer or shorter than the " blue-green " region in the spectrum. As the image is moved through this zone still nearer to the fovea its effect will be described as if its wave-length had been gradually varied from the yellow (or blue) region toward its actual value, and finally a paracentral region will be found in which the normal response will be made.

The extents of these zones, measured in terms of angular separations from the fovea, vary according to the wave-length, brightness and purity of the stimulating light and also according to the retinal area covered by the image. In general the greater the area and brightness, the wave-length composition being constant, the wider the normal zone. Abney's measurements on the horizontal extent of the normal zone may be formulated as follows: If E represents the extent of the normal zone in circular degrees from the fovea, and B represents the brightness of the image on the retina, and C and K, constants whose values are different for different wave-lengths, then for stimuli of constant area, $E = c. \log B + k$. That is, for a given wave-length and a given area, the horizontal extent of the normal zone varies as the logarithm of the brightness of the stimulus. The extent of the normal zone depends also on the area of the retinal image. It is constant for areas exceeding $5°$ but diminishes according to the logarithm of the reduction of area below $5°$.

It has been found that certain wave-lengths can be chosen whose normal zones are coextensive and which are reacted to as if they were neutral in all parts of the peripheral field outside the normal zone. According to Baird these stimuli are: (1) A bluish-green of about 490 mμ; (2) an extreme red mixed with a little blue; (3) a yellow, of about 570 mμ; and a blue of about 460 mμ. Stimulus (1) is the complement of (2) and stimulus (3) is the complement of (4). These are called "stable" stimuli and they correspond to the two pairs of "primaries" selected by Hering. It has been argued by some color-theorists that as compared with the central zone the extreme peripheral retina is color-blind, and the intermediate dichromatic; but, as appears above, the evidence does not support this view.

Some Temporal Aspects of Visual Response.—If a reflecting or transmitting surface is alternately exposed to a light source and shaded from it the subject will describe the surface as "flickering" if the frequency of alternation is sufficiently slow. If the frequency be sufficiently increased a critical value will be found at which the subject will react as if the illumination were steady but reduced in intensity.

The critical frequency for flicker F_c, depends on the brightness of the intermittently viewed surface as appears from the formula

$$F_c = C \cdot \log B + k$$

in which B represents the absolute brightness of the surface, and C and k constants whose values depend on the wave-length of the stimulus. For each wave-length the value of the constant c has two values: one for brightness below 0.03 millilamberts (below which the retinal cones are supposed to cease to respond and the rods become active), and the other for brightnesses between 0.03 and 100 millilamberts. These facts are of importance in that they make it possible to compare the brightnesses of two surfaces whose colors are so different as to make simultaneous comparison of their brightness very difficult and unreliable. In determining the " visibility factor " advantage is often taken of this method rather than the method of direct comparison described on p. 91.

It has been established that if two images having the same wave-length composition are alternated on the retina at varying speeds the flicker-effect will vanish for both at the same rate if the two images are equally bright. It is further *assumed* by some investigators that the same law holds when the two images have different wave-length compositions as well. On this assumption this method (called the method of flicker photometry) is widely used as a means of equating the brightnesses of two fields of different color. The results obtained by this method are much more constant than those obtained by the method of direct comparison or by the method of critical frequency; but the results obtained by the three methods do not agree perfectly. It will be readily seen that if the assumption just mentioned be sound the principle of the flicker photometer involves a different law from that established for critical frequency. One of the ablest exponents of the flicker method, H. E. Ives, indeed asserts that this is the case. As a method of making possible the *reproduction* of stimulus conditions to a high approximation to exactness the flicker method has great value whether it measures true brightness or not.

In general if two or more surfaces of different brightnesses
are viewed in succession at a rate above the critical frequency
for flicker, the brightness of the fused images will be the mean
of the brightness of the several images weighted according to
their respective durations. This formulation is known as the
Talbot-Plateau law [13] and is of extreme importance. On its
validity depends the use of the rotating sectored disk as a
means of reducing the effectiveness of a beam of light to a known
degree. When extended to include chromatic effects, the law
also authorizes the use of the " color-wheel " in demonstrating
the laws of color-mixture.

After-Images.—If a small portion of the retina be stimulated
by homogeneous light for a short time and then shaded, the
subject will often behave as if the retina were still being stimulated either (1) by the original light or (2) by its complementary. In case (1) the effect is called the positive after-image
and in case (2) the negative after-image. The two effects can
be made to alternate by alternately stimulating the eye with
diffused white light and then removing the stimulus. Under
suitable conditions these effects may persist for a long time but

---

[13] Every-day illustrations of its application may be seen in the moving-
picture houses; and also in vision under illumination from tungsten lamps
operated on alternating current. As the direction of the current through
the lamp is alternated (usually) 60 times a second, the current passes
through a maximum and also through zero 120 times a second. Thus the
filament is alternately heated and cooled and the illumination which it
produces consists of a series of intense flashes separated by intervals of
relative darkness. The net effect, however, is that of a steady illumination
whose intensity is the mean of all the instants of the cycle. If one uses
a lamp whose filament is very fine and therefore cools rapidly, small
moving objects will be responded to as if they occupied several discrete
positions at the same time. An electric fan rotating at high speed under
such illumination will appear to be rotating slowly forward or backward.
If a given blade occupied exactly the same position at one flash which
it or another blade occupied at the preceding flash, the fan would appear
to be stationary. These effects are called stroboscopic. They have been
utilized in the construction of an interesting instrument called the Lorenz-
Seashore tonoscope, for demonstrating and measuring the fluctuations of
pitch of musical tones as produced by different instruments and by singers.

they gradually diminish both in intensity and saturation. They are capable however of being revived to an intense degree many hours after they have disappeared if the eye is adapted to darkness. They may have quite a deal to do with the character of dreams and so-called "mental imagery," and may play an important part in hallucinatory experiences. If the original stimulus is very intense the after-images may not be simple, positive or negative, ones but the subject may behave as if the affected area were being successively stimulated by "red," "yellow," "green," "blue" and "purple" lights in varying orders.

Under ordinary conditions the after-images of one stimulus, being superposed on the primary images of succeeding ones, serve to modify visual responses unfavorably and to a large degree. In such practical problems as the distribution of illumination and the selection of wall-papers and paints due regard must be paid to the conditions of their production if high efficiency of performance is to be had.

The effectiveness of a photic stimulus is manifestly a function of three variables: (1) Its brightness, (2) the area of the retina to which it is applied, and (3) its duration. Cobb has shown that if (1) be kept constant the product of (2) and (3) is constant for threshold effectiveness. If the area be kept constant, and small, the reciprocal of the duration necessary for threshold effectiveness is nearly proportional to the logarithm of the brightness between the limits of 1 and 107 millilamberts; but the necessary duration is much less than the duration of the normal resting period of the eye at a brightness of one millilambert. The advantages of the higher brightnesses are therefore doubtful.

Adaptation.—If a subject is brought from a brightly lighted room into one that is very feebly lighted he will at first be either unable to distinguish objects or else will react only to very large objects which present a large difference in brightness from their background. After a time, which may vary from a few minutes to one or two hours, he will be able to respond to the same objects with quickness and certainty. If he is now suddenly brought into a brightly lighted room he will probably again be unable to see clearly and may make efforts to shield the eyes from light. After a short time, varying from a few seconds to a few minutes, he can again make normal responses. The changes which occur under these conditions are called *adaptational* changes and are of capital importance.

The sensitivity of the normal subject is capable of enormous modification. He is capable of making visual responses of some sort at general levels of brightness which vary relatively between 1 and 1,000,000,000. Furthermore, responses can be made *with about equal effectiveness* at brightness levels varying between 1 and 1000 millilamberts, provided the subject has been allowed sufficient time for adaptation. Below the level of 1 millilambert the effectiveness of vision begins to fail (cf. Fig. 15-G). Thus the practical question of how much light one needs to see by is a meaningless question unless the subject's state of adaptation be taken into account.

Just what determines adaptation is not clearly known. The total light admitted to the retina is a function of the area of the pupil (cf. p. 117) other conditions being constant. The pupil in very dim light tends to dilate to a diameter of about 8 millimeters. On sudden exposure to a brighter surface it usually contracts to a diameter of about 2 millimeters but may later assume a larger value. As the areas of the opening are proportional to the squares of the diameter it appears that the pupil may operate to vary the relative intensity of illumination on the retina between the limits of 1 and 16. This, however, is almost an insignificant part of the total range of adaptation. Some authors have assumed that the photosensitive structures in the retina have their sensitivity altered so that they tend with adaptation to excite neural impulses with about the same frequency under intense and weak stimulation. Some have assumed that this action is due to the rate of consumption of a sensitizing substance present in the receptors or their surrounding media. This hypothesis however is affected by the fact of binocular adaptation. Dunlap has shown that if a restricted area in one eye is continuously stimulated until it ceases to respond, the " corresponding " area (cf. p. 123) in the unexposed eye is likewise affected, and in the same degree. This suggests that a central mechanism is essential to the process. There are certainly efferent pathways leading to the retina, which might make such control possible.

It has been shown that in certain of the lower vertebrates the pigment in the epithelial cells of the retina (which dove-tail with the rods and cones) migrates forward under high illumination, and retreats in darkness. On the other hand, under high illumination the rods elongate, so that their sensitive portions are well shielded by the pigment layer, while the cones contract. In darkness the reverse seems to be true. The facts are not perfectly consistent, due, perhaps, to shortcomings of the technique. Furthermore the exposure of only one eye results in similar changes in the shielded eye, thus suggesting a central control. These facts tempt one to construct a theory of adaptation based at least in part on an assumed tendency of the epithelial pigment to admit a constant density of illumination to the rods and cones. Such an hypothesis is in accord with the facts and offers a simple explanation of them, but it suffers from the disadvantage that all attempts as yet made to demonstrate pigment-migration or contraction of rods and cones in the mammalian eye have failed. There is some probability that this failure is due to defective methods of fixing the histological preparations but meanwhile the hypothesis can hardly be pressed too far.

Other students have assumed that the rods and cones, by their contraction and elongation, may weaken and strengthen their synaptic connections with the bipolar cells, so that fewer impulses aroused in the former would be transmitted to the bipolar cells. Evidence as to this point is completely lacking and the view is out of harmony with the belief of eminent neurologists in the permanence of physical connections at the synapses. Still others have assumed that the frequency of retinal response may be the same for strong and weak stimulation but, due to the action in inhibitory centers some of the neural impulses themselves may be blocked.

8

According to the duplicity theory, the rods and cones are two separate and alternative mechanisms, the former functioning at very low brightness, and the latter at high ones. There is a range of brightness within which both rods and cones function after a fashion but above and below this range only one mechanism is operative. The fovea, which contains only cones, is completely blind under dark-adaptation; birds which have only cones are helpless in low illuminations; the evidence of critical frequency for flicker, etc., all points to a double mechanism.

Many industrial accidents result from inattention to the fact of adaptation. Persons who have to pass from brightly lighted rooms to dimly lighted rooms where there is complicated machinery, or who, after working on a well lighted part of a machine have to look into a dense shadow to operate another part, are especially exposed, since the eye cannot be adapted, even in tolerable degree, to two widely different levels of brightness at the same time.

While it is possible under special conditions to produce local adaptation in restricted areas of the retina in practice this process seldom proceeds very far on account of eye-movement. Everyone has noticed that it is impossible to discern objects in a daylight room when one is standing outside the building and looking through an open window; the reason being that the eye being adapted to the brightness-level of the sun-lit sky, clouds, earth, and wall of the building, will not function well at the much lower brightness level of the room. On the other hand the observer on the outside can distinguish the objects with ease at night, when the room is much more dimly illuminated by artificial sources, but the observer's surroundings are relatively dark. As a rule the brightest surfaces in the principal part of the visual field, if they are fairly large, tend to determine the state of adaptation of the eye. Hence, it is of great importance that the average brightness of the objects under special observation be at least as high as any of the other surfaces within the field of view. Cobb and Johnson by very different methods have independently shown that vision is impaired by approximately 20 per cent. by making the surroundings only twice as bright as the test object; and the impairment is increased to the order of 65 per cent. by making the surroundings ten times as bright as the test field. In some factories the workers are required to face diffusing glass windows whose brightness may be 100 times as high as that of the work material. The result, if the operation requires much of vision, is a tremendous insult to safety, efficiency and health of the worker.

Color Theories.—The principle facts of vision have been related to as many as 80 different hypotheses invoked to explain them. The spatial limits of this book preclude an adequate discussion of any of them, and the student is referred to more copious works. Perhaps the best general reference at the present date is J. H. Parsons: An Introduction to the Study of Color Vision (Cambridge, 1915). The hypotheses formulated by Helmholtz, by Hering (especially as modified recently by E. Q. Adams) and by Christine Ladd-Franklin are the most used; that of Ladd-Franklin probably having the most to commend it.

STRUCTURE OF THE EYE.

Structure of the Eye as a Whole.—The eye as a whole functions somewhat like a camera. In a camera there is a lens for focussing an image upon a sensitive plate, and a diaphragm for controlling the intensity of the light. In the eye there is a lens, and a similar diaphragm, the iris. The sensitive plate of the camera becomes the retina of the eye. In the retina must lie the photochemical substances which are assumed to exist. Here the analogy stops. The action of the chemical substances in the retina ends in a neural impulse which passes through the central nervous system and out to an effector organ. Each eye-ball is almost spherical. It is made up of concentric coats, modified in a special way in certain parts, a crystalline lens and two fluid masses—the aqueous and vitreous humors. The lens and fluids occupy the interior of the eye-ball. Fig. 16 shows the more important features of the eye as a whole.

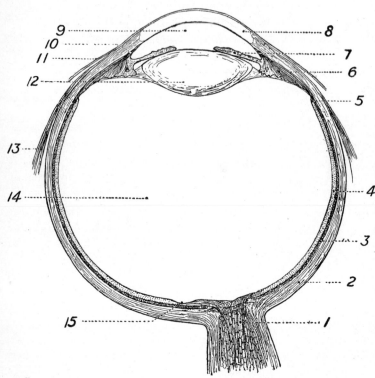

Fig. 16.—Schematic drawing of eye, in cross-section. 1, The optic nerve (really the optic tract); 2, sclerotic coat; 3, choroid coat; 4, the retina; 5, ora serrata, termination of retinal structures; 6, ciliary muscle; 7, iris; 8, cornea; 9, aqueous humor (camera oculi anterior); 10, attachment of choroid to sclerotic forming a fixed point towards which the ciliary muscle draws when contracted; 12, the crystalline lens; 13, tendon of rectus lateralis; 14, vitreous humor (corpus vitreum); 15, fovea centralis.

Coats of the Eye.—(1) The outside coat of the eye is a tough fibrous membrane which gives the eye its form. The posterior portion of this coat, the sclerotic, is opaque; the anterior portion, the cornea, is transparent. (2) The middle coat, the choroid, is a black, soft, extensible and easily disrupted membrane. It is composed largely of vascular and muscular tissue. The posterior portion of the choroid is pigmented; the middle portion is muscular (for the control of the lens), while the anterior portion, the iris, is a perforated membranous diaphragm placed just in front of the lens and immediately behind the cornea. The opening in this diaphragm is called the pupil. The iris contains connective tissue fibers arranged radially to the pupil. Near the margin of the pupil there are also smooth muscle fibers which form a sphincter muscle. There are also smooth muscle fibers radially disposed that act antagonistically to the sphincter fibers. The size of the pupillary opening is determined by the action of these muscles. Strong light falling upon the retina produces relaxation in the radial fibers and contraction of the sphincters: the pupil grows smaller. When the light is decreased in intensity, or removed, the sphincters relax and the radial fibers contract: the pupil dilates.

The Lens and the Ciliary Muscles.—The crystalline lens (Fig. 16, 12) is biconvex. It is highly elastic and tends always, unless constrained, to become more nearly spherical. It is put under restraint by the transparent capsule which surrounds it. When the eye fixates objects upon the horizon, the lens becomes most flattened. When fixating objects at a distance of 14 inches, it becomes most nearly spherical. The mechanism which brings about the flattening of the lens is the ciliary muscle. The loose muscular coat of the choroid in the region of the ciliary muscle is firmly attached to the firmer sclerotic. The lens capsule is attached as shown in Fig. 16. When the eye fixates objects near at hand, the ciliary muscle contracts sharply and as the muscle pulls up towards the point where the choroid is attached to the sclerotic, the tension on the capsule is lessened. The lens, by virtue of its own elasticity, becomes more convex. When the object is far away, the ciliary muscle relaxes, thus dragging down the lens capsule, greatly increasing the tension. This exerts uniform pressure principally upon the anterior surface of the lens. The images for near and far objects thus fall accurately upon the retina in the emmetropic or normal eye. In a great many cases the action of the lens and muscle is not accurate. For example, in myopia (near-sightedness) parallel rays of light are brought to a focus in front of the retina; in hypermetropia (long-sightedness) they are brought to a focus behind the retina. These two defects are easily corrected with glasses. Often, too, there is a lack of perfectness in the cornea. It may not have the same radius of curvature in the upper and lower halves, or in the right and left halves. The effect on the path of the light is the same as that which would be obtained were the light passed through a lens made up by cementing together halves and quarters of lenses of different foci. In such cases of corneal defect no clear, complete image can fall upon the retina. This condition is known as astigmatism.

The Retina.—The retina (Fig. 16, 4) is a delicate inner membrane lining the eye-ball. It is cup-shaped, since it does not invest the anterior portion of the eye-ball. It ends near the ciliary muscle. Nerve cells lying in the retina send out their processes to form the optic tract. This tract pierces the choroid and sclerotic and takes its exit at the posterior pole of the eye-ball. Fig. 16, 1, gives a view of this relationship. It is usually spoken of as the entrance of the optic nerve. It is really the exit of the optic tract. The relationship of the nerve elements in the optic tract with the other elements in the retina is somewhat complicated. Indeed, the whole retina is far from simple. For descriptive purposes it is best to start with the actual receptors or sense organs. These are nearest the choroid and hence farthest away from the light. The light must pass through all the other layers here described before it can fall upon the receptors. The receptors are of two kinds, the rods and the cones. They are shown in Fig. 17. The outer segments of both rods and cones are made up of shining, doubly refractive substances, which can be split up by certain reagents into a series of discs. The inner member of both rods and cones is a fine varicose fiber which contains a

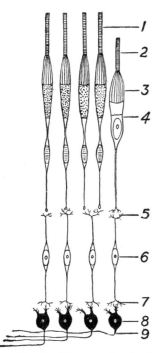

nucleus. The inner segments of the rods terminate in a rounded swelling, whereas the cone terminates in a swelling which splits up into fine processes. It can be seen that the cone is probably the more highly complex of the two structures, since by its branched ending it offers more chances for neural connections. We have already brought out the fact that in the fovea centralis, or spot of clearest vision, only cones are present. In the regions around the fovea there is a one-to-one relationship between rods and cones. As one passes from this region, one finds fewer and fewer cones. On the periphery only rods are present. The rod and cone layer may be called the outermost functional layer of the retina (that is, it lies next to the choroid). As in all other sense organs, the receiving structures must come in contact with neural structures. The rods and cones form no exception. The ends of their inner processes come into contact with the second functional layer of the retina, the layer of bipolar neurones (a neurone is a nerve cell with its outgrowth) (Fig. 17). This layer may be looked upon as the true peripheral optic nerve, although the neurones composing it are only a fraction of a

Fig. 17.—Diagrammatic sketch showing the three principal layers of the retina. The outer layer is the layer of rods and cones; the middle layer is the layer of bipolar neurones; the inner layer is the layer of ganglion cells with their axones. 1, Outer member of rods; 2, outer member of cone; 3, inner member of cone; the corresponding inner member of the rods is not indicated; 4, nucleus of cone; the corresponding nuclei of rods not indicated; 5, end processes of rods and cones coming into functional relation with dendrite of bipolar neurone; 6, nucleus of bipolar neurone (the layer of bipolar neurones is a true peripheral optic nerve); 7, axone of bipolar neurone terminating around dendrites of neurones which form the optic tract; 8, cell bodies of the latter neurones; 9, their fibers. All of the structures here shown lie within the retina itself.

mm. in length. The cell bodies in this layer give off at one pole an outer process which ends around the terminal processes of the inner structures of the rods and cones. At its other pole, it gives off a process which ends around the cell bodies that lie on the inner surface of the retina (next to the vitreous humor). These cell bodies with their processes should be looked upon as the third functional layer of the retina. This innermost layer consists of fairly large nerve cells, each of which gives off a single fiber which passes back to the pole of the eye. This fiber, regardless of the position of the cell body giving rise to it, takes a curved radial course and joins with all fibers of similar origin to form the optic tract. Their further course to the brain is described on page 163.

Summary.—We find that the light passes through all of the transparent structures just described and falls finally upon the outer members of the rods and cones. The rods and cones are stimulated, that is, some chemical change takes place in them, and a neural impulse arises in the nerve elements with which the rods and cones are in contact, the bipolar neurones. These neurones arouse in turn impulses in the ganglion cells (neurones of the optic tract) with which they are in contact. The impulse passes from here to the occipital cortex, then to the motor cortex and back to the muscles of the eyes, head, etc.

Action of Visual Purple.—Probably the most interesting physiological phenomenon observable in the eye is the action of the visual purple. It has been several times clearly shown that the outer members of the rods secrete a purplish-red pigment when the eye has not been exposed to light for a considerable time (two hours). Under the action of white or monochromatic light this purple gradually fades, passing through several changes in color, and disappears at the end of fifteen minutes. When first discovered it was hoped that a true physiological theory had been approached. Ebbinghaus actually formulated a theory of color vision in terms of the action of visual purple. In view of the fact that it does not appear in cones, the human fovea would thus be without any function, as would that of birds and other animals whose retinæ contain only cones. Nor does its assumed function as acting as a sensitizer for the rods in darkness adaptation fare much better, since many animals whose retinæ contain only cones

or mainly cones can still dark adapt, therefore the view is forced
upon us that the true function of the visual purple in the rods
has not been completely worked out.

Binocular Vision.—In our discussion of the eye so far, we
have considered it really as a single organ. But usually the two
eyes work together. In uniocular vision there is a lack of definiteness and perfectness in reactions to objects at varying distances
from the eye. If one eye is closed in a normal individual, the
reactions to objects at a distance are fairly accurate. On the
other hand, those to objects close at hand are very inaccurate.
Try this by having some one touch your finger, having one of his
eyes closed, or thread a needle or appose two sharp-pointed instruments. The adjustments are poorly made. The moment he
opens the other eye, the acts are accomplished with ease. It
should be mentioned in this connection that a little practice greatly
improves this type of adjustment, so that the man born with
only one eye functional, or who has had one eye removed, is not at
such a loss as might be supposed from these observations. When
the two eyes work together, there is (*a*) a greater extension of
the total vision field, since a part of the possible field of view
of any one eye is blocked by the nose. The true binocular field,
that is, that portion of the total field from which images reflected
into the eyes fall upon corresponding points, is smaller than the
sum of the fields of the two eyes; (*b*) in binocular vision, the
images falling upon the retina are more complete, since each eye
contributes certain elements, that is, there are two fixed points
of view; (*c*) the response to form, size and distance of objects
from the eye are more accurate; (*d*) defects in the one eye do not
disturb the adjustments of the subject when both eyes are stimulated. A reference to the blind spot will simplify this. If only
one eye is used, it is quite possible that the image of an object
might fall upon the blind spot. No reflex tendencies would be
released whereby the eye would be turned so as to receive the
object upon the fovea; the object would not be reacted to. When
both eyes are stimulated by an object, it is not possible for the
image to fall upon the blind spot of both eyes, hence reflex
tendencies will start in one eye at least and the other eye will be

forced to follow. The result will be a perfect focussing of the
object upon the spot of clearest vision in each eye.

Muscles of the Eye and Their Action.—The movements of
the two eyes are controlled by six large striped muscles attached
to each eye-ball. Their points of attachment are shown in Fig. 18.

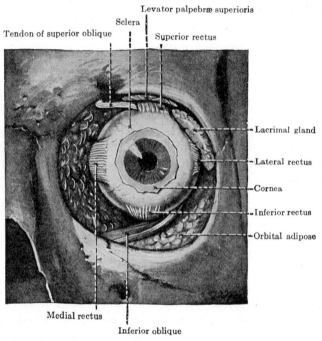

Fig. 18.—Dissection of the left orbit from in front. (Morris' Anatomy, Courtesy P.
Blakiston's Son & Co.)

The joint action of the medial rectus and of the lateral rectus
rotates the eye inward and outward. The superior rectus and
the inferior rectus rotate the eye upward and downward and
somewhat inward. The inferior oblique and the superior
oblique rotate the eye outward and upward or outward and
downward. These are the simple eye movements which result
from the action of pairs of muscles. In many cases three or more
muscles are involved and the relationships become very compli-

cated indeed. Attention is called to the fact that the muscular
system of the eye is at the same time a part of the kinæsthetic
system and indeed an extremely important part.

Condition for Single Vision.—Owing to the coördination and
balance existing in the eye movements, the two eyes become really
a binocular instrument. In order to have single vision with both
eyes functioning, it is necessary that the images of the objects
fall upon certain points in the two retinæ which are called "identical or corresponding points." Whenever this happens the subject reacts to a single object. In all cases where the images fall
upon disparate points, diplopia, or double images, results, that is,
the subject reacts to two objects. Occasionally one of these images
is so blurred and indistinct that its presence does not very much
disturb reaction. One can learn, of course, to react to either
image. This appears quite clearly in the use of a microscope. After
a little practice the individual becomes monocular in his use of
the microscope, and the image from the unused eye is "neglected." Corresponding points on the retina may be made clear
by making a paper image of the right retina and one of the left,
first dividing each into quadrants, and sliding the left model
into the right without rotating or otherwise disorienting them:
the corresponding quadrants in the two retinæ will be superimposed. The upper and lower nasal quadrants of the left eye
correspond respectively to the upper and lower temporal quadrants of the right eye; the upper and lower temporal quadrants
of the left eye correspond respectively to the upper and lower
nasal quadrants of the right eye. The most important corresponding points are the two foveæ.

Horopter.—In each fixed position of the eye there are a number of points in the field of view, images from which will fall upon
the corresponding points of the two retinæ. If we plot a figure
embracing all such points, the figure is called the horopter for
that position. If a distant point is fixated upon the horizon, the
two images of the point fall, of course, upon corresponding points,
namely, upon the foveæ. But it is found that even if this fixation is held, the images of many other objects above, below, right
and left, while not falling upon the foveæ, fall nevertheless upon

corresponding points in the retinæ. They are reacted to singly; the subject can enumerate them or name them correctly.

Visual Reactions Involve Habit Systems.—Attention must be directed to the fact that in our visual reactions to objects there are many complex non-visual factors. In the first place, visual reactions are really habit systems visually set off or initiated. We have in the past not only reacted visually to such objects; we have touched them in the dark, handled them, walked toward them, away from them, in intense illumination, in shadow and in fog, now with the eye in one position, now in another, now with one set or accommodation of the lens, now with another, with competing objects in the field of view, and again with few or none. Various habit systems thus grow up, so that if even a part of the original visual component is actually present, the absent motor elements are redintegrated or associatively aroused (there is undoubtedly present a vast system of conditioned reflexes). This can be seen very plainly in watching any complex motor act. With every change of movement in the performer there goes along a more or less complete change of tensions in the muscular system of the observer, so that he is thrown into the proper "attitude" to make the next adjustment. For example, in watching a fight, we tend to ward off a blow or to strike a blow. The inter-relations of these factors and the dependence of our immediate visual reactions upon past habits can best be seen, possibly, in the way an experienced hunter sets his rifle sights to bring down his prey. The novice, going into a clear mountainous country for the first time, sets his sights for a too close range and the bullet falls short. The experienced hunter has learned by trial and error that he must increase his range over that which he would use on the plains. In the same way habits grow up based upon the size of the retinal image and upon the presence or absence of a clear image upon the retina. The presence or absence, too, of intermediate objects in the field of view to which we have previously made adjustments markedly affect our visual reactions to any distant object. An individual unused to the sea may start out to row his boat to a distant object. The chances are that it will take him two or three times as long as he had cal-

culated. The point to be emphasized in all of our visual adjustments is that we are dealing with integrated habit systems and
conditioned reflex systems. Each time the visual receptor is stimulated, the kinæsthetic receptors (eye muscles, the ciliary
muscles controlling adaptation and other factors) are simultaneously stimulated and the complex of impulses resulting redinte-
grates the established habit systems. The reactions which we make,
whether a mere verbal reaction as to the form, size or distance
of an object, or the starting out to walk to a distant point, are
dependent upon such complex factors. It must be noted, too,
that we can give no verbal report about the various rôles played
by the different factors. A deer springs up in the fog, in shadows, in dim light, in the red light of early morning, in the clear
light of noon, on a mountain or on a plain : immediately the rifle
is raised, pointed at a varying distance ahead of the animal, and
fired. The animal falls. No hunter (not even a psychological
one) can give a verbal report that contributes one iota to the
event. We have made a visual motor adjustment and the complex factors involved in it all work harmoniously together.

The Stereoscope.—Since visual stimuli really touch off habit
systems, it follows that we can, by a very simple arrangement of
visual conditions, initiate reactions which really belong to another
general environmental setting. For example, if we obtain two
photographs of a landscape taken simultaneously with a twin
camera with the lenses fixed at the same distance apart as the
two eyes, or slightly wider, and place these photographs in a
stereoscope which allows the two images to fall upon corresponding points without fatigue of accommodation and without the
intrusion of lateral images, we have a close approximation to the
landscape situation as it stimulates the eye in nature—we obtain
the *"stereoscopic"* effect even though the stimulus in each of the
eyes is presented in one plane. The reaction obtained from the
subject is like that obtained in ordinary binocular vision. The
subject states that the various objects appear in different planes
and at different distances from the eye. On the other hand, the
visual conditions can be so arranged that the image which usually
falls upon the right eye has to fall upon the left, and *vice versa.*

When this is done, an inverted relief is reported. The pseudo-scope is an instrument admirably arranged to make the image ordinarily falling upon the right eye to fall upon the left and *vice versa*. Hollow objects are thus reacted to as solid objects, and solid objects as hollow.

Untrustworthiness of Vision.—The various "illusions" or errors in visual reactions to which the eye is subject probably

Fig. 19.—The Müller-Lyer figure.

depend to some extent at least upon a certain lack of balance and coördination in the functioning of the motor system of the eye. For example, the eye under-reacts to acute angles and over-reacts to obtuse angles. If the movements of the eyes are photographed while traversing the two forms above (Fig. 19), it will be seen that the movements are more extended on the right-hand figure (obtuse

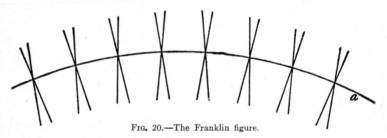

Fig. 20.—The Franklin figure.

angles) than on the left where they are acute angles. In the latter case the eye movement is checked. The two horizontal lines are of course equal. Again, if a subject is asked to draw equal horizontal and vertical lines (in the form of a cross) without the aid of a rule, it will be found that he draws the vertical line too short. This is supposed to be due to the fact that horizontal eye movements are made with less effort than vertical ones. Occasionally the eye is downright untrustworthy. Make up a drawing like that shown in Fig. 20; have some one hold the drawing flat at the level of the chin six or eight inches from the face, and tell him to fixate on the point of intersection of any two lines. He will tell you that there are three lines, two horizontal and a third line standing vertical to the drawing. This is really a very special case of diplopia or double vision. In the various text-books of psychology a great deal of attention is paid to these illusions, but little can be said about them at present which will be contributory.

Visual Hallucinations.—From "illusions" to "hallucinations" there is only a step. We have already said that the eye is always under stimulation. This is shown by the presence of action currents, the ideoretinal lights, and the hypnogogic images (long-continued after-effect of stimulation). Possibly also slight stimulation is afforded by each lens adjustment and by each change in convergence and divergence of the eye-ball. In addition, we know that there are centrifugal neural impulses reaching the eye from the central nervous system. The retina is peculiarly a sense organ that is never at rest and its activity is not wholly dependent upon outward stimulation of light. Attention, too, has been called to the fact that visual impulses of a very simple character sometimes touch off complicated visual-motor habits. It is small wonder, then, that, in pathological cases where the retina is probably over-active so far as these internal changes are concerned, as in fevers, delirium tremens and the like, we see the subject *reacting apparently to a visual object to which other persons present do not react.* In understanding this, attention is called to the fact that in normal persons, when there is a readiness of certain action systems to function the moment a certain visual stimulus appears, the action is often touched off by any visual stimulus; for example, a concealed enemy is ready to fire at the head of a soldier. The soldier, instead of exposing himself, holds up his hat or a dummy. The enemy's fire is drawn and a momentary respite is obtained with the chance to make the next objective. The higher the emotional tension, the easier it is to set off such premature reactions. This may account for the fact that a man in the throes of delirium tremens covers his head to shut out the vision of the snakes that squirm around the wall. His reading and his conversation with other imbibers have taught him that after drinking too much he will "see snakes." Long indulgence has made such habit systems ready to function. Any wavering of fixation, the presence of

sinuous shadows on the wall, the presence of any entoptic phenomenon may touch off both explicit and implicit types of reaction. We shall return to the fact again and again that visual
reactions may become short-circuited into word reactions. The
patient blind from birth can describe in appropriate words all
of the beauties of the setting sun. Provided such a person were
in the throes of delirium tremens and there were conditional
emotional reflexes of a proper kind present, there is some reason
to think that he might exhibit many of the characteristics of one
suffering from visual hallucination. We have no such factual
case at hand, be it said. This explanation would hold perfectly
well for the asserted cases of hallucinations appearing in patients
long after both eye-balls have been removed.

General Summary.—In considering, as has been done in this
chapter, the various factors which must be taken into account in
providing stimuli for the control of human action, it may be
argued that we have not offered to the subjects experimented
upon 'the same kind of situations they will meet in daily life.
Rarely are they stimulated with pure monochromatic lights, pure
tones, with two olfactory substances which balance or cancel one
another, and only rarely does the environment offer stimuli to
which they make the simple types of reaction that they make in
the laboratory. The laboratory obviously selects its problems and
investigates one phase of them at a time. For this it has been
criticised. The criticism would be justified if the laboratory made
no effort at other times to make good this defect. That this
science does attempt with some success to deal with larger human
problems, total situations and total reactions will appear from
some of the material we later present. Even granting the narrowness of our conclusions in sensory physiology, it is safe to say
that most of the facts we have presented here have been of service
and will continue to be of service to one or another group of
scientists outside of psychology. Findings in sensory physiology
are used by the physiologists themselves, by the neurologists, by
specialists in ear, nose and throat, by the surgeon, by the psychiatrist, and in the Army and Navy, as well as in the arts and trades.
To trace their use in these fields is beyond our present aim.

CHAPTER IV

THE ELEMENTARY FACTS ABOUT THE NEURO-PHYSI-
OLOGICAL BASIS OF ACTION

Introduction.—Having studied the receptors and found that their activity involves the initiation of neural impulses, our next problem is to learn something about neural conduction and the arrangement of pathways over which such impulses must pass in order to reach the effectors—the muscles and glands. We should say in the beginning that all neural impulses initiated in a sense organ have to pass either through the spinal cord or the brain or both of these organs before reaching the muscles and glands. Hence it is necessary for us to take up the elementary facts about their structure and functions. If we attempted to make a study of the whole nervous system, even in outline, we should find that our task could not be accomplished without going into a laboratory and actually working with neurological material. We can, though, apart from such laboratories, obtain a fairly good working notion of (1) many of the things which the nervous system as a whole has to do, (2) of the elementary neural structures and (3) the way the latter are chained together to form the reflex arcs that make possible our acts in daily life.

The Unit of the Nervous System.—The unit of the nervous system is the neurone. A complete neurone is shown in Fig. 21. It consists (1) of a cell body with (2) its axone and (3) its dendrites. The cell body is a somewhat complicated and not thoroughly understood structure. It contains a *nucleus* which does not differ greatly from the nucleus of any other cell. The most characteristic part of the cell is its *cytoplasm,* which is made up of neurofibrils, fine fibrils that are continuous throughout the axone, cell body and dendrites. The *perifibrillar* substance is a fluid-like substance that surrounds the neurofibrils. The cell contains in addition *chromophilic substance,* flake-like masses scattered

9   129

throughout the cell body and larger dendrites, but never in the axone or the axone hillock. These subdivisions are shown in Fig. 22. In the embryonic or developing nervous system the cell body which is called a neuroblast, first appears. If one were to watch the neuroblast develop into a partially complete neurone (as has actually been done), he would see the axone hillock first form and from it would develop the slender axone process, and later the dendrites.

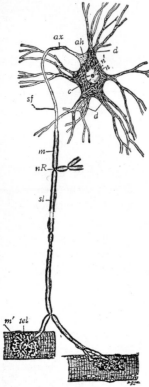

The axone, *ax*, Fig. 21, is a slender outgrowth from the cell body varying in length from a fraction of a mm. to more than a meter. Under the high power microscope it is seen to be made up of elementary neurofibrils. There is usually only one axone to a cell body. It is to be distinguished from the dendrites by its straighter course, its uniform diameter and smooth outline, Fig. 24. Shortly after leaving the cell body the axone may become myelinated, *i.e.*, covered by a fatty sheath whose function may be insulating or nutritive. It may possibly also be concerned with conduction. In addition to the medullary sheath, many of the axones are covered also with the more primitive sheath of Schwann or neurilemma. The sheath of Schwann is probably not found in the central nervous system. Certain axones, for example, those of the sympathetic neurones and of the

FIG. 21.—Scheme of peripheral motor neurone. The cell body, dendrites, axone, collaterals, and terminal arborizations in the muscle are seen to be parts of a single cell, the neurone. *c*, cytoplasm of cell body containing chromophilic bodies, neurofibrils and perifibrillar substance; *n*, nucleus; *n′*, nucleolus; *d*, dendrites; *ah*, axone hillock, free from chromophilic bodies; *ax*, axone; *sf*, collateral; *m*, medullary sheath; *nR*, node of Ranvier where branch is given off; *sl*, neurilemma (not present in central nervous system); *n′*, striated muscle fiber; *tel*, motor end plate. (From Bailey's Text-Book of Histology.) Courtesy Wm. Wood & Co.

olfactory, may have a sheath of Schwann without a medullary sheath. We have then two main divisions of axones: myelinated axones, with or without a neurilemma; and non-myelinated axones, with or without a neurilemma. The axone on ending usually splits up into a terminal brush. These brushes always end (1) around the dendrite of another neurone or (2) in a muscle or gland or (3) in some sense organ structure (if the peripheral process of an afferent neurone is classed as an axone) (page 116). On their course inside the central nervous system axones give off collaterals or side branches which end around dendrites of neurones whose cell bodies lie in the brain and cord.

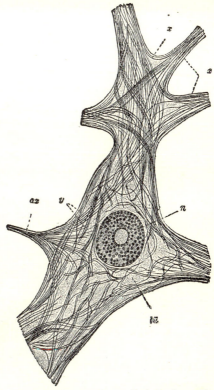

Fig. 22.—Diagram of a cell body from the ventral horn of the gray matter of the human spinal cord showing arrangement of neurofibrils. *ax*, axone; *lü*, interfibrillar spaces occupied by chromophilic substances; *n*, nucleus; *x*, neurofibril passing from one dendrite to another; *y*, similar fibril passing through the body of the cell. (Herrick's Introduction to Neurology.) W. B. Saunders Co.

The remaining parts of the neurone are the dendrites, *d*, Fig. 21. They have a structure similar to that of the cell body. They may be exceedingly numerous or lacking altogether. They exhaust themselves by subdivision and end near the cell body. To this general statement there is one exception: the dendrite of an afferent spinal neurone (Fig. 23) consists of a single process which is exactly like the axone—it runs a straight course, it is smooth and myelinated. However, it ends in a sense organ and conducts toward the cell body. We have learned that axones conduct the impulse centrifugally, that is, away from the cell body, and that the dendrites conduct centripetally. Hence the outgrowth from such a cell body as we are considering is an axone so far as structure is concerned but a dendrite in its function. Dendrites of all other types of neurones, since they are so intimately a part of the cell body, are probably important devices for securing nutrition for the whole neurone. They are beautifully contrived for this purpose since they offer many points of contact with their nutrient environment. The dendrites must also take part in conduction since the end of axones often comes in contact only with the dendrites.

The neurone as a whole is thus the anatomical, embryological, functional and

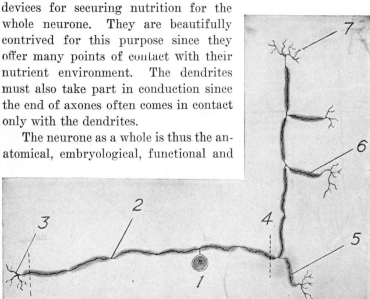

FIG. 23.—Schema of peripheral afferent neurone. 1, spinal ganglion cell; 2, dendrite (or peripheral axone process); 3, free nerve ending in epithelium; 4, line to show entrance of axone or central process into the central nervous system; 5, short caudal branch ending in the gray matter of dorsal column; 6, collateral of the cephalic branch likewise ending in the gray matter of the dorsal column; 7, end arborization of the axone; the axone may end around cell bodies in the medulla or turn in at any point to end around cells in the dorsal column.

trophic unit. There are no other structures in the nervous system, so far as we know, which take part in neural activity. Several types of neurones are shown in Fig. 24.

Those to be emphasized here are as follows: A, the peripheral afferent neurone; B, the peripheral motor neurone, and E, the

interconnecting central neurone (Golgi Type II).   There are
very many types of neurones not shown in this figure.

The Reflex Arc.—Although the neurone is a unit of the nervous system it cannot function alone.   It becomes functional from
a conduction standpoint only when its connections are established.   The functional unit of conduction is called a reflex arc.

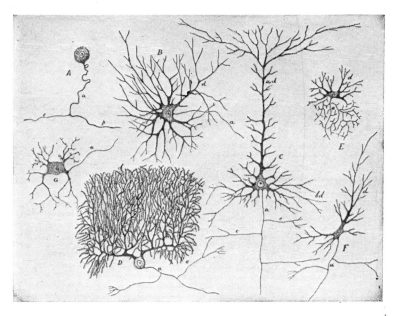

Fig. 24.—Showing some of the varieties of the cell bodies of the neurones of the human
nervous system including the dendrites and small portions of the axones, axone sheaths
not included. *A*, from spinal ganglion; *B*, from ventral horn of spinal cord; *C*, pyramidal
cell from the cerebral cortex; *D*, Purkinje cell from cerebellar cortex; *E*, Golgi cell type
II from spinal cord; *F*, fusiform cell from cerebral cortex; *G*, sympathetic. *a*, axone;
d, dendrites; *c*, collateral branches; *ad*, apical dendrites; *bd*, basal dendrites.   In the cell
marked *A p* is the peripheral process ending in a sense organ, *c* is the central process ending
within the central nervous system. (Morris' Human Anatomy.)

A schematic diagram of a reflex arc involving a segment of the
spinal cord is shown in Fig. 25.   It consists of a neurone of type A
in Fig. 24.   In Fig. 25 the neurone is marked 1.   One of its
processes (the dendrite) ends in a sense organ structure, *SS*, in
the periphery, while the other process (the axone) ends around
the dendrites of a neurone of type E above, numbered 2, the com-

plete neurone lying usually in the gray matter of the cord; and of a third neurone (spinal motor neurone) whose cell body lies in the gray matter (anterior horn) of the cord, but the axone of which ends in a motor structure, *MS*. This neurone is numbered 3. Occasionally possibly it may happen that a reflex arc is completed without the intervention of the intermediate central neurone. In such a case the peripheral sensory neurone, 1, may end, or one of its collaterals may end, directly around the dendrites of the motor neurone, 3. These are only schematic pictures, however. Usually many neurones are involved in any reflex arc.

The Synapse.—There has been a great amount of discussion

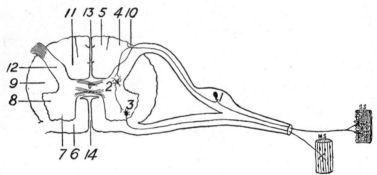

Fig. 25.—Schematic drawing to show neural elements involved in a simple reflex arc. 1, afferent peripheral neurone; 2, central or connecting cell; 3, motor neurone; MS, striped muscle; SS, sensory surface (skin).

as to the kind of connection existing among neurones. It seems safe to say that it is usually one of contact like that shown in Fig. 26—the end processes of an axone or its collateral come into more or less intimate contact with the bushy dendrites or cell body of another neurone. The place where functional contact occurs is called a "synapse." Many physiologists believe that the synapse is the most important part of the reflex arc. If the relation is one of contact there must be a surface of separation there, and this, it seems, in some way affects conduction. An impulse takes longer to traverse a reflex arc which always contains one or more synapses than to pass an equal distance over a nerve trunk. Furthermore, an impulse may travel in either direction along a nerve fiber, but it can travel in only one direction (forward) through the reflex arc, *i.e.*, from the axones to the dendrites. The idea has gained ground that the synapse can offer varying resistance to the passage of a neural impulse. It is assumed that an impulse coming from a sense organ might very well pass out to the muscles over either one of two neurones, but the momentary resistance at the one synapse may be so high that the impulse can pass out only over the other. It can readily be seen that this hypothesis may be of help in explaining habit, failure to obtain the predicted response, sleep, etc.

The All-or-None Law.—If the all-or-none law is established the conception of the synapse will have to be modified. The all-or-none law states that if a nerve fiber is stimulated it is stimulated maximally in each and in all of its parts. Hence grading of neural activity by the action of the synapse is not possible, for if the propagated disturbance (neural impulse) gets by the synapse at all, where it may suffer a decrement, it will become max-

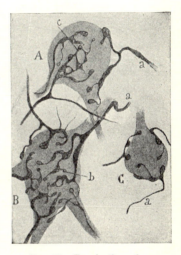

Fig. 26.— Termination of axones around cell bodies. *A*, *B*, and *C*, three cells with axones terminating upon them (from reception nucleus of cochlear nerve of rabbit); *a*, *a*, *a*, fibers of the cochlear nerve which break up into terminal arborizations upon the cells; *b*, *c*, terminal rings. The points of contact are called a synapse; the points of contact occur more frequently at the dendrites than at the cell body. (Bailey's Text-Book of Histology.) Courtesy Wm. Wood & Co.

imal again after a short distance. This can be shown quite clearly in the case where a nerve trunk is being stimulated electrically. The resulting action current is taken as the measure of the impulse and is registered by means of the deflections of the string of a galvanometer. If we partially anæsthetize the fibers in a stretch of a nerve trunk and measure the amount of deflection in the area so narcotized, the magnitude of the deflection is decreased; but if we measure the propagated disturbance (impulse) shortly after it passes out from this region where it underwent a decrement we shall find that the deflection of the galvanometer string has returned to its normal magnitude. Grading of a muscular response then must be a function of the number of muscular fibers thrown into action, and this is a function, in turn, of the number of axones bearing impulses to the muscle. Slight stimulation of a nerve trunk will produce a small contraction of the muscle because with a slight stimulus only a *few nerve fibers* are aroused. As soon as all of the fibers are bearing impulses no increase in the intensity of the stimulating current will produce a larger contraction. Our common experience teaches us that there is a rough proportionality between magnitude of stimulus and magnitude of response. But this grading is probably not a function of the synapse nor does it take place in the central nervous system.[1] The all-or-none law must still be looked upon as a research problem. If the various implications of the law are confirmed it will probably profoundly modify many of the present conceptions of neuro-physiology.

Some of the Facts Known About Neural Action.—It has been shown that the speed of the neural impulse in the motor nerve of man is about 125 meters per second. Apparently the velocity may be altered in various ways. Variations in temperature alter it most markedly. If one starts with a low temperature and tests the velocity it is found that for each 10° C. rise in temperature the velocity is doubled until the physiological limit is reached. Cooling a section of the nerve beyond a certain point will block the nervous impulse. Anæsthetics and narcotics may also be applied locally to the nerve, both decreasing its irritability and conductivity, or suspending them entirely. Conductivity and irritability may also be suspended by depriving the nerve of oxygen. With the restoration of oxygen these functions are restored. The questions as to whether activity can fatigue the nerve fiber as it is known to fatigue the cell body, and whether

---

[1] We shall see later, however, that impulses from the cerebral structures may inhibit action in lower motor neurones. This, however, is a function of the refractory phase of the neurone and of the time relations of the impulses impinging upon it.

nerve fibers show chemical change after or during activity, have not been answered with complete certainty.[2]   Certainly the nerve fiber is fatigued with the very greatest difficulty in ordinary laboratory experiments where the electrical current is used to excite it.   That both the resting and active fibers show metabolic change is becoming generally admitted.   Recent work tends to show that the resting fiber gives off CO_2, that it eliminates it faster during functional activity and that the elimination is as great per unit of weight as that of the cell body.   There can thus be little doubt that since oxygen is needed also by the fiber to maintain its functional properties, and since it gives off CO_2, functional activity in the fiber is connected with a chemical reaction of some kind.

Nature of the Neural Impulse.—The tendency is growing to regard the neural impulse as the rapid passage of a wave of chemical decomposition.   If a hair on the skin is touched it is assumed that the structure and composition of the surface film (surface films must exist between two structures which are in contact) of the axone ending around the hair is altered.   "The state of electrical surface polarization is thus changed; and the bioelectric circuit arising between altered and adjoining unaltered regions completes the activation" (Lillie).   These local currents extend for only a few centimeters, but at the point where they end there is the condition at hand for starting a new disturbance of film (between the portion of the nerve which has just been active and the resting portion which joins it) and the process is thus repeated the whole length of the conducting arc.   The speed of propagation of the wave or impulse is thus slow notwithstanding the

---

[2] The question of the fatigue in nerve cells, while generally admitted, has not been very well worked out.   There seems to be agreement that certain histological changes can be noticed after a cell has been made to function severely.   There is possibly an increase in the size of the cell, a diminution of the chromatic (Nissl) substance, and possibly even a displacement of the nucleus (Hodge).   In prolonged activity the chromatin may completely disappear.   Presumably in the cell body as in the active muscle lactic acid and CO_2 are formed.   Certainly oxygen is necessary for the proper functioning of the cell.   Very little can be said with certainty about the rôle the cell body plays during the conduction of the neural impulse.   It is certainly best to look upon the cell as a nutritive center of the neurone as a whole.

essential electric nature of the phenomena. Lillie gives the process as follows: ''The rapid passage of waves of chemical decomposition (probably oxidative in nature and involving some structural change) over the surface of the reacting element, followed immediately by a reverse change which restores the original or resting condition, is what appears to take place in a nerve or other living structure during conduction. Associated with the chemical process is a local electrical circuit by whose electrolytic action the chemical change is apparently determined.''

THE CEREBRO-SPINAL SYSTEM (SYSTEMA NERVORUM CENTRALE).[3]

Introduction.—The brain and spinal cord with their various peripheral connections may be looked upon as a unitary aggregation of simple and complex reflex conduction systems such as we have just considered. The brain and cord connected on the one hand with the sense organs and on the other hand with the muscles and glands afford a multiple connection system between the various receptors and the various effectors. No matter how minute the sense organ structure is which is stimulated, the impulse arising there can travel to the central system and produce a response of the whole organism which is entirely out of proportion to the actual energy applied at the sense organ. In other words, a stimulus applied anywhere on the body produces not only a local segmental reflex action, but it changes the system of tensions and secretions probably in every part of the body.

To understand how the nervous system is put together we must first spend some time upon the gross or macroscopic features of the brain and spinal cord, coming back finally to the discussion of internal architecture and inter-relations among the neurones themselves. Once the gross structures are found they will serve as landmarks in the description of the various pathways in the brain and cord.

The brain and cord together are known as the central nervous system (systema nervorum centrale), but as we have pointed out the central nervous system is connected on the one hand with a

---

[3] For the sake of ease in referring to the cuts where the scientific or Latin name of the part is given in the singular, we follow the same usage in the body of the text.

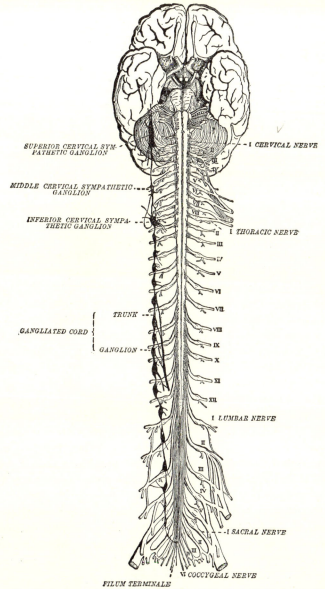

SUPERIOR CERVICAL SYM-
PATHETIC GANGLION

MIDDLE CERVICAL SYMPATHETIC
GANGLION

INFERIOR CERVICAL SYMPA-
THETIC GANGLION

TRUNK

GANGLIATED CORD

GANGLION

-- I CERVICAL NERVE

I THORACIC NERVE

I LUMBAR NERVE

-- I SACRAL NERVE

VI COCCYGEAL NERVE

FILUM TERMINALE

FIG. 27.—The human central nervous system from the ventral side illustrating its connections with the cerebro-spinal nerves and with the sympathetic nervous system (in black,
on right side only). The various subdivisions of the cord are shown. (Herrick's Introduction to Neurology.)

sense organ by means of the afferent peripheral cerebro-spinal neurones, and on the other hand with the muscles by means of the efferent peripheral cerebro-spinal neurones. These latter divisions are often spoken of as the peripheral nervous system (systema nervorum periphericum). Usually the sympathetic or autonomic system (systema nervorum sympathicum) is included as a part of the peripheral nervous system. We shall leave the sympathetic out of account at present, giving it a separate treatment on page 170.

Gross Features of the Spinal Cord (Medulla Spinalis).—The spinal cord is shown together with the brain in Fig. 27. The cord is about eighteen inches long and extends from the first cervical vertebra (more accurately from the foramen magnum of the occipital bone) to the lower part of the body of the first lumbar vertebra. Its upper portion is continuous with the medulla oblongata, which is the lowest part of the brain. The lower portion of the cord tapers conically and ends in a slender filament, the filum teminale. The cord is invested with three membranes. These are shown in Fig. 28: (1) the dura mater (dura mater spinalis) is a tough protective membrane which forms a lining for the bony cavity; (2) a thin intermediate membrane, the arachnoid (arachnoidea spinalis); and (3) finally a highly vascular membrane which closely invests the neural structures, the pia (pia mater spinalis).

The cord is almost cylindrical in shape with two enlargements, a cervical (intumescentia cervicalis) and a lumbar (intumescentia lumbalis) (Fig. 27). The spinal nerve roots leave from regular segments in the cord (Fig. 36). There are thirty-one such segments corresponding to the thirty-one spinal nerves. It will be noted that the cord in this respect is symmetrical in that there are thirty-one nerves on each side. The cord is divided into white and gray matter. The outer portion of the cord is composed of white matter (substantia alba) while the central H-shaped portion is composed of gray matter (substantia grisea). The white matter is made up largely of myelinated axones coming from the spinal ganglia (to be described on page 154) and the myelinated axones growing out of the cells lying in the gray matter. The gray matter is made up largely of nerve cells with their dendrites and of the unmyelinated end brushes of axones ending around these cell bodies. In Fig. 29 attention is called to the dorsal median septum (sulcus medianus posterior) and to the ventral median fissure (fissura mediana anterior). These structures serve to orient one immediately with respect to the ventral and dorsal aspects of the cord. The ventral aspect of the

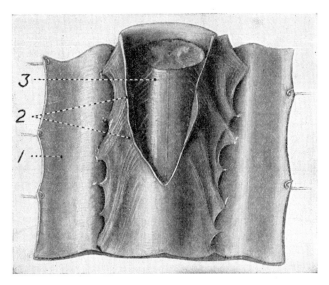

Fig. 28.—The membranes of the spinal cord. 1, the dura mater (dura mater spinalis); 2, arachnoid (arachnoidea spinalis); 3, pia (pia mater spinalis).   In the drawing the arachnoid is too strongly emphasized. Only rarely can one separate this membrane in a cord dissection. (Modified from Toldt.)

cord faces the ventral cavity of the body. Since the cord is symmetrical usually, only one-half of it is described. We can divide the white matter of each half of the cord as follows (Fig. 29) : (1) a ventral funiculus (funiculus anterior, 6), (2) a dorsal funiculus (funiculus posterior, 11), and (3) a lateral funiculus (funiculus lateralis, 9). The gray matter can similarly be divided into a (1) dorsal column—dorsal horn of gray matter—(columna posterior, 12), (2) ventral column—ventral horn of gray matter —(columna anterior, 7), and (3) lateral column—lateral horn of gray matter—(columna lateralis, 8).

Extending through the entire length of the cord there is a small central canal (canalis centralis) to be found in the substance of the gray commissure. It is the remains of the primitive ectodermal canal. The canal is the counterpart of the several ventricles in the brain, at least so far as origin is concerned. The canal and the fourth ventricle communicate at the calamus scriptorius.

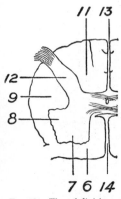

FIG. 29.—The subdivisions of the cord. 14, ventral median fissure (fissura mediana anterior); 13, dorsal median septum (Sulcus medianus posterior); 6, ventral funiculus (funiculus anterior); 11, dorsal funiculus (funiculus posterior); 9, lateral funiculus (funiculus lateralis); 12, dorsal column, dorsal horn of gray matter (columna posterior); 7, ventral column, ventral horn of gray matter (columna anterior); 8, lateral column, lateral horn of gray matter (columna lateralis).

Gross Features of the Brain (Encephalon).—The ventral aspect or base of the brain is shown in Figs. 30 and 31. The brain lies almost horizontally in the cranial cavity. We shall give a short description of the various features of the brain, beginning with the first or lowest structure. We shall try to describe together the various structures which belong together, but occasionally it has seemed better for the sake of clearness not to adhere too closely to the neurologist's divisions.

The Medulla Oblongata, Pons, Cerebellum and its Peduncles.—At the upper level of the cord and continuous with it is to be found the medulla oblongata (Fig. 30, 1). On the ventral aspect of the medulla we find the pyramids (pyramis) (Fig. 30, 26). Just lateral to the pyramids lie the olives (oliva) (Fig. 31, 3). On the dorsal aspect of the medulla (Fig. 32) are to be found the inferior cerebellar peduncles (corpus restiforme) (Fig. 32, 21), a band of fibers connecting the cord and medulla with the cerebellum. On the posterior aspect of the medulla one also finds two slight swellings, the tuberculum cuneatum (Fig. 32, 23) and the clava (Fig. 32, 4). At the upper border of the medulla and continuous with it is to be found the pons (Varoli) (Fig. 30, 8). The pons is really a great band of transverse axones coursing about the ventral aspect of the brain stem. Its fibers connect the two hemispheres of the cerebellum. The fibers are called commissural.[4] In addition to the superficial transverse axones, there are axones of many neurones to be found at this

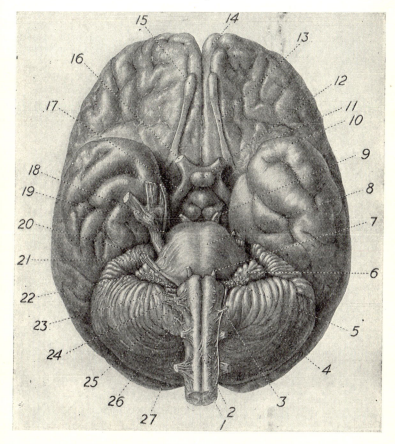

Fig. 30.—View of the base of the brain. 1, spinal cord (medulla spinalis); 2, decussation of pyramids (decussatio pyramidum); 3, spinal accessory nerve (n. accessorius); 4, cerebellum; 5, choroid plexus of fourth ventricle (plexus chorioideus ventriculi quarti); 6, flocculus; 7, abducens nerve (n. abducens); 8, pons (Varoli); 9, oculomotor nerve (n. oculomotorius); 10, temporal pole (polus temporalis); 11, fissure of Sylvius (fissura cerebri lateralis (Sylvii)); 12, hypophysis; 13, olfactory tract (tractus olfactorius); 14, frontal pole (polus frontalis); 15, olfactory bulb (bulbus olfactorius); 16, optic nerve (n. opticus); 17, optic tract (tractus opticus); 18, ganglion, root and branches of the trigeminal nerve (n. trigeminus); 19, trochlear or fourth nerve (n. trochlearis); 20, intermediate nerve (n. intermedius); 22, facial nerve (n. facialis); 23, auditory nerve (n. acusticus); 24, vagus and glossopharyngeal nerves (n. vagus, n. glossopharyngeus); 25, hypoglossal nerve (n. hypoglossus); 26, pyramids (pyramis); 27, first cervical spinal root.

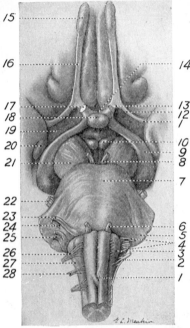

FIG. 31.—Ventral aspect of medulla and pons. 1. pyramidal decussation (decussatio pyramidum); 2, spinal accessory nerve (n. accessorius); 3, olive (oliva); 4, vagus and glosso-pharyngeal nerves (n. vagus, n. glossopharyngeus); 5, middle cerebellar peduncle (brachium pontis); 6, abducens nerve (n.abducens); 7, pons (Varoli); 8, oculomotor nerve (n. oculomotorius); 9, optic tract (tractus opticus); 10, mammillary body (corpus mammillare); 12, olfactory fibers (stria olfactoria lateralis); 13, trigonum olfactorium; 14, optic chiasm (chiasma opticum); 15, olfactory bulb (bulbus olfactorius); 16, olfactory tract (tractus olfactorius); 17, optic nerve (n. opticus); 18, hypophysis; 19, anterior perforated substance (substantia perforata anterior); 20, uncus of hippocampal gyrus (uncus gyri hippocampi)); 21, cerebral peduncle (pedunculus cerebri); 22, trigeminal nerve (n. trigeminus); 23, facial nerve (n. facialis); 24, intermediate nerve (n. intermedius); 25, acoustic nerve (n. acusticus); 26, hypoglossal nerve (n. hypoglossus); 27, lateral funiculus (funiculus lateralis); 28, motor root of first cervical nerve.

level which form connecting pathways between higher and lower levels of the central nervous system. The transverse fibers of the pons form the middle, cerebellar peduncle (brachium pontis) (Fig. 32, 20). In addition to the axone system in the pons, there are a number of gray cellular masses which serve as nuclei of reception for the sensory roots of cranial afferent nerves which enter in or near the pons and others serving as nuclei of origin of the motor nerves.[4]

The cerebellum or hind brain (Fig. 30, 4) lies dorsal to the pons and medulla and overhangs the latter. It in turn is overhung by the occipital lobes of the cerebral hemisphere (Fig. 35). The cerebellum is a fairly large structure weighing about 140 grams. We have already spoken of two of its peduncles, the middle or pons, and the inferior (the medulla and cord connection). It is connected with the higher brain centers by the superior

---

[4] A convenient way to describe the axone system is to use the terms (1) projection neurones, (2) commissural neurones, and (3) association neurones, meaning respectively (1) neurones ascending and descending in the central nervous system, (2) neurones connecting the two halves of any part of the central nervous system, and (3) neurones connecting distant parts of the same side of the nervous system.

peduncles (brachium conjunctivum). If the three peduncles
on each side are cut away the cerebellum can be removed. Fig.
32 shows the dorsal surface of the brain stem with the cerebellum cut away. The three peduncles are marked 19, 20 and
21. The two hemispheres of the cerebellum are connected with
each other by the vermis (Fig. 33, 18). The cerebellum has some
very important cell masses, for example, the dentate nucleus, the

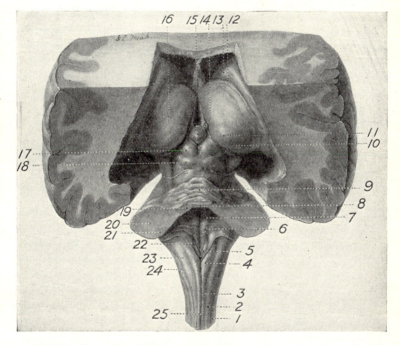

FIG. 32.—Dorsal view of brain stem, showing the regions of the 4th ventricle, the
corpora quadrigemina and the thalamus. 1, lateral funiculus (funiculus lateralis); 2 and 3,
dorsal funiculus [respectively, funiculus cuneatus (Burdachi) and funiculus gracilis (Galli)];
4, clava· 23, tuberculum cuneatum, marking the reception nuclei of the dorsal funiculus;
5, ala cinerea; 6, auditory striæ (striæ medullares); 7, colliculus facialis; 8, part of roof of
4th ventricle (velum medullare anterius); 9, lingula cerebelli; 10, medial geniculate body
(corpus geniculatum mediale); 11, pulvunar of thalamus; 12, stria terminalis; 13, caudate
nucleus (nucleus caudatus); 14, pineal gland (corpus pineale); 15, septum pellucidum;
16, body of thalamus; 17 and 18, corpora quadrigemina, made up of the colliculus superior
and colliculus inferior—each is continued into the thalamic mass by a brachium (brachium
quadrigeminum superius and brachium quadrigeminum inferius); 19, superior cerebellar
peduncle (brachium conjunctivum); 20, middle cerebellar peduncle (brachium pontis);
21, inferior cerebellar peduncle (corpus restiforme); 22, swelling marking nucleus of hypoglossal (trigonum n. hypoglossi); 24, swelling marking medulla portion of reception nucleus
of V nerve (tuberculum cinereum); dorsal median septum (fissura mediana posterior). The
cavities above and below thalamus show the lateral ventricle. Note origin of 4th nerve
(n. trochlearis) below inferior geniculate bodies.
    10

nucleus emboliformis, the nucleus globosus, and the roof nucleus (nuclei not shown). On the dorsal surface of the brain stem is shown the floor of the fourth ventricle (Fig. 32). The velum medullare anterius (Fig. 32, 8), together with the brachium conjunctivum, forms the roof of this ventricle. As has been pointed out, this ventricle is the remains of the embryonic medullary tube.

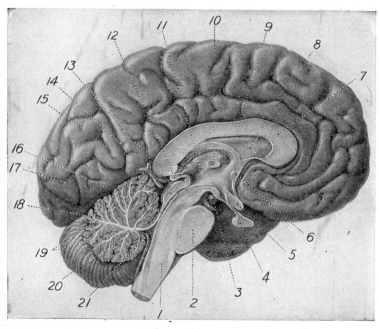

FIG. 33.—Vertical median section of adult brain. 1, medulla oblongata; 2, pons (Varoli); 3, corpus mammillare; 4, hypophysis; 5, optic chiasm (chiasma opticus); 6, anterior commissure (commissura anterior); 7, knee of corpus callosum (genu corporis callosi); 8, septum pellucidum; 9, foramen of Monroe (foramen interventriculare Monroi); 10, massa intermedia; 11, third ventricle (ventriculus tertius) and thalamus; 12, pineal gland (corpus pineale); 13, aqueduct of Sylvius (aquæductus cerebri Sylvii); 14, parieto-occipital fissure (fissura parieto-occipitalis); 15, corpora quadrigemina (lamina quadrigemina); 16, velum medullare anterius; 17, calcarine fissure (fissura calcarina); 18, vermis; 19, arbor vitæ; 20, corpus medullare cerebelli; 21, fourth ventricle (ventriculus quartus).

It is continuous with the central spinal canal, and with the third ventricle above by way of the aqueduct of Sylvius (aquæductus cerebri Sylvii) (Fig. 33, 13).

The Cerebral Peduncles (Pedunculus Cerebri) and the Corpora Quadrigemina (Colliculus Superior and Colliculus

Inferior).—Turning again to the ventral surface of the brain (Fig. 31), we see the two cerebral peduncles, 21 (pedunculus cerebri), just above the pons. They are nearly covered by the overlapping of the temporal lobes of the cerebral hemispheres. The cerebral peduncles are two large bundles of axones (right and left) connecting the parts we have just described with the parts yet to be described. They are close together when they emerge from the pons, but gradually separate as they pass upward, forming a recess which is occupied by the mammillary bodies (corpus mammillare) (Fig. 31, 10). These latter structures belong really to the forebrain. The term cerebral peduncle is very loosely used. In addition to the ascending and descending axones of which it is largely composed, there are to be found immediately dorsal to the fibers the *substantia nigra,* a pigmented cellular mass, and the *tegmentum,* in which are to be found many cellular masses serving as nuclei of reception for ascending and descending axones.

Fig. 33, which is obtained by splitting the brain symmetrically from front to back, thus dividing it into right and left halves, shows a medial view of the stem and mid-brain structures. One finds there the corpora quadrigemina, four (two on each side of the midline) small, but well-marked rounded masses (Fig. 33, 15). The lower two (right and left) are called the inferior colliculi, the upper two, the superior colliculi. They are much better shown in Fig. 32, 17 and 18. The two inferior colliculi are continued into the medial geniculate bodies (corpus geniculatum mediale, Fig. 32, 10) and thence into the thalamus by heavy strands of axones called brachia. In a similar way the superior colliculi are continued into the lateral geniculate bodies (corpus geniculatum laterale). The inferior colliculi and the medial geniculate bodies are a part of the auditory apparatus, while the superior colliculi and the lateral geniculate bodies are a part of the visual apparatus. The pineal gland (corpus pineale) is shown in Fig. 33, 12, and Fig. 32, 14.

The Thalamus and Related Structures.—We have already noted three of the structures belonging to the thalamic region, namely, the medial and lateral geniculate bodies and the pineal

gland. The thalamus proper is an ovoid, couch-like mass
which on its mesial surface forms the wall of the third ventricle.
Fig. 33, 11, shows the thalamus in the left half of the brain.
The massa intermedia (Fig. 33, 10) is a mass of gray matter
connecting the two thalami. The medial view does not show the
thalamus very well. Fig. 32, 16, shows the dorsal and lateral
extension of this most important structure. Fig. 44 shows a
coronal section through the thalamus. The dorsal surface of the
thalamus usually shows four eminences, indicating the nuclear
masses within. They are the anterior nucleus, the medial nucleus,
the lateral nucleus, and the pulvinar. Only the pulvinar can be
clearly seen in Fig. 32, 11. On the mesial surface near the thalamus are to be seen the pituitary gland (hypophysis cerebri)
(Fig. 33, 4). Note the ventral view of this same structure (Fig.
31, 18). The mammillary bodies (Fig. 33, 3) and the optic chiasma (chiasma opticum) (Fig. 33, 5) are indicated both in the
median section (Fig. 33) and in the ventral section (Fig. 31).
These structures belong really to the telencephalon, as do the
structures which are to be immediately described.

The Basal Ganglia.—Continuous with the thalamus but above
it and lateral to it is to be found in each hemisphere the caudate
nucleus (nucleus caudatus) (Fig. 32, 13, and Fig. 44, 13) and
the lenticular nucleus (nucleus lentiformis) (Fig. 44, 10 and 12).
They are two large cellular masses called the basal ganglia. Separating the two cellular masses is an axone band called the internal capsule (capsula interna) (Fig. 44, 20). These structures
are shown only in a coronal section. The three structures together are sometimes called the striate body. If the septum
pellucidum were torn away (Fig. 33, 8) one would see first into
the lateral ventricle, then the head of the caudate nucleus would
appear as one of the boundaries of the cavity. The internal capsule is of vital importance. In it are gathered together in a narrow space nearly all of the ascending and descending axones which
connect the cortex and the lower structures.

The Corpus Callosum.—The corpus callosum, which is an

enormous mass of commissural axones connecting the two cerebral hemispheres arches over the whole of the structures we have just been describing. It is plainly marked

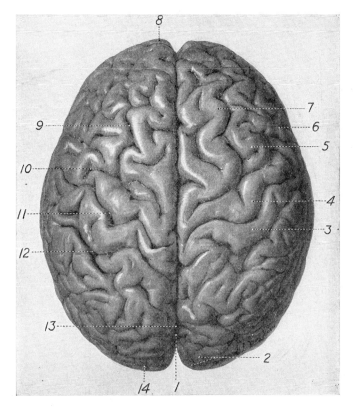

FIG. 34.—Convex surface of cerebral hemispheres as viewed from above. 1, longitudinal fissure (fissura longitudinalis cerebri); 2, occipital gyrus (gyri occipitales superiores); 3, postcentral gyrus (gyrus centralis posterior); 4, precentral gyrus (gyrus centralis anterior); 5, gyrus fontalis medius; 6, gyrus fontalis inferior: 7, superior frontal gyrus (gyrus frontalis superior); 8, frontal pole (polus frontalis); 9, superior frontal sulcus (sulcus frontalis superior); 10, precentral sulcus (sulcus precentralis); 11, fissure of Rolando (sulcus centralis (Rolandi)); interparietal sulcus (sulcus interparietalis); 13, parieto-occipital fissure (fissura parieto-occipitalis).

(Fig. 33, 7) and can also be seen in the coronal section (Fig. 44, 14). This system of axones can be seen quite easily if the two hemispheres are gently pressed apart: it appears as the floor of the great longitudinal fissure (Fig. 34, 1).

The Cerebral Hemispheres.—In man the cerebral hemispheres form the largest part of the central nervous system. Fig. 34 is a view of the hemispheres from above. They present an ovoid surface which corresponds to the inner surface of the vault of the cranium. The two hemispheres are separated from each other by the longitudinal fissure (fissura longitudinalis) which runs from the frontal pole to the occipital pole. A deep fold of the dura mater dips into the longitudinal fissure called the falx cerebri (not shown). It will be seen that when viewed from above the cerebral hemispheres completely obscure all other cranial structures. The cerebellum lies immediately under the occipital pole. There are three surfaces of the hemispheres: (1) the convex surface as seen from above (Fig. 34) or the side (Fig. 35), (2) the mesial surface, which can be seen only by pulling the two hemispheres apart (Fig. 33). The mesial surfaces bound the longitudinal fissure, or rather the falx cerebri lies between the two mesial surfaces. (3) The basal surface shown in Fig. 30.[5]

In addition to the structures described each hemisphere includes a *convoluted* and *infolded pallium* or mantle divided into *lobes* and *gyri*. The pallium consists of the gray outside surface called the *cortex*. The white matter of the cerebrum lies below the cortex. Only about one-third of the cortex is visible; the other two-thirds is found in the walls and floors of the sulci and fissures. The folds of the cortex are called gyri or convolutions. They are separated from one another by sulci or by the deeper furrows called fissures. The outside surface of each hemisphere (Fig. 35) (pallium) is divided into lobes; the frontal (lobus frontalis), parietal (lobus parietalis), occipital (lobus occipitalis), and temporal (lobus temporalis). The central lobe (insula) is concealed.

---

[5] The caudate and lenticular nuclei and the internal capsule (and the lateral ventricle), which we have already identified belong to and should be described with the cerebral hemispheres. We considered them with the more caudal structures so that we could describe continuous and adjoining parts beginning with the cord and ending with the corpus callosum.

In order to work out these divisions, first locate the great longitudinal fissure (Fig. 34, 1) separating the two hemispheres, then the fissure of Sylvius (fissura cerebri lateralis Sylvii), which is a lateral fissure, shown in Fig. 35, 4. The fissure of Rolando [sulcus centralis (Rolandi)] begins above, near the highest point of the hemisphere and courses outward and downward over the lateral surface of the brain (Fig. 35, 3) to the horizontal

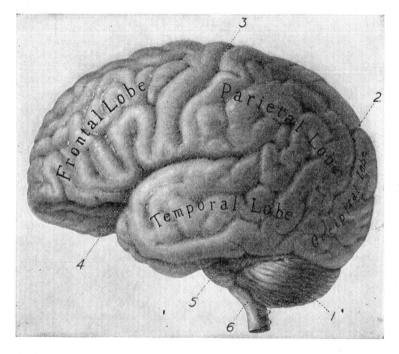

FIG. 35.—View of the left side of the adult human brain. 1, cerebellum; 2, parieto-occipital fissure (fissura parieto-occipitalis); 3, fissure of Rolando (sulcus centralis (Rolandi)); 4, fissure of Sylvius (fissura cerebri lateralis (Sylvii)); 5, pons (Varoli); 6, spinal cord (medulla spinalis).

fissure of Sylvius, which it rarely joins. The parieto-occipitalis (fissura parieto-occipitalis) fissure can be seen on the mesial surface (Fig. 33, 14). It runs from a cleft shown on the extended convex surface (Fig. 34, 13) downward and a little forward to join the calcarine fissure (fissura calcarina) (Fig. 33, 17). These two fissures enclose a wedge-shaped portion of the mesial cortex called the cuneus—an important visual station. Having located these more important fissures, we can divide the pallium into its lobes. (1) The frontal lobe has a convex, lateral and basal surface. The convex surface begins at the frontal pole (polus frontalis) and is bounded posteriorly by the fissure of Rolando. The mesial boundary is not well marked. The basal portion is shown in Fig. 30. Lying on its surface are to be seen the olfactory bulbs (bulbus olfactorius) and tracts (tractus olfactorius). (2) The parietal lobe lies behind the frontal in front of the occipital lobe and above the temporal. It is bounded frontally by the fissure of Rolando, and laterally by the fissure of Sylvius. Posteriorly it has no natural boundary, but a line drawn from the end of the fissure of Sylvius to the cleft of the parieto-occipital fissure will give a convenient boundary. Its mesial boundary is the parieto-occipitalis. (3) The mesial surface of the occipital lobe begins at this fissure and extends to the occipital pole (polus occipitalis). This lobe has a basal surface (that immediately above the cerebellum) and a lateral convex surface. (4) The temporal lobe lies below the fissure of Sylvius (a portion is concealed in the fissure of Sylvius). It has a convex surface, shown in Fig. 35, and a basal surface. (5) The central lobe (insula) is concealed. It lies in the floor of the fissure of Sylvius. It can be exposed by gently opening out the fissure. The location of the insula can be seen in Fig. 44, 11.

It is in definite parts of the cortical surface of these lobes that the various ascending projection fibers coming from the cord and brain stem, which are soon to be described, find their terminations, thus giving the nerves of special senses—visual, auditory and olfactory, etc.—a definite cortical representation. We shall find further that cell bodies lying in the cortex give rise to axones which form descending or returning pathways to the lower structures. To make clear this architecture we must turn to a study of the internal structure of the brain and spinal cord. We shall first consider the make-up or composition of the peripheral spinal and cranial nerves and then examine into the connections of these nerves with the internal structures of the cord and brain.

THE PERIPHERAL NEURONES OF THE CORD AND BRAIN.

The Peripheral Neurones of the Cord.—After this brief general discussion of the easily observable features of the nervous system as a whole, we are prepared to examine the system of pathways connecting the sense organs and the muscles. The first feature to study is how a spinal nerve is made up. We have already noted that there are thirty-one pairs of spinal nerves. Each nerve is made up of two roots, an efferent or motor root and an afferent or sensory root. The dorsal or afferent root (Fig.

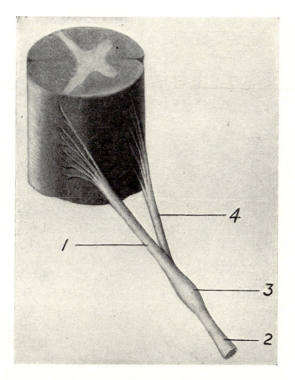

Fig. 36.—Segment of spinal cord showing origin of a nerve. 1, afferent or sensory root of nerve; 4, efferent root of nerve; 3, spinal ganglion; this gives rise to the axones which form the afferent root; 2, a spinal nerve; it is made up of motor fibers and afferent fibers (for simplicity the various subdivisions of the nerve such as anterior, posterior and recurrent are left out).

36, 1) plunges horizontally into the cord, roughly at the tip of the dorsal horn. The ventral root (Fig. 36, 4) enters (really emerges) at the same level.

Upon each of the thirty-one afferent roots there is situated a swelling called the ganglion (Fig. 36, 3). This is a structure

easily observable without the aid of a microscope. It contains
the cell bodies which give rise to the afferent peripheral processes
and roots. A complete afferent neurone is shown on page 132.
Attention was called there to the fact that these neurones have
no dendrites unless we call the processes running out to the
sensory surface the dendrite. The dorsal root (Fig. 36, 1) is
made up of the typical axone process from these cell bodies. In
man there are nearly one and a third million of axones in the
dorsal roots of the two sides of the spinal cord, but less than
one-half million in the ventral root. If the ventral root is followed back into the cord it will be found that it is really an outgrowth from cell bodies lying in the ventral column (of gray
matter). The genetic relations then are: cells in the ventral horn
give rise to axones which leave the cord at a given horizontal level,
the efferent roots. Each cell in the spinal ganglion at the same
horizontal level gives rise to a single afferent axone which
branches like a T or a Y, one process entering the cord as a
dorsal root fibre, the other process (dendrite) going to a
sense organ in the skin, muscle, tendon or joint. Just peripheral-
ward to the spinal ganglion the motor fibers join the sensory. The
combination is from then on called a nerve (Fig. 36, 2), for example, the first thoracic nerve on the right side. The nerve as a
whole runs in a dense sheath of connective tissue, the epineureum
(not shown). Somewhere in its course most of the afferent axones
leave the epineural sheath to end in receptors (of muscles, tendons, joints and skin). The efferent axones enter the muscles
and end in a typical way, shown in Fig. 47, page 177. Theoretically it should be possible to destroy all of the afferent supply of
neurones to a given skin and muscular area without destroying
the efferent neurones. According to Head, some afferent neurones, however, always run with the motor fibers so that in order
completely to rob an area of its afferent supply, both motor and
sensory nerves would have to be cut.[6]

---

[6] Head and Rivers have attempted to divide the cutaneous fibers up into
a protopathic group ("including cutaneous pain, a diffuse non-localizable
tactile sensibility, and the discrimination of extreme degrees of temperature") and an epicritic group ("light touch, cutaneous localization, discrim-

The Peripheral Neurones of the Brain.—There are twelve pairs of peripheral cranial nerves. Their superficial points of origin (efferent) or entrance (afferent) are shown on the ventral view of the brain (Figs. 30 and 31). The cranial nerves do not correspond at all closely to the pattern just described for the spinal nerves; some are wholly afferent, some wholly efferent, while others are mixed. The following table from Hardesty (Morris, Human Anatomy) gives the names and numbers of the nerves, whether they are afferent, efferent or mixed, and their distribution.

Name	Nature	General Distribution
Olfactory (I)	Sensory	Olfactory region, nasal epithelium.
Optic (II)	Sensory	Retina.
Oculomotor (III)	Motor { Somatic	Eye-moving muscles.
	Visceral	Ciliary body, iris.
Trochlear (IV)	Motor-Somatic	Eye-moving muscles.
Abducens (VI)	Motor-Somatic	Eye-moving muscles.
Trigeminus (V)	Sensory	Face, mouth and scalp.
Masticator (minor part or motor root of Trigeminus)	Motor-Somatic	Muscles of mastication.
Facial (VII)	Motor { Somatic	Facial muscles.
	Visceral	Salivary glands, vessels (?).
Glosso-palatine (*intermediate part of facial*)	{ Sensory	Tongue and palate.
	Motor-Visceral.	Salivary glands.
Cochlear (*auditory*) (VIII)	Sensory	Internal ear.
Vestibular (*equilibrator*) (VIII)	Sensory	Semicircular canals, utriculus, sacculus.
Glossopharyngeal (IX)	{ Sensory	Tongue, palate, pharynx.
	Motor { Somatic	Pharynx.
	Visceral.	Glands and vessels.
Vagus (X)	{ Sensory	Alimentary canal, lungs, heart
	Motor { Somatic	Larynx, pharynx.
	Visceral.	Alimentary canal, heart. larynx, trachea, lung.

ination of intermediate degrees of temperature, and some others"). The quotations are from Herrick. This work has been a great misfortune to neurology. It was accepted uncritically and on the basis of it the somatic conduction paths in the central nervous system have been delimited without sufficient confirmation. The works of Trotter and Davies and of Boring have cast doubt upon the wholesale generalizations made by Rivers and Head.

Hypoglossal (XII) ....Motor-Somatic ...Tongue-moving muscles.

Spinal Accessory (XI) ....Motor $\begin{cases} \text{Somatic: Neck and shoulder muscles.} \\ \text{Visceral .Pharynx, larynx and heart.} \end{cases}$

Each of the afferent nerves or the afferent portion of the mixed nerves has a ganglion corresponding to a spinal ganglion. The ganglion, however, may be at some distance from the point of entrance into the central system: the ganglion for the cochlear division of the VIII nerve lies in the modiolus of the cochlea (ganglion spirale); for the vestibular division it lies blended within the nerve at the bottom of the internal auditory meatus (ganglion of Scarpa) (Fig. 8, 3). In the I or olfactory nerve it lies in the mucous membrane of the nose. In the II or optic the relations are peculiar; the first neurone, cell body and axone lie in the retina (Fig. 17). The cranial nerve marked II (optic) is not a peripheral nerve but a central tract.[7]

The V or trigeminus springs from cells in the semilunar (Gasserian) ganglion—which lies in Meckel's cave, a cleft in the dura mater in the upper surface of the petrous portion of the temporal bone. The sensory fibers of the facial, VII (Glosso-palatine), spring from cells in the geniculate ganglion. This ganglion is situated within the canalis facialis (Fallopii). The superior ganglion and the inferior ganglion of the afferent part of the IX (Glossopharyngeal) lie in the jugular foramen. The X has two ganglia—jugular, which lies also in the jugular fora-men, and the ganglion nodosum, which lies below the base of the skull and in front of the jugular vein.

A discussion of the peripheral distribution and the central connections of these nerves other than those of the special senses is a task too vast to undertake outside of an anatomical labo-ratory. We shall, however, indicate some of the more important central pathways of the afferent nerves in our discussion of the ascending and descending pathways in the cord and brain.

Course of the Ascending Neurones in the Cord and Brain.— Turning to the study of the further course of the afferent roots inside the central nervous system, we find in the spinal cord that they may establish several connections upon their entrance. The afferent root may end at that level or above or below it. After entrance it usually divides by a Y division (Fig. 23) sending

---

[7] The reason for this depends upon the embryology of the eye. The retina with its optic stalk (becoming later the optic tract) was originally a part of the embryological brain.

one branch downward (caudal) in the dorsal funiculus and the
other branch upward in the dorsal funiculus (sometimes as far
as the medulla oblongata, where it ends in a nucleus of reception).   At various levels each of these branches gives off collaterals which end around the dendrites of cell bodies within the
cord.   The following relationships are known to occur: (1) such
a collateral may end around the dendrites of a motor cell in the
ventral horn on the same or on the opposite side, forming the

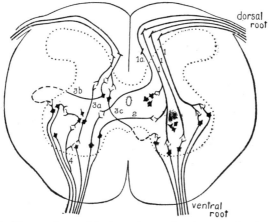

Fig. 37.—Diagram of some of the types of connections between the afferent fibers of
the dorsal root and the motor fibers of the ventral root (rabbit). The various fibers are
numbered: 1 and 1a represent collateral branches of the dorsal root fibers which run directly
to the dendrites of the motor neurones in the ventral column of the same or opposite side;
2, dendrites of ventral column cells crossing to the opposite side, meeting with the ter-
minals of 1 above (probably a very rare connection); 3a, 3b and 3c are central neurones;
these neurones may connect the sensory root ending with the motor neurone in the same
segment on the same or opposite side or they may send their axones to end at lower or
higher levels; 4 is a collateral of the motor axone returning to end in the gray matter
around other cells. (Herrick's Introduction to Neurology.) W. B. Saunders Co.

direct reflex pathway or the pathway for the crossed reflex, (2)
the dendrites of the ventral horn cells themselves may cross to
the opposite side in the central commissure and end in contact
with a collateral of an afferent root.   In either 1 or 2 above a
short central interconnecting neurone may be interpolated.   Its
cell body lies in the dorsal horn and its axone ends around ventral
cells of that or higher or lower levels.   Certain other relationships
which may occur will appear when we come to consider special
tracts in the cord.   Fig. 37 shows some of the possible connections.

Connection of Cord with Cerebellum (Ascending Neurones.)—Certain of the collaterals and axones of afferent roots end around cells in Clark's column (Fig. 38, 19), which is to be found in the posterior horn. Two tracts arise from these cells. They ascend in the lateral funiculus. One of the tracts (tractus spino-cerebellaris dorsalis, also called direct cerebellar tract and Flechsig's tract) (Fig. 39, 7), enters the cerebellum via the inferior peduncle, the other (tractus spino-cerebellaris ventralis) (Fig. 39, 5) enters the cerebellum by way of the superior peduncle. The two tracts carry impulses from the kinæsthetic sense organs to the cerebellum. We shall see later that the cerebellum is an important central station for all impulses connected with the maintenance of equilibrium and the tone of the muscles.

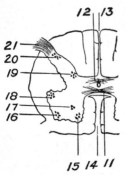

Fig. 38.—Diagram to show grouping of cell bodies in spinal cord. 14, ventral median fissure (fissura mediana superior); 13, dorsal median septum (sulcus mediana posterior); 12, posterior commissure (commissura posterior alba); 11, ventral commissure (commissura anterior alba); 21, entrance of dorsal root (radix posterior); 20, cell bodies lying in the dorsal horn; 19, Clark's column (nucleus dorsalis); 18, cell bodies lying in lateral column; these give rise to the preganglionic fibers, axones, which run to the sympathetic ganglia; 17, 16, 15, groups of cell bdoies giving rise to the peripheral motor neurone (radix anterior).

Connection of Cord with Medulla (and Cortex), Ascending Neurones.—The afferent fibers coming from the muscles, tendons and joints (kinæsthetic sense organs) enter the cord and take up a vertical position in the dorsal funiculi (posterior columns) and ascend without interruption (that is, without synaptical connections) as far as the medulla oblongata (first relay station). They end there around definite cell groups called nuclei of reception. The cells are so numerous that their presence is marked by an actual swelling shown in Fig. 32, 23 and 4. There are really two reception nuclei in each dorsal funiculus, the nucleus funiculi gracilis and the nucleus funiculi cuneati (the dorsal funiculus as a whole being divided into two fasciculi, the gracilis lying nearest the median septum and the cuneatus occupying the remainder of the space (Fig. 39, 10 and 9). The cell bodies lying in these nuclei give off axones (ascending neurones of the second order) which swing over to the opposite side, passing under the spinal canal, which in this region is near the dorsal surface (Fig. 40). This crossing is known as the sensory decussation (decussatio lemniscorum). The fibers after crossing form the medial lemniscus (lemniscus medialis), which can be seen in every cross-section from the medulla to the thalamus. The lemniscus is being constantly enlarged because ascending neurones of the sec-

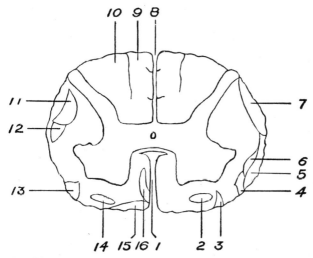

Fig. 39.—Diagram through spinal cord in mid-cervical region to show arrangement of various fiber tracts. 1, ventral median fissure; 8, dorsal median septum; 9, 10, show the two subdivisions of the dorsal funiculus, 9 being the fasciculus gracilis, 10, the fasciculus cuneatus; 2, one of the ascending tracts to the thalamus, tractus spino-thalamicus ventralis; 3, tract connecting spinal cord with the olives, tractus spino-olivaris; 4, tract connecting cord with the roof of the mid-brain, tractus spino-tectalis; 5, tractus spino-cerebellaris ventralis (part of the fasciculus antero-lateralis superficialis); 6, tractus spino-thalamicus lateralis; 7, tractus spino-cerebellaris dorsalis (fasciculus cerebello-spinalis).

ond order from the cranial afferent nerves (after decussating) are constantly joining. These ascending neurones in the medial lemniscus end around the cell bodies in the thalamus on the same side (second relay station). The cells there give rise to axones (ascending neurones of the third order) which pass through the internal capsule (Fig. 44, 20) through the corona radiata (Fig. 44, 16) then they ray out to end in the gyri behind the central sulcus—the so-called somæsthetic reception area in the cortex. Summarizing: In this system (*kinæsthetic*) the peripheral end of the first afferent axone terminates in a sensory structure in muscle, tendon or joint. The central end enters the cord, turns upward and reaches the medulla (ascending neurone of the first order). The neurones of the second order start in the medulla and end in the thalamus (of the opposite side). The neurones of the third order (the final neurones) start in the thalamus and end in the cortex.

Connection of Cord with Thalamus (and Cortex), Ascending Neurones.—Certain of the afferent neurones (spinal roots), instead of ascending in the dorsal funiculus (dorsal column), end in the posterior horn. The cell body of a central neurone lying there sends an axone across the cord (via the ventral commissure) to the ventral and lateral funiculi of the opposite side, forming the two spino-thalamic tracts (Fig. 39, 2 and 6). The axones in these tracts carry impulses from the *temperature, pain and pressure senses*. The fibers run directly up to their nuclei of reception in the thalamus (ventral and lateral nuclei of the thalamus). In other words, the temperature, pain, pressure pathway is relayed once, immediately upon entrance into the cord, and not again until the thalamus is reached (Fig. 40).

Above the level of the medulla they join the medial lemniscus and follow the same route as the axones just described, terminating probably in adjacent cortical regions (somæsthetic area).

Ascending Pathway of Afferent Cranial Neurones.—The afferent root of the V nerve (trigeminus) has its nucleus of reception (first relay station) in the gray matter of the pons. The reception nucleus is large at this level but tapers down, ending at the upper level of the spinal cord. The cells in this nucleus send axones which, after crossing, probably join the medial lemniscus (ascending neurones of the second order) and end in the thalamus (Fig. 40). There a second relay occurs and the axones from the thalamic cells (ascending neurones of the third order) pass up through the internal capsule and corona radiata and end in the somæsthetic area. It is probable that this ascending tract of the V remains fairly distinct from the fibers of the lemniscus (in Fig. 40 it is marked trigeminal lemniscus). The glossopalatine (afferent portion of VII, n. intermedius) entering under the inferior border of the pons (Fig. 31, 24), has its nucleus

of reception in the gray matter of the pons.   Cells situated there
send axones into the medial lemniscus to end in the thalamus.
Neurones beginning there continue the pathway to the somæsthetic area.   The axones here spoken of carry kinæsthetic and
cutaneous impulses from the tongue and palate.   The central

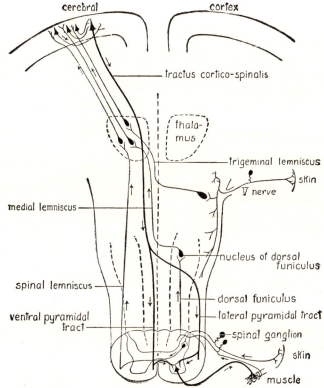

FIG. 40.—Showing some connections between the cord and brain. Explanation of figure
in text.   (Herrick's Introduction to Neurology.)

pathway of the glossopalatine axones carrying taste impulses
from the anterior two-thirds of the tongue is unknown.   They
may possibly run to the thalamus and after being relayed there
enter the gyrus hippocampus in the basal part of the temporal
lobe (Fig. 30).

The glossopharyngeal (afferent portion of the IX) and the

11

2

62   PSYCHOLOGY

afferent division of the vagus (X) enter the medulla lateral to the olive and end in the nucleus tractus solitarii and neighboring cells in the medulla. These cells send axones to join the lemniscus of the opposite side: they also bear cutaneous, kinæsthetic and organic impulses. The course of the gustatory axones through the brain stem (the glossopharyngeal innervates the posterior third of the tongue) and higher structures is likewise unknown.

Course of the Nerves of Special Sense and Their Cortical Terminations.—The auditory nerve (cochlear division) enters the medulla lateral to the olive (Fig. 31, 25) and ends around two reception nuclei in the tuberculum acusticum (Fig. 32). The cells from these nuclei send axones across the mid-line (stria medullaris acustica, Fig. 32, 6) and ascend along the sides of the medial lemniscus, forming the lateral lemriscus (lemniscus lateralis). These ascending neurones of the second order end mainly in the medial geniculate body of the thalamus (Fig. 32, 10). Some end undoubtedly in the inferior colliculus (Fig. 32, 18). By a short system of neurones the pathway of the latter group is continued to the medial geniculate body. The third (or, as the case may be, the fourth) order of neurones carries them from this point through the internal capsule (Fig. 44, 20) to the cortical reception station in the temporal lobe (gyri immediately below the fissure of Sylvius) (Fig. 35, 4).

The fibers from the vestibular portion of the eighth nerve enter the medulla at a slightly higher level than the cochlear branch (Fig. 31, 25). The fibers end around four terminal nuclei in the floor and wall of the fourth ventricle: Deiter's (nucleus nervi vestibuli lateralis) situated just internal to the restiform body; a superior, Von Bechterew's (nucleus nervi vestibuli superior) situated dorsal to Deiter's nucleus in the lateral wall of the fourth ventricle; a medial, Schwalbe's (nucleus nervi vestibuli medialis); and an inferior (nucleus nervi vestibuli spinalis). Axones from the lateral and inferior nuclei form paths to the spinal cord. Axones from the lateral and superior nuclei form a path to the roof nucleus of the cerebellum (nucleus fastigii) of the opposite side. Apparently there is no thalamic tract issuing from these nuclei. It would seem that most of the connections of the vestibular portion of the ear are thus made with the cerebellum and cord.

As was pointed out, the peripheral optic nerve lies in the retina (neurones of the first order). The layer of ganglion cells with their fibers are ascending neurones of the second order corresponding to the tract running from cerebellum to thalamus in the kinæsthetic system. These neurones are rightly named the optic tract (tractus opticus) (Fig. 31, 9). The axone system in part crosses at the chiasma (Fig. 31, 14). From the chiasma the fibers enter the brain in the region of the pulvinar of the thalamus. Reaching the pulvinar, the optic tract divides into a

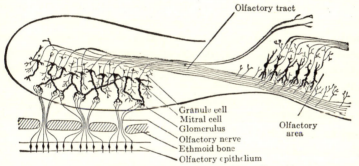

Olfactory tract

Granule cell
Mitral cell
Glomerulus
Olfactory nerve
Ethmoid bone
Olfactory epithelium

Olfactory area

Fig. 41.—Diagram of the connections of the olfactory bulb. (Herrick's Introduction to Neurology.)

lateral and a mesial branch. The lateral root contains the true visual fibers and these fibers end around cells in three regions, lateral geniculate body, pulvinar, and in the superior colliculus (Fig. 32, 11 and 17). The latter pathway serves to carry impulses (for releasing eye moving reflexes) from the retina to the nuclei of motor nerves (III and IV) whose cells of origin lie near. The cells in the lateral geniculate body and in the pulvinar send axones through the internal capsule to end in the visual cortical area—the gyri about the calcarine fissure of the occipital lobe (Fig. 33, 17).

The olfactory nerve has a very special course. The ganglion cells in the olfactory epithelium in the nose send axones (first order) to end around the mitral cells in the olfactory bulb (relay station). The mitral cells there send axones known as the olfactory tract (second order) to enter the hippocampal gyrus in the region of the uncus (Fig. 31, 20). The system is shown in Fig. 41.

Summary.—Schematically at any rate, the architecture we have been studying is simple enough. All of the tracts in the cord bearing cutaneous impulses (occupying ventro-lateral columns) and kinæsthetic impulses (occupying posterior columns) from the body are gathered together in the medial lemniscus, which ever increases in size from its beginning in the medulla due to the addition of fibers coming from reception nuclei of the afferent cranial nerves. It is soon joined by the axones from the reception nuclei of the auditory nerve (lateral lemniscus). All of these axones, including the optic, terminate in nuclei lying in the corpora quadrigemina or thalamus. These nuclei send axones directly (or by addition of a short central neurone) to the sensory projection areas in the cortex, for example, the somæsthetic, visual and auditory. In this summary we neglect only the olfactory, which does not appear in any of these levels, and the gustatory, about whose central connections we know little or nothing.

Connection of Sensory Projection Areas with the Motor Area in the Cortex.—From our study of behavior we have found that many objects can stimulate more than one sense organ, and that when we have learned to respond in a certain way to that object, the same response may be initiated by stimulation of any one of the sense organs: for example, the stimulation of vision, smell, taste or touch effected by an apple may lead to the same final movement, the reaching out and grasping of the apple and the carrying of it to the mouth. If the formation of habit (acquired forms of reaction) involves the cortex, then we should expect to find that the cortical reception area of each sense organ should be in close connection with the cortical motor area. Entirely apart from behavior studies it was early established by Fritsch while operating upon a wounded soldier in the Franco-Prussian War, that if the galvanic-electric current is applied to certain parts of the brain, movement of the limbs occurs. Careful experiments during recent years have shown that the pre-central gyrus is the main cortical motor area. Stimulation there is followed by the contraction of a particular group of muscles on the opposite side of the body. The diagrammatic sketch (Fig. 42) shows what motor parts are moved. Since we know that the peripheral, spinal and cerebral motor neurones run to these muscles and directly control them, we may be sure even before we examine the architecture that the motor area is connected with the cell bodies which give rise to the lower motor neurones. Between the motor area or motor projection "center" and the sensory projection areas lie the so-called association "centers." These areas do not directly receive the final neurones from sense organs nor does a weak electrical stimulation arouse muscular

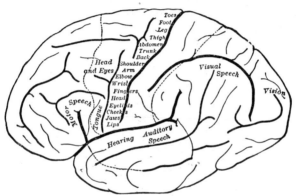

Fig. 42.—The human cerebral hemisphere seen from the left side, upon which the functional areas of the cortex are indicated. The area marked "motor speech" is Broca's convolution. (Starr, "Nervous Diseases," Lea & Febiger.)

movement. They are the "silent areas." Entirely too much has been made of them (and of the whole localization of function as well, page 170). Try to look upon them as more or less non-specialized brain areas which contain interconnecting neurones. It may be safe to say—it is often said—that every gyrus is connected with every other gyrus on the same side by association neurones and with every gyrus on the opposite side by commissural neurones (corpus callosum).

Connection of Cortex with Lower Centers.—Histological examination shows that in the precentral gyrus (motor area) there exist a large number of giant pyramidal cell bodies on each side. The cells are shown in Fig. 43. It has been shown

that these giant cells give rise to axones which without relay pass
to all levels of the spinal cord. Other cells located there send
axones to the nuclei of origin of the cranial motor nerves. This
vast system is schematically shown in Fig. 44 and can be

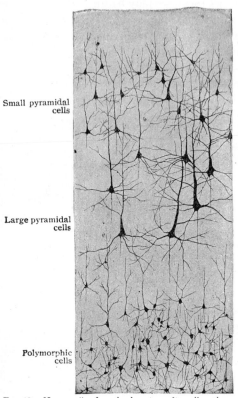

Small pyramidal
cells

Large pyramidal
cells

Polymorphic
cells

followed there pass-
ing through the cor-
ona radiata, through
the striate body and
through the thala-
mus; it takes up a
ventral position on
the cerebral peduncle
and passes through
the transverse fibers
of the pons to the
medulla   oblongata,
where it forms the
right and left pyra-
mid on its ventral
surface. This system
is called the pyram-
idal tract (fascic-
ulus   cerebro-spin-
alis) (Fig. 44, 24
and 26). The fur-
ther course of these
fibers is continued in
the next paragraph.
In addition to this
system of descending
neurones, the cortex

Fig. 43.—Nerve-cells of cerebral cortex, after silver im-
pregnation.   ×70. (Preparation by Prof. T. G. Lee.)

of the frontal lobe sends a direct system of axones to the red
nucleus (nucleus ruber) in the cerebral peduncle (this nucleus
lies in the tegmentum above the peduncles and just ventral to the
corpora quadrigemina)—the cortico rubro tract (the red nucleus
in its turn probably sends up an ascending system of neurones
which end in the frontal region). We know, furthermore, that

axones from cells in the frontal, parietal and occipital association regions form descending pathways to the cells in the pons—the cortico-pontile tracts. Many of the descending pathways are far too complicated to study without neurological material.

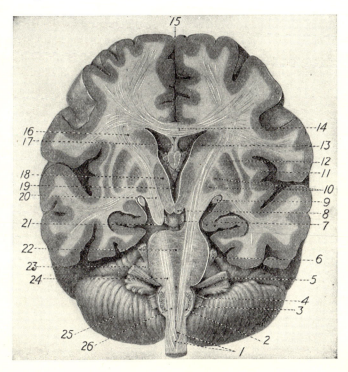

Fɪɢ. 41.—Coronal section through cerebral hemispheres and brain stem. 1, pyramidal decussation (decussatio pyramidum); 2, nucleus olivaris inferior; 3, n. vagus; 4, n. glossopharyngeus; 5, nn. facialis et acusticus; 6, n. trigeminus; 7, n. oculo-motorius; 8, corpus mammillare; 9, optic tract (tractus opticus); 10, globus pallidus (part of nucleus lentiformis); 11, insula; 12, putamen (part of nucleus lentiformis); 13, head of nucleus caudatus (caput nuclei caudati); 14, corpus callosum; 15, longitudinal fissure (fissura longitudinalis cerebri); 16, corona radiata; 17, septum pellucidum; 18, thalamus; 19, third ventricle (ventriculus tertius); 20, internal capsule (capsula interna); 21, cerebral peduncle (penduculus cerebri); 22, superficial fibers of the pons; 23, middle cerebellar peduncle (brachium pontis); 24, pyramidal tract passing through pons (fasciculi longitudinales pontis); 25, cerebellum; 26, pyramidal tract in medulla (pyramis medullæ oblongatæ). (Modified from Toldt.)

Descending Tracts in the Spinal Cord.—The pyramidal tract is the most conspicuous tract in the cord. At the lower end of the medulla the fibers begin to decussate (Fig. 44, 1). After decussation they take up two positions in the cord. A part of the fibers from one motor cortex continue down to the ventral funiculus of the same side, the direct pyramidal tract (fasciculus cerebro-spinalis anterior) (Fig. 45, 16). The majority of the fibers swing over to the opposite side and descend in the lateral funiculus, forming the lateral pyramidal tract (fasciculis cerebro-spinalis lateralis) (Fig. 45, 11). The direct pyramidal tract is soon exhausted. The fibers reach a certain level and turn at right angles to end around motor cells in the ventral horn. The

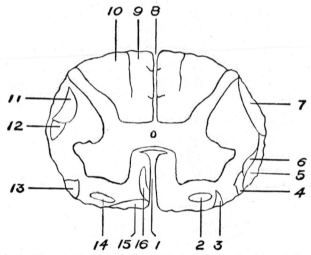

Fig. 45.—Diagram of cross-section of spinal cord through mid-cervical region to show the arrangement of the fiber tracts. 16, tractus cortico-spinalis ventralis, the direct pyramidal tract (fasciculus cerebro-spinalis anterior); 11, tractus cortico-spinalis lateralis, lateral or crossed pyramidal tract (fasciculus cerebro-spinalis lateralis); 15, tractus vestibulo-spinalis; 14, tractus tecto-spinalis; 13, tractus olivo-spinalis; 12, tractus rubro-spinalis. (The tracts are discussed in the text.)

lateral or crossed pyramidal tract can be identified down to the lowest level of the cord. As the tract descends it gets smaller and smaller, due to the fact that some of the fibers turn at right angles to end around motor cells at each successive level. The pyramidal neurones and the peripheral motor neurones thus together form a very direct path between the motor area in the brain and the muscle.

There are several other descending tracts in the cord. The

most important ones only are here mentioned. A. Tractus-rubro spinalis (von Monakow's tract) (Fig. 45, 12). This is a tract running from the mid-brain (nucleus ruber) to the cord. Its fibers terminate in the dorsal portion of the ventral horn. It is a joint cerebellar and thalamic system. Axones of cells in the cerebellar cortex run to the nucleus dentatus in the cerebellum : cells from this nucleus send axones to end in the nucleus ruber; this nucleus in turn sends axones to form the rubro-spinal tract. It brings the motor cell in the cord under the influence of the thalamus and the cerebellum. B. Tractus vestibulo-spinalis (Fig. 45, 15). This tract originates in the reception nuclei of the vestibular nerve lying in the medulla—Deiter's nucleus. It was pointed out that this nucleus receives impulses both from the cerebellum and from the semicircular canals. The axones in this tract also terminate around the ventral horn cell. We thus see that there are adequate connections both ascending and descending by means of which the cerebellum can serve as an equilibrating and toning organ for the muscles.

A General Caution.—This short sketch of the cerebro-spinal system should teach us that every sensory structure studied in our last chapter can, when stimulated, excite a segmental reflex, a reflex involving neighboring segments, or a reflex involving practically the whole of the central nervous system. All of this complexity is needed to serve as a neural basis for the complex types of reflex, instinctive and habitual acts man performs. We shall see when we come to study the motor side of the organism that sustained integrated acts such as are involved in eye-hand or ear-hand, such as those involved in walking or swimming, require that the peripheral motor neurones should be under the influence of many distant parts of the central nervous system. While we wish to emphasize the importance of the central nervous system, we do not wish to make a fetish of it. Due to the studies on the localization of function and of the disturbances which occur when injury is done to the sensory projection centers in the cortex, there has grown up in neurological circles a kind of scientific phrenology. The main fact about the central nervous system is that it affords a system of connection between sense organs and

glands and muscles. Interrupt the pathway in any place and
the organism no longer acts as a whole; some phase of the behavior pattern will drop out. Nor should the nervous system be
overemphasized. The whole motor and glandular systems in each
and every part do the reacting. A sudden stooping or rotation of
the head, or a loud noise, probably changes the tonus of every
muscle in the body, striped and unstriped, and starts a wealth of
glandular activity. But action cannot take place without the
participation of the bones. Action again means an increased
food supply, an increased strain upon the heart, and the elimination of waste product. A simple eye-hand coördination, the
picking up of a pin from the ground, brings about a well-ordered
and integrated response of the organism as a whole. Such a well-
ordered response will not take place without a central nervous
system, but it must be said with equal truth that it will not
take place without a heart, without bones, and without glands
and muscles.

THE SYMPATHETIC NERVOUS SYSTEM.

Introduction.—So far in our discussion of the nervous system we have neglected the sympathetic system, but we have
spoken of the peripheral motor neurones. The sympathetic system must be looked upon as an *extension of the peripheral motor
nervous system*. The peripheral motor nerves belonging to the
cord and brain are distributed to the striped muscles of the body
(page 176). But the striped musculature of the skeleton represents only a part of the efferent organs. The viscera in the thoracic,
abdominal and pelvic cavities and certain structures in the head
region contain unstriped or smooth muscle tissue and glands.
The sympathetic system which in nearly every case is under the
dominion of the motor nerves of the cord and brain controls the
smooth muscles of the viscera and glands. The sympathetic is
thus wholly motor. Afferent neurones are distributed to the
tissue which the sympathetic controls, but these *afferent neurones
belong to the afferent peripheral cerebro-spinal system which we
have already studied—the organic sense organ. There is no substantial evidence to show that the sympathetic system has an
afferent supply of its own.* It may be true from an evolutionary

point of view that the cerebro-spinal system is an adjunct to the sympathetic, but the development of the former has reached such a point that it now is the "tail that wags the dog." There has been a tendency in recent years to exploit the sympathetic system at the expense of the cerebro-spinal. This has been done largely in the interest of giving a neurophysiological basis to certain psychoanalytic principles. When one considers the enormous development of language habits and of the vast system of integrations existing among the reflex arcs controlling the striped musculature of the body as a whole, one cannot take such a view seriously, even though he himself is prepared to yield an ever-increasing importance to the system. Emotional activity is important, hunger, thirst, micturition, defecation are also important factors, as we have tried to show—especially when disturbances in those mechanisms occur. But after all the sympathetic mechanisms which underlie such functions are simply a part of the body as a whole. To overemphasize it is to neglect our facts in the interest of theory.

The Ganglia of the Sympathetic (or Autonomic) System.— Fig. 27 shows (in black, on right side only) (1) a chain of sympathetic ganglia that run parallel on each side of the spinal cord. The ganglia appear on each of these trunks at fairly regular intervals. Each trunk runs from the second cervical vertebra to the first piece of coccyx. The two trunks unite in one ganglion at the coccyx—the ganglion coccygeum impar. It will be understood that these ganglia, as do all other sympathetic ganglia, lie wholly outside of the central nervous system. (2) The cephalic or brain portion of the sympathetic consists of four main ganglia on each side, but not appearing in regular segments as do those considered above—the ciliary ganglion (ciliary muscle in the eye, sphincter of the iris, etc.), sphenopalatine (vaso-motor, secretory), the optic (vaso-motor, etc.) and the submaxillary (glands of mouth, etc.). There are also numerous other small ganglia. These ganglia are not shown. (3) Ganglia scattered through the visceral organs, in the cavities of the thorax, abdomen and pelvis—the heart, lungs, liver, alimentary tract, pancreas and sex organs. The most important of these ganglia are found in connection with the cardiac plexus, cœliac (solar) plexus and the hypogastric plexus (abdominal and pelvic). None of these is shown in our drawings.

Structure of the Sympathetic Ganglia.—The ganglia consist of gray matter, cell bodies giving rise to axones, and of ends of axones coming from other neurones. The axones of the sympathetic are rarely myelinated throughout their course, but they are occasionally myelinated for a short distance after leaving the cell body. Most of the axones are covered with a sheath of Schwann. The dendrites are numerous and similar in structure to those we have studied in the central nervous system.

Distribution of Sympathetic Neurones.—The axones of sympathetic neurones, after a shorter or longer course, end finally in the glandular tissue, in the heart muscle, in the blood-vessels, and in the *non-striated muscular tissue* of the body wherever it is found. We see the system in action in the bristling of hairs, dilatation and constriction of the pupil, secretion of saliva, inhibition and acceleration of the heart, flushing, goose-flesh, peristalsis, defecation, urination, tumescence in the sex organs, etc. Sympathetic neurones thus are motor and control the so-called vegetative functions.

The Control of the Central Nervous System Over the Sympathetic System.—The neural connection of the central nervous system with sympathetic ganglia is shown in Fig. 46. It is seen there that cell bodies in the gray matter of the cord (lateral horn), and this is true also of the brain, send out axones through the motor roots, which end in a near or distant sympathetic ganglion. The synaptical connection is like that in the central nervous system. The axone breaks up into an end brush and ends around the dendrites of the sympathetic neurone. The neurone (Fig. 46, 8) running from the spinal cord or brain to the sympathetic ganglia and ending there is called the *pre-ganglionic* neurone (the axone is also called the pre-ganglionic axone or fiber). This pre-ganglionic neurone is myelinated and is similar in all respects to motor neurones with the possible exception of its size; in general it is slightly smaller. The sympathetic neurone (Fig. 46, 5) running from the ganglion cell to end in the gland or smooth muscle tissue is called usually the *post-ganglionic* neurone.   We thus see that the whole sympathetic nervous system is under the control of the central nervous system by means of the pre-ganglionic neurone.

(The white ramus communicans consists of pre-ganglionic axones on their way to enter a sympathetic ganglion.   There is also a gray ramus communicans consisting largely of axones of

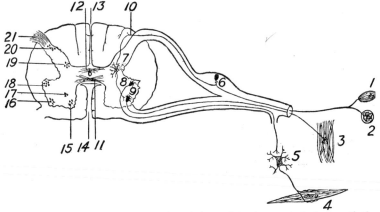

Fig. 46.—Diagrammatic cross-section of the cord to show control of sympathetic by cerebro-spinal system.   In addition the diagram shows the reflex arc from skin to striped muscle.   6, spinal afferent neurone with peripheral ending and sensory structures 1 and 2 with central ending in the cord; a collateral from this neurone ends around the central cell marked 7, whose axone in turn ends around motor neurone 9, whose axone ends in the striped muscle 3; neurone 8 has its cell body in the lateral horn of the gray matter; the axone, however, ends in a sympathetic ganglion, in the drawing around 5, a sympathetic neurone; the sympathetic neurone ends in smooth muscle cell 4.

sympathetic neurones which must get out of the visceral cavity in order to run to the sweat glands of the skin, the muscles of the hairs and blood-vessels.   These post-ganglionic fibers join the spinal nerves and run a common course with them.)

The Afferent or Return Connections of the Sympathetic.— Notwithstanding the work of Dogiel and Huber and others, more recent investigations show that the sympathetic has no afferent system of its own.   The peripheral afferent system of the brain and cord (spinal and cranial ganglia) affords the sensory innervation for the tissues controlled by the sympathetic.   The peripheral process from a spinal or cerebral ganglion cell, instead of running towards the skin or kinæsthetic structures, turns to enter the white ramus and pass along with the pre-ganglionic fiber. But instead of ending in a sympathetic ganglion, where the pre-ganglionic fiber ends, it passes through or alongside of the ganglion without making functional connections and ends in the motor or glandular tissue that is under the control of the post-ganglionic or sympathetic fiber. This is the usual relation. Possibly an illustration will make this clearer. The sweetheart of a boy comes suddenly into the room. His face flushes. The neural situation in outline is as follows: The optic impulses pass back over the optic tract and upon reaching the central system arouse an impulse in pre-ganglionic neurones. These neurones carry the impulse to the sympathetic neurones which dilate the blood-vessels of the face. But this sudden change in the temperature of the face arouses the ordinary nerve endings in the skin which are sensitive to warmth, etc. In the viscera the conditions are probably not at all different.

Divisions of the Sympathetic System.—Most authors divide the sympathetic as a whole into two divisions, oftentimes into more. The most recent and satisfactory division seems to be as follows (Ranson): (1) The *thoracico-lumbar autonomic system* is that division of the sympathetic the pre-ganglionic fibers of which make their exit from the spinal cord through the thoracic and upper lumbar nerves. (2) The *craniosacral autonomic system* is that division of the sympathetic system the pre-ganglionic fibers of which make their exit from the cerebro-spinal axis (brain and cord) through the III, VII, IX, X, XI cranial nerves and the II, III and IV sacral nerves. Most of the structures innervated by the autonomic system receive a double supply, a portion from part 1 above and a portion from part 2. When this occurs the two sets possess opposite functions; for example: autonomic system 1 dilates the pupil, while autonomic system 2 contracts it; again, autonomic 1 increases secretion in the submaxillary gland, autonomic 2 decreases it. Finally, autonomic 1 accelerates the heart, autonomic 2 inhibits it.

Concluding Statements.—Although the material presented in this chapter has possibly seemed detailed we have done little more than present the elementary conduction systems which connect the sense organs with the central nervous system and the latter with the muscles and glands. We have had to leave out of account all discussion of the special functions of the cerebral cortex, thalamus, caudate nucleus, nucleus lentiformis, the cerebellum, and the gray cellular masses in the brain stem. If what has been presented has been followed, the student should carry away with him an increased knowledge of what kinæsthetic motor responses, visual-motor responses, and organic-motor responses are, and what is meant by the integration or tying together of long and short reflex arcs in such a way that concerted, controlled and sustained action in the muscles may be obtained. This knowledge is fundamental if the factors underlying human behavior are sought.

The sympathetic system should not be confusing. Every sense organ is the beginning of an arc which ends in a muscle. The organic sense organ is no exception. The afferent portion of this system is similar in all respects to that of the kinæsthetic or cutaneous, but on the motor side it takes both the pre-ganglionic neurone and the post-ganglionic (sympathetic) neurone to establish connections with the effectors. In other words, the pre-ganglionic neurone belonging to the central system has to be "lengthened" or "supplemented" in order to reach and stimulate the motor organs belonging to the organic system. This is, of course, an oversimplification in the interest of making the anatomical relation clear. Whether neural action in neurones belonging to the sympathetic system is in all respects similar to neural action elsewhere is a problem which we need not attempt to study here.

CHAPTER V

THE ORGANS OF RESPONSE: MUSCLES AND GLANDS

Introduction.—In order to complete our sketch of the mechanisms involved in human response, it remains for us to study the effectors. So far we have studied receptors or sense organs and their stimuli, and the system of conductors stretching out between receptors and the effectors, or acting organs. The motor neurones of the cord and brain end directly in skeletal muscle or *indirectly* (through the intermediation of a sympathetic post-ganglionic neurone, page 173) in the smooth muscles of the body and the glands. Our sketch would be incomplete if we failed to get a good working notion of action in skeletal muscles, smooth muscles, and glands. In the sketch which follows we have omitted all details and have summarized only the most important features of such action, and the features with which psychology has most to do. We can study the effector system under three general divisions: I, the striped muscles; II, the smooth muscles; III, the glands.

I. STRIPED MUSCLES.

Structure of the Striped Muscles.—The skeletal or striped muscles constitute the principal mass of the body as a whole. Each muscle is more or less of an organic whole, which can assume various shapes and sizes. The morphological unit of a muscle, however, is a muscle fiber or muscle cell. Each muscle consists of a large number of thread-like cells which usually lie parallel to the long axis of the muscle. At one or both ends, the muscle tapers down and forms a junction with a tendon. The tendons in turn are attached to the bone. The fibers of the muscles are grouped into larger and smaller bundles, each bundle being bound with connective tissue. A sheath, or perimysium, surrounds the muscle as a whole.

The individual muscle fibers vary greatly in diameter and length. They are rarely longer than 36 mm., and the diameter varies from 0.1 to 0.01 mm. The fibers are cylindrical in shape.

176

Each fiber is inclosed in a thin homogeneous elastic membrane called the sarcolemma. The material inside the fiber is striated. It is supposed to be of a semi-viscous consistency. This material is the muscle plasma. The muscle plasma is made up of fibrils which run the whole length of the intervening sarcoplasm. The fibrils seem to be made up of alternating dim and light discs.

Neural Endings in Muscles.—The peripheral motor and sensory neurones end in the muscles. We have already spoken of the

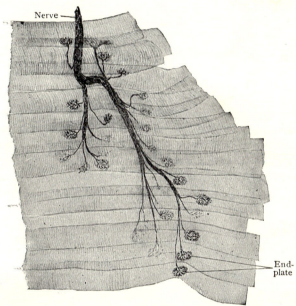

Nerve

End-plate

Fig. 47.—Ending of motor nerves in striped muscle. The axones pierce the perimysium, lose their medullary sheath and end in a plate-like formation on the individual muscle fibers. (Piersol's Anatomy.)

sensory endings in muscles on page 59. The axones of the motor nerves upon reaching the muscle lose their medullary sheath and break up into numerous fine fibrils. These fibrils spread out in plate form (motor end plates) and pass to each muscle fiber. Fig. 47 shows the ending in striped muscle fibers of axones of efferent neurones.

In addition to the afferent and efferent supply coming from the central nervous system, the muscles receive sympathetic fibers, *i.e.,* the axones of post-ganglionic neurones end in the

12

muscle. The function of the sympathetic neurones there, however, seems to be that of controlling the blood supply to the muscles.[1]

Relations of Muscles to Bones and Tendons, etc.—The bones of the body, about 200 in number, are the passive organs in reaction. The muscles are the active organs. The bones are more or less rigid structures, well adapted to their function, combining the maximum amount of rigidity with the least amount of weight. All of the long bones are hollow and filled with a substance rich in fat. The bones are united rigidly, as those of the skull, or else in a way to permit movement the one upon the other. The bones united by cartilages are semi-mobile, for example, the bones of the pelvis, ribs and vertebræ. The bones united by articular capsules are semi-mobile, mobile or very mobile, as the elbow, knee, shoulder and hip. In the true articulations the heads of the bones are covered with a large cartilage to which is attached the fibrous articular capsule which connects the two bones. External to the capsule lie the strong protective ligaments. In each capsule there are epithelial cells which secrete the synovia, a transparent viscous mass which lubricates the articular surfaces. Most skeletal muscles have tendons at each end. The tendons end in two contiguous bones. The majority of the muscles thus *cross one joint*. Whenever this condition is met we have a lever. The skeleton is built up of a vast number of such levers. Whenever the organ moved must have speed but needs to overcome but little resistance, the force is supplied to the shorter arm of the lever; whenever, on the contrary, speed is not essential, but great force is required, the power is applied to the longer arm. An example of the first case is a movement of the forearm; of the second case, the raising of the body upon the toes. For all the finer movements of the more mobile parts of the body there are both flexor muscles and extensor muscles. These two are antagonistic. The one will flex or bend the arm, for example, at the

[1] Hunt maintains that the sympathetic fibers also go to the muscle plasm. Kempf and also White have accepted this extremely problematical conclusion, and have tremendously overemphasized the importance of the sympathetic system.

elbow; the other will straighten it out, extend it. Since both
muscles are elastic and always under tension, the mobile organ is
always delicately balanced. A slight impulse to the flexor draws
the arm up smoothly, and a slight impulse to the extensor will
straighten it just as smoothly. It has been shown that whenever a
motor impulse goes to a flexor causing its contraction, there goes
also a neural impulse to the extensor muscle causing it to
lengthen or relax. Likewise, when the extensor is contracted the
flexor is relaxed. The muscles around a joint are thus set in
opposed groups, one group relaxing while the other contracts.

The Nature of Muscular Activity.—In normal reaction the

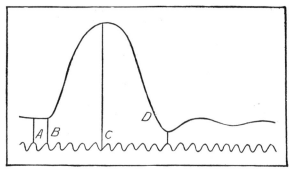

Fig. 48.—Schematic drawing of contraction of frog's gastrocnemius. Time tracing
from tuning-fork giving 100 vibrations per second. *A, B,* latent period; *B, C,* phase of
contraction; *C, D,* phase of relaxation.

muscle is contracted (shortened) by a neural impulse passing to
it over its own motor nerve. The muscle itself, however, is irritable, as is shown by the fact that when separated from its nerve
supply it can be made to contract by a stimulus applied directly
to it. It can be aroused by a blow, by a sudden change in temperature, by chemical stimuli and by electrical stimuli. The electrical stimuli are most convenient to use.[2]

Simple Contraction.—The contraction of a muscle to a single
stimulus shows three phases; a schematic tracing is shown in

---

[2] By irritability is meant that a tissue can be made to exhibit its own
particular form of activity whenever and however it is stimulated; *e.g.,*
the muscle cells contract no matter how stimulated, whereas the gland cells
when stimulated secrete.

Fig. 48. The muscle is stimulated electrically at *a*, it begins to contract at *b*, reaches the apex of contraction at *c*, begins to relax rapidly, then more slowly, becoming normally relaxed at *d*. The time line is indicated below the curve. The interval from *a* to *b* is (1) the latent period. Although stimulated, no movement can be observed. The time of the latent period is very short, possibly not over 0.005 sec. It varies greatly in the different muscles. The condition the muscle is in also causes it to vary, as do temperature, fatigue and the load the muscle has to raise.

The interval *b–c* is (2) the phase of the shortening. The muscle shortens at first slowly, then rapidly, then more slowly. This interval is about 0.04 sec.

The interval *c–d* is (3) the elongation or relaxation phase. Relaxation is rapid at first and then slows down. This interval is about 0.05 sec. A good many factors alter the time of these last two phases. Temperature affects both the shortening and relaxation phases. At 0° C. the muscle loses its irritability; at about 9° C. the contraction phase is high. From there it falls off slightly, then begins to increase again at 18° C., becoming maximal at 30° C. The contractions then die out, heat rigor taking place at 37° C. or above. In no case does the muscle (or other protoplasmic tissue) withstand a temperature higher than 45° C. The duration of contraction is prolonged by low temperatures. As the temperature rises the duration of the contraction as a whole decreases until at 18° C. it becomes constant. Certain drugs greatly affect the simple contraction. The alkaloid veratrin has the following effect: (1) The phase of shortening is not altered, but the phase of relaxation is much prolonged. After the height of the shortening has been reached there is a brief relaxation, followed by a second slower contraction.

We discussed on page 119 the relation of strength of stimulus to response in nerve tissue. We found that in the nerve the "all-or-none law" seemed to hold and we mentioned the fact there that it held in the muscle as well. If a single muscle fiber is contracted it contracts to its full capacity; increase of stimulus merely brings more muscle fibers into operation. As soon as all are stimulated the response of the muscle is maximal. Gradation of muscular activity is thus brought about by the number of fibers at work and not by the intensity of the stimulation.

Effect of Repeated Contraction.—If instead of stimulating the muscle with a single induction shock we give it repeated stimulations all equal in intensity and equally spaced in time, we find that the first contraction (shortening phase) is highest, then there follows a decrease for about four contractions. The muscle decreases slightly in irritability; irritability then increases and the shortening increases again for some time. The effect of activity is thus beneficial to the muscle. After a time under repeated stimulation, the muscle begins again steadily to lose its irritability. The height of contraction becomes less and less. Finally the muscle ceases to shorten. This condition is known as "*fatigue.*"

Tetanic Contraction.—Most muscular responses brought about by the action of motor neurones are unlike the simple twitch we have thus far studied. The impulses come so rapidly that the muscles cannot react to them separately. There is no time for relaxation. The muscle then contracts and stays permanently in that phase as long as the stimulus endures. This is called compound contraction or *tetanus*. It can be produced in the laboratory by sending in separate electrical shocks very rapidly to the muscle. The number of stimuli per second required to produce tetanus varies with the muscle and with the species of animal from which the muscle is taken. Twenty to thirty stimuli are required for mammalian muscles. Of course, all of the conditions mentioned above which tend to slow the relaxation phase tend to produce tetanus with less frequency of stimulus.

Summation of Stimuli.—The most interesting phenomenon to be observed in compound contraction or tetanus is summation. If conditions are so arranged that a second impulse strikes the muscle just at the instant that it is most shortened, it will still further shorten. If three instead of two stimuli are thus properly timed, a still further shortening will occur. It thus becomes possible in a muscle completely tetanized to obtain two to three times the extent of shortening that can be obtained in the simple twitch.

Muscular Contraction in Habit Responses.—In habitual activity, boxing, swimming, tapping, for example, is there a compound contraction, tetanus, or a simple twitch? Most movements of this character are so long continued that they must be of the tetanus type. It has been recently shown that even the most rapid trills that can be made upon a musical instrument are of this type. How do sufficient impulses reach the muscles to produce tetanus? Investigation shows that the motor nerve has its own rhythm of discharge. When a muscle is in tetanic contrac-

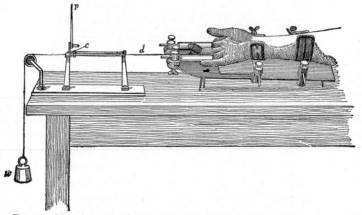

FIG. 49.—Mosso's ergograph: *c*, carriage moving to and fro on runners by means of cord *d*, which passes from the carriage to a holder attached to the last two phalanges of the middle finger (the adjoining fingers are held in place by clamps); *p*, writing point of the carriage, *c*, which makes the record of its movements on the smoked drum; *w*, weight to be lifted. (Howell's Text-Book of Physiology.) W. B. Saunders Co.

tion the separate impulses do not observably change its form, but under such conditions the muscle (1) emits a musical note which has a frequency that within certain limits corresponds to the frequency of the impulses reaching it. The same phenomenon can be detected by the string galvanometer. The number of impulses reaching the striped muscles in habit contraction varies with the muscle—from 47 in the flexor of the arm to 100 in the masseter (jaw). The various motor cells of the central nervous system thus have very different rates of discharge. If the frequency of the impulses reaching the muscles is greater than the above, the muscle cannot keep in step. It, however, maintains its intrinsic rhythm.

Muscular Work.—Fig. 49 shows the ergograph, an instrument by means of which we can study graphically the curve of work of certain muscular organs.

Fig. 50 shows the curve of work of the flexors of the middle finger of the right hand, lifting a load of three kilograms at intervals of two seconds. This curve is usually called a fatigue curve. It will be noticed that the height to which the load is raised is great at first, that it decreases rapidly for a time, then

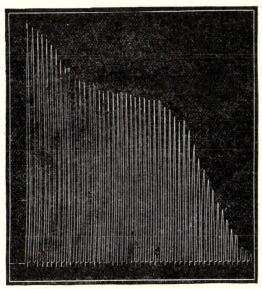

Fig. 50.—Normal fatigue curve of the flexors of the middle finger of right hand. Weight 3 kilograms, contractions at intervals of 2 seconds. (Howell's Text-Book of Physiology.) W. B. Saunders Co.

much more slowly, decreasing very rapidly thereafter until fatigue results. If now the load is lightened the muscle again is capable of doing work. The ergograph thus does not afford a means of completely determining the amount of work a muscle can do. Certain interesting facts have been obtained with the ergograph: (1) If a sufficient rest period is allowed after each contraction, no fatigue occurs; (2) after complete fatigue with a given load, a rest of two hours is required for the muscle's complete recovery; (3) if after complete fatigue abortive contractions are continued for some time, the period of rest must be much longer than two hours. This shows the deleterious effect of attempting to continue much muscular activity in a fatigued condition; (4) loss of sleep, hunger, and anæmia of the muscles lower the amount of work which can be done; (5) improved circulation produced by massage, better foods and sugar solutions increase the muscular work; (6) the total amount of work done is greater with small loads than with large; (7) fatigue of one set of muscles, for example, those in the leg, will decrease the amount of work which can be obtained from another muscle due to the circulation of fatigue products in the blood.

Muscle Tone.—We have several times spoken of muscle tone. This is poorly understood in physiology. That a muscle is never fully relaxed in the normal state appears from the fact that when the muscle is cut the two ends draw away from each other. Tone in both flexors and extensors is generally supposed to be due to a reflex through the central nervous system (without assistance of sympathetic neurones). It is supposed that when the muscle relaxes to a certain point, afferent endings in the muscle are stimulated. These in turn arouse motor impulses in the central nervous system which pass directly to the motor end plates and are distributed to each motor fiber. Certain authors have recently suggested that the sympathetic system contributes the tone: that the answering impulses to the afferent stream from the muscle goes out from the cord over the pre-ganglionic fibers, then to the post-ganglionic (sympathetic) and to the muscle. Sectioning of the white rami is said to destroy muscle tone. The whole matter is still a research problem.

Fatigue Products.—When an individual exercises, CO_2 is given out by the muscle. It is absorbed into the blood stream, carried to the lungs and then given off in the expired air. Twice as much CO_2 is given off on a working day as on a resting day. The further products as a result of activity are lactic acid (derived probably from sugar, the sugar in turn being obtained from the glycogen), and possibly acid potassium phosphate. If extracts are made from the muscles of a fatigued animal and administered to a rested animal, the latter shows signs of fatigue.

Functioning of Reflex Arcs: The "Final Common Path".— We have on page 133 already touched upon reflex action. Now that we have studied all of the elements comprising a reflex arc, it would be well to consider a little more closely some of the phenomena which appear when reflex arcs function. From our survey of the sense organ structures, it becomes clear that there are many more points where afferent impulses can be aroused than there are separate motor outlets. Indeed, a count of axones shows that there are about five afferent neurones to one efferent (cerebro-spinal axis as a whole). Hence we must look upon each motor neurone as the possible outlet for impulses aroused at many different sensory points on the bodily surfaces. It is the sole outlet, the final common path for impulses which are on their way to the muscle in which the given motor neurone ends. Certain consequences result from this relationship. Two sensory impulses aroused at points a and b upon a sensory surface might pass out over a common path to a given muscle, but the impulse aroused at a if acting alone might excite one type of motor response, say, a contraction of the flexors, whereas that aroused at b if acting alone might excite the muscle to act in a wholly different way, for example, produce the contraction of the extensors. Obviously both flexion and extension of the leg do not and cannot occur at the same time. What usually occurs is that either the one or the other reflex appears; or if both flexor and extensor muscles do contract trembling will occur. In observing the behavior of others, we see their separate acts taking place in an orderly way, although we know it is not usual for one stimulus to begin to act at the moment another ceases to act. A host of stimuli act concurrently, but the organism reacts now to one, now to another, depending upon which group of stimuli becomes prepotent. To give the reasons for now the one, now the other group of stimuli becoming prepotent is to give an outline of the whole of physiology and psychology. Although we cannot profitably discuss this question, it is possible for us to examine certain close relations existing among different reflex arcs.

Allied Reflex Arcs.—Certain reflexes combine harmoniously, being mutually reinforcing reactions. This can be shown most easily in the scratch reflex of the dog (Sherrington). If at the moment the scratch reflex is being elicited by stimulation of a skin point on the shoulder, another point 10 cm. distant is stimulated, the result is favorable to the action already in progress. If the two stimuli are each made just subliminal so that the reflex cannot be obtained by stimulating either the one or the other of the skin points, the reflex can be obtained by simultaneously stimulating the two points. The greater the similarity in the type of action each stimulus separately applied would call out, the greater the reinforcement when both stimuli are applied simultaneously. We may look upon the whole skin area (or skin and kinæsthetic area) from which variations of the same reflex can be obtained as the receptive field of the reflex. These receptive fields are quite extended. In the scratch reflex, the different points in the receptive field when touched all produce variations in the scratching reaction. Such reflexes are called type reflexes. There is thus a completely harmonious relationship existing among all of the separate reflexes comprising a given type.

Antagonistic Reflexes.—Many of the reflexes which can be aroused by the use of the same common path are thus allied. But many arcs are antagonistic when functioning. If while the scratch reflex is in progress with the left foot, due to a stimulation of a skin point of the left shoulder, the right foot is stimulated, the scratch movement is halted. Depending upon the time relations of the stimuli, the contact applied to the right foot can interrupt the scratch reflex, cut it short or delay its progress. The stimulus to the right foot does not have to be very intense in order to produce this result. We have here an example of interference between two reflexes. The final common path used by the scratch reflex is used also by the reflex elicitable from the right foot. The latter reflex has as a result extension at the left knee. In other words, stimulation of the right foot arouses the extensors at the left knee and simultaneously inhibits the flexors. The scratch reflex involves a rhythmical use of the flexor neurones. There is thus a definite conflict in use of the flexors. The scratch reflex involves them in action four times per second, whereas the stimulus from the right foot would block action in them altogether.

The Knee Jerk in Man.—Entirely aside from the subject of allied and antagonistic reflexes the fact is worth considering that apparently any form of reflex action taking place under the impulse of a given stimulus may and probably is altered by the presence of another stimulus if the application of the latter is timed with respect to that of the first. This can be illustrated by the reflex knee jerk, which occurs when the tendon is struck. If the extent of the jerk of the leg is being measured, it will be found that blowing upon the eye, or squeezing a dynamometer with the hand at the instant that the blow is struck on the tendon augments the extent of the jerk. If the reinforcing action (or stimulus) precedes the blow on the tendon by too great an interval, the extent of the jerk is decreased: there is inhibition. Inhibition begins to appear when the reinforcing act (squeezing the dynamometer with the hand, for example) precedes the blow on the tendon by .22 sec. to .6 sec.; the maximum inhibiting effect is obtained at from .66 to .9 sec. If the interval is greater, inhibition becomes less noticeable. At 1.7 sec. to 2.5 sec., the reinforcing stimulus has no effect.

Latent Time in Reflex Arcs.—After a reflex arc has conducted an impulse, it shows a resting or unstimulable phase for a short time. Stimuli impinging upon the afferent nerve endings will no longer excite the muscle. This is known as latent reflex time. It seems to be never longer than one second or thereabouts. It is sometimes much shorter; in the knee jerk, 10σ; in the reflex eyelid closure, 45σ.

General Considerations.—This completes our survey of the efferent motor control of the system of skeletal muscles. We have entered somewhat into the details of reflex action in order that we may have before us some of the factors which may later on throw light upon the phenomena we meet with in instinct and in habit. We have gained in the various parts of the text some little insight into such physiological factors as (1) fatigue in cell body and possibly in axones; (2) the nature of simple and tetanic contractions in muscles (latent period, shortening and relaxation phases, and summation of stimuli); (3) the nature of work, fatigue and fatigue products in the muscles, and finally

(4) the nature of simple allied and antagonistic reflex action. If there were space at our disposal, we should find it helpful to consider the compounding of reflexes, coördination of reflexes, and the so-called laws of reflex action. The final explanation of many of these topics in sensory physiology is still in question, but most of the phenomena actually appear in the behavior of organisms, whatever their final explanation in terms of neural action may be. We cannot apply in detail all of the data we have gained from this study. Man's acts from day to day are too complicated. We see him running to catch his train, tossing pennies to his newsboy, speaking fluently, meeting his family, playing, painting, building and running mechanical contrivances. It does help us not a little in observing these acts to have some insight into the factors we have studied, even though we cannot put our finger from moment to moment upon a reinforcement, an inhibition, or action in a partially fatigued group of muscles.

II. The Nature and Function of Smooth Muscle.

The most important area of unstriped muscle is to be found in connection with the alimentary canal and the other visceral

Fig. 51.—Showing smooth muscle cells arranged to form a membrane. (From Piersol's Anatomy.)

organs. The gross divisions of the alimentary canal are the mouth, pharynx, œsophagus, stomach, the small and the large intestine. The unstriped muscular tissue is to be found mainly in the lower portion of the œsophagus and throughout the stomach, the large and the small intestines. These latter structures have (1) an inner lining of epithelial cells supported by a fibrous tunic and a thin layer of smooth muscle, (2) a muscular coat composed of two layers of smooth muscle, one circular and the other longitudinal; this muscular layer propels the contents along the canal, and (3) an outer fibrous coat (several subsidiary coats are

not given). Smooth muscle is found almost exclusively in the
veins and arteries throughout the body, in the bronchi, in the
genital and urinary organs, and to some extent in the skin
(muscles attached to hairs, ducts of sweat glands, for examples).
The structure of the smooth muscle differs markedly from the
striated. It consists of minute spindle-shaped cells (Fig. 51)
with a single nucleus. These cells generally unite to form membranes as in the intestines. Fig. 52 shows
the details of the construction of the
nucleus.

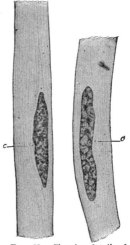

**The Nerve Supply of Smooth Mus-
cles.**—In general the smooth muscles are
under the control of the sympathetic system, that is, of the post-ganglionic
neurones (page 170). They can also, as
will be shown later, be stimulated to action
by secretion from the ductless glands, and
by other chemical agents. They are thus
under two forms of control: under a
nervous control, and a secretion control.
The endings of the post-ganglionic neurone are like those shown in Fig. 46, but
the afferent endings have not been surely
differentiated from the sympathetic. The
endings at times are quite complicated.

Fig. 52.—Showing details of
nucleus of smooth muscle cells.
(From Piersol's Anatomy.)

Attention is called to the fact that several of the efferent neurones of the brain and cord are (apparently) distributed to the
visceral organs controlled by the smooth muscles. It is generally
supposed that these pre-ganglionic neurones of the central system are never distributed directly to smooth muscles fibers or
glands (the adrenal gland being possibly an exception). They
end in the various plexuses around cell bodies of post-ganglionic
neurones (sympathetic ganglia). Emerging from these plexuses
are the post-ganglionic neurones which control the bladder, sex
organs, and the contraction and dilatation of the intestines.

Importance of the Action of Smooth Muscles.—A little observation shows that the vegetative life of the organism is con-

trolled by smooth muscle. Its integrity and smooth working condition all of the functions of the organism as a whole. We have emphasized certain of these factors on page 66.

Contraction in Smooth Muscles.—Speaking broadly, the general phenomena of contraction already discussed in connection with the skeletal muscles appear here. The most important difference is that of sluggishness in the changes. The latent period in smooth muscle is long, sometimes 100 to 500 times longer than in striped muscle. The phases of shortening and relaxation are also prolonged, summation effects appear as well as tetanic contractions. It maintains any tone given to it for a much longer period of time than striped muscle. Intestinal muscles show rapid increase in tone upon little stimulation, particularly when evoked by chemical stimuli, and maintain it against pronounced resistance with slight production of heat. They show, under proper conditions of stimulation, rhythmic activity. This is seen in the hunger contractions, in the ureters, and in the bladder.

III. GLANDS AND THEIR ACTIONS.

In addition to the skeletal muscles and the smooth muscles, there is another group of effectors or expressive organs—the glands. These organs are fundamental to animal existence, since they play the principal rôle in the digestion of food and in the control and the regulation of growth and metabolism (secretion), and in the elimination of certain waste products of the body (excretion). While each cell in the body must abstract from the blood and lymph its own nutrient material and give off its own waste products, still in all complex animal forms certain cells are grouped in the glands which either secrete certain substances for the use of other organs, or else eliminate waste products from the bodily fluid. There are many scattering groups of cells which perform these functions for the body as a whole that are not grouped into glandular structures, but we shall have to neglect any lengthy discussion of them and confine our survey to the most important and largest of the gland structures. We may divide glands into (a) duct-glands, which have a well-

marked opening or outlet through which their products are delivered, and (*b*) ductless-glands, which have no outlets. Their
secretion is absorbed directly into the blood stream and is distributed by it to other bodily tissues.

A. THE DUCT-GLAND (EXTERNAL SECRETION).

The duct-glands were studied earlier than the ductless-glands,
and their action was thought to be better understood. Recent
investigation has thrown a great deal of light upon the action
of these glands and new points of view have been obtained. It is
now generally recognized that their activity is very complex
indeed. There are so many problems connected with the action
of duct-glands that we can survey only certain features which
are at the present moment of most interest to objective psychology. Due largely to the work on animals carried out by Pavlow
and his students in Russia, and to that of Lashley on man in this
country (page 30), it has been found that the action of certain
duct-glands can be profoundly modified by habit influences.

The Salivary Glands.—The principal glands which at present have been found to show this influence (conditioned reflex)
are the glands of the stomach and the three pairs of glands in
the mouth cavity—the parotid, the sublingual and the submaxillary. The latter three pairs of glands are shown in Fig. 53.
They manufacture and secrete jointly the fluid called saliva,
which they pour directly through ducts into the mouth cavity.
The saliva is thus the first digestive fluid with which the food
comes into contact. These glands are made up of several types of
secreting cells (epithelial). Contained in the glands besides the
secreting cells are blood-vessels, connective tissue, smooth muscle
tissue and nerve endings. The nerve supply is complex. The
motor neurones actually ending in the glands are post-ganglionic,
but the pre-ganglionic fibers belong to both autonomic systems
(thoracico-lumbar autonomic and cranio-sacral autonomic).
There are, too, medullated afferent endings present (cerebro-
spinal). The glands are excited usually reflexly (normal
reflex) by food substances coming into contact with the lining of
the mouth. They seem to possess in addition to their function

as digestive organs a certain protective function. Small pieces of rock fail to excite the glands, but if the rock is powdered, copious fluid appears which apparently makes the spitting out of the indigestible substance more feasible. Strongly irritating substances, acids, salts, etc., produce a copious flow of saliva which reduces their irritating action. As has been brought out

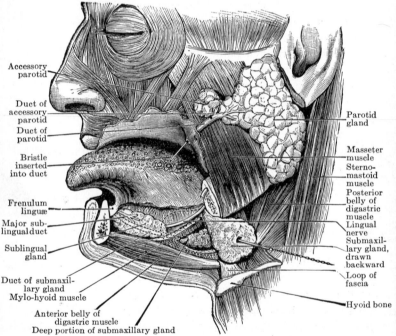

Accessory
parotid

Duct of
accessory
parotid
Duct of
parotid

Bristle
inserted
into duct

Frenulum
linguæ

Major sub-
lingual duct

Sublingual
gland

Duct of submaxil-
lary gland
Mylo-hyoid muscle

Anterior belly of
digastric muscle
Deep portion of submaxillary gland

Parotid
gland

Masseter
muscle
Sterno-
mastoid
muscle
Posterior
belly of
digastric
muscle
Lingual
nerve
Submaxil-
lary gland,
drawn
backward
Loop of
fascia

Hyoid bone

Fig. 53.—Salivary glands. (Morris's Human Anatomy.) P. Blakiston's Son & Co.

on page 32, conditioned reflexes can be aroused through the nose, the eyes, the ears, etc. This proves that definite reflex arcs control the action of the glands. This can be shown even more clearly by cutting the cranial pre-ganglionic fibers (lingual nerve or the chorda tympani) and electrically stimulating the peripheral stump. A copious, thin, watery secretion results after an appreciable latent period and at the same time there occurs an increased flow of blood through the gland. Excitation of the post-ganglionic fibers belonging to the sympathetic (thoracico-lumbar autonomic) also produces secretions of saliva. The amount is relatively small, is thick and turbid and contains many solids. At the same time the glands become pale, thus indicating that vascular constriction has occurred. It can be shown that secretion is not dependent upon the blood-pressure in the glands, since if the blood supply is cut off the glands will still secrete if its nerves are stimulated. In the above illustration, physiologists call the first set of fibers which produces the large supply of thin, watery secretion and the influx of blood secretory nerve fibers, whereas they call the other set which causes the formation of organic constituents of secretion trophic, since it influences the metabolism of the cells.[3]

Glands of the Stomach.—The food after being moistened through the saliva is swallowed and is next acted upon by the glands in the stomach. The mucous membrane of the stomach as a whole contains secreting epithelial cells grouped into small glands distributed throughout the mucous membrane. If the membrane as a whole is examined, minute depressions, just visible to the naked eye, are seen, the so-called gastric pits. These are the openings of the glands. The glands at the pyloric part of the stomach (junction with small intestines) have a different structure from those at the fundic end of the stomach, the details of which need not be entered into. The glands in the fundus have two kinds of secreting cells: the central or peptic cells, and the cells of the border, the parietal cells. The peptic cells are contained only in the glands of the pyloric part of the stomach. The peptic cells of the pyloric and fundic glands furnish apparently two digestive enzymes, pepsin and rennin; the parietal cells secrete hydrochloric acid. Until recently the nerve supply of the stomach glands was in doubt. It is now known that their action is controlled by reflex arcs as in the case of the glands just considered. Special secretory nerves are pres-

---

[3] The saliva as a digestive fluid acts mainly upon the starch. It contains an active enzyme, ptyalin. Ptyalin acts readily upon boiled starch, converting it into sugar and dextrin. In addition to its digestive function, the saliva moistens the food and makes it suitable for swallowing, and the mucin acts as a kind of lubricator.

13

ent. This is shown quite clearly in the phenomena which occur when a gastric fistula is made; at the same time the œsophagus is divided halfway up to the neck, and subsequently made to open out upon the skin surface. When the animal is fed the food drops out again through the now external œsophageal opening. The food thus never reaches the stomach. When an animal thus prepared is made to chew and swallow food (sham feeding) a marked secretion of gastric juice appears some five to six minutes later. This proves very definitely the existence of a reflex arc system. It has been shown further that these glands show conditioned reflexes (habit influence) similar to those exhibited in the case of the salivary glands. The secretory fibers to the stomach belong to the vagus (pre-ganglionic fibers). The experiments described above upon dogs have also been made upon human beings where a surgical operation for disease has made such an arrangement necessary. These conditioned reflexes play an important rôle in the course of digestion.

Pancreas.—After the food leaves the stomach it enters the small intestine. The upper ten inches of the small intestine is known as the duodenum. In the duodenum the contents of the alimentary tract are next subjected to the action of the secretions from the pancreas. The main duct of the pancreatic gland (duct of Wirsung) opens directly into the duodenum together with the common bile duct. The pancreas is a compound tubular gland like the salivary gland. The gland as a whole is long and irregular in shape. It is 12 or 13 cm. long and weighs from 66 to 102 grams. The gland is under definite neural control, the postganglionic fibers coming directly from the cœliac plexus. The origin of the pre-ganglionic fibers is not so clear. Pavlow claims that the mechanical or electrical stimulation of the vagus or splanchnic gives a marked flow of pancreatic juice. As in the case of the other glands studied, conditioned reflexes may be operative in the pancreas, although the evidence is not so sure. Secretion seems to begin the moment food enters the stomach, which must be due to a neural impulse transmitted through the afferent nerves of the cerebro-spinal system and then out through the vagus to the cœliac plexus (sympathetic) and thence over the post-ganglionic neurones to the gland. It is possible that the gland may be stirred to activity also by the action of a hormone, although this is contested. Starling states that the normal method of arousing the pancreatic secretion is not through reflex arcs, but by chemical action; the acid of the gastric juice, upon reaching the duodenum, produces secretin. This in turn is absorbed by the blood, carried to the pancreas and stimulates this organ to activity (hormone action). It is said that the secretion brought about by nervous reflexes and by the action of the secretin are different. The former is thick, opalescent, rich in enzymes and protein, but poor in alkalides; the trypsin is secreted in active form. The secretion is stopped by atropin and started by pilocarpin. The chemical secretion is thin and watery, contains few enzymes, and is rich in alkalides. The trypsin appears in inactive form. The secretion is not affected by atropin. The digestive action of the pancreatic secretion depends upon its three enzymes, trypsin, diastase and lipase. Besides the glandular secretion pouring into the small intestine through the pancreatic duct, other secretions arise in this region from the small tubular glands which exist in the mucous membrane of the intestine itself. This region of the intestine is the place where the most active absorptions of the products of digestion (carbohydrates, fats, proteins) take place.

The Liver.—At the same time that the contents of the alimentary tract are acted upon by the pancreas, they are also acted upon by secretions from the liver. As has been pointed out, the opening of the duct (bile) from the pancreas is common to the liver. This gland is really a gigantic structure, weighing close to 1600 grams. The liver is an organ receiving the very highest respect of the physiologists. It seems to be a laboratory for very complex chemical operations. The preparation of the bile, which is stored in a gall bladder and then injected into the duodenum, is probably only a secondary function. Post-ganglionic neurones end in the liver and probably also afferent fibers belonging to the cerebro-spinal system. The formation of bile is not activated by the mere presence of foodstuffs in the gastrointestinal tube, that is, the presence of food in the stomach does not arouse a neural impulse which excites the liver cells to increased secretion. The alimentary substances must be absorbed into the blood; they are passed by it through the portal vein and thus reach the liver, exciting it to secrete bile. A protein meal at the end of thirty minutes produces a marked increase in bile secretion, which reaches its maximum after four hours. A meal of fat similarly produces the secretion of bile. Carbohydrates produce only a slight secretion. Apparently the liver is also induced to secrete bile by an increased flow of blood. Interruption of the blood stream arrests its secretion.

From our standpoint the most interesting phenomenon connected with the liver is its power to convert the sugars into glycogen and to store it against a time of need. The function of glycogen and its formation is touched upon on page 219.

The Kidney and Skin as Excretory Organs.—The main function of the kidneys is to purge the blood from the products of katabolic processes. Its excretory activity, then, must stand in intimate relation with the composition of the blood. Two theories are held as regards the formation of urine which the kidneys secrete. It is held (1) that the urine is formed by the simple physical process of filtration and diffusion, since certain structures in the kidney (glomeruli) seem to be favorable organs for such a process. The theory holds that the water is filtered through them from the blood, carrying with it both the inorganic salts and the specific elements (urea, etc.) of the secretion. (2) The other view holds that the water and inorganic salts are produced by filtration in the glomeruli, but that the urea and related bodies are eliminated through the activity of certain epithelial cells found in the convoluted tubes of the kidneys. Physiologists are somewhat divided in their adherence to these views, although the majority seem to side with the second. The kidneys receive a rich supply of nerve fibers, but their reflex function and connections are not well understood. There is some evidence that the secretion of urine is controlled through chemical stimuli (hormones).

The urine, which is very complex in its structure, is secreted continuously and carried to the bladder through the ureters, and

is ejected from time to time from the bladder through the urethra
by the act of micturition.

The excretory glands of the skin are the sweat glands and sebaceous glands; the former are particularly abundant in the palms
of the hand and the soles of the feet (Fig. 6). There are probably
two millions in the whole cutaneous surface. The secretory cells
lie in the deep tissues of the skin. The duct is composed of
smooth muscle cells. It opens upon the surface of the skin in
pores. The average quantity of sweat eliminated in twenty-four
hours may amount to two or three liters. The existence of secretory fibers running to the sweat glands has been definitely shown
(post-ganglionic neurones).

The sebaceous glands are found on cutaneous surfaces associated with the hair. They secrete an oily semi-liquid material. It
is supposed that this secretion serves to protect the hairs from
becoming too brittle and too easily permeated with moisture.
The oiling of the skin which occurs by their action prevents
an undue loss of heat from evaporation of the sweat. Similar
glands are present in the sex organs.

B. DUCTLESS GLANDS (INTERNAL SECRETION).

Within recent years the ductless glands have become increasingly a subject of physiological experimentation. Many of the
results which have been obtained throw light upon problems in
behavior. The closest contact between this field and objective
psychology is in the realm of emotional behavior.

The study of emotions has always been backward in psychology, mainly because the psychologist could not get any way of
envisaging them. Observation shows that the human organism
does not always act in the same dead level way that he would
presumably act if only the organized reflex pathways belonging to the central nervous system were functioning. Man goes
about his daily duties with a varying amount of what, in a slangy
way, has been called "pep," and what has speculatively been
called "drive" by scientific men. "Drive" is not a satisfactory
word, because it seems to add something to the organism which
comes in from the outside, whereas the term "pep" belongs peculiarly to the organism. The term "libido" has been used by

the Freudians in a somewhat similar way, but always with definite sex implications. This term likewise for psychological use
is not very satisfactory, however well it may work in psychopathology. The main facts which can be obtained by observation
seem to center around the following: (1) The human being seems
at times to work at a higher level of energy than at other times
(page 218) ; (2) at times the individual works with a persistency
far beyond that ordinarily displayed; (3) the individual seems
totally unable to accomplish his daily duties, execute his stable
habits; we speak of him as being excited, flighty, or else depressed.
These are not meant as characterizations of the various emotional types or states. Attention is called to them merely to
show that the organic tone changes from time to time, and that
the individual displays an increase or decrease in emotional tone.
It is thought that a study of the endocrine glands may help us
to understand these factors. The following chapter takes up
emotional response in detail.

The Endocrine or Ductless Glands.—The endocrine glands
differ from the duct glands which we have just considered in
that they have no external outlet. The material which they
manufacture is absorbed into the blood stream and carried to
other organs. The active materials secreted by ductless glands
have been termed hormones, which means etymologically "I stir
up." A good many of the hormones, though, inhibit action, so
that certain authors prefer a different terminology. The term
hormone as first used (by Starling) really meant any substance
produced by cells in one part of the body and carried by the
blood stream to more distant parts. According to this usage,
there are a great many hormones not secreted by ductless glands,
such as water, urea, glucose and inorganic salts. It seems better
then to drop the term hormone and adopt the new term used by
Schafer, autacoid substance, or simply autacoid. An autacoid
is a specific organic substance formed by the cells of one organ
and passed from it into the circulatory fluid to produce effect
upon other organs *similar to those produced by drugs* (the internal secretions of the endocrine glands apparently act like
drugs). Further there are excitatory autacoids and those which

restrain or produce inhibition, inhibitory autacoids. The former would come under the definition of a hormone, and the latter Schafer designates by a new word, chalone. The nature of autacoidal action is not well understood. We know that the active material is not injured by prolonged boiling. In general the autacoids have not been isolated. One, however, has been isolated and appears in crystalline form, adrenin. Two or three others may possibly have been isolated, for example, thyroxin. We know that they have an effect upon the sympathetic nerve centers, a direct effect upon smooth muscle and upon the secretion of other glands.

The Chief Endocrine Glands.—We may divide the endocrine glands into five principal divisions: (1) The thyroid apparatus, which consists of the two thyroids and the four small parathyroids, two on each side. (2) The suprarenal apparatus; and (3) the pituitary apparatus. (4) The thymus and pineal glands. (5) The sex gland. There are several other glands which unquestionably secrete autocoid substances, as the pancreas and the alimentary mucous membrane.

The Thyroid Glands.—Fig. 54 gives one view of the thyroid apparatus. It consists of the two lobes of the thyroid situated on either side of the larynx and windpipe, and of the connecting lobe (not shown), and of a superior and inferior parathyroid on each side. The superior parathyroid is in close contact with the thyroid and sometimes imbedded in it. The inferior parathyroid may lie in contact (ventral aspect) or be removed to a greater or less distance. Occasionally accessory thyroids, quite small in number, may occur. The thyroid is an organ made up of small closed vesicles; each vesicle is lined with epithelial cells. The vesicles are generally filled with a viscid fluid "colloid." There are very numerous blood-vessels, the thyroids being among the most vascular organs of the body. The gland is innervated by the sympathetic (thoracico-lumbar) and by the vagus (pre-ganglionic). The nerves are distributed both to the blood-vessels and directly to the secreting cells (epithelium). The colloid is insoluble in alcohol, water or ether. It doubtless contains the active principle and probably serves as a storehouse from which the organism from time to time draws out a needed supply. The colloid of the human thyroid appears always to contain iodine.

The parathyroids are very small, about 6 mm. in length, 3 to 4 mm. broad. Each parathyroid is a mass of epithelium-like cells. These are arranged in strands with numerous capillaries

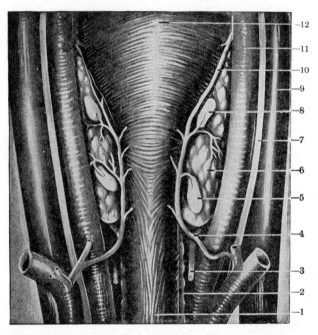

Fig. 54.—1, Œsophagus; 2, trachea; 3, inferior laryngeal nerve; 4, inferior thyroid artery; 5, inferior parathyroid; 6, thyroid (lateral lobe); 7, vagus nerve; 8, superior parathyroid; 12, pharynx. (Morris's Human Anatomy.) P. Blakiston's Son & Co.

running between or around them. These glands contain some plain muscle fibers. Small vesicles are also present containing colloid material. The innervation is the same as the thyroid, the nerves ending both on the cells and on the blood-vessels.

Effect of Removal of the Parathyroids.—If the four small parathyroids are removed, the animal usually dies within a few days or at most in a few weeks. For the first day or two, the only symptom is loss of appetite. The reflexes then become exalted, and later cramp-like contractions occur and eventually convulsive fits. The body temperature may rise two or three degrees during the fit. The paroxysms are accompanied by rapid gasping respiration, sometimes by vomiting and diarrhœa. The picture as a whole is sometimes called tetany (tetania parathyreopriva, not to be confused with normal tetanic contraction, page 181). It is assumed that the parathyroids yield an autacoid of a restraining type which tends to prevent overexertion or discharge of nerve cells. Besides these apparent neural effects, there is a widespread effect on metabolism which can be noted in the few cases where the animal survives the operation for some length of time. In the young animal the calcification of the teeth is delayed, the skeletal bones remain smaller than in the controls. There is thus some reason for believing that the parathyroids furnish a second autacoid which is able to influence calcium metabolism.

It has been found that the bad effects of removal of the parathyroid can be partly relieved by the injection of the extract of parathyroid. Extract of pituitary is also said to keep the organism alive. But so far a satisfactory way of keeping the animal alive for any considerable length of time has not been found. We shall see that the reverse is true when the thyroid is removed and the parathyroids are left intact.

Removal of the Thyroid.—In removing the thyroid, at least two of the parathyroids must be left intact. The results of the removal of the thyroid, or of spontaneous atrophy of that organ, are most clearly marked in young animals. The following symptoms appear: The growth of the body as a whole, and especially of the skeleton, is arrested; the development of the generative organs is delayed; the integument is swollen, the skin remains dry and the hair thin; in the young human the face is pale and puffy and the abdomen is swollen; the fontanelles remain open; deaf-mutism is common; there is an arrest of the development of the cells in the cerebral cortex: This is the typical picture of cretinism. In the thyroid atrophy of the adult human (myxœdema) a similar picture is presented. There is thickening and swelling of the integument, drying of the skin, falling out of the hair, low body temperature and a general impairment of sensibility; the level of behavior is low; metabolism is diminished; there is a considerable deposition of fat with a diminution of sex function, and an increased tolerance for sugar. Myxœdema may be produced when goitrous tumors (the tumor destroying the secreting cells) are removed. This is called post-operative myxœdema (cachexia strumipriva). This may show itself in a few days or months or even years after the operation. Unless the parathyroids are removed with the thyroid, symptoms of tetany do not appear.

It is interesting to note that the above symptoms, whether due to atrophy or to surgical removal of the gland, may be made to disappear or be allayed by the administration of thyroid substance, either hypodermically or by the mouth. Persons can be completely restored to health and kept normal by eating the thyroid substance. If the treatment is omitted the symptoms again appear. The effects are therefore due to the absence of an autacoid that actively influences metabolism.

Effect of Excess of Thyroid Secretion.—The effect of a too great amount of the thyroid autacoid can be tested by administering thyroid extract by injection or by the mouth. The immediate results of intravenous injection are slight. When given by the mouth, there is a lowering of blood-pressure, rapid pulse, with some irregularity, nervous excitability, flushing of the skin, increased perspiration and increase of nitrogen metabolism. If the feeding is long continued, the body fat is diminished and glycosuria may appear. In extreme cases there may be dilatation of the pupil, great excitement, sleepiness, and tremors of the limbs. In short, we have the symptoms which appear in exophthalmic goitre, where there is an enlarged gland (with no destruction of tissue) with a great oversecretion of the thyroid autacoid.

Exophthalmic goitre is more common in women than in men, a fact which may be related to the enlargement of the gland when the female reaches puberty and during pregnancy.

Chemical Isolation of the Thyroid Hormone.—Investigators for many years have been interested in the hormone or active principle produced by the thyroid gland. Many efforts have been made to isolate this hormone. As early as 1895 Baumann showed that the thyroid was rich in iodine. Until his work no one had thought that such an element as iodine existed in the body. This work was immediately fastened upon as showing that the active principle of the gland was iodine and that food containing iodine had to be supplied to the body. Investigators following Baumann isolated various iodine compounds from the gland. These have been given various names and their discoverers have claimed that they are just as efficacious in myxedema as is the feeding of the whole gland. The matter was not settled until E. C. Kendall, working in the Mayo Foundation in Rochester, succeeded in isolating the active principle in the gland in its pure form. Nearly nine years of continuous research were spent in making this isolation. He calls it " thyroxin." It contains no less than 60 per cent. of iodine. Thyroxin is now extensively used in the treatment of thyroid deficiency. Kendall claims never to have found a case of thyroid deficiency that has not responded to an intravenous injection of thyroxin. The response to thyroxin is apparently a quantitative one. One-third of 1 m.g. of this substance increases the metabolic rate of a one-hundred-and-fifty pound individual 1 per cent. If the basal metabolic rate of an individual of this weight is 30 per cent. below normal (hypoactive thyroid) the administration of 10 m.g. will raise the rate to normal. By the administration of greater amounts of this substance the basal metabolic rate may be raised to a figure just as high as is compatible with life. As the metabolic rate is raised, the fundamental changes noted in the text occur, such as pulse rate increase, pulse pressure increase, utilization of body sugar. Fats and proteins will be used up in greater amounts than normal. The carbon dioxide output will be increased, as will the oxygen consumption, and there will be an increase in nitrogen elimination. Administration of " thyroxin " will relieve subnormal activity of tissues; i.e., myxœdema will disappear. If by the administration of " thyroxin " the metabolic rate is carried high enough, a condition like that found in hyperthyroidism will result.

The Adrenal Apparatus.—The secretions from the suprarenal capsules or adrenals have a profound effect upon many of the tissues of the body. Attention was early directed to the adrenals because of their connection with Addison's disease.

The adrenals, which are closely attached to the kidneys, consist of two parts: (1) cortex, and (2) medulla which in man are anatomically joined, but which in some animals are completely separated (fish).

The (1) cortex of the adrenal is composed of epithelium-like cells arranged in columns. There are a number of lipoid granules, yellowish in color. The (2) adrenal medulla is composed of cells which have a different form and structure from those of the cortex. It is described as a solid cell mass permeated by capillaries and venous spaces somewhat similar to liver tissue. The cell protoplasm contains a number of granules and imparts a yellowish-brown color to the medulla when the adrenals are fixed in any solution containing chromic acid salts. Oftentimes there are a number of accessory glands which have a similar structure to the medulla (paraganglia or chromaffine).

The suprarenals are richly supplied with nerves and blood-vessels. The blood supply to these glands is greater than that of any other organ in the body (except the pituitary body). The nerve supply is also rich. No less than thirty-three small bundles approach it (post-ganglionic neurones from the cœliac, phrenic and renal plexuses and from the splanchnic). The nerves enter the adrenal cortex supplying both the blood-vessels and its secreting cells, but the great majority pass into the adrenal medulla.

Little is known regarding the functions of the cortex. It may partly prepare the material with which the medulla works. Some authors suggest that there is a close connection between the development of the sex organs and the adrenal cortex.

Function of the Adrenal Medulla.—In animals death follows the removal of both glands. There is little disturbance noted at first, but at the end of a few days the animal becomes lively and begins to manifest signs of muscular weakness and incoördination. The body temperature becomes lowered, weakness becomes extreme, pulse feeble and blood-pressure low. Since death always follows the removal of the adrenals, experimental surgery even in pathological cases is not resorted to in the human being. Addison's disease, however, seems to be due to a degeneration of the adrenal gland (usually tubercular). This disease is characterized by languor, general debility, weakness and loss of tone of the skeletal, vascular and visceral musculature. The heart action is feeble; there is a loss of appetite and a disturbance of the digestive tract with extreme emaciation. The bronzing of the skin is the most striking characteristic of Addison's disease. The disease is nearly always fatal, but the life of a patient suffering from it may be prolonged for some years.

So far it has been found to be impossible to secure beneficial results in Addison's disease, or in the case of animals whose adrenals have been removed, by the administration of suprarenal extract. Nothing seems to take the place of the internal secretion of the gland. Nor has it been found possible to get an implanted adrenal to grow.

Effect of Administering Suprarenal Extract.—The most striking effect is the marked rise in blood-pressure which is caused by the contraction of the peripheral arteries. The heart's action is also slowed. Adrenin seems to have a direct effect upon the sympathetic nerve endings in the unstriped muscular tissue, causing especially tonic contraction in the case of peripheral veins, and rhythmic contractions of the superior vena cava near the heart. Other unstriped muscular tissue, supplied by sympathetic fibers, is also affected: The spleen, the vagina, the uterus, vas deferens and the retractor penis are contracted, whereas there is inhibition in the intestines, the stomach, the œsophagus and the gall-bladder. A heavier flow of saliva results. The skeletal muscle has an increased excitability. The autacoid has been found to be able to defer the onset of fatigue in muscle and to assist in its recovery (page 243). It is thus seen that in this autacoid we have a direct influence upon the unstriped muscular tissue which is supplemental to, and possibly regulatory of, the nervous (autonomic sympathetic) control. The muscles which the sympathetic contracts, adrenin contracts; those it inhibits, adrenin inhibits. The autacoid from the posterior pituitary contracts (stimulates) the smooth muscles directly without regard to what action the sympathetic may have.

Relation of the Adrenal Apparatus to the Other Glands.— There is a close relationship between the sex glands and the adrenal. During pregnancy the whole gland undergoes enlargement, especially the cortical portion. The secretion of bile is increased by the adrenin. Furthermore, the autacoid of the medulla rapidly converts the liver glycogen into sugar which passes into the blood (page 241).[4] Removal of the suprarenals affects the pancreas, producing a flow of pancreatic juice. If adrenin is injected this flow is stopped.

The Pituitary Apparatus.

It is only within recent years that the pituitary body (hypophysis cerebri) has been satisfactorily investigated. It is a small organ, weighing less than half a gram. It lies at the base of the brain just posterior to the optic chiasma. It is connected with the floor of the third ventricle by a hollow stalk, the infundibulum. The whole structure is shown on the ventral surface of the brain (page 143). It is divided into an anterior portion and a posterior portion. The anterior part is richly supplied with blood-vessels. It is even more vascular than the adrenal. The two lobes have a different embryological history. The large anterior lobe is formed by invagination of the buccal ectoderm. It is a truly glandular structure. A part of the posterior lobe has the same origin (pars intermedia). The other part of the posterior lobe (pars nervosa) is really an outgrowth from the floor of the third ventricle of the brain.

Function of the Pituitary Body.—When extracts from the posterior lobe are injected into the circulation, the heart rate is slowed and the blood-pressure raised, but the effects are less

---

[4] It is thought that glycogen forms a temporary reserve supply of carbohydrate material which the body requires in large amounts. It is supposed that during digestion the carbohydrate food is absorbed into the blood (portal system) as dextrose and galactose. If these passed directly through the liver unchanged, there would be an excess of sugar secreted by the kidneys, but it is assumed that as this blood rich in sugars passes through the liver, the excess of sugar is extracted by the liver cells. It is dehydrated and exists there in the form of glycogen. Under the action of the nerves or of adrenin, the glycogen is reconverted into dextrose and is then carried by the blood to whatever point it may be needed. This conversion of the stored glycogen into sugar is known as glycogenolysis. We have therefore in the liver a large supply of food which can be easily converted and quickly utilized. The way it may be utilized in emotional stress where great muscular activity is called for will be described later.

marked than in the case of adrenin. These extracts seem to exercise a stimulating effect upon the involuntary muscles of the body; the intestine, bladder and uterus are all made to contract directly. It was pointed out on page 205 that adrenin may give either contraction or relaxation, depending upon the action the sympathetic autonomic has upon these fibers. The posterior lobe extract produces contraction in all cases. This excites other glands, the kidneys, mammary glands, and apparently accelerates the process of sugar conversion in the liver.

The anterior lobe extract produces no noticeable effect when first administered.

Removal of the whole pituitary body produces death in a few days. There is a fall in temperature, an unsteady gait, rapid emaciation and diarrhœa. Apparently this will happen when the anterior lobe alone is removed. Removal of the posterior lobe alone is not necessarily fatal. The animal shows greater tolerance for sugar; fat is increased. When the operation is made on young animals, there is an arrested development of the sex glands. Clinical observation shows that when the gland is overactive the chief effect noticeable is gigantism. The growth of the skeleton is much greater. If the condition occurs in adults, there is a very great enlargement of the bones of the face and extremities (acromegaly). When there is a diminished secretion due to pathological conditions there is obesity and sexual infantilism. Gigantism is supposed to be due to an overactive anterior lobe; obesity and sexual infantilism to the lack of secretion of the posterior lobe. The anterior lobe would thus seem to furnish an autacoid which stimulates skeletal growth and the connective tissues, and in addition exercises a wide influence upon metabolism in general. The posterior lobe furnishes one or several autacoids which stimulate the plain muscle; excite the secretory activity of other glands; hasten the conversion of glycogen into sugar, and produce a regulatory action of the reproductive organs.

The Pineal and Thymus Glands.— The pineal gland is one of the brain structures. It is found on the posterior aspect of the brain stem just anterior to the corpora quadrigemina (Fig. 32, 14). It is a glandular structure in man possibly functional throughout life. It seems to exert its main function however early in the life of the individual. In children, if the functions of this gland are disturbed, there is a rapid development of the reproductive organs, precocity and an increased growth of skeleton. It is thus supposed that the gland furnishes an inhibitory autacoid. The thymus, situated in the neck near the thyroid is another gland which apparently is of chief importance in childhood. Although it, like the pineal, may possibly function throughout life, it increases in weight and size up to the end of puberty and then gradually gets smaller. The function of the thymus is in dispute. Dr. Walter Timme links the pineal and the thymus into a related system which dominates the life cycle from birth to puberty.[5]

The Sex Gland as an Endocrine Organ.—The organs of reproduction—the sexual glands—furnish both an external secretion contributing to the reproduction of the species, and an internal secretion. The cells producing the two secretions are to be found together but they are entirely distinct in their functions. The external secretion is produced by the true sex cells or gonads. The internal secretion is produced by the so-called interstitial cells (sometimes called " puberty gland ").

The hormone from the interstitial cells exerts a marked influence upon bodily development. This is shown by the growth changes that take place when the sex glands are completely excised in the male before puberty. The youth grows to be quite tall; the larynx fails to develop; hence the childish soprano voice never changes; the skin is poorly pigmented; layers of fat accumulate; the breasts increase in size. Such individuals are beardless. They apparently approach the " neutral " in type. These changes are due apparently solely to the lack of the hormone coming from the puberty gland.

On the behavior side there is in the eunuch a lack of sex

---

[5] Before taking up the study of the sex glands, it is well to point out that it is now well established that the pancreas furnishes an internal secretion which inhibits glycogenolysis. This may, through conditioning, play an important rôle in emotional reactions (account for exhaustion after certain emotional responses).

aggressiveness and of all other forms of positive sex behavior. Our information, however, upon the general behavior changes necessarily resulting from castration is almost nil. Such individuals have always been set aside by society for certain inferior duties—keepers of the harem, male sopranos and the like. They are told by word of mouth and by what they read that there is something lacking in their make-up—that they are inferior. Of course, the lack of habits based upon sex activity even in the absence of social stigmatization marks them off from the general run of men.

So far these individuals have apparently escaped the hands of the mental testers. Hence we know little about their I.Q. The fact that many eunuchs have attained distinction along intellectual lines would seem to indicate that progress in ordinary academic subjects may take place at the normal rate.

The results of castration upon the female are not so well known. There are few cases where the ovaries have been removed before puberty. Animal experiments seem to establish the fact that the hormone from the ovaries exerts a tendency upon the part of the female to revert to the male type. For example: if the ovaries are removed from the duck and the pheasant, male plumage is assumed.

In the adult (both male and female) the hormone from the puberty gland seems to be mainly responsible both for sexual vigor and sex aggressiveness, and for the youthfulness and activitation of all the other glandular systems of the body. At any rate, there is a growing tendency on the part of investigators (possibly in the absence of critical proof) to believe that man is as old as his glands. And since the remaining glands apparently cannot stay youthful in the absence of a sufficient output from the puberty glands, it is only natural to connect senescence or old age with a decline in the output from this gland.

Methods of Increasing the Hormone Supply from the Puberty Gland.—For years the dream of man has been to find eternal youth. Brown-Sequard (1889) thought he had found

14

it through the effects to be had from the injection of extracts obtained from the gonadal system of the ram. These extracts he claimed restored his youth and vigor. Other investigators could not confirm his finding and this great physiologists fell into disrepute.

During the past three years new light has been thrown upon this problem. Steinach has shown that it is possible, even after the onset of old age, to increase the output of the puberty gland. Lygation of the *ductus deferens* combined with vasectomy cause the sperm cells (reproductive) that produce the external secretion, to atrophy and finally to disappear. The interstitial cells (puberty gland), however, not only *do not atrophy subsequent to the operation but may actually increase in number and in size.* An increased output of the sex hormone takes place which reactivates the entire endocrine system of the patient, causing clinical results, varying from nothing more than an " endocrine tonic " to an almost actual " rejuvenation."

The effects of the operation may not fully appear under six months. The length of time improvement may continue has not yet been determined due to the recency of all such operations.

This operation is performed when there are indications of a lack of active functioning of the gonadal system—as is the case both in senility and in premature senility. It should be noted that while individuals undergoing this operation lack the external sperm secretion, the sex reflexes are otherwise quite normal (tumescence, orgasm, etc.).

The Method of Testicular Grafting.—An entirely different method of supplying the body with the gonadal hormone has been devised by Dr. Serge Voronoff of Paris. He transplants in the senescent animal the whole or a part of the testicle from a young and vigorous animal of the same species. This testicular graft can be transplanted under the skin or in the peritoneum—theoretically into any part of the body.

With suitable technique the graft " takes." Quite often, however, the graft is expelled or is reabsorbed. When the graft lives and begins to function, the interstitial cells (puberty gland) begin to supply the blood stream with their characteristic hormone. (It should be noted that in such grafts the sperms cells soon disappear.)

The following experiment of Voronoff on an animal, quoted from Harrow (*Glands in Health and Disease*, p. 109) is most enlightening:

" In another experiment a ram 12 to 14 years old—corresponding to about 80 years in man—which could hardly totter, had implanted the fragments of a testicle obtained from a young man. Two months after the graft had been effected the animal was completely transformed. His urinal incontinence had disappeared; so had tremblings of the legs; and he no longer looked afraid. His bodily carriage had become magnificent, he behaved in a lively and aggressive manner. The old ram had taken on the appearance of remarkable youth and vigor. He was isolated in a small stable, together with a young ewe-lamb, which afforded the opportunity for observing not only the awakening of his sexual instincts, which he had lost years ago, but also the following more tangible result: the ewe-lamb covered by him in September, 1918, dropped a vigorous lamb in February, 1919. There is nothing in the fact to cause surprise. Old animals, like very aged men, occasionally still possess spermatozoids which are altogether alive, but it is the atrophy of the internal secretive glands which prevents their experiencing the sexual appetite and manifesting their virility."

" Doctor Voronoff's next procedure with the rejuvenated animal was excellent from the scientific standpoint. He removed the graft. Three months later the animal had completely aged. Then he reimplanted another graft from the testical of a younger animal. Once again the animal showed signs of rejuvenation. Nothing in the whole book approaches in value this particular experiment."

Similar experiments upon man have been tried by Voronoff and others. Apparently in some cases the graft takes with beneficial results. A search of the literature, however, fails to reveal very many cases where the results of such operations have been critically tested.

Even granting the successful nature of the operation, suitable human material for grafting will always be hard to obtain.

This has led to experiments on the transplantation of testicular grafts obtained from the higher apes. Investigators are still skeptical of the success of this work. Thorek (*Endocrinology*, November, 1922, p. 771) claims to have devised a surgical method which gives perfectly satisfactory results in transplanting the testes of higher apes to man.

There seems to be some doubt about the possibility of lengthening life by such experiments but there is reason to believe that ultimately man will be able to lengthen the span of sex activity.

Some of the Important Social Consequences of Rejuvenation:
1. It will decrease the amount of invalidism. Invalidism is often resorted to after sex competition has been given up as hopeless or through actual failure of sex functioning. Competition in sex, business and in science will be prolonged. The 50-70 year age-span will be useful and happy.

2. The tremendous pressure to accumulate wealth between the years of 20–60 may be somewhat relieved. Old men retaining their energies will hold their positions for a much longer period of time. They should be far more valuable to society than younger men because of their richer experience.

3. If this psychological pressure of the fear of impotence at fifty is relieved, such experiments may bring a more leisurely journey through the 20–30 year period giving time for culture and for laying more enduring foundations for scientific, business and artistic careers.

4. The most interesting phase of the prolongation of youth will take place in the domain of marriage. Economic pressure now postpones marriage and enables the older man to compete with younger men. Only the fear of possible impotence with the onset of age keeps this competition in check. The older man has considerable in his favor—experience, social position, wealth, poise. Even in the absence of rejuvenation, older men to-day are younger than they were a few decades ago. With the spread of knowledge about rejuvenation the marriageable age limit for men will be still further advanced.

5. Coincident with these important changes in sex habits will come new legislation, and considerable changes in the present laws concerning the sex control of individuals.

Concluding Statements on the Glands and Muscles.—In the present chapter, as in the preceding one, we have been dealing with parts of the organism and their functioning. It remains to call attention to the fact that only rarely do the various parts function in an isolated way. Any stimulation strong enough to reach the motor side of the central nervous system brings about not only narrow reflex and associated activities (segmental reactions) but widespread changes in the organism as a whole. Even so simple an activity as putting on our clothes and lacing up our shoes in the morning involves a most complex series of adjustments of a motor and glandular kind such as the proper relations of action between extension and flexion, changes in autonomic activity such as are seen in the regulation of the pupil and in respiration and circulation. Our study of the glands has taught us that muscular activity cannot go on for any length of time without involving changes in those organs; sweat begins to form, sugar is released to serve as food for the muscles, adrenin is contributed to the blood stream, which not only neutralizes fatigue products but also acts upon the autonomic system in such a way as to increase the flow of blood to the muscular organs in operation. The thyroid glands secrete and affect not only other glands, either increasing their output or checking it, but also possibly all of the cells of the body as well. The eating of the simplest meal starts another widespread series of changes in the body as a whole, beginning the moment food enters the mouth and continuing until the products of digestion are absorbed and stored for future use and the waste products eliminated.

The material we have gathered in the last three chapters should emphasize the difference between physiology and psychology. The science of physiology deals with part reactions whereas psychology deals with the adjustments of the organism as a whole. We have entered into these psysiological studies in order to get a better grasp upon what is meant by *whole organism*. Our remaining studies will deal with activities which require the coöperation of the body as a whole.

13

CHAPTER VI

UNLEARNED BEHAVIOR: " EMOTIONS "

Introduction.—In the last three chapters we have been concerned with the details of sensory-motor adjustment. We turn next to man as a reacting organism, and specifically to some of the reactions which belong to his hereditary equipment. Human action as a whole can be divided into *hereditary* modes of response (emotional and instinctive), and *acquired* modes of response (habit). Each of these two broad divisions is capable of many subdivisions. It is obvious both from the standpoint of common-sense and of laboratory experimentation that the hereditary and acquired forms of activity begin to overlap early in life. Emotional reactions become wholly separated from the stimuli that originally called them out (transfer, page 234), and the instinctive positive reaction tendencies displayed by the child soon become overlaid with the organized habits of the adult. This process of masking or dovetailing of activities is a part of the general process of organization. The separation between hereditary reaction modes and acquired reaction modes can thus never be made absolute. Fortunately in most connections psychology is not called upon to draw a sharp distinction between hereditary and acquired reactions. In making laboratory studies, however, it is sometimes necessary for us to study the details of hereditary response. We find it simpler in such cases to overemphasize for the time the definiteness of the separation. This is unquestionably a legitimate mode of procedure in science. Few biological problems permit of any other treatment. In order to accomplish this at all we have to adopt a genetic method. We have to start with the baby's advent (we would start before if it were not for possible injury to mother and child) and follow his development step by step, noting the first appearance of the hereditary forms of reaction, their course and effect upon the moulding of the child's whole personality; and the early beginnings of acquired modes of response. Undoubtedly learning

214

begins *in utero* (there is no reason to suppose that conditioned reflexes do not begin there), and probably several hereditary modes of action (particular types of reflexes) run their entire course *in utero*. But we are entering here upon a field which just at present is purely speculative.

What Is an Emotion?—Hard and fast definitions are not possible in the psychology of emotion, but formulations are possible and sometimes help us to group our facts. A formulation which will fit a part of the emotional group of reactions may be stated as follows: *An emotion is an hereditary "pattern-reaction" involving profound changes of the bodily mechanism as a whole, but particularly of the visceral and glandular systems.*[1] By pattern-reaction we mean that the separate details of response appear with some constancy, with some regularity and in approximately the same sequential order each time the exciting stimulus is presented. It is obvious that if this formulation is to fit the facts, the general condition of the organism must be such that the stimulus can produce its effect. A child alone in a house on a stormy night with only a dim candle burning may display the reaction of fear at the mournful hoot of an owl. If the parents are at hand and the room is well lighted, the stimulus may pass unreacted to. Stimulus then in this sense is used in a broad way to refer not only to the exciting object but also to the general setting (page 10). There is implied also the fact that the general state of the organism must be sensitive (capable of being stimulated) to this form of stimulus at the moment. This condition is very important. A young man may be extremely sensitive to the blandishments of every female he meets while in the unmarried state and may show considerable excitement and

---

[1] Throughout the chapter we have introduced physiological concepts into the behavior study of emotions. It is possible that we have given the impression that we are writing a physiology of the emotions. Such is not the case. It is perfectly possible for a student of behavior entirely ignorant of the sympathetic nervous system and of the glands and smooth muscles, or even of the central nervous system as a whole, to write a thoroughly comprehensive and accurate study of the emotions—the types, their interrelations with habits, their rôle, etc. We have tried to connect emotional activity with physiological processes because it seems that such formulations are now practical and no longer purely speculative.

over-reaction on such occasions. In most cases, he becomes considerably less sensitive after being happily married. This formulation may seem somewhat roundabout—somewhat like saying that a stimulus is an emotional stimulus only when you get the pattern-reaction, but this is very nearly the case. Possibly we can illustrate most easily what we mean by choosing an example from animal life. When the naturalist comes suddenly upon a young sooty tern under four days of age, it lies stock still (it is capable of very rapid locomotion): It can be pushed about or rolled over without explicit forms of response appearing. The moment the intruder moves away, the fledgling may hop to its feet and dash away or give one of its instinctive cries. The pattern-reaction, that is, the explicit observable pattern, is very simple indeed—a death feint or posture. Such a type of response is quite common in the animal world. In order to bring about such a tremendous variation in behavior in an animal usually so active there must be a profound modification of the organic processes. We shall see later that the locus of the effect (the implicit side, page 198) is principally in the visceral system. Often, however, the skeletal musculature is involved in the pattern. A serviceable way to mark off an *emotional* reaction from an *instinctive* reaction is to include in the formulation of emotion a factor which may be stated as follows: The shock of an emotional stimulus throws the organism for the *moment at least* into a chaotic state.[2] When in the first shock of an emotional state, the subject makes few adjustments to objects in his environment. In contrast to this stand the instincts as we shall see farther on. The subject in an instinctive act usually does something: he

---

[2] It is most interesting that with many psychologists and with a good many physiologists and neurologists the newer conceptions of experimental zoölogy make slow progress. Experimental biologists and students of animal behavior have begun to put the emphasis upon accurate statements of what really happens in hereditary adjustments rather than to seek in them the exposition of the dogma that they exist because they are useful or serviceable. No one who has watched animals display their hereditary forms of activity from birth to the adult stage could hold that more than a few, considering the thousands which exist, fit such a philosophic and really vitalistic mould. The case of the human infant is not different.

throws his hand up for defense, blinks his eyes or ducks his head; runs away; he bites, scratches, kicks and grasps whatever his hand touches. We may express our formulation in convenient terms somewhat as follows: when the adjustments called out by the stimulus are internal and confined to the subject's body, we have emotion, for example, blushing; when the stimulus leads to adjustment of the organism as a whole to objects, we have instinct, for example, defense responses, grasping, etc. Emotions seldom appear alone. The stimulus usually calls out emotional instinctive and habit factors simultaneously.

Additional Formulations.—The above formulation fits only the more stereotyped forms of emotional response as seen, for example, in the states popularly called blushing, anger, fear and shame. When we take into account the whole group of phenomena in which we see emotional manifestations in adults, a pronounced modification is necessary. Apparently the hereditary pattern as a whole gets broken up. At any rate it largely disappears (the parts never wholly disappear) except under unusual conditions, and there *can be noted only a reinforcement or inhibition of the habit and instinctive (exaggerated and depressed reflexes, for example) activities taking place at the moment.* We mean to imply here only the generally observed facts typified by such popular expressions as "He is working at a low ebb to-day," "His tone is low," "He's a gloom"; in psychopathology when this phase is more marked, *depressions* are spoken of. The opposite picture is popularly portrayed by such expressions as "Jones is full of pep to-day," "he is excited," "happy," "he is working with a punch "; in psychopathology, the exaggerated type of this behavior is termed *manic*. It will be noted that these expressions refer to the activity level at which all of an individual's acts are accomplished, that is, they do not refer to the pattern type of emotion. Only in pathological cases, or in the case of normals in periods of a cataclysmic nature, such as war, earthquake, and the sudden death of loved ones, do we get a complete return to the original and more infantile type of emotional response.

Observation would seem to suggest the following formulation: Organized activity (hereditary and acquired) may go on and usually does go on at a given level. We may call the most usual *the normal level* or level, of equilibrium. It varies with different individuals and one can determine it even with respect to a single individual only after observing him for a considerable time. We may note further that an individual at one time may exhibit more energy, push or pep than normal, for example, during and immediately after a cold shower; we may call this the excited level. Again at times he works at a level lower than normal, for example, when in trouble, after money losses or illness; we may call this the *depressed level*.

Without neurologizing too much, we may venture the assumption that in adults environmental factors have brought about the partial inhibition of the more external features of the primitive pattern types of emotion. The implicit, mainly glandular and smooth muscular side of the pattern, remains. The emotionally exciting object releases important internal secretions which, without initiating new (part) reactions, reinforce or inhibit those actually in progress. This hypothesis would account for changes in level. Only in rare cases do we see mere changes in level. Usually when such changes occur, certain auxiliary or additional part reactions appear, such as we see in whistling while at work, keeping time with the feet, drumming on the table, biting the finger nails. These types of reaction are singled out and spoken of in some detail under the head *Emotional Outlets* (page 236).

The Genetic Study of Emotion in the Child.—Unfortunately for the subject of psychology, few experiments have been made upon the emotional life of the child under anything like as favorable conditions as obtain in the study of animals. Our observations upon the child are similar to those which were made upon animals before Thorndike and Lloyd Morgan introduced the experimental method. Until very recently, in spite of volumes written upon it, discussion has been of the armchair variety. The superstition that the human infant is too fragile for study is giving way to a more sensible viewpoint. It has proven practicable in some laboratories to take infants from birth and to study them from the same point of view that animals are studied, giving due consideration to those factors in behavior which do not appear in animal response. But unfortunately this work is handicapped because there are no facilities in maternity wards for keeping the mother and child under close observation for years, a condition which is indispensable for real systematic work.

Summary of Positive Results; Early Types of Emotional Reactions.—After observing a number of infants, especially during the first months of life, we suggest the following group of emotional reactions as belonging to the original and fundamental nature of man: *fear, rage* and *love* (using *love* in approximately the same sense that Freud uses *sex*).[3] We use these terms which are current in psychology with a good deal of hesitation. The student is asked to find nothing in them which is not fully statable in terms of situation and response. Indeed, we should be willing to call them emotional reaction states X, Y and Z. They are far more easily observable in animals than in infants.

Fear.—What stimulus apart from all training will call out fear responses; what are these responses, and how early may they be called out? The principal situations which call out fear responses seem to be as follows: (1) To suddenly remove from the infant all means of support, as when one drops it from the hands to be caught by an assistant (in the experiment the child is held over a bed upon which has been placed a soft feather pillow); (2) by loud sounds; (3) occasionally when an infant is just falling asleep or is just ready to waken, a sudden push or a slight shake is an adequate stimulus; (4) when an infant is just falling asleep, occasionally the sudden pulling of the blanket upon which it is lying will produce the fear responses. (3) and

---

[3] This list is identical with James' list of *coarser* emotions except for the omission of grief, which James puts first. Grief we look upon as being a *reactive state* (connected with love, really) in which the object or situation which usually calls out in the subject the reactions of love is suddenly removed. The state of grief must be looked upon as a mal-adjustment period, where the objects and situations which have usually called out both the original love responses and the conditioned reflexes built upon them are lacking. The state (in normal cases) disappears as soon as new objects are found or new conditioned reflexes have been entrained.

(4) above may be looked upon as belonging under (1). The responses are a sudden catching of the breath, clutching randomly with the hands (the grasping reflex invariably appearing when the child is dropped), sudden closing of the eye-lids, puckering of the lips, then crying; in older children possibly flight and hiding (not yet observed by us as "original" reactions). In regard to the age at which fear responses first appear, we can state with some sureness that the above mentioned group of reactions appears at birth. It is often stated that children are instinctively afraid in the dark. While we shall advance our opinion with the greatest caution, we have not so far been able to gather any evidence to this effect (page 226). When such reactions to darkness do appear they are due to other causes; darkness comes to be associated with absence of customary stimulation, noises, etc. (they should be looked upon as conditioned fear reactions). From time immemorial children have been "scared" in the dark, either unintentionally or as a means of controlling them (this is especially true of children reared in the South).

Rage.—In a similar way the question arises as to what is the original situation which brings out the activities seen in rage. Observation seems to show that the *hampering of the infant's movements* is the factor which apart from all training brings out the movements characterized as rage. If the face or head is held, crying results, quickly followed by screaming. The body stiffens and fairly well-coördinated slashing or striking movements of the hands and arms result; the feet and legs are drawn up and down; the breath is held until the child's face is flushed. In older children the slashing movements of the arms and legs are better coördinated, and appear as kicking, slapping, pushing, etc. These reactions continue until the irritating situation is relieved, and sometimes do not cease then. Almost any child from birth can be thrown into a rage if its arms are held tightly to its sides; sometimes even if the elbow joint is clasped tightly between the fingers the response appears; at times just the placing of the head between cotton pads will produce it. This was noticed repeatedly when testing eye coördinations in infants under ten days of age. The slight constraint put upon the head by the soft pads would often result in a disturbance so great that the experiment had to be discontinued for a time.

Love.—The original situation which calls out the observable love responses seems to be the stroking or manipulation of some erogenous zone, tickling, shaking, gentle rocking, patting and turning upon the stomach across the attendant's knee. The response varies. If the infant is crying, crying ceases, a smile may appear, attempts at gurgling, cooing, and finally, in slightly older children, the extension of the arms, which we should class as the forerunner of the embrace of adults. The smile and the laugh which Freud connects with the release of repression (we are not denying in the case of adults this may be true) we should thus class as original reaction tendencies intimately connected from infancy with the stimulation of, in our opinion at least, the erogenous zones.

These types fit fairly well the general formulation we gave on page 215. There is a reaction pattern; there is a definite stimulus, which has its peculiarly exciting character (the reason for which must be sought in biology); the radius of action is small; no particular adjustment is made to any object in the environment. It is admitted, however, that the responses contain both explicit and implicit components, that is, involve the skeletal musculature, the visceral system, the smooth muscles and glands. It is probable, though, that if the exciting stimulus were sufficiently strong—strong enough to produce "shock"—or if continued for a sufficient length of time, the subject would tend to take on more and more the purely vegetative type of existence illustrated by the example of the young tern. In rage, the child becomes so stiff, and holds its breath for such a long time, that it is often necessary to soothe it. The final stage in any great emotion would seem to be paralysis or the "death feint." Approximations to this condition are seen in the paralysis of fear, in the fainting under strong emotional excitement, in the stereotyped reactions of the stoics and martyrs when they unflinchingly endured the torch. Individuals on the battlefield, likewise, are able to withstand operations, wounds, and injuries without complaint. It must be admitted that there is a constant tendency for the

organized habit response of the individual to disappear under
the extremes of emotion. So far as we can see, this tendency
towards stereotypy, paralysis or the death feint under the immediate effect of a strong emotional excitement has no biological
or adaptive value (see page 243), however, on post-emotional
state). The organism exhibiting it is at the mercy of its enemies,
whether on the battlefield or in the struggle for food among savage tribes, and is at a disadvantage in the race for a much-sought-
after woman, or in the fight for business and scientific reputation.

Negative Results of Experimental Study.—Three babies
from the Harriet Lane Hospital were put into various situations,
the types of which are illustrated below, for the purpose of finding out whether there is a wider range of stimuli that may arouse
an emotional reaction than the one we cited a moment ago.
These babies represented splendid, healthy types. Their mothers
were the wet nurses belonging to the hospital. They were 165,
126 and 124 days of age. The first two, whose ages are given,
were put through the more numerous tests. The experiments
are interesting for the reason that the babies had never been
out of the hospital and had never seen an animal. A summary
of the tests on Thorne, a girl 165 days of age, is given below.[4]

A very lively, friendly *black cat* was allowed to crawl near
the baby. She reached for it with both hands at once. The cat
was purring loudly. She touched its nose, playing with it with
her fingers. It was shown three times. Each time she reached
with both hands for it, the left hand being rather more active.
She reached for it when it was placed on a lounge before her but
out of reach.

Then a *pigeon* in a paper bag was laid on the couch. The
pigeon was struggling, and moving the bag about on the couch
and making a slight rattling noise. The baby watched it intently
but did not reach for it. The pigeon was taken out of the bag on
the couch before her, cooing and struggling in the experimenter's
hands. She reached for it again and again, and failing, of course,
to get hold of it put her hands in her mouth each time. She was
allowed to touch its head. The pigeon moved its head about with

---

[4] These experiments on the reactions of infants to various objects should
be read again in connection with the theory of positive and negative
reactions, p. 269. It will be noted that most of the responses were positive.

quick, jerking movements. It was then held by its feet and allowed to flap its wings near the baby's face. She watched it intently, showing no tendency to avoid it, but did not reach for it. When the bird became quiet she reached for it, and caught hold of its beak with her left hand.

Test with a rabbit. The animal was put on a couch in front of her. (The child was sitting on her mother's lap.) She watched it very intently but did not reach for it until the experimenter held it in his hands close to her; then she reached for it immediately, catching one of its ears in her left hand, and attempted to put it into her mouth.

The last animal presented to her was a *white rat*. She paid little attention to it, only fixating it occasionally. She followed it with her eyes somewhat when it moved about the couch. When held out to her on the experimenter's arm, she turned her head away, no longer stimulated.

April 24, 172 days old. The baby was taken into a dark room with only an electric light behind her, not very bright (faint illumination). A stranger held the baby. The mother sat where she could not be seen. A dog was brought into the room and allowed to jump up on the couch beside her. The baby watched intently every move the dog made but did not attempt to reach for it. Then she turned her head aside. The front light was then turned up and the dog again exhibited. The infant watched very closely every move the dog and the experimenter made, but did not attempt to catch the dog. Exhibited no fear reactions, no matter how close the dog was made to come to her.

The *black cat* was then brought in (both lights on). The cat rubbed against the baby's feet and put her front paws in the baby's lap, touching its nose to her hand. The baby watched intently and reached for it with her left hand. The front light was then turned out. The experimenter held the cat closer to her, and she reached for it with both hands.

Rabbit. She reached for it with both hands as soon as the experimenter came into the room with it in his arms. The front light was turned on. The rabbit was held out to her. She reached for it at once with both hands, trying to put her fingers in its eyes. She caught hold of a piece of fur above the rabbit's eye and pulled hard.

Pigeon. The front light was turned out. She reached for the bird with her left hand before the experimenter was ready to present it to her. The pigeon's wings were released and it fluttered violently just in front of the baby's eyes. She continued to reach for it with both hands, even when the wings brushed her face.

When the bird was quiet it was presented to her again. She reached for it even more vigorously. She tried to take hold of the pigeon's beak with her left hand, but failed, because the bird continually bobbed its head. The front light was then turned on. The pigeon again flapped wildly. The baby looked at it intently with widely opened eyes, but this time did not reach. She showed no fear, however. It was then held out to her again when it had become quiet. She reached for it at once with both hands, held the feathers and tried to put her fingers into its eyes.

April 27, 175 days old. The baby was placed in a small chair and tied in, and put behind a screen, so that she could not see any of the people in the room. The dog was allowed to walk suddenly around the screen in front of her. She showed no fear when the dog rubbed against her legs. She did not reach for him, however. While she was still in the same position, the experimenter held the pigeon in front of her and allowed it to flap its wings. She reached for it with both hands the moment it was presented to her, and did not withdraw her hands while the bird was flapping its wings. She continued to reach as the bird was moved out of her range.

The cat was then brought around the screen and placed on the couch just in front of the baby's chair. She did not reach for it, but followed it with her eyes. It was held very close to her. She reached for it with her left hand and touched its head. The cat was then moved away, but she continued to reach for it. Then the cat put its front feet in her lap. She reached with her left hand and followed with her right, touching its ears.

Rabbit. She reached with her left hand at once when the rabbit was still too far away to touch. When it came close to her she reached with her left hand and touched it.

She was then taken into the dark room with both lights turned out and seated in a small chair. A newspaper was lighted before her and allowed to burn in a large metal bucket. She watched it intently from the moment the match was struck until the flames died down. She showed no fear, but did not attempt to reach.[5]

While being tested in the large room for eye-hand coördination, the dog suddenly began to bark at some one entering the room. He was quite near the baby. He barked loudly and jumped about at the end of the leash. The baby became perfectly still, watching intently with widely opened eyes, blinking at each bark, but did not cry.

---

[5] When tested seven days later with this she wet her napkin, but no general fear reaction appeared (possibly normal bladder reflex).

May 1, 178 days old. She was taken out to Druid Hill Park in an automobile for the first time in her life. She was wide awake the whole time. She was carried rather rapidly through the grounds of the small zoo at the park. The camel was braying and came up to the fence as we approached, rubbing rather violently against the fence, coming within a few feet of the baby. This produced no fear reaction and no constant fixation. She was then taken to the cages containing the cinnamon and black bears. She gazed at them from time to time, but with no constant fixation. We then took her into the monkey house which contained also a large number of parrots and other smaller birds. The monkeys came to the sides of the cage, and from time to time attacked the wires. Three or four times they came up and made threatening movements, and actually caught the experimenter by the arm. The child did not seem to be in the least afraid. The peacocks were making their rather uncanny sounds within twenty feet of her, but she did not turn her eyes towards the source of the sound. She was then taken back to the camel yard, and the camel again "performed" nicely. Two camels came up to each other and rubbed noses and put their heads over the dividing fence. The baby was within two or three inches of the camel's nose on several occasions, but while she followed the movements with her eyes, she showed no pronounced reactions of any kind. She was then taken to the Shetland pony, who put his nose through the wires and showed his teeth. She was within a few inches of his mouth. Outside of following movements of the eyes, no reactions were observable. She was taken near two zebras. They came to the edge of the fence, within a few inches of the baby. The zebras were possibly followed slightly more intently with the eyes, but there was no other observable reaction. While the baby was watching the zebras an ostrich came close to her and brought its head to the wire but did not strike the wire violently. During approximately half of the experiment the baby was carried by her mother and the rest of the time by the experimenter's assistant. She had never been carried by this individual before. At times the mother was kept out of the range of the baby's vision.

Baby Nixon, a girl, 126 days of age, had just learned the eye-hand coördination. She was put through exactly the same series of situations. Slight differences appeared, *e.g.*, when the cat rubbed its head against the baby's stomach, there was a distinct start, a tendency to stiffen. While the experimenter was out of the room getting the rabbit, three persons were left with the baby in the dark room (dim light). All were sitting very quietly.

15

She was being held by a stranger. Suddenly the baby began to cry, and had to be given to the mother for a few moments. She quieted down immediately. Again when the pigeon flapped its wings near the baby's face, she gave a distinct jump, but did not cry or show other signs of fear. When the dog was made to bark (lighted room), the baby blinked her eyes at every bark, but gave no other reaction. She smiled throughout most of the situations. She smiled all through the burning of the paper in the dark room.

It is thus seen that this unusual opportunity of testing children's reactions to their first sight of animals yielded few definite results. At least we can say that the older statements which maintain that violent emotions appear must be very greatly modified. Of course, it is always possible that the children were too young, but this has not very much weight, since we have tested children from birth through to 200 days. These children left the hospital shortly after the tests and further experimentation could not be made. As a control test, similar observations were made upon a colored baby girl (Lee) 200 days of age, who had been under observation from birth. She lived in the city under the usual environmental conditions. Exactly the same results were obtained. There was practically no evidence of fear.

Are There Other Original Emotional Patterns?—It is thus seen that so far our attempts to bring out emotional patterns distinct from those enumerated on page 199 have been barren of result. If it were possible to continue such experiments through a much longer span of a child's life, and if we could face him with a much larger number of situations that more nearly touched his daily life activities, it might be possible to extend the list. It is realized that we are working here with very young members of the human species. A good deal of organization and development takes place after two hundred days. Some very complex situations have yet to be faced, such as masturbation (and in boys especially, the first masturbation after puberty); the first menstruation period in girls; complex situations connected with family life, such as quarrels between the parents, corporal punishment and the death of loved ones, all of which have to be met with for a first time. We know from later observation that these do become hitched up to emotional reactions; whether they are original or transferred does not appear from our studies. It would be especially desirable to study the reaction states we now designate by the names of shame and shyness and embarrassment in this connection. We are of the opinion that most of the asserted emotions are of the consolidated type (that is, emotion plus instinct, plus habit) or emotional attitudes. These are discussed on page 238.

Attention is called here to the limitations of the genetic method. As long as we can keep the baby under constant observation, a great deal of simplification can be obtained in the study of the emotions, but the human infant is a part of a social group and must sooner or later be returned to it. Things happen so fast then that a separate tabulation of events cannot be made. Under ordinary conditions, the emotions take care of themselves in a normal child, that is, society, including, of course, the parents and the family group, furnishes its own corrective for failure to react emotionally, for wrong emotional reaction and for over or under reactions. All too often, due mainly to defective environment, seldom to defective heredity, the emotions may go wrong. The genetic method is not of service. The emotional life of the individual must then be studied by the psychopathologist. Again, in business and professional life (especially in the Army and Navy), more and more emphasis is being placed upon what may be called emotional temperament. It is thus evident that the applied psychologist must have some means of making studies of emotional activity in adults. Finally, the scientific psychologist, for methodological and purely technical reasons, devises methods for the study of emotions in the hope that they will yield scientific results, or that his methods may prove of such value that they can be employed by the psychopathologist, by the criminologist and by the applied psychologist. A short account of the methods which can be used where the genetic method is not applicable follows.

Methods Employed in the Detection of Implicit Emotional Response.—The explicit portions of the pattern reaction in emotion are, as we have tried to indicate, usually the least important constituent. When they appear, systematic observation enables us to note them with sufficient scientific accuracy. In the study of criminals, of psychogenic disorders and of normal individuals, often all explicit emotional manifestations disappear. The exciting situation is complex. On the one hand, it inhibits overt vocal response, but initiates a train of (visceral) implicit activity. Questioning the subject may reveal nothing. He may deny that the stimulus produced any reaction whatever, and yet the next moment he may drop his cigarette, bite his nails, or hesitate or stumble over a word. Popularly we speak in such cases of deceit, concealment of the emotion, "repressions," etc. In many cases, however, the individual would report his observations upon himself correctly, if he could observe them, but the movements may be of such a fleeting character as to escape observation, or his intellectual level may be of such a low grade that he cannot make the observation. In such cases there are often so many disturbing factors that self-observation is not possible. Several methods are in use by means of which we can detect the implicit side of emotion.

(1) **The Word Reaction Method; Free Type.**—The subject is told to respond immediately with a word to a given visual or auditory word stimulus. The stimulus words are made up before the test. Some of the words are neutral words, the others are the "significant" words which refer to the emotional situation. The indicators of implicit response or tension obtained from the subject are unduly long reactions (with occasional appearance of explicit forms such as the giggle, dropping the eyes, a flush); significant response words, showing that the stimulus word was a part of the emotional setting; repetition of the same word; too rapid responses; low level responses; failure in responses (there are several variations in this method).

(2) **The Continuous Type.**—The subject is started on any selected word, possibly a fragment from a dream, and told to "speak the words as they come." He begins. For a time the words come freely and then they fail. There is blockage. New associated lines are begun. Sooner or later, however, in disturbed cases all lines seem to converge and blockage occurs

whatever the start may have been. The blockage seems to occur at the point where the words relating to the emotionally exciting object belong in the associated train of words.

(3) Dream study and analysis often reveal emotional tension. They may be studied by the common-sense method of questioning the patient now from one angle, now from another, but they are often analyzed by employing the two methods described above singly or in combination. Dreams are a part of a person's sum total of reactions. They are as good indicators of the nature of his personality, of his stresses and strains and emotional life generally, as are any of his other activities. We have already stated that we can judge the emotional level of an individual by watching his daily routine of activity. To make this statement complete, the dream activity in sleep and day-dreams must be taken into account. These are word reactions but not isolated reactions or reactions of the muscle-twitch kind. They are connected and associated activity, fully as complete oftentimes as housebuilding, delivering a lecture, or putting through a big business deal. The study of dreams, since the dream language is extremely symbolic, requires individuals especially trained in that field.

(4) The study of slips of word or pen, poor adjustments, over and under reactions, bodily postures and attitudes. These can be studied by general observation and by the methods which are employed in the study of dreams.

In discussing these methods, it should be stated that the psychologist busies himself with them principally from a methodological standpoint, that is, by determining the range of applicability, their reliability, the best technic, etc. The psychopathologist uses them for practical purposes. The reshaping and rebalancing of a personality often depends upon the finding of situations connected with an emotion, or upon finding out whether there is an emotion where normally there should be one. He uses all of the above methods, and in addition his common-sense, combining it all with general observation of the patient's whole personality. In gathering his data, it is often necessary and desirable for him to question the patient upon the significant events of his life history; the things he is naturally inclined to do and inclined not to do (positive and negative reaction tendencies) ; the books he has read, the way they affected him; the types of situation in real or dramatic life which influenced him most; his main emotional assets; the easiest way to get an emotional rise out of him; the trend of his day-dreams and the types of air-castles he builds; what his chief lines of sensitiveness are; his conflicts and temptations, and the way he finds himself meeting these difficulties. A full discussion of these factors requires more space than we can give. We return to them again on page 423.

In addition to the above methods, others are being developed.

(5) The determination of increased sugar in the blood or urine before and after presentation of a stimulus when there is reason to infer that the stimulus is not without significance (page 241).

(6) The emotional questionary of Woodworth, and the various character analysis outlines. The subject answers by "yes" or "no" a series of questions, such as: Were you considered a bad boy? Were you shy with other boys? Do you know of anybody who is trying to do you harm? Did you ever make love to a girl? Have you ever had any great mental shock? Does it make you uneasy to have to cross a wide street or an open square? Did you ever feel a strong desire to steal things? Did you ever have the habit of biting your finger nails? Do your feelings keep changing from happy to sad and from sad to happy without any reason? Have you ever been afraid of going insane? If there is unstable emotional temperament, the fact is supposed to be revealed by the nature of the answers.

(7) The so-called psycho-galvanic reflex. Here the subject sits in a quiet room with two non-polarizable electrodes upon two parts of the body. The electrodes are connected to a sensitive galvanometer. A definite deflection of the needle is obtained. Emotional stimuli are then given, and their effect noted by the deflection of the needle. So far in our laboratory this method has not been found serviceable. It is hoped, however, that with an improved technic, the action currents in the heart revealed by the string galvanometer can be made to yield serviceable results.

(8) The so-called expressive methods. These consist of the

recording of the respiratory changes, vaso-motor changes; auto-matic writing and drawing (planchette). Such methods in general have proven of slight value. The respiratory curve is a very sensitive indicator (showing conditioned reflexes quite clearly), but it is subject to so many influences that the significant changes are often obscured and their interpretation is made difficult. This is equally true of vaso-motor changes.

Conditioned Emotional Reactions.—Under the action of environmental factors (habit influences) situations which originally did not call out emotional response come later to do so. This enlargement of the range of stimuli capable of calling out emotional activity is responsible largely for the complexity we see in the emotional life of the adult. Until recently no experimental work has been done which would show such conditioned emotional responses in the making.

Recently, in the Hopkins laboratory, the following experiments were tried upon Albert B., an eleven-month old infant weighing 21 pounds. This infant was rather stolid and phlegmatic, but extremely well and healthy.

Albert was the son of one of the wet nurses. He had lived his entire life in the hospital. He had been under continuous observation by the experimenters almost from birth.*

To start the experiment it became necessary to use some simple native or fundamental stimulus which *would* produce fear (corresponding to the electrical shock). We have already pointed out that loud sounds are the most potent of all such stimuli. We determined to take Albert and attempt to condition fear to a white rat by showing him the rat and as soon as he reached for it and touched it to strike a heavy steel bar behind him. We first showed by repeated tests that Albert feared nothing except loud sounds (and removal of support). Everything coming within twelve inches of him was reached for and manipulated. This was true of animals, persons and things. His reaction, however, to the sound of the steel bar was charac-

* For a fuller report of this experiment see "Studies in Infant Psychology," John B. Watson and Rosalie Rayner Watson, *Scientific Monthly*, December, 1921, p. 493.

teristic and what we had been led to believe is true of most if not all infants. When it was suddenly sounded behind him for the first time there was a sudden intake of the breath and an upward fling of the arms. On the second stimulation the lips began to pucker and tremble, on the third he broke into a crying fit, turned to one side and began to crawl away as rapidly as possible with head averted.

The result of this observation showing that the loud sound would call out the fear response gave us hope that we might be able to use this stimulus for *bringing about a conditioned emotional response* just as the electric shock combined with the sight of a colored object brings about in the end a conditioned motor response of the finger. Our laboratory notes showing the progress of this test are most convincing.

Eleven months, three days old. (1) White rat suddenly taken from the basket and presented to Albert. He began to reach for rat with left hand. Just as his hand touched the animal the bar was struck immediately behind his head. The infant jumped violently and fell forward, burying his face in the mattress. He did not cry, however.

(2) Just as his right hand touched the rat the bar was again struck. Again the infant jumped violently, fell forward and began to whimper.

In order not to disturb the child too seriously no further tests were given for one week.

Eleven months, ten days old. (1) Rat presented suddenly without sound. There was steady fixation but no tendency at first to reach for it. The rat was then placed nearer, whereupon tentative reaching movements began with the right hand. When the rat nosed the infant's left hand the hand was immediately withdrawn. He started to reach for the head of the animal with the forefinger of his left hand but withdrew it suddenly before contact. It is thus seen that the two joint stimulations given last week were not without effect. He was tested with his blocks immediately afterwards to see if they shared in the process of conditioning. He began immediately to pick them up, dropping them and pounding them, etc. In the remainder of the tests the blocks were given frequently to quiet him and to test his general emotional state. They were always removed from sight when the process of conditioning was under way.

(2) Combined stimulation with rat and sound. Started, then fell over immediately to right side. No crying.

(3) Combined stimulation. Fell to right side and rested on hands with head turned from rat. No crying.

(4) Combined stimulation. Same reaction.

(5) Rat suddenly presented *alone*. Puckered face, whimpered and withdrew body sharply to left.

(6) Combined stimulation. Fell over immediately to right side and began to whimper.

(7) Combined stimulation. Started violently and cried, but did not fall over.

(8) Rat alone. *The instant the rat was shown the baby began to cry. Almost instanlty he turned sharply to the left, fell over, raised himself on all fours and began to crawl away so rapidly that he was caught with difficulty before he reached the edge of the table.*

This was as convincing a case of a completely conditioned fear response as could have been theoretically pictured. It is not unlikely had the sound been of greater intensity and the child more delicately organized that one or two combined stimulations might have been sufficient to condition the emotion. We thus see how easily such conditioned fears may grow up in the home. A child that has gone to bed for years without a light with no fears may, through the loud slamming of doors or through a sudden loud clap of thunder, become conditioned to darkness. We can easily explain how it is that a sudden flash of lightning finds you all set and tense, often times with the hands over the ears, before the clap of thunder, which is the true stimulus to such action, occurs. We can thus see further how it is that the sight of a nurse that constrains the movements of the youngster or dresses it badly may cause the infant to go into a rage, or how the momentary glimpse of a maiden's bonnet may produce the emotional reactions of love in her swain.

Transferred Conditioned Emotional Reactions.—The experimental question arose as to whether Albert would be afraid henceforth only of rats, or whether the fear would be *transferred* to other animals and possibly to other objects. To answer this question Albert was brought back into the laboratory five days later and tested. Our laboratory notes again show the results most convincingly.

Eleven months, fifteen days old. (1) Tested first with blocks. He reached readily for them, playing with them as usual. This shows that there has been no general *transfer* to the room, table, blocks, etc.

(2) Rat alone. Whimpered immediately, withdrew right hand and turned head and trunk away.

(3) Blocks again offered. Played readily with them, smiling and gurgling.

(4) Rat alone. Leaned over to the left side as far away from the rat as possible, then fell over, getting up on all fours and scurrying away as rapidly as possible.

(5) Blocks again offered. Reached immediately for them, smiling and laughing as before.

The above preliminary test shows that the conditioned response to the rat had carried over completely for the five days in which no tests were given. The question as to whether or not there is a *transfer* was next taken up.

(6) *Rabbit* alone. A rabbit was suddenly placed on the mattress in front of him. The reaction was pronounced. Negative responses began at once. He leaned as far away from the animal as possible, whimpered, then burst into tears. When the rabbit was placed in contact with him he buried his face in the mattress, then got up on all fours and crawled away, crying as he went. This was a most convincing test.

(7) The blocks were next given him, after an interval. He played with them as before. It was observed by four people that he played far more energetically with them than ever before. The blocks were raised high over his head and slammed down with a great deal of force.

(8) *Dog* alone. The dog did not produce as violent a reaction as the rabbit. The moment fixation of the eyes occurred the child shrank back and as the animal came nearer he attempted to get on all fours but did not cry at first. As soon as the dog passed out of his range of vision he became quiet. The dog was then made to approach the infant's head (he was lying down at the moment). Albert straightened up immediately, fell over to the opposite side and turned his head away. He then began to cry.

(9) Blocks were again presented. He began immediately to play with them.

(10) *Fur coat* (seal). Withdrew immediately to the left side and began to fret. Coat put close to him on the left side, he turned immediately, began to cry and tried to crawl away on all fours.

(11) *Cotton wool.* The wool was presented in a paper package. At the ends the cotton was not covered by the paper. It was placed first on his feet. He kicked it away but did not touch it with his hands. When his hand was laid on the wool he immediately withdrew it but did not show the shock that the animals or fur coat produced in him.

He then began to play with the paper, avoiding contact with the wool itself. He finally, under the impulse of the manipulative instinct, lost some of his negativism to the wool.

(12) Just in play W. put his head down to see if Albert would play with his hair. Albert was completely negative. The two other observers did the same thing. He began immediately to play with their hair. A Santa Claus mask was then brought and presented to Albert. He was again pronouncedly negative, although on all previous occasions he had played with it.

We see that the conditioned fear to the rat, which was experimentally set up, transferred to many other objects. The transfer was immediate and without any additional experience in connection with these other objects. In these transferred emotional reactions we thus would find a reason for the widespread change in the personality of children and possibly even of adults once even a single strongly conditioned emotional reaction has been set up to any object or situation. It accounts for the many unreasonable fears and for a good deal of the sensitiveness of individuals to objects for which no adequate ground for such behavior can be offered in the past history of that individual. The importance of such a factor in shaping the life of the child needs no further emphasis from us.

The most important question for the applied psychologist is " How can these conditioned fear, rage and love responses be removed? " The conditioned love responses are probably more serious even than the fears and tantrums, since they are not only tolerated by society but even encouraged by it. In our opinion conditioned love responses, especially those directed towards the mother and father, *breeding too great dependence upon the parents as they do* (p. 250), are probably the most sinister factors in the whole system of human organization. Even if psychoanalysis could re-condition the individual, it would be too late—these attachments, beginning in infancy and continuing throughout the adolescent period, thwart and block organization along other lines. The adult possessing these infantile habits is and must remain unbalanced from the standpoint of his total organization. The research psychologists in the infant behavior laboratories, once they are established will in time learn how to remove these conditioned emotional reactions. Emotional re-conditioning bids fair to become as important to society as medicine. But until parents in turn are trained in the rearing of children, re-conditioning will be an andless process. The parents can establish new entanglements for the helpless child faster than the behaviorist can break them down.

Summary of Experimental Findings.—In general, then, it seems safe to say that when an emotionally exciting object stimulates the subject simultaneously with one not emotionally exciting, the latter may in time (often after one such joint stimulation) arouse the same emotional reaction as the former. It is probable that conditioned reflexes of the second, third and succeeding orders are also continually arising. In the process, the reaction pattern probably gets broken up to a large extent. Part reactions belonging to love, rage and fear might all appear in the reaction to such a substituted stimulus.

In addition to this sudden and abrupt type of substitution, which undoubtedly belongs in the class of conditioned reflexes, there are the "attachments" and "detachments" to persons, places and things which come by the slow process of habit connection. They probably do not differ in origin from the type just considered except for the increased length of time required for their formation.

Emotional Outlets: Diffusion.—On page 217 we spoke of changes in the general level of activity due to emotional disturbance. We spoke there of a normal, of a high and of a low level. Probably if an individual were perfectly balanced, the distribution of emotional activity would be uniform and all organized activity would share equally, that is, there would be a mere change in level. But few individuals possess that perfect balance which would make this possible. Furthermore, society and one's own organization often make emotional outlets impossible along certain lines. When emotional expression is blocked in any one region, outlet seems to take place somewhere else. An illustration will make the point clear: *A* is insulted by a larger man, or by an older or a younger man, or by one from whom he is receiving his daily bread. The instinct and habit organization of *A* would lead to an attack, or at least to its equivalent—a strong verbal retort. But other features in the total situation (the fact that he is larger, older, younger, etc.) inhibit these outlets. The emotional pressure, however, has been aroused. He may proceed to his office, fire his bookkeeper or office boy or terrorize his stenographer. One's family often suffers most in such cases. If a man's wife causes the emotional rise, the children are apt to suffer. The outlet, however, may not always be a harsh word or a blow. If the emotion partakes of the fear or rage components, the blow or harsh word is most frequent. If the thwarted emotion is of the love type, the final outlet may be exhibited by showering kind words or benefits upon some one other than the person calling out but thwarting the love emotion. If the thwarting is brought about by the death of the loved object, the outlet may be found in grief or suicide.

Human life is full of such outlets. If society as a whole puts on too many restrictions (rage) and the thwarted individual is not well-balanced, the outlet may be through burglary or vandalism. In balanced individuals it may have its outlet through swearing or in privately railing at the restrictions of society.

In certain individuals, either through inferior constitution or the narrowness or restrictiveness of their environment, no external outlet seems to be possible. The emotional drainage expresses itself in some form of attitude (page 239); by withdrawing or shrinkage from contact with fellow humans of any kind; in drink or drugs; in ruminations, day-dreams and air-castles—that is, there is a language outlet.

The point which rationalizes all such behavior seems to be, namely, that the individual by so reacting gets relaxation and freedom from emotional pressure. Popularly we speak of "working off" the emotion, that "one's rage is cooled" by this or that. The study of these various outlets when they assume pathological form and interfere with the remaining actions of the individual or of those organized functions which society demands of each individual, and of the reshaping of such individuals, belongs to psychiatry. We see, however, the same factors at work even in "normal" individuals, and our training as psychologists is not complete until we are able to note the signs of emotional mal-adjustment.

We have not the evidence at hand to affirm the view that all of the phenomena seen in diffusion belong to the conditioned reflex realm. The activity seems to be too little stereotyped and entirely too complex to belong in that category. The attachment is not focalized. Probably the simplest way of stating the generally observed fact is that too great emotional pressure is drained off through whatever channel environmental (social) and hereditary factors make possible.

Consolidation Among Emotion, Instinct and Habit; Attitudes.—Observation seems to show that combinations or integrations occur among emotional, instinctive and habit activities. Our discussion of these integrations will be handicapped to some extent by our not having had opportunity to study instinct and habit. Possibly the activities we see in "anger" or its more active attitude, "fighting," best illustrate the points to be presented. Anger as we see it exhibited in the insect world probably remains on the emotion-instinct level (hereditary). Habit activities are at a minimum in these animals (though not wholly lacking). In the human race certainly the exciting stimulus is usually one which hampers, jostles, crowds or constrains the individual—the stimulus to rage. The instinctive factors are striking out with the arms and hands, grasping, running toward the object, probably biting it, the while unfleshing the teeth. Defensive movements also occur of the instinctive kind. The habit factors express themselves in the scientific "form" of attack and defense: the way the arms are held to avoid giving the enemy an opening, planting the blow on a vulnerable spot—the eyes or the solar plexus, etc.—and in the stance of the feet. The whole group is integrated, the part reactions work together. The individual becomes a fighting-defending, unitary action mass. If the environmental factors are such that actual fighting cannot occur, the subject assumes the "defiant" attitude. All three factors are still present even in the attitude. Many of the emotion, instinct and habit action tendencies are constrained by social factors. The emphasis has then, of course, to fall back on the implicit emotional components of the action mass.

In the above, rage predominated as the emotional constituent, the hereditary attack and defense movement as the instinct, and the trained activities as the habitual. Probably all other forms of emotion—those of the native or more fundamental type, as love and fear, and the broken up, combined and consolidated types which we get through substitution—show the types of combination shown above. To attempt to list these, to show their history and formation through the process of substitution and consolidation, would require a volume (and a very necessary one) of its own. Only a few will be touched upon here. The so-called submissive or inferiority attitude shows itself at once as having fear as the most prominent emotional element. The instinctive factor may not be clearly overt, but it is in general. It manifests itself in shrinking, submission and avoiding —sometimes with the body as a whole, sometimes with special organs, as the lips or eyes. The habitual factor shows itself especially in the language behavior of the adult—hastening to agree, avoiding an argument, and the hesitant voice.

In the sphere of love there are numerous attitudes as shown by the popular expressions "lovelorn," "lovesick," "tenderness," "sympathy." More fundamental and prominent attitudes are those of "shyness," "shame," "embarrassment," "jealousy," "envy," "hate," "pride," "suspicion," "resentment," "anguish" and "anxiety." There are many combinations of emotional habit and instinctive factors in all of these attitudes. They actually function by limiting the range of stimuli to which the person is sensitive. For the individual they are fundamental attributes of character, as much a part of him as his arms or legs or his method of attacking a new problem.

This very superficial analysis is not at all commensurate with the rôle these attitudes play in the life of the individual. In studying the life history of any person we can see how they have oftentimes furthered or hindered his life work and disturbed his personal balance. Shyness and the inferiority attitude may keep a man tied all his life to an accustomed but unremunerative job. They have oftentimes prevented his marriage or brought about a poorly adjusted marriage or kept him out of a wider

social circle. On the other hand, in other cases too much aggressiveness has just as often made impossible a man's chances of
making good business and social connections.

**Results of the Physiological Study of Emotions. A. Duct
Glands and Smooth Muscles.**—On page 31 and again in the
discussion of the duct glands of the mouth and stomach (page
194), we brought out the fact that when the human or animal subject is under the influence of the stimulus of hunger (rhythmical
contractions of stomach muscles) conditioned secretion reflexes
occur when food (food positively reacted to) is allowed to stimulate the animal visually or olfactorily.

Under the influence of emotional stimuli these part activities
are often blocked. This aspect of the phenomena of secretion and
movement of the smooth muscles of the stomach is undoubtedly
a part of the physiological study of emotion. A number of observers have shown that emotionally exciting situations do check
the functioning of the glands. If a child with a gastric fistula
is shown food and is then badgered by first handing it to him and
then taking it away and then causing it to disappear from vision,
crying and other definite signs of an emotional state appear. The
secretions are checked. Similar conditions obtain in the case of
dogs: if they are put in strange surroundings or if they are
fastened in a holder, or finally if they are shown their natural
enemy, the cat, the flow of secretion is checked. If the emotional
state is long continued, in both man and animals even the uncon-
ditioned reflexes may fail for some time, that is, the actual
contact of the substance may fail to arouse the flow of the
gastric juices.

A similar phenomenon appears in connection with the peri-
staltic movements of the stomach, and indeed of the movements in
the muscular layer of the whole alimentary canal. Restraining
the animal and covering its mouth and nose with the finger, check
the stomach contractions very quickly. But we have just seen
that stimuli of this kind produce the emotion of rage. The same
phenomena appear in the case of man. People under the influence of fear and rage frequently do not digest their food (due
to the checking of secretion) and the food remains in the stomach

(due to lack of movements necessary to pass the contents of the canal along).

Excitation of the pain receptors has the same effect as emotional disturbance (probably is a stimulus to rage) both upon secretion and upon the stomach contractions. It is probable that any of the highly exciting emotions act in the same way as those discussed above. Sex emotions aroused by salacious photographs and pictures have a definite inhibitory effect upon the rate and amount of secretion of the parotid gland and upon certain reflexes (swallowing, for example).

B. Effect of Exciting Stimuli upon the Ductless Glands.— Apparently one of the most important effects that emotional stimuli exert is the release of adrenin. The adrenin in turn liberates sugar from the stored supply in the liver, often in amounts greater than the body can consume. Glycosuria results, that is, the excess sugar passes over into the urine. This phenomenon often occurs in battle and in extreme emotional situations of any kind (depressing or exciting). Cannon states that young male cats when fastened in a holder become quite frantic, with eyes wide open and pupils dilated; the pulse is accelerated and the hairs of the tail become more or less erect; they snarl and growl as they try to free themselves. Whenever this excited condition occurs there is glycosuria (in from forty minutes to an hour and a half). When a small dog is allowed to bark at the cats, causing them to become excited, the glycosuria manifests itself. Similar results occur in the case of the human being. After hard examinations or exciting athletic contests, students show temporary glycosuria.

When glycosuria occurs, it is an indication of an increased supply of sugar in the blood, since so long as the kidneys are uninjured the sugar cannot pass out through the urine until an excessive supply of sugar is at hand. Testing for sugar in the urine is really a very coarse method of detecting the emotional effect of a stimulus. Recently very sensitive methods have been discovered for detecting the presence of increase of sugar in the blood. A large amount of material has collected in our laboratory as the result of blood sugar tests. It is unquestionably a very

16

delicate indicator and revealer of emotional changes. It has been used in connection with the association word reaction method. This joint method may be utilized as follows: One individual does a certain act while a second subject remains quietly in another room. The two return to the experimental room and the experimenter must decide from the word responses (hesitations, etc.) which one of the individuals performed the act in question. A small amount (few drops) of blood is obtained from both individuals both before the test is made and after, and the percentage of blood sugar is determined in all four specimens. The individual having committed the ''crime'' shows as a result the greater increase in blood sugar. The blood sugar reaction can thus be used as a supplementary method of detecting ''guilt.''

The method is probably delicate enough to decide whether a given individual is emotionally aroused by the mere presence of another individual. These results were obtained by Dr. N. D. C. Lewis in our laboratory. They have not yet been published. It has been shown conclusively in animals that if the adrenal glands are removed emotional stimuli will not cause this increase in sugar either in the blood or in the urine. The conclusion is well sustained, then, that emotional stimuli through a reflex mechanism set free adrenin which in turn acts upon the supply of sugar in the liver and converts it into a form which can be used by the muscles after it gets into the blood stream.

In addition to its sugar conversion effect upon the liver, adrenin acts in conjunction with the sympathetic nerves and produces vaso-constriction and hence an increased blood-pressure. It has been shown that when a given muscle is active, its blood-vessels dilate, thus tending to decrease arterial pressure. If many muscles are called into action at any given moment, these dilated vessels may so reduce arterial pressure that the muscles fail to get their proper food. Waste products also accumulate in the muscles. Adrenin because of its reinforcing effect upon the vaso-constrictor nerves produces heightened arterial pressure, which increases the food supply to the muscle and removes waste products. The blood is driven out of the vegetative organs of the interior into the skeletal muscles, which have to meet the extra demand when the animal is fighting and struggling to free itself.

C. Specific Effect of Adrenin.—There seems to be general agreement that the free adrenin in the blood acts directly upon the muscle in such a way as to neutralize fatigue products. "What rest will do only after an hour or more, adrenin will do in five minutes or less" (Cannon). This result is in addition to adrenin's function in producing a greater food supply to the muscle and increasing the amount of blood circulating through the muscle. After a muscle has been fatigued, that is, has lost its irritability, the injection of adrenin in the blood (or stimulation of the splanchnic nerve) will rapidly restore the muscle to its resting condition. Cannon maintains that the presence of adrenin also hastens clotting of the blood, which in wounded animals might be advantageous. His results in this respect have not been wholly confirmed.

Apparent Conflict Between Formulations.—There seems to be a conflict between our early statements about emotion and those gathered from the physiological studies just reported. We first expressed the view that if the emotional stimulus was strong enough or continued for a sufficient length of time paralysis or the death feint would occur. The state attained here is surely not adaptive. The result of the physiological study seemed to show that the organism under the influence of exciting stimuli often takes on a bettered state, one in which greater muscular activity and less fatigue is possible. The conflict can be harmonized. The "improved" physiological state is apparently due to the action of the autacoid substances. We saw on page 182 that such substances act like drugs. If a small amount of a certain drug, say strychnine, is administered, increased appetite and increased muscular activity ensue. A bettered general physiological condition may result. On the other hand, if too large an amount is given, the muscles may become rigid and the subject may die. Possibly a similar thing happens in the case of the autacoids. If the substances are set free in too large amounts, there is one type of action, namely, the paralyzing effect. If set free in physiologically serviceable amounts, their action may produce a combined series of reflexes, the total result of which may be a bettered physiological state.

The physiologists have unquestionably overemphasized the ''adaptive'' character in all of the major emotions. From Cannon's work it is easy to see how under the emotions of rage, fear and pain stimulation the possibility of increased muscular effort might aid the organism in fighting or in flight. On the other hand, it is difficult to see how this physiological state plays any serviceable rôle in adjustment unless the organism is in a situation where the increased muscular possibilities are to be used; but such situations are rare. A man in the army receives a letter telling him that his wife has given birth to a son. The news is undoubtedly a strong stimulus; excitement takes place and examination shows the presence of sugar in the urine, and naturally an increased supply in the blood, but his routine of camp activity happens to be such that no great muscular demand is made of him. We may grant Cannon's general position and yet maintain that it is not a very serviceable concept for the ordinary routine of daily life. We are no longer living in a frontier country, and outside of an occasional war, there is not much opportunity to bare our teeth and struggle for existence in the good old primitive way of our ancestors. Cannon's appeal to the biological serviceableness of the emotional reaction needs modification.

There would seem to be no question but that the immediate effect of the exciting stimuli upon organized activity, as was brought out on page 216, is always disruptive. If an individual is preparing a lecture or writing a book or rendering a musical selection, any strong emotional stimulus at least temporarily disrupts and blocks organized activity. The same thing would occur in the case of a group of officers if while preparing plans to make an attack on the enemy the following day, a shell were to burst and tear down a portion of the building in which they were working. It would thus seem necessary to state that the immediate effect of an exciting stimulus is ''unadaptive,'' disassociative and disruptive. The immediate effect may endure for an extremely short time, or for a longer time. We have found that the increased blood sugar may endure for several hours even after fairly slight emotional stimulation. There is thus a *post-shock* or *post-emotional* state. Apparently the post-emotional state may be of such a character that (1) the organism is left less well adjusted and less capable of carrying out organized activities. As an example of this, the death of a child may leave the mother in a depressed and apathetic condition which may endure for months. On the other hand, (2) the post-emotional state may be of such a character that the organism is in a bettered physiological state; the activities going on before the emotional stimulus appeared may be resumed under a condition of facilitation and reinforcement. An example of this occurs when a parent punishes a child: there may be immediate improvement noticeable in his whole behavior (but the reverse may also happen; the child may be thrown into a sullen state which might endure for some time). As a less ambiguous example, take the case of an individual working at a low ebb. He receives a letter containing a check which, while it blocks his activity for the moment, has as its post-emotional effect a tremendous influence upon the speed and accuracy of his work for the remainder of the day or even for a longer period. In general we may say that the effect of an emotion arousing stimulus upon the general level of activity may produce facilitation or the reverse; or it may leave the level unchanged. What result will occur depends upon a great many factors: the nature of the exciting stimulus, the individual's character, his general bodily state, etc.

Rôle of Emotion in Daily Life.—The main fact about emotion seems to be that the human organism is built to react in emotional ways. We stated in the beginning that those ways are inherited modes of action. Consequently it is not incumbent upon us as psychologists to give any detailed statement as to their biological serviceableness in keeping the race alive. We should be content with describing the facts and pointing out the rôle that emotion plays in our development and in our daily life. Of course, if one is terribly overawed by Darwin, one cannot rest until he has pointed out in detail the utilitarian value of every reaction. We are inclined to believe that in both instinct and emotion there are many part reactions which are of no adaptive value to the organism whatsoever. We find here what we shall find more strongly emphasized in our discussion of instincts, namely, that if the organism possesses enough hereditary structures and modes of reaction to enable it to get along in its environment, the process of evolution (selection or elimination) allows it to possess many luxuries in the way of reaction possibilities.

We do not mean to assume by these precautionary remarks that emotions are without significance in daily life. We would emphasize the point that they can and do exist whether biologically they are *always* useful, or useful only at times. (1) Even though they were mere luxuries, so far as biological fitness is concerned, they keep the individual from existing as a machine that runs the same way everyday. They give him his ups and downs, make the exact prediction of his acts more difficult (troubling the psychologist and psychiatrist thereby), and in general make him a more delightful personality with whom to work, fight and play. The world would be a sorry place indeed, from an artistic and human standpoint, if the distress of the child, of the weak and downtrodden move no eye to tears. Fame and ambition would be sorry crowns if the multitude were not moved to acclaim. If all hearts were calm, the great artists would have lived in vain. In a sense society hangs together because of the possibility of emotional rapprochement. (2) As regards their effect upon the possibilities of the achievement of the individual, we are inclined to agree with William James in his *Energies of Men,* that in very exceptional cases the heightened state which comes *after* a great emotional crisis may bring about a degree of achievement that could not be dreamed of at the ordinary working level of the individual. Poe, De Quincey, Byron, Goethe and George Sand would probably never have produced their masterpieces under a humdrum régime. One can take selected cases and marshal an imposing array of such instances. On the other hand, one must preserve one's balance in making the assumption that because a few geniuses have produced great works under heightened emotional tension, such exalted states make for or produce genius. The point seems to be that occasionally under a great tension all part reactions hang together and mutually facilitate one another— every asset and every resource of the individual, as long as the effect of the emotional state persists, are marshaled for the work in hand. Such occasions are rare. The next emotional shock might as its after-effect leave the individual trembling, enervated and flat; totally incapable of accomplishing anything except the merest routine. We all know from our own diaries of ourselves that under ordinary circumstances if we have a fine piece of work to do, a championship game to play, a delicate piece of apparatus to manipulate, a fine surgical operation to perform, we would not willingly expose ourselves to any strong emotional situation; and yet the brilliancy of our performance might be increased thereby. Certainly in history such achievements have been accomplished under such conditions. Possibly the sheltering which comes from civilization has built up an attitude of timidity, thereby lessening our readiness to take the chances which our predecessors had to take. Society more and more guards against the presence of strong emotional stimuli, since the weak and possibly even the individual of average ability cannot withstand their effects, however well the genius may thrive under their influence.

It is true that the illustrations in which we see the bad effects of emotional shock have been chosen from activities that demand gross, explicit forms of adjustment. Would the case be different with more constructive language types of activities? Would the plan of a novel, the writing of a poem, the painting of a masterpiece, the composition of a great opera, be facilitated, or the reverse, by producing in the artist some great emotion? We shall hazard no answer. (3) In observing the daily life of a great many individuals, we seem to see the following factors at work: One individual has reached a low level of adjustment; he can typewrite so many words a minute, or telegraph so many words a minute, or make so many entries in his journal: if this low level of adjustment gives the individual his daily bread, he does not depart from it. His social relations at home and on the outside are on the same dead level. His emotional attitudes are stereotyped. One takes the attitude of suffering at everything; another the religious attitude; still another the hard-done-by, and the downtrodden attitude. There seems to be a wall around these people. Is there no way of breaking through this wall and getting the individual to reach a higher level of achievement? Emotionally exciting stimuli occasionally seem to accomplish it. The sudden accession of responsibility or wealth; the enforced demands which come with marriage and the rearing of a family; sometimes even a strong rage or fear, may break through the stereotyped and habitual mode of response, and arouse the individual to the point where he can accept and profit by intensive training (acquisition of greater skill in his field) and eliminate his errors, work longer hours, and plan his work in a more systematic manner.

Practical Study of Emotion and Control of Emotional Reaction.—At the present time as never before, individuals representing authority or control over developing human beings are striving to find out enough about the normality and abnormality of emotional life to be of help in shaping that phase of the character of those under them. By individuals representing authority we mean explicitly the parent, the physician, the teacher and the employer.

Before attempting to be of help to others in the control of emotional reactions and attitudes, it would seem to be the most logical procedure to examine for a time one's own emotional equipment. The simplest way for the student just beginning psychology to approach this problem is for him to make a study of his own emotional reactions. All the student is asked to do here is to note his own activities from moment to moment. He should begin to keep a diary of his day: What stimuli most usually call out emotional activities; do these activities show the more infantile type of phenomena that we see in fear, rage and love, or is there only a change in level? What are the immediate and the more remote effects upon efficiency and learning? Naturally, we should include here as a part of his total activity *thinking, planning,* since these processes show the functioning of language organization. He should determine whether the number of emotional rises are increasing in number, whether they are becoming more stereotyped and consolidated into attitudes, or whether they are decreasing as he becomes better balanced and adjusted. After such a study the student should come out with a much better estimate of his own character than he now has. Very few of us have faced ourselves (indexed our own reactions) in this way during the formative period of life, and we realize often too late that certain overemphasized attitudes have made life's adjustments very difficult for us. Some of the more serious defects in emotional adjustment (especially those connected with the sex life) will escape the student's own observation. Because of this it is extremely worth-while to have another person make systematic observations upon you, which must extend over some period of time. Our measure of normality or balance is not a mathematical or quantitative one, but a common-sense one.

From such studies we arrive at the conclusions: (1) that there is normal emotional adjustment; (2) that the majority of individuals are not perfectly balanced, but their weaknesses are so compensated for by other factors (habit) that it is safe to predict that no break-down will occur unless the crisis is very unusual or severe; (3) there are emotionally unstable individuals. So many wrong attachments and detachments have been made, so many unsafe outlets have been formed, so high or so low is the level of activity, so persistently do these levels appear and so easily are they provoked, that we cannot fail to conclude that the person exhibiting them is in need of medical attention—the advice of modern psychiatrist should be sought. The parent, the teacher and the employer are, however, brought face to face constantly with individuals belonging in this last class under conditions where it is not possible to obtain the advice of a properly trained psychiatrist. Some kind of practical safe and sane way of controlling these factors must be sought. After the unstable individual has been studied and the main factors connected with his lack of balance have been found out, there are two ways of possibly doing good without introducing the element of harm: (1) the environment may be altered; (2) the individual may be retrained.

Summary of Practical Aspects of Emotion.—Sometimes the conditions antecedent to emotional disturbance are quite simple when discovered. (1) There may be ordinary factors, such as wrong diet, overindulgence in certain foods, overeating, lack of regularity in sleep and insufficient sleep. It is assumed, of course, that the individual has been in the hands of a physician and that organic disturbances and deficiencies have been corrected as far as possible (including hyper- and hypo-activity of the glands of internal secretion). A change of routine often succeeds in bringing about the disappearance of the mal-adjustment. (2) In children especially there are factors of a very different character which can produce disturbances. The parents by giving way to the child, noting its every pain and woe, doing things for it which it should do for itself, failing to force it to form the early habits every child should put on (thereby putting it out of adjustment with its mates); now railing at the child and scolding it, the next moment displaying entirely too violent an attachment for it—this condition soon breeds a series of attitudes (dependence, inferiority, rage, depressions); which many times cannot be corrected until the child is removed from that environment. (3) As the child grows older, a still more complicated set of causal factors comes in. It is called upon to react to a world of situations connected with sex. They are made peculiarly sensitive to such situations by their own developing bodies. The stimuli from without are hurled at them in such conflicting ways that proper associations have no time to form, and there are no preëxisting organized channels for appropriate reaction. Wrong sex theories are built up; harmful attachments are made and poor outlets are formed. We have in mind here the complex conditions which are at hand around the age of puberty. The youths have to face a mass of sex stories and wrong conceptions of how children come into the world. Sometimes these come from associates of their own age, but often from older children who for the younger represent authority. Unless these theories are straightened out by the parents (or teacher or physician) they get out of touch with their environment. Most healthy children pass safely through this period; some, however, do not emerge unscathed. Improvement can be obtained in such cases if the parents are able to establish a perfect rapport with the child and to talk such matters out quite frankly. A true education process is begun. Appropriate systems or ways of responding to the sex situation are prepared. If the mal-adjustment has gone on for any great length of time, it may be necessary to remove the child for a time from the persons, places and things around which his poorly adjusted reactions cling. (4) One other especially trying period occurs when the young man and woman break home attachments and ties and leave a sheltered environment to face a world which they must build for themselves. They have their occupations to choose and master and their mates to select and adjust to. How they meet this new world depends very largely upon the emotional attitude they bring with them from the childhood and adolescent periods. If their repertoire includes the attitude of seclusiveness, suspicion and inferiority, or if the sheltering process has gone on too long, healthy adjustments of the type demanded are hard to form and actual psychoses may ensue. A process of retraining must take place. The factors involved in retraining belong in the chapter devoted to habit.

CHAPTER VII

UNLEARNED BEHAVIOR: " INSTINCT "

Introduction.—In our discussion of emotion we brought out the fact that there is no sharp line of separation between emotion and instinct. Both are hereditary modes of action. On page 194 we stated that in emotion the radius of action lies within the individual's organism, whereas in instinct the radius of action is extended in such a way that the individual as a whole may make adjustments to objects in his environment. While the radius of action in instinct is extended, the action at the same time is particularized—narrowed down to some specific form of adjustment, *e.g.,* nursing, wiping off an offending substance, grasping the covers or any small object with the hands, etc. If the above distinction could be made to apply wholly without exception it would be equivalent to saying that in emotion the action is *implicit mass action,* whereas in instinct it is *explicit definitized and localized action.* But in the previous chapter we found that while the reaction in emotion involved mainly a general response in the visceral motor and glandular side of the organism (implicit), movements of the striped musculature (explicit) were involved to some extent. Notwithstanding this exception, the distinction suggested above is serviceable. We can hardly escape the fact that in emotion the *implicit* factors predominate. We shall see from our present study that in instinct the action is *explicit* and capable of being observed in general without instrumentation. Probably every stimulus which leads to a definite instinctive act leads at the same time to some change in emotional tension. It seems easier to believe that emotion can occur without overt instinctive response than that instinctive action can occur without at the same time arousing emotional activity.

Definition of Instinct.—We should define instinct as an hereditary pattern reaction, the separate elements of which are movements principally of the striped muscles. It might otherwise be expressed as a combination of explicit congenital responses un-

252

folding serially under appropriate stimulation. The following is an illustration: At a fairly early age, the child will respond to a rapid threatening movement of the hand or some other object as follows: A definite sharp blink of the eyes (which does not appear until about the 100th day), an upward movement of the hands and a backward movement of the head. In every instinct of the more complicated type, we see that the human animal does the same thing, makes some kind of an adjustment. The fact accomplished (what he does) may or may not be adaptive. Many of the hereditary acts are, of course, adaptive, but many of them are non-adaptive and even anti-adaptive. William James has made some statements about instinct which are as nearly true now as when he wrote them:

"The actions we call instinctive all conform to the general reflex type; they are called forth by determinate sensory stimuli in contact with the animal's body or at a distance in his environment." And again: "The older writings on instinct are ineffectual waste of words, because their authors never came down to this definite and simple point of view, but smothered everything in vague wonder at the clairvoyant and prophetic power of the animals—so superior to anything in man—and at the beneficence of God in endowing them with such a gift. But God's beneficence endows them, first of all, with a nervous system; and turning our attention to this makes instinct appear neither more nor less wonderful than all the other facts of life."

The simplest way for those beginning the study of instinct is to look upon every definite act that the infant performs at an early age, and hence without learning, as an instinct. If the pure instinctive activities are to be isolated we must here also adopt the genetic method. In advance it may be said that if we look upon all untutored activity of the child as instinctive, we shall have to admit that man has a large repertoire of instincts, but we shall see that they are not all of the full-fledged pattern type. We do not see the very young infant fighting, running, swimming and burrowing, but we do find him performing a goodly number of less spectacular acts, some of which we shall soon describe. At a later age we do find the youth running, fighting, swimming and doing many other things that the animals do. We are not at this age dealing with pure instincts, however, but with instinct plus habit. The question is pertinent as to why we wish to make distinctions among the instinct, habit and emotional activities. The answer here as it was in the case of emotions is that such an abstraction is necessary if we are ever to be in a position where we can understand and use instinctive factors to the fullest extent. We shall by no means neglect the instinct-habit consolidation. We shall take up in detail such consolidations and show that they function very much as do "pure" instincts.

The Distinction Between Reflex and Instinct.—The term reflex is a convenient abstraction in both physiology and behavior. In clinical neurology we speak of testing a patient's reflexes such as the patellar, the movement of the pupil under the action of light, the adjustment of the lens, the plantar, etc. In physiology we speak of the reflexes connected with circulation, respiration, digestion, etc. We mean by reflex when used in this way that action takes place under appropriate stimulation in some fairly circumscribed glandular or muscular tissue. It is an abstraction because reflex action in the eye, the leg, hand or foot can never take place in isolation. Action is altered in other parts of the body as well. We brought some of these factors out in our discussion of the knee jerk. The clinician and the physiologist, however, are not interested for the moment in action in any part of the body other than in the particular motor organ which is under observation. Our schematic drawing on page 118 showed the fewest neural connections necessary for a reflex, but action of such simplicity never really takes place. The term reflex, however, is an extremely convenient one and by it we mean the simplest type of activity that can ordinarily be produced. Theoretically we might have a pure reflex if we were to stimulate a single neuro-fibrillar ending of an afferent neurone and had a single neuro-fibrillar strand of a motor neurone connected with a single muscle fiber. This dissection has never been made nor has any one been interested in making it. We defined instinct above as a "combination of congenital responses unfolding serially under appropriate stimulation." When we are interested in analyzing instinct into its lowest terms, it is simplest to look upon each such element of activity in the pattern as a whole as a reflex.   Loeb states, for example, that an instinct is a system of chained reflexes.   As a mere schematic outline of the instinct we have no objection to such a definition.

The Attempt to Classify Human Instincts.—No one as yet has succeeded in making even a helpful classification of instincts. It is far more difficult to make such a classification in the human realm than in the animal.   Fairly serviceable classifications in the animal world are food-getting, home-building activities, attack and defense, migration, etc.   In man there may be rudiments of many of these activities, but long before the organism is in a situation to exercise such integrations, habit has overlaid everything.   Such a classification as the above has been attempted for the human being, but without much success.   Another attempt at a classification is seen in the splitting up of hereditary instinctive action into positive reaction tendencies and negative reaction tendencies.   We give a separate discussion of some observations on this point on page 269.   Several efforts have been made to enumerate the human instincts.   The most noteworthy example of this is to be found in Thorndike.   In a serviceable way he describes the reaction and then defines the stimulus or situation to which the reaction is made.   We present this enumeration on page 275.   The difficulty with this method of procedure is due to the fact that we have not the genetic data at present to make either the enumeration accurate or the definition of the stimulus at all complete.   Only long and careful study by the genetic method will yield a scientific classification.   We shall show in a later paragraph some of the preliminary results which have been obtained by a genetic study of instincts.

Some of the Problems in Instinct.—A point which should be emphasized here is that in order to make a profitable study in the field of instincts we should come to it with a definite problem before us.   It is believed that when the human infant has been gone over more thoroughly from the standpoint of special interests, rational lines of cleavage in instinct will appear.   Instincts should be studied from the vocational, social, pedagogical and psy-

chiatric points of view. We might emphasize here just a few of
the definite problems which interest the behaviorist: (1) Is handedness congenital or merely social? If congenital, will any serious consequences result if left-handedness is changed to right-
handedness? (2) Are there important variations in instinctive
equipment? May these variations be made use of in the later
development of the child? It is believable, at least, that the positive reactions of the child may from earliest infancy point toward
definite vocational interests. His negative or indifferent reactions may be just as important factors. A good deal of popular
material has been collected upon this, but little of scientific value
has appeared. (3) It is just possible that we may succeed in
working out the life history of groups of instinctive activities in
such a way that an index may be obtained of the child's normality
of development at certain ages, since certain instincts appear
haltingly at first, ripen or develop, and then disappear. We know
very little about the types and level of behavior the child should
show at six months, at a year, and at two years, etc. The Binet
scale does not help us. (4) We should know enough about the
normal development and functioning of instinct to be able to
detect instinct distortions. We should know, for example, at
what point to break or socialize instinct by habit. We mention
here nursing, continence of urine and fæces, etc. (5) Sex differences in instinct—is there a differentiation of activity between
the male and the female child, or is the differentiation wholly
social (such differentiation, of course, begins almost at birth).
This is involved in (2) above. Some material has been collected
upon this point, but not under wholly trustworthy conditions of
investigation.

What at present deters us from making the more circumscribed studies is the fact that we have really no orientation as
yet in the field. The first need is for a rough survey of a useful
kind. Such a survey should be made upon more than one child
and under a better controlled situation than is to be found in the
ordinary home and school conditions. In the general section
below on the genetic study of instincts we summarize some of the
types of instincts which have been studied under reasonably con-

trolled conditions. This study must be looked upon merely as the beginning of the general survey suggested above.

THE GENETIC STUDY OF INSTINCTS

Early Sensory Responses.—A large number of observations have been collected in our laboratory upon the early sensory responses of infants. If the infant's breathing and hand movement are being recorded during sensory stimulation, evidences of sensitivity can be obtained. From birth the infant responds to loud noises, to the tearing of paper and to the scraping of one object upon another (Fig. 55, A). The responses have been partially considered under the emotion of *fear*—the catching of the breath, spasmodic movements of arms and legs and the closing of the hand are the responses to be observed. Sensitivity to tuning forks and other musical instruments is not marked. Unless placed very close to the ear or made very loud, no response can be obtained. Similar undifferentiated responses have been obtained by stimulating with different olfactory substances, such as oil of peppermint, asafœtida, butyric acid and ammonia (Fig. 55, C). Most of the responses were obtained from substances which stimulate the fifth nerve, which is a tactual nerve. No very sure results have been obtained from the milder perfumes. Pinching, sticking with a pin, warm and cold objects, twisting and turning of a joint (contact and kinæsthetic), all will produce changes in respiration and in the rate, amplitude and form of the movement curve obtained from the hands. Vision so far has been tested only with respect to the infant's ability to fixate a white light (page 264). This occurs at birth. Color sensitivity has not been tested. It can be determined, but only with difficulty.

The First Thirty Days of Childhood.—Infants often *sneeze* immediately upon being taken from the mother. *Hiccoughing* may begin after the first few hours. *Yawning* has been noted five minutes after birth. *Crying* is also one of the earliest responses. The birth cry occurs at the moment the respiratory centers are stimulated after birth. In some cases it is necessary to stimulate the infant with hot and cold plunges in order to start

17

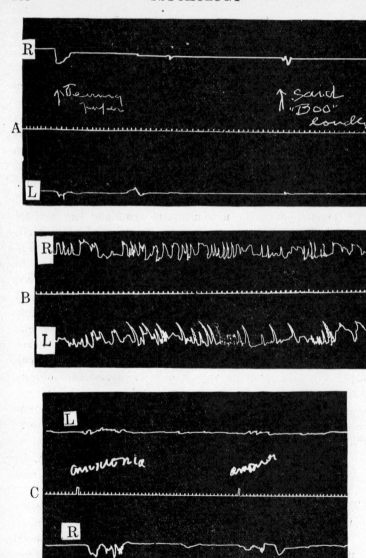

Fig. 55.—Showing wrist and arm movements under stimulation. A shows the arm reaction when auditory stimulus is given. The first stimulation was tearing paper. The second was the word "Boo" said loudly. B is a graphic record of the left and right wrist and arm movements during "free" activity. C is the reaction of the right and left wrist and arm movements to two faint ammonia stimulations. (Infant less than one day of age.)

breathing. The cry often comes an instant after the infant touches the water. The mechanisms involved in the *erection of the penis, voiding of urine* and *defecation* are functional at birth or very shortly thereafter. *Tears* apparently are shed within the first few hours after birth. Children, however, often fail to shed tears until several days after birth. Some dates are as follows: *S* showed dampness in corners of eyes after crying on the 13th day; *L* on the 15th, crying with a copious flow of tears on the 34th day. *Smiles* are rare at an early age. Under observation some first dates are as follows: *S*, 4 days; *O'K*, 7 days; *K*, 8 days; *C* smiled repeatedly on the 28th day. Tickling under the chin and stroking other parts of the body will occasionally bring out a smile. Children at an early age can *turn the head* when placed face down on a pillow. *C*, 30 minutes old, rotated her head in such a way as to leave her mouth and nose free. Several other infants did equally well at 1½ hours of age. *Raising the head* may occur at any time after birth. These head movements appear most clearly if the infant is supported by placing the open hand under the stomach and supporting its back with the other hand. In observed cases subjects ranging from 2 to 15 days could support their heads for times varying from one to six seconds. *Hand movements: Spreading of the fingers* and *closing* of the hands occur at any time after birth. *Repeated movements of many kinds are made with legs, feet and toes.* It is often asserted that babies can cling with their toes, but this has not been observed. *Kicking with the legs and slashing with the arms are almost continuous during active moments from a few minutes after birth. Turning over:* Subject *T* at 7 days turned repeatedly from face to back when not impeded by clothing. *Stretching:* Begins very early in life and varies from a mere raising of the arm to a complete stretching of the legs and toes, arching of the back and abdomen, etc. (Summarized from Mrs. Blanton's study).

Some Instincts Singled Out for Study.—(1) *Nursing.* If either cheek or the chin is touched lightly with the finger, an infant shortly after birth will move the head in such a way as to bring the mouth in contact with the finger. In deep sleep it apparently disappears. After feeding it is also very hard to elicit.

During hunger it is very easy to elicit, the infant often moving with such surprising quickness that it catches the finger in its mouth. Again, if one taps lightly above or below the corner of the mouth of a sleeping baby the lips are pursed into a nursing position; occasionally the tongue will protrude and complete suck-

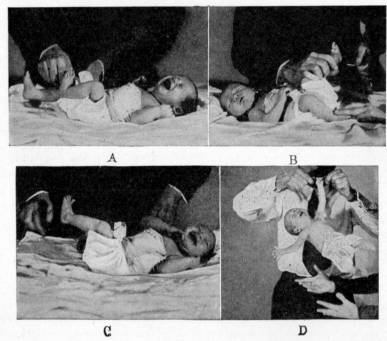

Fig. 56.—Showing some infant reflexes. A, defensive reflex with left foot to slight pinch on inner surface of right knee. B, stimulation for Babinski. The blunt end of a match is rubbed across the sole of the foot. The result is shown in C. The great toe shows extension, whereas the small toes show "fanning" or flexion. (This is a very variable reflex so far as the pattern is concerned.) D shows the grasping reflex (infant 12 days old.)

ing movements will appear. Children a few hours after birth seem to be able to get the fingers and hands into the mouth. The sucking instinct as a whole seems to be well coördinated by the end of the first half-hour. The series of reflexes as a whole is made up of tongue, lip and cheek movements, swallowing being the final link in the chain of activities. Although the evidence is not complete as yet, failure in the ability to swallow is suggestive

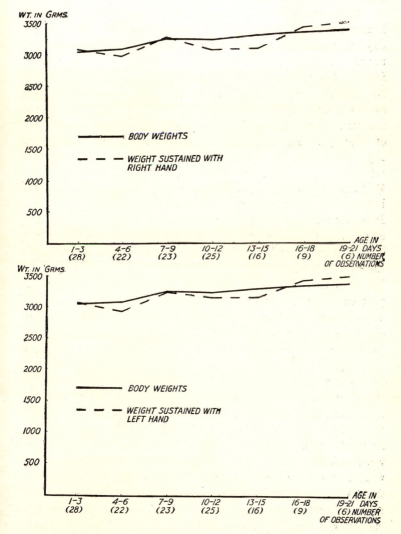

Fig. 57.—Showing the strength of the grasping reflex for the first 21 days.   The curves show that the strength of the right and left hand is approximately equal.

of retardation. Children born of defective parents seem to have
difficulty with swallowing.

(2) *Grasping reflex.* Records of tests on approximately one
hundred babies in Baltimore ranging in age from birth to 150
days show that the grasping reflex is present in practically all
normal cases. There have been only three or four exceptions
found. The method of testing the babies is shown in Fig. 56, D.
Not all babies will support the full weight. Most of them, however, will support the full body weight for a longer or a shorter
time and with either hand. The results for the first twenty days
of infancy are shown in Fig. 57. Our records from the twentieth
day onward are not yet complete, but samplings show that the
reflex is present in more or less perfect form up to about the
120th day or longer. It seems to give way about the time the eye-
hand coördination is formed. This habit is discussed on page 296.
In abnormal cases, rickets, mal-nutrition generally, oversupply
of fat, illness, etc., the reflex is apparently lacking. In one baby
born without a cerebrum the reflex was practically perfect up to
the day of its death at 18 days.

(3) *Right- and left-handedness.* This method opens up the
problem of testing whether handedness is an instinct or a socially
acquired habit. Those babies which will support their full weight
on any given day will cling for a longer or a shorter time with
either the right or the left hand. A wide series of records has
been kept and a large number of babies has been followed through
day by day, but the application of statistical method shows that
there is not any steady predominance in either right or left hand
in the length of suspension. The problem of handedness has also
been attacked in another way. The baby is laid flat on its back;
its hands are attached by means of a linen thread to two pivoted
writing levers in practically frictionless bearings. No matter
whether the infant moves its hand down or up, to the right or to
the left, or to any intermediate position, a vertical tracing is
recorded upon a smoked drum. Fig. 56, B, shows such a tracing. It was hoped by this method to obtain a constantly greater
or less amount of activity with either the one or the other hand
in a given period of time. In making the test both the random

activity (intra-organically aroused) and activity extra-organically aroused by midline contact stimulation were recorded. The method has not as yet yielded any very decisive results. Although the child is stripped it is almost impossible to keep it lying in such a way that the one or the other hand is not given more or less freedom. Still another method for determining handedness has been tried, namely, the anthropometric one of measuring the diameter of the right and left biceps, the length of the left and right forearms from the elbow to the second joint of the middle fingers. The preliminary report of this method shows that the right biceps is larger and the length of the right forearm is slightly greater than the left. These results probably cannot be trusted. We are thus left without conclusions as to the problem of handedness. In early infancy there is certainly no preferential use. The early habit coördinations, too, seem to form about as readily with the left as with the right hand, and yet we know that so far as adult activity is concerned, about 96 per cent. of individuals are right-handed.

(4) *Defense movements.* Early defense movements have been rather thoroughly tried out in a large number of infants, but by a very crude method. The nose is lightly pinched and the length of time it takes the child to touch the experimenter's fingers is recorded. A few sample records are given:

B. 4 days. Hands went up at once, and pushed at experimenter's fingers in three seconds.

H. 12 days. Movement started rapidly. Struck experimenter's fingers in three seconds.

BE. 3 days. Right hand struck experimenter's fingers in 18 seconds on the first trial, 2 seconds on the second trial.

T. 8 days. Struck experimenter's fingers with the right hand in 3 seconds and with the left in 4 seconds. On the next trial, struck first with the left hand in 5 seconds, with the right in 6.

Another interesting defense movement may be noted as follows: If the baby lies on its back with legs extended and the inner surface of one knee is lightly pinched, the opposite foot is brought up almost with the regularity seen in the reflex frog. (Fig. 56, A, shows the reflex.)

T. 8 days. Left knee pinched. Right heel struck experimenter's fingers in 3/5 second. Right knee pinched. Left heel struck experimenter's fingers in 20 seconds. Several abortive attempts were made.

M. Less than one day. Pinched left knee. Right foot struck in 35 seconds. Pinched right knee. Left foot struck in 48 seconds.

H. 5 days. Pinched left knee. Right foot failed to reach experimenter's fingers. When right knee was pinched, the left foot struck in 10 seconds.

These are only samples of a very large number of records. The records as a whole run closely similar to these samples. It will be noticed that we have here an interesting opportunity to study rapidity of habit formations in even the one-day-old infant. Such experiments have not yet been conducted. The pinching is never made severe enough to produce any mark and there is not the slightest injury or danger in making the experiment. In fact, it may be made to serve as a very useful exercise at the hands of a considerate experimenter.

(5) *Absence of swimming movement.* Some speculation has been entered into as to whether the new-born infant would show coördinated swimming movements (see recapitulation theory, page 287). Some definite experiments have been carried out a few minutes after birth. A small galvanized iron tank was filled with water to a height of about ten inches and maintained at the body temperature in readiness for the test. After breathing was established, the infant was lowered slowly into the water and supported on the back by the experimenter's hands. Violent expression of fear—a cry, checking of breathing followed by deeper inspiration and rapid, entirely uncoördinated slashing of hands and feet were all that could be observed. In making the test the greatest care was used not to let the baby's head sink so low as to allow water to enter the nose or mouth. The infant's behavior is in marked contrast to that observed in certain other young mammals, some of which swim moderately well the first time they are placed in the water.

(6) *Orientation to Light.*—The following experiment was

made on approximately 20 children at varying ages from birth to several days of age: the child was laid flat on its back and its head held horizontally by means of two cotton-wool pads. Immediately above the head was fastened a perimeter, the radius of which was one-half meter. A small carriage bearing a light could be made to travel from one portion of the perimeter to another. The position of the light immediately above the baby's eyes was called the zero position. From that position the light could be carried to any desired number of degrees to the right or to the left. The tests were, of course, carried out in the dark room. The light was just bright enough for the dark-adapted observers' eyes to note whether or not orientation occurred. Two observers had to agree that it had occurred. A few sample records only are offered. The times given represent the interval from the moment the light was exposed until orientation occurred:

Infant *B*, 14½ hours old:
    10 degrees to the left, 15 seconds;
    10 degrees to the right, 10 seconds;
    15 degrees to the right, 12 seconds;
    15 degrees to the left, 6 seconds;
    25 degrees to the left, failed in two trials;
    25 degrees to the right, failed.

In the last two cases, of course, the extent of the eye movement demanded is so great that it was not expected that the child could attain it.

Infant *C*, 17 hours old:
    10 degrees to the right, 15 seconds;
    10 degrees to the left, 13 seconds;
    20 degrees to the left, cried and closed eyes in two trials;
    20 degrees to the left, 30 seconds (after a slight rest in the light);
    10 degrees to the left, 5 seconds;
    20 degrees to the right, 12 seconds; the right eye turned perfectly, but the left did not seem to follow synchronously.

Similar tests were carried out with perimeter swung so that the object would appear in the upper and lower meridians. Naturally the infants do not make these movements so well.

Definite orientation was not found in every trial, but in a group of twenty or more infants selected at random, one infant 17 hours of age, and one other that never could be kept awake long cnough to make the tests failed to give positive results. In many cases the infants would go so fast asleep that the tests on any given day would have to be abandoned.

We thus see that the child at birth has at least a well developed mechanism for turning the eyes toward the lighted half of the visual field. That true fixation occurs is not maintained. That we are dealing here with a native mechanism is probable, since the infants had had little opportunity in their darkened room to form visual habits. The true fixation of people's faces and definite objects in a well-lighted room occurs at a much later date; at just what date has not been determined upon any large number of children.

(7) *Blinking.*—Blinking, which may be considered a part of the general avoiding movements, and which in older children and adults is followed by the backward throw of the head and preparatory movements for stepping backward, is not present at birth. A number of children have been consistently tested for the purpose of determining its incidence. Some random examples are given here:

S. 174 days, perfect.
W. 72 days, absent.
Y. 47 days, absent.
B. 55 days, absent.
Y. 75 days, slightly present.
B. 83 days, present on half of the tests.
F. 124 days, present.

Lee, one of the youngsters most carefully tested, blinked twice on the 87th day; would not blink on the 127th day; on the 129th day blinked on the first two stimulations, but failed on the next four. On the 136th day, blinked at every stimulation, eight times. Thus, in her case, blinking was not firmly established until the 136th day.

The earliest the reflex has been noted is at 55 days. It seems to vary as a rule between 75 and 120 days, although this has not been very accurately determined. There seems to be, too, a developing or ripening period.

(8) *The Babinski Reflex.*—The Babinski has been tried out

several hundred times, but at present we are not prepared to give any detailed report of the life history of this reflex. At birth and for some months thereafter if the sole of the foot of the infant is stroked with the blunt end of a match (Fig. 56 B), the great toe shows extension, whereas the small toes "fan" or else show flexion as in the adult. The total result is shown in Fig. 56, C. The reflex is connected by physicians with lack of medullation in the pyramidal tract. It is assumed that as soon as medullation is complete in the tract the reflex disappears. As a whole the pattern of the reflex is a very variable one.

(9) *Crawling.*—Whether crawling is an inherited pattern reaction is, we should say, somewhat doubtful. Our results again are not as yet secure. If an infant from birth is put down upon a thin mat fastened tightly to a table top, it will at the end of ten minutes have slightly changed its position. Very shortly after birth a *regression* of as much as four inches has been noticed. Long before anything like the coördinated movements of legs and arms that are so necessary in the complete set of crawling movements occur, slashing movements of legs or arms or of both will throw the infant's trunk to the right or to the left. Systematic tests were begun upon L at 87 days of age. The method in general was as follows: A single cotton blanket was stretched tightly to a table top. A small piece of wood was then pushed up against the feet. In a minute or two she had pushed this away as far as the toes would reach. This position was then marked. A piece of candy was put in front of her face. On the 87th day, "climbing" movements with the legs were fairly well coördinated. The right leg would struggle forward and then the left; then one or both would be kicked out. The hand and arm movement showed no coördination. No advance was shown up to the 115th day. Definite progress was noted on that day in the use of the arms. There was some slight use of the elbows. The fore part of the body was considerably raised. From the 87th day on, the head was well raised for the first two or three minutes. It would gradually sink down. On the 115th day, she made a forward progress of two inches in nine minutes. Circus mo-

tions were present, and the body would be rocked from side to side. This rocking movement seemed to net the gain rather than the progressive movements of the legs and arms. On this date for the first time, she grasped the blanket ahead of her and apparently pulled herself slightly forward. Even on the 220th day crawling was not much further advanced, although she had been tested every week from the 87th day. At that time the experiment had to be discontinued. (The mother reports that one week after the above date this baby began to crawl, and during that week she learned to pull herself up by holding on to objects.) Subject N at the end of 163 days had made little more progress. T, a fine, well-developed baby, at 182 days had not learned to crawl, although on that date she had learned to stand alone, supporting herself on the bars of the crib after her mother had helped her up. F, another well-developed baby, up to 131 days had not made the slightest effort to crawl. When placed upon the mat he would usually lie still with head resting on the table and with the left cheek down. Feet and arms were sprawled out. M, the son of one of the instructors, was watched very carefully for the first ten months of his life. On the 280th day, the infant took hold of a side of its bassinet and raised itself to its feet for the first time. This he practiced incessantly for a week, standing for as long a time as he could, then sitting down to rest and then repeating the process. This general method of reaching out for an object, pulling himself up to it if it were fixed, standing up, sitting down, reaching out again, gave him a method of locomotion, but he did not crawl in the ordinary sense. When placed on the floor in the crawling position on the 284th day, he began to twist and turn, to sit up and roll over, and to go through any movement which would produce locomotion except crawling. Crawling in this child was never an instinctive process. Two other children of my colleagues never crawled in the ordinary sense of that term. M had a system all her own. Locomotion was effected practically by the use of her left arm, which she very speedily learned to use without making circus movements. This endured up to the walking period at 380 days. J adopted a most curious and unusual method of locomotion. He would sit up, put his hands forward on the floor and slightly raise and slide his body along. He would come to a rest and again reach out his hands and repeat the process. He became very adept in this, moving at no mean speed. His success probably delayed his walking, which did not take place until he was 510 days of age. Even after learning to walk, when he was in a hurry he would resort to the more primitive method of locomotion. While we do not affirm that crawling may not have a definite time of appearance and that it is not a definite instinctive pattern in some cases, we are prepared to affirm that it is *not* anything like as prevalent an instinct as is commonly supposed. Walking has not yet been brought under observation in our laboratory.

(10) *Positive and Negative Reaction Tendencies.*—The method of making tests on this very important subject is to establish first the eye-hand coördination. This is done usually by means of a stick of old-fashioned red striped peppermint candy. When this was established perfectly, the infant was offered a series of objects to which it had not reacted before. Some test cases are given: L completed eye-hand coördination at about the 129th day. She reached for stop watch, dark ink eraser (136 days), pipette with red bulb and for candle (150 days). The reaction to the candle was most pronounced. She held out both hands for it and reached out as far from her mother's lap as was possible. She was tested with a round metal ball and reached for it immediately. Attention has already been called to the fact that this child reacted positively to small animals. On the 169th day, she was tested for the presence of the washing or wiping reaction (so-called instinct of cleanliness). We first rolled up a ball of library paste, making it just as sticky as possible. After it had been warmed in the experimenter's hands it was offered to her on a piece of paper. She took hold of the edge of the paper with both hands, but did not roll the paste down to her hand. The paste was then held out to her between the experimenter's fingers. She caught it at once with both hands and carried it to her mouth. She was checked and her hands were washed. She repeated the reaction on the next trial. On the third trial

she *manipulated it with her fingers,* fixating the process with her eyes very continually. She did not attempt to put it into her mouth. With one piece in her right hand, she reached out for an additional piece with her left hand. There was not the slightest tendency to wipe off her fingers and hands. A cake of wet soap was next offered her. She reached for it with both hands. She rubbed her fingers up and down on it and tried hard to grasp its slippery surface. She reached her head forward and downward and tried to get her mouth to the soap. She tried hard to grasp it first with the right hand, then with both hands, and made peevish, querulous sounds when she failed to get hold of it. There was not the slightest avoiding tendency, or wiping or washing tendency present. A large bunch of cotton wool was held out to her. She reached for it first with the left hand and then with the right, smiling as she stroked it. She reached for it repeatedly. A smooth thick piece of glass, a lens without mounting, was held out to her. Her reactions to it were much like those made to the soap. Positive reaction tendencies were observed to an electric light bulb and to many other small objects. She played with a bunch of violin bow hairs in much the same way that she had played with the cotton wool. In her case at the ages studied, it will be seen that practically no avoiding tendencies were instinctive. We can summarize as is generally done and say that once the reaching coördination has been formed, infants respond positively to nearly all small objects which are given a high stimulating value by moving them.

No definite avoiding tendencies have been noted at this age, except those mentioned under *blinking* and *defense reactions.* These tests have been repeated upon two other children of approximately the same age who had never previously been stimulated by such objects. The whole series of tests would be pointless if habit formation had been present with respect to these objects.

Theory of Positive and Negative Reaction Tendencies.— Although we are not prepared to insist upon it we are inclined to believe that man is originally endowed with various kinds of positive reaction tendencies, but with few negative reaction tendencies. The few negative tendencies are to be seen in the "avoidance'' of loud-sounding objects, the struggle to escape from those which excite rage and fear generally, and the guarding or fending movements used in connection with any object or person that tends to injure the subject's own tissue.   In addition there are many objects which are not reacted to at all, or reacted to only with the eye, for example, such as objects too far away to reach, etc.   Taken as a whole, however, the child reacts positively to hundreds of objects where it reacts to one in a negative way. Negative reaction tendencies (with exceptions noted) as we see them are the products of training such as we see in conditioned reflexes or training of the most highly integrated and associated types.

We are inclined to think that as the individual grows older persons, places and things tend to become generally associated with organic responses of one kind or another and to some extent specifically with those connected with love (page 221).   The individual cannot usually put the connection in words; he cannot state, for example, why he reacts positively to this person or thing but negatively to that person or thing.   We might state the general theory of positive and negative reactions very much as we stated it in 1914.   Every object either by virtue of the original constitution of the individual or through associative connections of one kind or another (conditioned reflex or habit) calls out, in addition to the ordinary overt or delayed response in the striped musculature, a definite and complex group of reflex activity in the erogenous zones.   When thus stimulated this area may according to the way in which it has been excited arouse two fundamental kinds of impulses, (1) a group connected with tumescence, rhythmical contractions of other muscular tissue, and with increases in the quantity of the various secretions. This group, if functioning alone, would lead to the positive seeking movements, and ultimately to the unfolding of the instinctive mechanism of the act of reproduction.   (2) A group connected with detumescence inhibition and relaxation of other muscular tissue and with inhibition of secretions.   These impulses gaining the motor centers would, if no inhibitory factors were present, release the movements of avoidance.   In order to make this matter

definite, let us turn to animal psychology and take the neuro-
physiological situation at the moment of sex excitement.

When a definite sex object (female) appeals to any distance
receptor, the eye or the ear of the male (granting a certain
physiological condition of the animal, *i.e.*, the proper season
of the year, period of sex excitement, etc., in general; since
seasonal rhythms are not so marked in the male, the animal
must be in a receptive condition for such stimuli), at least two
sets of arcs begin to function: (*a*) one leading from the distance
receptor (aroused by the sex object) to the striped muscles, tending to produce a heightened tone in the skeletal muscles; (*b*) the
other, leading likewise from the distance receptor, passes out
(via the white rami) to the appropriate sympathetic ganglia.
When these neurones are stimulated changes are produced in the
circulatory, glandular, secretory and muscular mechanisms, possibly of the character described in (1) above. As soon as these
effectors are thrown into activity, they set up a characteristic
group of afferent impulses which upon reaching the motor centers
complete the initiation of *overt-seeking* movements. When the
situation is prolonged and contact receptors become stimulated by
the result of the seeking movements, the complex sex act follows.
On the other hand, if the general physiological condition is
different (organism not receptive to sex stimuli), there again
arises (*a*) an increased tonus in the striped muscles and (*b*)
activity in the sympathetic mechanisms, but in this case there
is a checking of secretion, lack of tonicity in the muscles, etc.
(2 above), which arouse in turn a definite group of afferent
impulses that tends definitely to set free the *avoiding reaction*.
Since the mechanisms involved in sex are fundamental, it seems
reasonable to suppose that every object, either instinctively or
through habit, tends to throw them into one or the other form
of action of which we have just spoken.

Certainly many objects (non-emotion producing stimuli,
stimuli distantly or not at all connected with sex) do not in
the beginning arouse these groups, *but through the ordinary
mechanism of habit and the formation of conditioned reflexes
come later to arouse faintly or overtly the one or the other.* There

is evidence in sexual pathology to show not only that such habit connections are formed, but also that they can become more fundamental than the primal instinctive pathways, as is shown in the use of phallic symbols, fetishes, etc.

This theory has been objected to on the ground that it seems unduly to emphasize the instinctive factors connected with love. It in a way maintains that action is determined and evaluated by such factors. But our use of the term love here is entirely different from that ordinarily employed. We use the term in the modern way in which it is used in psycho-pathology. Nearly every one will admit that there are such factors at the bottom of home life, in our general social life and even in our vocations. We work long hours, try to improve our position and bring in more money, in order that our home life may be carried out upon a broader scale. The activities centered around loved objects and persons from infancy to old age are easily the most important factors in our life as a whole. It is no wonder that our acts should be connected with and evaluated by such a reference as we have indicated (the connections lying usually below the language level).

The Order of Appearance of Various Instincts.—While the field of animal instincts has been worked over with a good deal of care with respect to the time of appearance, time of disappearance, and the cyclical character of inherited activities, no one has as yet made a similarly careful study of the temporal aspects of instincts in man. We have some data upon this subject, as was brought out in our genetic study. The principle can at least be illustrated, *e.g.*, by the grasping reflex which appears at birth, increases in definiteness and disappears, probably gradually, at about 120 days; by blinking, which does not appear until about the 100th day and which endures for life; and by the final group of instincts connected with the sex acts proper (coition), which appears at puberty and continues indefinitely. As a rule, an instinct shows a waxing or developmental stage which may be short or extend over some time. In those instincts which die out after a time there is probably a similar waning period. The sex instinct illustrates (but none too well) the periodical or cyclical character of instincts. It is about the only example of it we find in man if we neglect the periodic functioning of the vegetative instincts. We see the cycles in instinct very clearly in the animal world in those activities connected with nest building, migration, hibernation, etc.

When the instinct-habit consolidations, discussed on page 238, are considered, some interesting pedagogical and moral conclusions are often drawn. William James has expressed this idea in his own inimitable way in connection with the discussion of the transitoriness of instincts:

Leaving lower animals aside, and turning to human instincts, we see the law of transiency corroborated on the widest scale by the alternation of different interests and passions as human life goes on. With the child, life is all play and fairy-tales and learning the external properties of ''things''; with the youth, it is bodily exercise of a more systematic sort, novels of the real world, boon-fellowship and song, nature, travel and adventure, science and philosophy; with the man, ambition and policy, acquisitiveness, responsibility to others, and the selfish zest of the battle of life. If a boy grows up alone at the age of games and sports, and learns neither to play ball, nor row, nor sail, nor ride, nor skate, nor fish, nor shoot, probably he will be sedentary to the end of his days; and, though the best of opportunities be afforded him for learning these things later, it is a hundred to one but he will pass them by and shrink back from the effort of taking those necessary first steps the prospect of which, at an earlier age, would have filled him with eager delight. The sexual passion expires after a protracted reign; but it is well known that its peculiar manifestations in a given individual depend almost entirely upon the habits he may form during the early period of its activity. Exposure to bad company then makes him a loose liver all his days; chastity kept at first makes the same easier later on. In all pedagogy the great thing is to strike the iron while hot, and to seize the wave of the pupil's interest in each successive subject before its ebb has come, so that knowledge may be got and a habit of skill acquired—a headway of interest, in short, secured, on which afterward the individual may float. There is a happy moment for fixing skill in drawing, for making boys collectors in natural history, and presently dissectors and botanists; then for initiating them into the harmonies of mechanics and the wonders of physical and chemical law.

We are far from agreeing with James that in the above description he is dealing with instinct as such. He is rather

describing the changing situations that confront the developing youth, the onset and course of habit, the effect of social and
economic pressure, etc., than the transitoriness of instinct.

Lack of Pattern Instincts in Man.—No fair-minded scientific
observer of instincts in man should claim that the *genus homo*
possesses anything like the picturesque instinctive repertoire
of the animal. Yet even James maintains the contrary. If we
neglect the vegetative (including the sex act proper here) and
the direct life conserving functions, such as attack and defense,
there are few complete and perfect instincts in man yet observed.
Instinct and the capacity to form habits, while related functions,
are present in any animal in inverse ratio. Man excels in his
habit-forming capacities. So quickly are habits formed upon the
basis of whatever instinctive activity is present, that man is
usually accredited with as long a list of instincts as the animals.
We turn next to a consideration of this list.

Some Asserted Instincts in Man.—The following is a more
or less conventional list of human instincts. The account is taken
largely from Thorndike's *"Original Nature of Man."* While
there are certain additions of his own, the list was originally
compiled from Preyer, Schneider and William James. Not all
of the instincts listed by Thorndike are given here.

Acquisition and Possession.—To any not too large object and
to one which does not arouse fear, the original response is approach, or if the child is within reaching distance, reaching, touching, grasping. Then follows putting the object into the mouth,
or manipulation. To the situation of a person or animal grab-
bing or making off with an object which one holds or has near him,
the response is a tightening of the hold upon the article, pushing,
striking and screaming at the intruder.

It will be seen that reaching and grasping are put down as
part reactions. Reaching, grasping and release of object, while
they have instinctive elements, nevertheless must be tremendously modified by habit before they are of any service. See
the work on *Lee*, page 296, on reaching for the candy and
the candle.

Hunting.—To a small escaping object, man, especially if
hungry, responds apart from training by pursuit. When near
enough he pounces upon it and seizes it. If seized, he inspects,

manipulates and dismembers it. If the object is larger, he responds much the same way, only he is more likely to throw himself upon it and bear it to the ground, choke and maul it until it ceases to move.

No one has ever made any such observation as this. The only hunting we know anything about comes long after differential responses with respect to animals have been developed. Thorndike's description is undoubtedly true with respect to animals, but it is a mere word picture so far as human activity goes. I have seen infants and children and monkeys pull and rotate any moving organ of an animal, poke at the eyes, etc. By the time the infant is strong enough to really dismember an animal, the seizing-pulling-pouncing activities have been overlaid by habit, and oftentimes with distorted habits which go by the name of cruelty (unfortunately the limits of this volume do not allow us to treat of sadistic and masochistic tendencies). All that we can see in the "hunting" instinct until habit modifies it is a *positive reaction* towards certain objects dead or alive, and *manipulation*.

Collecting and Hoarding.—It is assumed that there is a "blind" tendency to take up any positively reacted to object and carry it home. This crystallizes into collecting and storing objects, such as money, marbles, string, tops, postage stamps, picture post-cards, valentines, etc.

If the psycho-analysts are to be believed, collecting and hoarding are indicative of a great many factors which are anything but instinctive. Our own comment is that there is little here which might be called instinctive. ⟨Children will grow up in a rather sheltered environment, with no tendency to collect or hoard. So far as we can observe, their reactions are more like those of the monkey: they do reach out and grasp and manipulate everything, but they drop or throw down the first object and reach for the next until the attendant is wearied. As soon as constructive habits are formed, hoarding may occur. It is usually, though, a struggle from infancy to get the child to keep its playthings collected. One of the hardest habits in the world to form is that of neatness—putting things back into the hoard, both as regards toys and personal belongings. The tendency is all the other way—toward the monkey, scattering type of behavior. With money the situation is much the same. Insurance statistics show that only about 4 per cent. of men at 60 years of age have "hoarded" capital enough to give them a living income for the rest of their expected lives. When children start out into the social group, they hoard what the others hoard. For one or two months the youngster's pockets are weighed down with marbles, two months later it may be tops. They usually collect whatever the group is actually using. Tops give way to roller-skating, an activity in which hoarding is certainly not essential. The earliest hoarding noticed in two children under our observation was of post-cards and letters from the parents and then from friends. But this was done under the very evident suggestion of the attendants.

Habitation.—We quote James: "There can be no doubt that the instinct to seek a sheltered nook, open only on one side, into which he may retire and be safe, is in man quite as specific as the instinct of birds to build a nest. It is not necessarily in the shape of a shelter from wet and cold that the need comes before him, but he feels less *exposed* and more at home when not altogether unenclosed than when lying all abroad. . . . Habits of the most complicated kind are reared upon it. But even in the midst of these habits we see the blind instinct cropping out; as, *e.g.*, in the fact that we feign a shelter by backing our beds in rooms with their heads against the wall, and never lying in them the other way."

There are a great many unanalyzed factors in James' statement. For example, he does not tell us at all what the situation is which leads to such acts. His observation of the way people sleep is certainly superficial. Babies and children apparently sleep just as well with the crib or bed in one location in the room as another; as they grow older the habit is formed of sleeping in such a way that vision is not obstructed. Vision is interfered with unless we back "our beds in rooms with their heads against the wall." Were it not to keep warm or cool, or to be protected from insects, animals and marauders, there would probably be exhibited no tendency to sleep in a bed in an enclosed place. The argument might be turned around just as well: "There is a strong instinct in man to keep away from all habitation and to sleep out in the open." Just as good a case can be made out for it. His whole description seems to be an endeavor to find something in the acts of the human being which corresponds to such acts in the animal. This is very curiously present in all writings on instinct. It is the opposite of the anthropomorphic description in animal behavior. There we try to make the animal into a human; here we try to make the human a lower animal.

Migration.—It is often asserted that there are two closely related but opposite instincts, one for migration and the other for domesticity. Upholders of these asserted tendencies cite the tramp. Says Flint (quoted from Thorndike) : "I have known men on the road who were tramping purely and simply because they loved to tramp. They had no appetite for liquor or tobacco, so far as I could find, also were quite out of touch with criminals and their habits; but somehow or other they could not conquer that passion for roving. In a way this type of vagabond is the most pitiful that I have ever known; and yet it is the truest type of the genuine voluntary vagrant—to reform him it is necessary to kill his personality, to take away his ambition—and this is a task almost superhuman. Even when he has reformed he is a most cast-down person."

The superficiality of this analysis is clearly evident. There are a great many factors mixed up which are more fundamental than any instinct towards migration, such as homosexuality, pederasty, the reaction against authority, etc. While it is true that a great many children, some as young as two and three years, begin to break bounds and to stay away for several hours at a time, and from seven years on begin to stay away at night, there are usually upon analysis complicating home factors, the example of older boys, etc., to be taken into consideration, which considerably weaken the argument for a pure migratory instinct.

Fighting.—Fighting is listed as one of the principal instinctive tendencies. We have already in part discussed this under emotions, page 239. Where the overt, explicit activity is emphasized, it is properly classed as an instinct, and an all-important one. It has been so well discussed in psychological literature that it need not detain us here.

Maternal Instincts.—Thorndike says: "To a woman who has given birth to a child, a baby to see and hold and suckle is perhaps the most potent satisfaction life can offer, its loss the cause of saddest yearning. To a woman who has given birth to a child, the baby she sees, holds and nurses appeals almost irresistibly when it gives a cry of hunger, pain or distress, the start of surprise, the scream of fear, the smiles of comfort, the cooing, and gurgling and shouting of vocal play."

A great many other psychologists also idealize the parental behavior in this way. To those who work in maternity wards the situation is sometimes seen to be quite otherwise. We have observed the nursing, handling, bathing, etc., of the first baby of a good many mothers. Certainly there are no new ready-made activities appearing except nursing. The mother is usually as awkward about that as she can well be. The instinctive factors are practically *nil*. The emotional activity of both parents may be intense, but this is often the result of many factors. The infant thus comes as a "loaded" stimulus. Very often the mother who is unshackled by social conventions behaves quite differently from the way she should behave if Thorndike's pictures were correct. Even in cases where the woman is duly married and there is no reason for a loading or a transfer of an emotional state of an adverse kind upon the child, little maternal behavior of the type described above appears. Society puts the strongest pressure upon a conventional attitude with respect to the proper care of the youngster and the emotional attitude which should be displayed with reference to it. We are not denying, however, that there are some instinctive factors here. It should be recalled that the nursing of the child and the fondling of it is not without a sex stimulating effect upon the mother.

There is a stronger and stronger tendency among educated women to break away from the sentimental drivel connected with the rearing of the child and to make a scientific problem of it. Just to the extent to which convention permits it, rationalization occurs. This is a strong argument that maternal behavior is not mainly instinctive. Rationalization does not mean that strong attachments of the type we have already discussed may not grow up between parent and child. But regardless of its ultimate analysis we should be the last to undervalue the tremendous rôle maternal behavior plays in society as a whole.

Gregariousness.—The activities displayed by children and adults brought about by the stimulus of being left alone are often called the gregarious instinct. The observed responses are wandering from place to place, restlessness, verbal complaint and actual seeking movements. If long continued the situation leads even the adult to break all bounds and to overcome many obstacles in order to mix with his fellow-man. Caste and social distinctions are broken down, and the most exalted person will fraternize with the humblest. When actually with the group the restlessness dies away even though the individual does not enter into any kind of social relation with his fellows, but merely idles along with them from place to place. Often the presence of a dog or a cat or of another human being far too young to serve as a real companion will suffice to cause the restlessness and seeking movements to disappear. Solitary confinement is one of the severest of punishments. These tendencies have been well worked out in McDougall's *Social Psychology* and in Le Bon's *The Crowd*. It is possible to analyze still further the instinct into simpler factors, but it is so well consolidated and so generally recognized (although there are many exceptions) that analysis seems to be out of place. Our cafés, boulevards, churches and county fairs are dependent upon it to a certain extent.

Other So-Called Social Instincts.—Social psychologists have overemphasized the instinctive factors in the activities enumerated below. Man is supposed to exhibit special instinctive tendencies in his *behavior to other human beings.* It is asserted that the human face is too early singled out by the child from all other objects for the process to be anything but instinctive. Our insight into the early functioning of the conditioned reflexes teaches us to expect that the baby would "single out" the person handing the bottle (or giving the breast) before all other persons. There are certainly very slight grounds for assuming instinctive factors here. Any object, a moving dancing manikin, for example, that could feed the infant, keep it dry and warm, pet it, etc., would be singled out just as early. Young ducks hatched out by the hen follow her around, single her out and learn her haunts, but surely no one would claim that there was anything more present than the following instinct plus habits which had been built up. Similar conclusions with respect to the lack of many instinctive factors must be drawn in the cases of the so-called *"attention getting," "responses to approving and scornful behavior," "mastering and submissive behavior," "display,"* etc. These are all important aspects of man's total behavior, but there seem to be no just grounds for assuming that the activities are carried out at the instinctive level. Undoubtedly just after birth conditioned reflexes begin to form with respect to the attendants and parents long before systematized habits begin to form. In other words, there is a genuine conditioned reflex level of functioning lying between the reflex-instinct level and the organized habit level. Many of the connections described in the older texts as instinctive are formed during this period. We have already shown how quickly and at what an early age children learn to control the parents' actions—crying when left alone, when put down in the dark, when put to bed, etc., is a favorite trick. Retching and vomiting at the *sight* of certain foods is another; going into a rage when something is taken away from it is another (the parent often returns the object, thus "giving way" to the child). This conditioning of activity occurs so early that it is no wonder many observers have created "attention-getting" and other instincts.

Imitation.—Psychologists and students of animal behavior generally are more or less divided in their opinion as to the presence of any function to imitate both in animals and in man. The analysis of the instinct has been very superficial. Thorndike's characterization of the stimulus and response is probably as accurate as any we have. It is as follows: *"Smiling when smiled at, laughing when others laugh, yelling when others yell, looking at what is observed, listening when others listen, running with or after people who are running in the same direction, running from the focus whence others scatter, jabbering when others jabber and becoming silent as they become silent, crouching when others crouch, chasing, attacking and rending what others hunt, and seizing whatever object another seizes."*

Manipulation.—This instinctive tendency is sometimes exalted by calling it constructiveness. That there is an original tendency to reach out for objects, to scrape them along the floor, to pick them up, put them into the mouth, to throw them upon the floor, to move back and forth any parts which can be moved, is one of the best grounded and best observed of the instincts. From our point of view this instinct to manipulate, even though it must be supplemented, as we brought out above, by certain habit factors, *is probably the most important of all original tendencies in view of the fact that nearly all later habit formations are dependent upon it.* When we say most important here, we are neglecting for the moment the instincts connected with bodily functions, as sex, the eliminative functions, etc. Curiosity is often listed as one of the important human instincts. The activities seen in curiosity are embraced in those connected with manipulation. Veblen, the economist, uses the instinct of workmanship as a pillar for his economic theories. It is doubtful whether there are any instinctive factors there which are not embraced in manipulation, positive and negative reaction tendencies, etc.

Other Asserted Instincts.—Other asserted instincts are *greed, kindliness, teasing, tormenting, bullying, cleanliness, adornment.* Further observation and analysis of these activities are necessary before it can be decided to what extent instinctive factors are present. Psychologists persistently maintain that *cleanliness* is instinctive, in spite of the filth of the negro, of the savage and of the child. It is a fight with most children from birth until the competition of sex occurs to get them to properly wash their hands and face and body as a whole, not to speak of smaller matters such as washing the ears, keeping the teeth brushed and the nails cut and cleaned. Even the adult, highly conventionalized individual omits his daily plunge and lets his beard grow when living in an unsocial environment. The functioning of the instinct is supposed to occur when slimy, sticky substances are grasped. Our own observations on this point are cited on page 269.

Play.—Play is a form of instinctive activity the stimulus to which is unquestionably in doubt. Play as a whole seems to be made up really of a variety of activities, all functioning more or less together. Manipulation is one of the most easily observable of the activities; then, too, there are rapid shifts of facial expression, vocalization, running toward and away from, crawling, hiding, etc. The activities under the influence of social factors soon become organized into the various games, or individual habit activity such as the making of mud pies, building with blocks, caring for, playing with and feeding small animals, etc.

We undoubtedly see in the play activities of children the embryonic activities of the adults, playing house, cooking, petting dolls, etc. Here the shaping or training activities of a parent are easily observable. If a young human were to grow up in isolation, it is probable that he would play, but the form of the play would, without doubt, be entirely different from that observed in children brought up under modern conditions of civilization. Kipling has with some skill pictured the growth of Mowgli, who was suckled by the wolf and brought up in the forest with animals as playmates.

Groos has advanced a biological theory of play. Play, according to him, is a biological tendency. The young animal engages in those functions which will be of service to it in later life. He sees in the running, jumping, tumbling, fighting, early sex responses, etc., the perfecting of those activities which the animal will use when the struggle for food, mate, etc., begins. This theory really has nothing to recommend it.

General Comments on the Above Instincts.—We are inclined to take the point of view here also that most of these asserted instincts are really consolidations of instinct and habit. In certain of them, such as manipulation, the original activities predominate. In certain others, e.g., adornment, hunting, habitation, etc., the pattern as a whole is largely composed of habit elements. It should again be reiterated here that so far as the functioning and value of these attitudes to the organism, so far as the rôle they play in daily life, so far as their backward and forward reference in the life history of the individual are concerned, it makes not a whit's difference what factors these capacities are analyzable into. The geneticist is likely to overemphasize the number of original tendencies; the psycho-analyst, to underestimate them. He reduces instincts almost as a class to a few stereotyped factors connected with the (from his standpoint, fundamental) sex phenomena. The fact of the matter seems to be that in most cases there is no need of detailed analysis of these attitudes. Those that we have cited and many others function as wholes in the daily lives of all individuals. They are as potent and real as if they were inborn and began to function in earliest infancy with all the completeness they exhibit in adult life.

The Instinctive Sex Responses.—The subject of the complete manifestation of the instinct of sex is too vast for brief treatment. We have already discussed some of the implicit factors in connection with the emotion of *love*, and indicated there how attachments (conditioned reflexes) might grow up to persons and objects that stimulate the erogenous zones of the child, as in bathing, rocking and petting. We are dealing here, though, with a primitive order of habits and not with instincts. There seems to be no original tendency to approach the sex organs with the hands as there is to approach the mouth. In some five hundred observations of infants varying in age from birth to three hundred days we have never seen any instinctive tendency on the part of the child to approach the sex organs with the hands. Observation shows that even when the child is pinched or scratched on the sole of the foot the tendency for the hand is always upward and toward the face and rarely downward. The finding of the sex organs seems to be something of a genuine discovery, like the finding of the feet and toes (which occurs, of course, much earlier—150 days). Once discovered, habits of distortion may possibly grow up. Undoubtedly there are a large number of purely instinctive responses connected with those organs.

The sex instinct as a whole has very many ramifications. Habits of the most varied kinds are built upon and around it. The study of the normal sex "sublimations" leads us into the whole field of human activity from folk-lore to philosophic and artistic productions. The study of sex perversions leads us very quickly into the field of the psychoses.

Inhibition and Control of Instinct.—The problems connected with the breaking down of instincts and their replacement by habit are of both practical and theoretical interest. Where instincts are distorted they must often be broken down before normal activities can be given an opportunity for development. Furthermore, many of the perfectly normal instincts must be brought under social control before the individual is prepared to mingle with his fellow-men. One of the earliest examples of the socialization of normal instinctive acts is illustrated by the teaching of the infant continence with respect to its eliminative functions. Here the instinctive activities are left intact so far as the pattern is concerned, but the situation for the release of these activities is made more complex. The mother starts the process of control very simply by taking the child to the toilet every two hours or oftener and leaving it there until those acts are performed, and then bringing it back to its more customary and normal environment. The association grows up rapidly in normal children. Thereafter, the intra-organic stimulus (pressure of urine and fæces) leads the child to make some sign, usually a vocal one, which stimulates the mother to gather it up and carry it to the proper place for the performance of those functions. As the child grows older, the pressure of such stimuli touches off the act of going to the proper place of his own accord. The extra-organic stimulation (the new situational factor, the sight and contact of the toilet) leads to the act of evacuation. There are thus a large number of habit activities built up around the instinctive function, but the latter as such is left practically untouched except for a momentary initial inhibition (sphincter control).

A case in which the pattern itself is altered to some extent can be illustrated most simply from animal life. The bird dog when taught to retrieve, at first instinctively bites the bird when he grasps it, especially if it is wounded and fluttering. It is often difficult to get this part of the pattern broken up. It can be done by filling the dead bird with pins. If the dog then mouths the bird at all severely, the points prick him and it is necessary for him to close down very gently indeed when he brings the bird in if he is to avoid pain stimulation. Dogs and cats often suck eggs, which is a purely instinctive function with dogs at least. They can be cured by filling the egg with quinine or

cayenne pepper. In these illustrations there is the actual breaking down of a part of the reaction pattern by reason of the
changes introduced into the stimulus. The stimulus becomes
other than it was. Instead of leading now to action a + b + c
+ d, for example, smelling at, licking the egg, cracking the shell
and lapping up the contents, it leads to action a + x, *i.e.*, to
smelling and avoiding. Some children suck the fingers instinctively from birth. If not corrected, it may continue long after
the infancy period. The most usual way of breaking the instinct
is to place something upon the fingers that will lead to another
reaction (quinine, pepper, etc.), or else to make the action impossible by putting a cardboard tube on the arm so that the elbow
cannot be bent. The instinct dies here because the act cannot be
completed. Society puts a good deal of emphasis upon right-
handedness. If handedness is instinctive as is most generally
assumed, we have in the breaking up of left-handedness a study
in the displacement of an instinct. Everything is offered to
the child's right hand, people shake hands with it with the right
hand, the parents place everything in such a way that the right
hand will be used much more frequently than the left. All habits,
then, are built up around the right hand and left-handedness dies
by inanition, *i.e.*, through lack of stimulation. Habits of a pernicious character are often as difficult to break up as are instincts.

Summarizing the general principle by means of which we
break up or control instinct, we may say that we may break up
an instinct by (1) arranging the environmental factors in such
a way that the instinct cannot take place; the organism is restrained to such an extent that although the movement is initiated, it cannot be completed. Examples, tying down the hand
of the child, muzzling the dog, harnessing the cow (to prevent
its sucking its own milk). While the animal is restrained, we
build up habits with respect to those objects which have hitherto
been instinctively reacted to—the burglar often feeds the watch-
dog in the daytime and speaks gently to him while the animal is
tied up, hoping that when released at night the friendly habits
with respect to himself will inhibit the instinct to rend and tear.
(2) On the other hand, we can *alter* the stimulus, as shown by

the illustrations of the doctoring of the egg, putting pepper on the baby's fingers, etc. The stimulus then touches off once at least and usually several times the old reaction, but the new elements added to the stimulus touch off something in addition to the old instinct pattern, *viz.*, an avoidance reaction, possibly also vomiting, hanging out of the tongue to cool it, etc. This phase of the stimulus may become so emphasized that the avoiding reaction may be the first to appear the next time the stimulus is presented.

In adult life the process of ''habituation'' is probably the most potent factor in eliminating especially the instinctive fear tendencies (even though many such reactions are conditioned, they are often fully as powerful factors as if they were native). The movie of a workman going out over a single iron beam twenty stories up from the ground produces many fear reactions on our part and sometimes nausea. If forced actually to walk such a beam suddenly yourself for the first time, it would produce fainting and falling without much question. When led gradually to it, it is soon done as readily as any other act. So with climbing to high places, rushing into burning buildings, taming lions and tigers, etc. Habit gradually makes the thing possible.

An interesting example of the breaking up of an instinct by experimental methods is cited by Partridge. On a visit to Central Park in New York he noted that the observers around the snakes' cage blinked and jumped back (defensive reflex) each time one of the cobras struck the glass. In order partially to duplicate the situation for an experiment on the breaking up of the instinct he set up a piece of heavy plate glass in front of his subjects and devised a mechanism which would release a rubber-faced wooden-headed hammer for striking against the glass. The hammer struck the glass at the level of the subjects' eyes. At first, of course, the subject blinked and drew back each time the hammer approached the eye. As the subject became more habituated to the situation inhibition occurred. The following figures refer to the number of times the wink was inhibited in each of a series of four hundred trials: 6, 14, 38, 65, 268, 352. That is, inhibition occurred only six times in the first four hundred trials, whereas it occurred 352 times in the last four hundred trials.

The Recapitulation Theory.—Under the influence of several non-biologically trained psychologists, a rather persistent but nevertheless pernicious theory of the stages of childhood activity has grown up. This is known as the recapitulation theory. It holds, in short, that ontogeny repeats phylogeny—that the developing child must pass through all the stages that the race has passed through. He should thus by rights pass through a fish stage of activity, a monkey stage, a primitive man stage, etc. Certain psychologists have seriously subscribed to such statements as the following: "A babe a few days old . . . made peculiar paddling or swimming movements." "In children and adults . . . we find swaying from side to side or backward or forward, not infrequent. This suggests the slow vacillatory movements used by fish." The best corrective for such harmful conceptions is a real genetic study of the child and a deeper knowledge of biology.

Principal Rôle of the Unlearned Activities.—Though the perfect native pattern responses in man be few in number, his wealth of native, *partially organized reactions* is quite important. In general it seems safe to summarize their rôle in the organization of man as follows:

1. Man is supplied with a large number of directly adaptive life-conserving activities which care for the intake, digestion and distribution of food products and for the elimination of waste and for procreation. These purely vegetative functions serve him as they serve animals lower than man and are possibly just as " perfect."

2. Man at birth and at varying periods thereafter is supplied with a series of protective attack and defense mechanisms, which while not nearly so perfect as in animals, nevertheless form a substantial repertoire of acts. They need supplementation by habit before being of direct utility to the individual in his struggle for food, against enemies, etc. These are the protective and defense reactions—the unlearned part activities at first predominate.

3. Then follow the occupational activities (manipulation) consisting mainly of habit—seen in collection, hoarding, building of blocks, hammering and the use of tools generally, drawing, modelling in clay, etc. In the crude stage of these activities, instinctive factors may be operative but their presence is hard to demonstrate. The instinctive factors are, even if they exist, soon lost sight of in the technique of the skilled workman, the artist and the collector. These variations in activities are seen at very early ages in children. Modern school methods, and especially the college, tend to break down these desirable childhood slants towards manipulations and occupations. One rarely finds a lad of twelve who cannot tell exactly what he wants to become, what he is fitted for and why he is fitted for it. By the time he has had all of his earlier attained manipulative organization cultivated out of him in college, he can rarely tell what he is fitted for, and he drifts now into this work, now into that, depending upon his father's business, temporary openings, the traditions of the school, or the aspirations of his parents or other backers.

4. Individuality seems in some way to depend upon man's unlearned behavior, not upon the presence of completed pattern types of responses, since these do not exist in any large number, but apparently upon factors which, when taken singly, are difficult to detect, but which when taken together are most important. There is not much experimental evidence for this conclusion, but there is a great deal of common-sense data. We have in mind such differentiation as follows: Two men with similar and equal training and approximately equal in ability in any skilled field, each capable of turning out fine work, will show individuality in workmanship, design and method of approaching their problems. Two equally skilled pitchers or catchers in baseball show this very well. Two men working upon lathes, or modelling in clay, or making drawings of the same microscopic slide illustrate it. Apparently there are differences in the part activities which have persisted in spite of instruction. We dignify these in the artist by the terms " touch ", " technic ", " individuality ", etc. The fact that they have persisted seems to prove mainly that we are all put together differently—nervous sys-

tems-circulatory, respiratory-glandular, all differ in detail. Again our muscular, tendinous and bony structures differ— some of us are put together with long fingers, some with thick, stubby ones; some with flexible joints, some with stiff ones. Many of the behavior differences are but the natural correlates of inherited structure—it hardly seems fair to call these differences instinctive.

5. As may be inferred from this whole chapter, and we shall still more clearly bring the matter out in the following chapter, the principal rôle of all unlearned activity, neglecting the vegetative and procreative (the latter especially is not lacking in habit supplementation), *is to initiate the process of learning.* In an object does not call out either a positive or a negative response, the formation of a habit with respect to that object is impossible unless we take measures to condition a response.

CHAPTER VIII

THE GENESIS AND RETENTION OF EXPLICIT BODILY HABITS

A. Acquisition.

Introduction.—In the preceding two chapters we have dealt with the hereditary assets of man—his untutored ways of acting. It was clear from our study that if man were forced to make adjustments with only his inborn equipment his behavior would be lacking in that complexity and variety which we know exists in the adult. In habit we come to a higher and more varied level of functioning. For some reason a misconception has grown up in regard to habit. Many regard the term in a somewhat sinister way—as implying something that is inevitable, invariable and indeed somewhat fatal. To them it means the drug habit or alcoholism or some other pathological manifestation of activity. It is best to clear away such misconceptions since habits in our sense represent the bulwark of human organization.

A Conditioned Reflex Level of Functioning.—Between the purely instinct-reflex level of activity seen at birth and the level represented by definite habits of the type we are about to consider there is a stage of activity of the habit kind deserving more consideration than it has hitherto received. Not until the child begins to handle and generally manipulate objects, to build with blocks or clay, to crawl or walk from spot to spot and to put on language habits is it a going human concern. But it is unthinkable that a mass of individual acquisitions is not put on before this level is reached. We have discussed this phase of activity in several places—in the attachment and detachment of reactions to emotional stimuli and in connection with the positive and negative reactions which develop at a very early age. It remains to call special attention to it in connection with habit. The pattern of this early activity is not complex and for this reason it is often spoken of as being the putting on of new instinc-

tive part activities. Our own view is that they are of the conditioned reflex type and are therefore acquired. The whole
level should receive a far more extended study since the pedagogical aspect for parent and teacher is most important. To
dwell for any length of time upon it here is out of place. But
it is believed that the child is often made or broken at just this
stage. One needs only to call attention to the mass of objects that
gets tied up with the fear responses, or the way the eighty-day-old
infant learns to control its attendants by crying and giving way
to rage. We recall these statements made in other connections in
order to emphasize the point here that habits of the type we
shall now consider are not the earliest to develop.

The Nature of Habit.—Any definite mode of acting, either
explicit or implicit in character, not belonging to man's hereditary
equipment, must be looked upon as a habit. It is an individually
acquired or learned act. We have already pointed out that
from the moment of birth the infant when not sleeping is
moving almost ceaselessly the arms, hands, legs, eyes, head,
and indeed the whole body. Stimulate him in any way and
these movements become more frequent and increase in amplitude.
Under the influence of intra-organic stimulation as seen in the
hyperactivity of the smooth-muscle contractions in hunger and
thirst, and especially in the hypersecretion of the ductless glands
in rage, fear and other emotional activity, these movements become
much more numerous. In pain, likewise, the number of movements is increased. It can be maintained from our experimental
work on habit that the autonomic system furnishes the restless
seeking or avoiding movements of the body as a whole which
lead the organism to display the instinctive repertoire out of
which habits are composed. The question as to whether the exteroceptive sense organs (eyes, ears and nose) ever furnish this
initial drive in the absence of autonomic activity is not so easily
answered. It is maintained by psychologists generally that the
moving, the flashing of bright objects, the sounding of noises,
and in general the application of distance receptor stimuli, can
increase the number and amplitude of these initial movements.
It must be remembered, though, that such stimuli arouse the

sympathetic nervous system which stirs up the smooth muscles and glands. It may be the return afferent impulses from these organs which set the seeking activity in the striped muscles in motion. The whole series of questions involved can be focalized by asking whether a hypothetically eviscerated animal depending upon the reflex arcs ending in the striped muscles alone would ever display that activity which would lead to habit formation. Our own view is that habits would not be formed. It seems equally probable, though, that once they were formed in a normal animal they could be called out after evisceration if in some way the animal could be kept alive.[1] Fortunately we do not have to answer such a question, since we are working with our animal as a whole and since the slightest observation will show that the habit-forming activities in a human being are present at birth and in all probability before birth.

---

[1] The whole matter can be put in another way by stating what is meant by an adjustment. We will use a simple illustration: Suppose that the animal has been without food for some time: rhythmical contractions begin in the stomach which serve as stimuli for arousing the animal as a whole to activity. We call such activity "restless," "positive" or "seeking." They continue until by some customary or chance act food is grasped, carried to the mouth and eaten. The moment the food touches the stomach the rhythmical contractions in its walls die away and the restless seeking activity disappears. The animal is said to be adjusted—but only with respect to food. If the environment does not permit the act which will bring the cessation of such movements—that is, if he is restrained from acting or no food is at hand—he may do something else, for example, walk until exhausted. In time, however, the restless movements may disappear without food having been eaten; that is, the rhythmical contractions end of their own accord after a certain period—adjustment has taken place, but not of an organically safe kind. In our illustration the original, oftentimes called driving or compelling stimulus, was organic activity. Such are sometimes designated as needs or hungers. There is a strong tendency now to hold that the organism is always acting, even when displaying highly organized habits, under the influence of an organic stimulus—we have already brought out the fact that such stimuli in the glands and smooth muscles are very varied—and that man's ordinary reactions to things and people are the equivalents of his taking food in the above illustration. He becomes adjusted only when he reacts in such a way as to bring about the disappearance of the particular organic stimulus which is acting at the moment.

Certainly at birth or shortly thereafter the elements or unit acts out of which every habit is formed can be noted. We mention the contraction and flexion of the fingers, of the lower and upper arm, raising and lowering of the head, rotation of the head, bending the trunk from side to side and backward and forward, well-systematized movements of the legs, and a host of others. The conclusion is forced upon us that in habit no new elementary movements are needed. There are enough present at birth and more than will ever be combined into complex unitary acts. Since so many of the psychological texts speak freely of the formation of "new pathways" in habit it seems well to call attention to the simple mathematical fact that the number of permutations and combinations of, say, one hundred unit acts is a staggering number. Such speculations, though, are futile. One needs only to examine the five- or six-day-old infant to be reasonably convinced that there is no need for the formation of additional reflex arcs to account for all later organization.[2] The new or learned element in habit is the tying together or integration of separate movements in such a way as to produce a new unitary activity. And by unitary activity we mean nothing more than the every-day acts of life, such as reaching out the hand for an object that stimulates the eye, picking the object up and carrying it to the mouth or laying it on the table; or picking up a hammer in the right hand, a nail in the left, holding the nail with the left, hammering with the right until the nail is started, then withdrawing the left hand and completing the process by driving the nail home. These are simple and elementary acts to be sure, seemingly far different from building a model airplane or writing a novel so far as complexity is concerned. But it probably takes the child a longer time to learn to drive a nail well than it takes an adult engineer to build an airplane.

Instinct and habit are undoubtedly composed of the same elementary reflexes. They differ so far as concerns the origin

---

[2] In stating the view this way we are of course neglecting some of the late appearing elementary reflex movements such as blinking, extension of the great toe in place of flexion when the sole of the foot is touched, and the late sex reflexes.

of the pattern (number and localization of the simple reflex arcs involved) and the order (temporal relation) of the unfolding of the elements composing the pattern. In instinct the pattern and order are inherited, in habit both are acquired during the lifetime of the individual. We can define habit then as we did instinct as a complex system of reflexes which functions in a serial order when the child or adult is confronted by the appropriate stimulus, provided we add the statement that in habit the pattern and order are acquired, whereas in instinct they are inherited. It would follow from this definition that so far as the observance of a single adult performance is concerned we should not be able to tell an instinct from a habit, so that here again the genetic method is required to determine the relationship between the two. It should be noted that, usually, instinctive response is tied down fairly well to a definite particular stimulus or situation, whereas in acquired activity one and the same object can call forth from an educated man literally hundreds of different actions depending upon slight differences in its setting or upon his needs at the moment. Think of the number of activities that can be called out from one and the same individual by a piece of lumber, leather, stone, marble or metal.

Explicit and Implicit Types of Habit.— On page 14 we divided habit into explicit and implicit types. The examples we gave of explicit habits were unlocking a door, tennis and violin playing. We should add talking, lecturing, writing, working at any vocation and, in fact, doing the thousands of things that we see individuals and groups doing from the moment of waking to the moment of sleeping. We deal here with overt activity which can be observed without instrumentation (the subject matter largely of ordinary observation). While the whole body is involved in these acts, the most conspicuous and most easily observable phase of the activity is the combination of movements we see in the arms, legs and other motile organs of the striped-muscle system. So far no enumeration of the total acquisitions of this character has ever been attempted for the adult. A slight indication of their number can be gathered from investigating the word repertoire of individuals. The exceptional five-year-old child of a cultivated family can probably use more than two thousand words (page 343). Many uneducated adults never learn to use more than this number. The educated university man employs possibly five thousand words, the accomplished lexicographer can probably use appropriately ten to fifteen thousand words, giving the derivation of many of them. The number of acts, not counting the use of words, which have a name (for example, hammering, sawing, eating, reading) which an individual living a complex life does in the course of a week is enormous. When we contrast this wealth of possession with that of the infant of a hundred and twenty days, the age at which the simple eye-hand coördination is forming, it can be seen what a tremendous journey the young individual must take in order to arrive at that stage of organization which is called for by society as a matter of course. The hereditary pattern acts fade into insignificance so far as concerns their number and complexity.

The implicit-habit systems which we cannot observe except with the aid of instruments are probably equally as numerous if not more so and oftentimes more complex than the explicit. Many of the implicit habits have already been discussed under the heading of conditioned reflexes in the glands and in the unstriped muscles. Of the implicit habits involving mainly the striped bodily musculature little is known except those connected with throat, tongue and larynx. That a great many of the activities involved in thinking are really implicit bodily movements, for example, of the shoulders, hands, fingers and other moving organs, is probable. A slight wave of the hand, the flicking of an eyebrow, the upward fling of the lip, a faintly muttered "humph" is the only organized immediate reaction we make towards many situations in life. Certainly in the deaf-mute not trained to speak the behaviorist assumes that all thinking is carried out in terms of the nascent movements involved in the deaf and dumb alphabet, the Braille reading system, and in the bodily musculature as a whole. That there are many abridged processes there is as true as in the thinking of a normal adult. In the normal individual the great mass of implicit habit systems are formed in the laryngeal, tongue and throat muscles. They are in general word processes or the abbreviations of such. Naturally there are as many of these organized implicit activities as there are overt word responses and probably many more.

For ease of presentation only the acquisition of explicit bodily habits and their retention will be discussed in the present chapter. In Chapter IX the acquisition of explicit speech habits and the various forms of implicit habits will be taken up.

The Acquisition of Explicit Bodily Habits.

Genesis of Some Eye-Hand Coördinations.—Systematic tests were begun upon L on the 80th day. She was carefully tested each week thereafter in such a way that progress in eye-hand coördination could be observed. The method was as follows: The baby sat in the mother's lap facing the experimenter. The mother supported her by placing her two hands upon the baby's waist, thus leaving both arms entirely free. The experiments were carried out in a brilliantly lighted room, in the same room with all shades pulled down, and in the dark-room as occasion demanded. A stick of red peppermint candy of the old-fashioned kind, half an inch in diameter, was suspended in front of her within easy reaching distance. After dangling the candy for a minute or two it was put into her mouth by the experimenter if she failed to reach for it. This was done invariably, following the method found so serviceable in animal psychology. On the 94th day, having failed to reach for the candy on any preceding test, the candy was placed in the left hand in order to see how long it would take her to put it into the mouth. At the end of two minutes she had failed to make the adjustment with the left hand. When the candy was placed in her right hand she put it into her mouth immediately. Another trial with the left hand failed, another with the right hand was immediately successful. (We began to think that the child was right-handed).

Age, 101 days. Candy dangled in front of her as before. She fixated the experimenter rather than the candy. She failed to reach for the candy on five presentations. On the last trial she seemed to open her hand and to make tentative striking movements. One interesting observation was made upon the way she put the candy into her mouth. After it was placed in her hand whenever she grasped the candy near one end and poked the long end into her mouth, she would push it far back into her throat so that gagging ensued. She did this three times. It was evident that the contact of the object against the lips and tongue did not check the movement. The fingers had to reach the mouth before movement ceased.

108 days. No advance in manipulation could be noted.

115 days. Not much further advance in reaching. We ended the experiment by putting the candy first in the right hand and then in the left, recording the time it took her to put the candy in her mouth.

Time (in seconds):

Right	12	Left	2
	21		12
	2		5

The left hand was thus fully as successful as the right in getting objects into the mouth.

122 days. No evidence of reaching with the hands on first tests. Candy was placed on the tongue and then quickly removed, then advanced again toward the face. The head was almost immediately thrust forward with the lips pursed and the beginning of sucking movements took place. As the mouth approached the candy both hands were raised, one touching the experimenter's hands. After an interval candy was again offered on the string. *Grasped at it with left hand while pursing the lips.* It was again offered. Grasped at it with left hand, catching it and putting it into her mouth. On the next trial she made the effort to grasp it with her left hand but failed.

129 days. Tested with candy suspended as before. At first would not fixate. Dangled it within six inches of the eyes. Slight movement was made with the right hand. The candy was then swung away and slowly brought back. Followed it with her eyes and when it was six inches distant from her face, she struck the candy with the back of her hand in two seconds, then pushed it over to the other hand, then to her chin, finally worrying it into her mouth. On the next trial there were no false movements in reaching. The right hand went slowly up and grasped the candy, and she pushed it up into her mouth without aid from her left hand. On the next trial she again reached definitely with her right hand and put it into her mouth. After these definite results we did not make any further tests because we wished to see if the first trials one week later would be just as definite.

The grasping reflex was always tested at the end of each day's test. On the 122nd day she was made to grasp the rod with difficulty and then only with her right hand. She swung for some seconds with this hand. On the above date she made no effort to grasp the rod at all, but by "worrying" her we succeeded in getting her to hold on for $3^3/_5$ seconds (her time from the 35th to the 70th day would average around 12 to 15 seconds).

136 days. Candy held as before. The right hand started up immediately, grasped the candy and carried it to the mouth. Time, 8 seconds. On the next trial the right hand was used. Time, 10 seconds. On the succeeding trial the right hand was used. Time, 8 seconds. The left hand did not assist in any of these adjustments. The thumb was not used. The whole act was quite clumsy. The mother was then made to shift the baby's position slightly on her lap. When the candy was presented, both hands started out, but the right hand grasped and took the candy to the mouth.

The grasping reflex was gone. Tested four times with the rod, but she could not cling. Defensive movements appeared. The right hand actually slapped the rod away. The left hand once momentarily grasped the rod, but she released her hold the moment she began to be lifted.

143 days. From this point on the detailed notes will not be given. In her reaching to-day the arms were outstretched at right angles to the body. She had the greatest difficulty in flexing the arm at the elbow. She would reach for the candy on her back and in the position for crawling.

150 days. Movement quite definite, mainly with the right hand. Occasionally the left assisted. The whole process of reaching required in general about three seconds.

164 days. Left hand started first on nearly every test, but right hand succeeded in grasping the candy each time. The last five tests brought success in two seconds each for the whole operation.

171 days. Succeeded first with the left hand, then twice with the right, then with both hands, then again with the right. The coördination was so well established after this that the details are not instructive. On the whole, *L* used the right hand much more frequently than the left. At the age of two and a half years *L* was again tested. She is a well-developed child, walking and talking. She is completely right-handed.

Reaching for the Candle.—While the tests on reaching for candy were being conducted she was tried frequently with an ordinary lighted wax candle. She was tested first on the 150th day (reaching for candy had been established, see above). The room was darkened. She reached immediately with the right hand, advancing the whole upper part of the body. She then held out both hands, reaching as far out from her mother's lap as possible. Heat did not seem to make her withdraw even when the flame was held as close to her hand as an eighth of an inch. The candle was then held at a distance of one meter and moved in a circle at that distance. It was then slowly brought toward her face. She followed it definitely with the eyes. At a distance of 20 centimeters she reached for it immediately with the right hand. On the second trial she started to reach at a distance of half a meter. On the third trial she began to reach at 30 centimeters. On the last three trials her hand was allowed to touch the flame, causing flexion of the fingers, but this did not deter her from reaching. On the succeeding trial she reached immediately with the right hand, the flame touching the fingers and again causing flexion. The definite reflex withdrawal of the whole hand occurred sharply on this trial, but the child did not cry. Twenty-five trials in all were given. In most cases the hand was allowed to come close enough to cause flexion of the fingers.

157 days. Tested in the dark-room. When the candle was

two meters away no attempt was made to reach for it, nor did she reach for it when it was held at one meter's distance. When held at 20 centimeters she reached for it first with the left and then with the right. Many tests were again given on this day. She was often allowed to stick her fingers near enough to the flame to cause not only contraction of the fingers but actual withdrawal of the hand.

164 days. A similar set of tests was given. She would reach continually for the candle, regardless of the fact that her fingers were often scorched.

178 days. Definite progress in avoidance was noted. When the candle was presented she reached out with her left hand, but only after an appreciable interval, during which she sucked her fingers. On the next trial she reached with her left hand immediately. On the next she reached with the left and scorched her fingers; again, left hand was started toward the candle but was checked. On the final trial she would not reach for it, but looked at it and sucked her fingers.

220 days. Reaching for the candle persisted during the early trials. Her final reactions on this day were as follows: Left hand started out but was withdrawn. She then slapped at the light with her left hand. On the next trial she refused to reach for it, holding her left hand against her breast with the right clasped over it. On the next trial she started to reach out but pulled the hand back. Several other trials were given, but in only one did she actually reach out and grasp at the flame. The tests on this day show that the avoiding reaction is fairly well established. (In all, probably 150 trials were required to perfect the coördination to the extent just noted.)

These tests with the candle are given somewhat in detail both because of their intrinsic value in showing the rise of an avoiding reaction and by reason of the fact that a great deal of speculation and theorizing has been entered into in regard to the infant's reaction to the candle. Holt has recently developed an ethical theory which centers around such a reaction as we have described.[3] It will be seen that the building up of the coördinations requires a long time when the flame is held near enough to produce the avoiding reaction. The habit as a whole grows up like any other habit. Whether the process would have been greatly hastened by allowing the child to be burned severely on the first test is, of course, not settled. Fear would have been produced very likely which would not only have extended to the candle but possibly also to the experimenter and to the whole experimental situation. Further tests of this kind would thereafter have been impossible. As it was, the baby did not cry on any of the tests.

We have carried out similar tests both on reaching for candy and for the candle upon several children (at least fifteen) with results wholly similar to the above. Experiments upon *T, F* and *N* were carried through with some detail. The beginning of reaching as tested by our method was noticed in nearly every

[3] "On seeing a candle the child puts out its hand; the second reaction (of withdrawal) is touched off by stimulation of the heat-pain nerves in the hand, and the moment at which this will happen depends on the sensitiveness of the heat-pain end-organs, and the openness of the path connecting them with the muscles that retract the arm; of which probably the openness of path is the modifiable factor. The warmth of the candle begins to stimulate this retraction reflex, and stimulates it more, and at an increasing rate of increase, as the hand approaches the candle. All that is needed to save the child from burning its hand, and this is what Meynert's scheme aims to explain, is an openness of the retraction reflex path sufficient to stop the hand before it actually reaches the flame. If the act of extension excited through the eye is not too impetuous, *the retraction reflex will from the outset protect the hand;* but if the former is a very open path, the advancing arm may get a momentum which the retraction reflex will not be sufficiently quick and strong to counterbalance in time to save the hand from being burned. *A few repetitions of the experience* will give retraction an openness which will safeguard the hand for the future; and this process is aided by the prolonged pain yielded by a burn, which continues the retraction stimulus for a considerable period and so 'wears' down the retraction path more than a great many merely momentary stimuli could do. In this way a single experience of burning is often sufficient for all time. Thus experience establishes a balance between the two opposed reflexes, of extension and of pain avoidance, such that the organism carries on its further examination of the candle in safety."—Holt, E. B., "The Freudian Wish." (Italics ours.)

case around the 120th to the 130th day. In poorly developed children it is apparently delayed.

Formation of Habits in Adults.—The process of habit formation in adults is marked off in several ways from that just studied in the infant. In the first place the muscles of the infant are poorly developed. The finer muscles of his moving members have not yet been coördinated into habit systems of general utility, action is lacking in definiteness and sharpness. His learning to reach for the candy and to inhibit reaching for the candle are organizations which will not only serve in this particular situation but also in nearly every other future habit he may form. There is some evidence to show that neuro-physiological growth processes are actually taking place since it is generally affirmed that the large movements of shoulder, elbow, wrist and hand come into prominence long before the finer movements of the fingers. We have gained some evidence for this in our study of the apposition of the thumb and first finger. This earlier development of the large muscles is taken into account in the primary grades in teaching children to write by employing large movements and then gradually progressing to the finer. Whether this is a justifiable pedagogical procedure is questionable, since by the time they reach the writing age fine finger movements are undoubtedly possible: the child merely has to learn a double set of habits. It was shown early in the history of psychology that differential contact reactions are finer in the child than in the adult. This is due to the fact that the child has all of the afferent endings developed, and since his hand is smaller than that of the adult the endings lie nearer together. The same argument can be advanced, of course, for the kinæsthetic endings in the muscles. Here again, though, we enter into the realm of research rather than into that of established fact.

In the adult many thousands of experiences like these we have just been considering have brought organization, and most of the habits he has to learn employ in part at least the organization gained from previous habit formation. This in a way is his strength and at the same time also his weakness. Our habitual ways of exercising our muscles so fixes them that unusual or totally new modes of activity are acquired with greater difficulty than if our muscles were not set in such habitual molds. It is difficult for the man of thirty-five to learn to dive well or to use his wrist perfectly in lobbing a tennis ball; it is practically impossible for a woman to learn to be a ballet or toe dancer unless she began practicing at ten years of age or younger. We shall see later though when we come to consider the effects of age upon habit formation that the concept of the rigidity of the muscles of the middle-aged has been overrated. There unquestionably are differences in the possibilities of acquisition of the adult and the adolescent, but we shall discuss this subject on page 388.

In observing the 120-day infant we saw that instinctive factors came into play as soon as it was faced by a situation to which it was not adjusted. In man in a similar situation, instead of the infantile random activity appearing, the habitual unitary activity previously learned appears. Suppose we try to teach him to play tennis. He grasps the racket accurately but possibly not at the right place. He swings it awkwardly enough, possibly as he would a baseball bat or a board—he does the thing which he has in the past most frequently done to objects of that type. In general, when put in new situations he tries first one old act and then another. When these fail to work, splitting and partial reactions appear. The situation may become an emotional one at any time, especially when his past organization fails to help him. He then falls back upon infantile types of reaction: he may throw the thing down, stamp on it, pull, twist and manipulate any part of it at random, finally breaking the object in his raging. Occasionally, but rarely, the infantile reactions lead to the adjustment, since in emotional excitement a larger number of random acts is released than when the individual is working at an organized integrated level. Usually in adults the display of activity in new situations is, as we have mentioned, orderly. The adult attacks the simpler things first, combining them as he can, each combination making the succeeding step easier until finally the problem is solved.

Learning to Shoot with the English Long Bow.—The stages

can be illustrated by an experimental study on learning to shoot the English long bow (Lashley). The bow used for the study was six feet in length, requiring a pull of forty-four pounds to draw the arrow to the head. The arrow was the regulation feathered, steel-tipped, twenty-eight-inch arrow used in tournament work. The target was four feet in diameter with a ten-inch bull's-eye placed at a distance of one hundred and twenty feet. The subject was given the bow, told how to nock the arrow and only enough more to keep him from injuring himself and others. He had to learn how to adjust his fingers to the string and to the arrow, to get his stance, to raise the bow properly, to get the arrow aligned, to point the arrow up far enough to counteract its parabolic flight (sighting or aiming), to hold the bow with extreme steadiness, to release so as to get the full power of the string, to hold the bow so that the string after the arrow was released would not strike the wrist and finally to brace himself for the recoil. It would be impossible for us to trace these part adjustments through in detail. At first the shooting is very wild, so wild that only rarely is the target hit. A wide background of cotton sheeting had to be placed behind the target in order to provide a method of marking the errors. The arrows at first are likely to fall short because of the difficulty in pulling the arrow back to the piling or in aiming too low. In counteracting this the subject begins to shoot entirely too high. On account of the wobbling of his arrow he also shoots to the right and left as well as above and below. Little by little the part reactions begin to fall in place, the subject begins to hit the target and to come closer and closer to the bull's-eye. In one group studied, the average of the first 20 shots was 56.9 inches away from the bull's-eye. The average of the last 20 shots when 360 shots in all were given was 27.1 inches. While this shows considerable progress it is really very far away from the record of the expert. The championship score at the forty-yard range between 1890 and 1908 varied from about 8–11 inches from the bull's-eye. One interesting thing appearing in this as in most habits is the fact that initial progress is quite rapid but that all later progress is slow. One might think at first sight that if a

beginner can change his score from 57 to 27 inches in 360 shots
he ought to be able to drop to 11 inches after a few hundred more
shots. But such is not the case. The 11-inch record is one which
few individuals can ever attain no matter what amount of practice they have had. In one exceptionally good subject we got a
final record of 15 inches at the end of 1300 shots. This brings
out the fact that in every act of skill there is what is called a

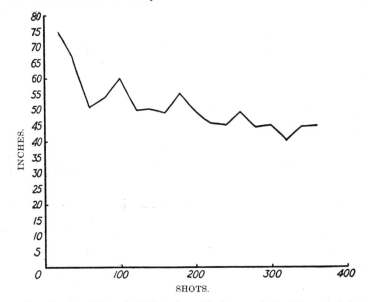

Fig. 58.—Acquisition of skill in archery (12 shots per day). The vertical line or
ordinate shows the average error in the shot, that is, the average distance in inches from
the bull's eye. The horizontal, abscissa, shows the number of shots. Each point on
the curve is an average of 20 shots.

physiological limit of accuracy or speed beyond which the individual cannot go. We find a good example of this in typewriting,
where the individual rarely exceeds a sustained speed of over 64
words per minute of straight copy. The same thing has been
brought out in rifle shooting, billiards, golf, and in fact in every
act of skill which has been investigated.

Above we give a curve (Fig. 58) of acquisition of skill in
archery. It shows the method of constructing charts and tabu-
lating results and the main features to be learned from such
20

a tabulation. The horizontal line, the abscissa, shows the amount of practice (number of shots); the vertical, the ordinate, shows the number of inches each shot was distant from the bull's-eye. From such a curve one can determine the total amount of improvement by subtracting the average of the first 20 shots from the average of the last 20 shots. In the curve under consideration the improvement was from 75.4 inches to 45.1 inches. One can also determine the rate of improvement between any two points, and finally the limit of improvement for the given amount of practice; for example, in this curve the subjects were finally shooting at an average of 45.1 inches. This learning curve is typical of most curves. Note (1) that initial accuracy was low, the average of the first 20 shots being 75.4 inches; (2) that improvement through the first 60 shots was very rapid indeed, from an average of 75.4 to an average of 51.5 inches; (3) that during the next 80 shots there is little total improvement. These long periods of no improvement are called plateaux; shorter periods of no improvement are called resting places. It will be seen that the curve ends on another plateau, the last 40 or 50 shots showing a decrease in accuracy. Note (4) that just before the 200th shot has been taken a period of marked improvement occurs which continues with slight irregularity to the 320th shot, where the second plateau begins. From what we know of such curves we can be reasonably sure that after a longer or shorter time of no improvement the curve would again take a decided drop, since the limit of improvement had by no means been approached. If the practice had continued, for example, to the 5000th shot the plotted curve would have been checked as the physiological limit for those particular individuals was approached. As soon as this limit was reached the curve would become, except for slight variations, a straight line. Certain individuals would find their limit probably at 15 inches and others at 12. It is, of course, possible even in as small a group as this (six) that an exceptional individual might be included. If so, a final record of 8 inches might have been attained. In Chapter X we shall discuss in detail a great many of the factors which affect the shape of such curves, the total amount and rate of improvement and the limits of improvement. The permanence of the improvement for curves of this type is discussed in the present chapter (page 327).

Single Adjustments and Partial Habits of Every-Day Life.—Only rarely in every-day life are acts of skill acquired in the systematic manner we have outlined. Our practice periods are sketchy, and are repeated only after long intervals. The best example of the ordinary way in which skill is attained in daily life is the behavior of an individual when he gets stuck on a problem. He solves the problem or leaves it, as the case may be, without mastering all the details. Possibly we can illustrate this by an actual example from motor-boating, which will fit the various automobile troubles fully as well. Suppose we take the following situation: The new gas engine in a motor-boat runs smoothly for a short time, then begins to miss and to lose power. Certain of the spark-plugs begin to heat up, and a valve or two sticks. The boat may run again smoothly for a mile or two, and then again get cranky. The owner stops the boat and looks at the engine, and undoubtedly "thinks" in the sense of acting with his language organization rather than with his hands. Previous scraps of reading and instruction are (kinæsthetically) reinstated, as for example: "when the engine misses, clean the spark-plugs." This intra-organically aroused stimulus leads to the act of taking out the spark-plugs and cleaning them. That done he puts on his spark and starts the engine. Again the miss. That leads to his investigating the gas supply. It is sufficient. He runs the boat to the dock, takes the magneto apart and sandpapers the points for luck. Still the miss. He next cleans the carbureter and the feed-pipe. Not being successful, he opens up the engine and looks at the valves. They are now cool, and are working properly. This exhausts his own organization. He takes the boat to a local "expert." The expert goes over everything in much the same way as the owner has already gone over it. He tells the owner that the engine is no good. The owner takes the boat back to the dock, his every act showing his depressed emotional level. At the dock he becomes infantile in his reactions, trying first one thing and then another, pushing this part, pulling that, finally lying down exhausted. Night comes on and he leaves the boat to eat and sleep, coming back to it next morning in a better physiological condition. He starts the engine up slowly, leaning over it and watching the various parts as they work. He sees the heads of the bolts which fasten the engine to the bed moving up and down. Like a flash he stops his engine, tightens the four bolts and sails off to tell the engine expert that he is fit only to patch up holes in rowboats.

Many of the mal-adjustments of the day are of this type. We have used thinking here in advance of our special study of that type of activity, but we mean only the language activity which corresponds in all respects to other kinds of organized motor activity. We pointed out earlier that the number of such language habits is far in excess of all others. Hence when stuck or in difficulty there is a constant shifting from overt language (talking to one's self or to one's companion) to implicit language (thought), and to overt activity in arms, hands and fingers. The words he has read or that others have spoken to him are reinstated; they become in turn adequate stimuli for the arousal of overt activity. We thus see that overt activity constantly arouses the implicit and the latter in turn arouses the overt. All the way through the individual in our illustration has been acting constantly under the guidance of extra-organically or intra-organically aroused stimuli or under both simultaneously.

It may be objected that our illustration is not a habit. This is true in the sense that after making such an adjustment as the above we cannot immediately try the man out in a similar situation. But our illustration does correspond, in some respects, to the first trial in our previous example of acquisition of skill in archery. Given enough similar situations and the owner could always spot a gas engine that is loose upon its bed. If we continue varying the situation, putting the trouble now in the valves, next in the magneto and then in order in the pump, piston rings and oiling system we could finally build up by this trial and error process such a series of specialized habits that given the sight or sound of an improperly working engine he could at once dive to the troublesome part. We would have then the practically trained expert gas engineer. But life is too short for us all to become experts in all of the activities in which we occasionally engage. We become Jacks-of-all-trades in lines other than those by means of which we earn our daily bread. The number of abbreviated habits possessed by any given individual in the different spheres of life, as in music, painting, drawing, lecturing and engineering, is very large indeed.

Cross Education.—One of the interesting and significant things in connection with habit formation is the fact that when a habit is established which utilizes any particular organ of the body, for example, the right hand and arm, the bilaterally symmetrical organ, the left hand and arm, shares in the training. The improvement does not seem to be confined wholly to the bilaterally symmetrical organ, since training the right toe to tap increases most markedly not only the ability of the left toe to tap, but also the improvement extends to the right hand and to the left hand. This phenomenon was noticed very early in sensory physiology (differential reaction to two contacts), but it has been more recently investigated by several psychologists. The method in brief is as follows: A measure of initial accuracy of a given function is tested in two symmetrical organs. One organ is then practiced until high skill is attained. The unused organ is then retested. The initial score made by this organ is compared with its later score and the difference in the two gives the measure of the amount of improvement (less, of course, the small practice effect gained by giving the original test). In this way it has been found that lunging at a target with a foil one hundred times with the right hand produced an improvement in the left hand about three-fourths as great as in the right (Davis). Woodworth has shown that practice with the left hand in hitting dots greatly improves the ability of the right hand in the same performance. Swift found that after training the right hand in tossing and catching balls the ability of the left hand improved. Starch found that when the right hand has been practiced in tracing the outline of a six-pointed star seen in a mirror the improvement in the left hand was about nine-tenths as great as in the right hand.

Certain individuals have used these results as an argument in favor of a general transfer of training, a subject which we consider below. Although we do not know the various physiological factors involved in cross education there seems to be no justification for extending our conclusions beyond the facts that can actually be observed.

The So-Called Transfer of Training.—The problems involved in the controversy as to whether training along any specific line produces a general transfer effect upon other lines are as old as are the school systems and older. The whole question at one or another time has centered around the problem as to whether training in the classics and in mathematics facilitates the acquisition of all other subjects. The experimental literature is large and extremely controversial. The results of a few experiments only are given here. Thorndike and Woodworth trained their subjects in estimating weights of 40 to 120 grams. This practice produced only a slight improvement in the ability to react correctly to weights ranging in weight from 120 to 1800 grams. Foster, working with adult students, each of whom spent 40 hours in practice distributed over 10 weeks, measured and analyzed the improvement in drawing objects, pictures and nonsense drawing. He concludes: ''That training in these experiments has made the observers noticeably better observers or memorizers in general, or given them any habits of observing closely or reporting correctly, or furnished any ability to meet better any situation generally met with, neither we nor the observers themselves believe. . . . It seems, therefore, as if the value of formal training of our kind has been greatly overestimated.'' Gilbert and Fracker tested two individuals for quickness in moving the fingers (1) to a sound stimulus, (2) to an electric shock, (3) when a blow was given, and (4) when a blue surface was shown. Under the conditions of the experiment, which we cannot enter into here, a spread of training seemed to be secured. Coover and Angell tested four adult subjects in typewriting before and after training in sorting cards, but their records show little gain which cannot be accounted for by the special improvement accruing from the practice in typewriting the test material.

Most of the experiments have been carried out upon the improvement in one language function due to the previous training in another. The subject, for example, would be trained on learning "Paradise Lost" and then tested on his ability to learn the "Coming of Arthur," or trained on learning nonsense syllables and tested upon the learning of ordinary words, or trained on learning poetry and tested on history. It is assumed, of course, in such experiments that a measure of the subject's ability to learn the material upon which later he is to be tested has been obtained. In general it may be stated that students of experimental education are inclined to admit the fact that improvement in one function may bring about improvement in another function, but they maintain that there is no general transfer of training (there may be just the reverse) of the kind usually insisted upon. In acquiring skill in any one function part adjustments are made, such as the control of the eye movements, formation of systematic habits of study, ways of looking up words in the dictionary, etc., which can be directly used in acquiring skill in certain other functions. These part adjustments have been called "identical elements" by Woodworth and Thorndike. Where there are no identical elements in the two functions, training in one does not hasten the process of acquisition in the other.

Increasing the Complexity of the Object Beyond the Point Where Adequate Reaction Can Be Made.—In a narrow sense this problem has been investigated in the laboratory by means of the tachistoscope. This is a device for exposing a series of words, figures or objects simultaneously for a period of time less than that of the reflex eye movement. The experimenter begins by exposing two letters, figures, words or numbers. If the subject can name those correctly or write them down or draw them, the number of objects exposed is increased until his limit is reached. As might be expected, considering the way our word habits and other habits are formed, as many separate words can be reacted to correctly as isolated letters. In general, it has been found that no more than six items can be properly reacted to. The limit, as a rule, ranges between four and six. In hearing, a practical test can be made by getting the subject to repeat a list of numerals given to him orally. The number of numerals presented is increased to the point where errors (omissions, displacements, wrong numerals) begin to appear. In the case of normal adults 6–8 numerals can be correctly repeated; in the case of children, defectives, and of certain psychopathic individuals this number cannot be attained. In, making any of these tests upon a sense organ the stimuli may be presented either simultaneously or successively without materially changing the results. The contact sense may be tested by touching the body simultaneously at several different places. The number of separate points stimulating the individual can be correctly enumerated if they are not in excess of six.

The Number of Habits Which Can Function Simultaneously.—The inability of the subject to react adequately to a, stimulus which has more than a certain complexity leads us at once into the discussion as to the number of separate activities or habits which can be exercised simultaneously. The fact seems to be that in the broadest sense since the individual acts as a unit only one thing can be done at a time. There seems to be an obvious contradiction in fact in this statement. It will be immediately remarked that women can knit, quilt or sew while engaging in a lively conversation. The answer to this is that the knitting and talking have been learned together and hence they form a part of an organized system. It is more difficult to talk and telegraph or to talk and play the piano, yet this, too, can be done. It is extremely difficult to talk and typewrite at the same time, yet possibly if the activities were originally learned in that way it could be done. In making all of the finer coördinations as in rifle shooting, expert balancing or trapeze work the final adjustment is always made without conversation.

Such considerations lead almost at once into the field of automatic writing. So far as the principles in automatic writing are concerned, there is no theoretical difficulty in holding that they are closely similar to knitting and talking, although, of course, the reaction system as a whole is far more complicated. The process of double acquisition, or, better, double functioning, has been experimentally studied by Downey and Anderson. After considerable work they acquired some skill in the double process of writing a stanza previously memorized while maintaining either silent reading or reading aloud. Two years after acquiring this skill the function was retested. There was considerable retention with rapid re-learning. It is safe to say that on account of the effort and tremendous strain involved in simultaneous double acquisition such learning will never become popular.

In psycho-pathology we find many examples of the independent exercise of part reactions, some of which become highly systematized. We see this systematization possibly in the so-called cases of "multiple personality" or "split personalities": nearly every human being has something in his organization both of Dr. Jekyll and Mr. Hyde. If we assume that for one reason or another the more socialized reactions of Dr. Jekyll so come in conflict with one another that inhibition of reaction on that plane occurs, action will take place through the outlets which are not in conflict. If this goes on for a sufficient length of time there seems to be no reason, according to the general principles of habit formation, why the individual should not become organized upon the level of Mr. Hyde. (Indeed, if enough suggestions are given to the patient, he may systematize on two or three such levels.) If by the alteration of the individual's environment or by his reëducation, the conflicts in the socialized reaction tendencies of Dr. Jekyll are removed, we may once more see him reacting permanently as Dr. Jekyll.

There is a purely practical question possibly involved in this discussion. For example, in the cotton mills of the South, children from fourteen years of age and on are taught to run one loom. As they grow older and become more adept in their work they are given more and more looms to manage. The adjustment required is fairly simple, but it involves great eye-strain and extreme nimbleness of movement. There are a number of duties in the electrical world which demand a similar type of adjustment. The question as to the possible number of such operations which can be carried out at one time is, of course, important. In the first place the larger the number of separate

operations the individual can conduct simultaneously and efficiently the greater is the advantage to the manufacturer, and to
the employee if paid on a piece-work basis. On the other hand,
it may be extremely detrimental to the organization of the individual himself. So far no investigations have been made which
show just how many such operations can be carried out without
loss in efficiency; or whether the number can be increased by the
adoption of special training methods; and finally whether the
effect of such a splitting of activity is detrimental to the individual himself.

Habit Fixation.—At the present time there is no satisfactory
way of giving an account of the formation of a habit in terms of
cause and effect. A good many monographs and special chapters
have been devoted to its explanation, but although we know a
great deal about the factors which influence the formation of
habits, as we shall see later, we cannot state in detail what the
course of events is in the inception of any individual habit.
Habits start, as we have seen, with the so-called random movements (if the object fails to arouse either positive or negative
reaction tendencies no habit can be formed). Among those
random movements is one group or combination which completes
the adjustment, the "successful" one. All others, from a superficial standpoint, seem to be unnecessary. But it must be remembered that the organism cannot respond in any other way than
his equipment allows him to. When put in front of a problem
the solution to which cannot be effected by an immediate instinctive act or by one belonging to his past habit acquisitions, the
whole organism begins to work in each and every part but without working together. Not only are the arms, legs and trunk
active but the heart, stomach, lungs and glands as well. We
know that when the new habit is formed the organism as a whole
acts smoothly, each part reaction hangs together with every other
part reaction, all tending to facilitate and make possible the
smooth working of the group of acts effecting the final adjustment. The formation of the simplest habit is an enormously complicated affair. We are prone to think that the successful act is
only a small group of movements involving, for example, only

the hands and the fingers. This is not true. Even so apparently simple a thing as firing a rifle successfully requires many facilitating part adjustments all over the body. As the right hand picks up the rifle the body parts begin to fall into line—a certain stance is taken so as to brace the body, the back muscles take on a greater tone, the left hand and arm begin to take on the position of grasping the end of the barrel, the shoulder muscles contract, finally the instant before firing respiration is blocked and as the trigger is pulled the body gets ready to withstand the recoil.

The production of such a close-fitting and well-timed group of activities all working together, the end result being the hitting of the bull's-eye or the felling of the deer, requires in the beginning naturally the display of a large number of "useless" movements. But probably on each succeeding attempt to hit the bull's-eye some of these part reactions fall together in such a way as to facilitate succeeding movements. The whole learning stage is thus an active one and something is gained each time the individual goes through the process. Hence the so-called useless movements are useless only when looked at from the standpoint of the completed habit. They are all necessary in view of the fact that the successful movements could not have appeared in any given trial unless they had been preceded by just those acts which did precede.

Some attempted causal explanations of the process of fixation are as follows: (1) In most cases where random activity finally leads to success the successful group of acts is always the last one to appear; hence when the next trial is given the last group active in the preceding test (the successful one) is thus the one most recently exercised, therefore, other things being equal, it will be the one most likely to occur first or at least early in the second trial. (2) In view of the fact that the random acts are infinitely varied the successful act is the only one performed each time the stimulus is presented. It, therefore, becomes the most frequently performed movement. (3) By reason of the fact that the final group of acts always brings food, water, removes an irritating object, lessens emotional tension, etc., the new state (attained by the result of the action of the final group) brings heightened metabolism. It is conceivable that those neuro-muscular elements which have just been active, in completing the adjustment have a slightly dilated system of blood-vessels, consequently they share more generously than the group functioning earlier in the increased and bettered blood supply. (4) It is possible that when the final group of movements functions and the adjustment is completed, the situation as a whole becomes an emotion-producing one; internal glandular secretions are set free which serve as reinforcers. It is possible to suppose, due to the increased dilatation of the blood-vessels in the elements which have just functioned, that they receive a slightly greater ''reinforcement'' (possibly increase in metabolic rate as a result of the increased blood flow to the parts in active use) from the autacoid agencies than the groups which functioned earlier. One pictures here, of course, the possible action of adrenin in neutralizing fatigue products. It should again be emphasized that these are little more than mere speculations. The fact, however, that we must confess to no ready-made explanation of this problem should detract in no way from our zeal in studying the other factors involved in habit formation.

Neural Basis of Habit.—Man is principally a visual and aural animal so far as the acquisition of habits is concerned. We mean by this that these two sense organs initiate the majority of the impulses to which he reacts in a motor way during the acquisition stage of all habit. This is far from saying that the other sense organs are not utilized in the same way or that they may not be. Certainly the contact and the kinæsthetic senses are important factors in every habit even in the initial stages. Nevertheless, the human animal, if left alone, brings vision to bear wherever possible in forming a habit. When considered purely schematically the relationships involved are quite simple. Watch any adult try to use a visible typewriter for the first time. Give him the printed word CAT. He looks over the keyboard and as soon as C stimulates the eye he strikes the key and looks at the result. He looks back at the copy, repeating the procedure until each letter is written. The activity is initiated at every step by vision. Some activities are necessarily always largely executed in the terms in which they were learned, but most acts, regardless of the sense organ used in acquisition, tend as time goes on to approach the kinæsthetic stage. An accomplished piano player rarely looks at his instrument. The "touch" stenographer never looks at the keys but only at the copy. Her hands literally run themselves (practically segmental reflexes) unless a breakdown occurs. The moment the wrong letter is struck the chain as a whole is broken and visual-motor adjustment takes place. On page 58 we called attention to the fact that every muscle is both a sense organ and a motor organ. The facts we studied there will explain how activities of great complexity can be executed wholly or largely in motor terms. Consider the following purely schematic illustration. Let A, B, C, D, E, F, etc., represent a series of visual objects to each of which we respond with a given group of movements; movements 1 to A, movements 2 to B, movements 3 to C, etc. If the series of responses is learned in an invariable way, the individual after a time gets to the point where only the first member of the visual series is necessary to produce the responses 1, 2, 3, 4, 5, etc., in their proper order.[4] How does this come about? What change has there been in the system? When visual stimulus A is presented movement 1 occurs. But when response 1 is made there arises a kinæsthetic impulse. This kinæsthetic impulse has been associated so long with the visual impulse B that it can rouse movement 2 without the visual object B actually striking the eye (substitution of stimulus). Similarly, movements in muscle 2 arouses the kinæsthetic impulse which throws muscle 3 into activity. We have outlined the matter so far with respect to normal individuals. The acquisition of habits in defectives of the blind deaf-mute type is very different. Cutaneous impulses take the place of vision and audition during the process of acquisition. This principle which we have so briefly discussed is one of the most important in the whole of psychology. By means of im-

---

[4] The so-called touch methods of teaching typewriting abbreviate learning apparently from the start. Contact and kinæsthesis take care of the movements from the beginning of learning, and the eyes are left free to follow the copy. There is no loss in time due to shifting the eyes from copy the keys and *vice versa.*

pulses from the muscles themselves man becomes partially independent of the impulses from the so-called higher senses. We
see the advantage of this when we have to act in the dark or
when we actually lose the use of one of the higher senses. We see
the final perfection of the process in thought where we have a
substituted word process for practically every object in our
environment. These substituted word processes can initiate general bodily movements exactly as do the visual or auditory stimuli
for which they stand.

**Possible Short-Circuiting in the Central Nervous Sys-
tem.**—The question arises, of course, as to whether there is a similar short-circuiting process in the central nervous system,
whether the cortex is involved in both the acquisition and the
performance stage of habit. It is conceivable, of course, that the
cortex is involved in the acquisition stage, but that as training
goes on the lower centers may short-circuit the process. We cannot answer this question definitely at the present time. It is certainly generally assumed that in the acquisition of a habit the
so-called sensory (and motor) areas in the cortex are involved,
and further that those parts of the brain must remain intact if
the habit is to exist undisturbed. For example, it is assumed
that in a visual-motor habit the visual and motor areas in the
cortex must be intact, that in an auditory-motor habit the auditory and motor areas must be without lesion. From some work
which Franz and Lashley are doing we are called upon to modify
to some extent this general view. Franz has shown that in individuals of the aphasic and paralytic types with serious destruction of nervous (brain) tissue a fairly respectable group of habits
may be built up—the subjects can be taught to speak, to knit and
sew and to play baseball. This is true even though their speech
and motor habits may have been lost for years. Lashley and
Franz, working upon the formation of habit in the rat, present
the view that one-third of any portion of the cortex as a whole
(motor area excluded) can be destroyed without interfering seriously with the animal's ability to form habits. If large portions
of the cortex are destroyed after the habit is formed, far less
serious disturbance is caused than we have been led to believe

hitherto. This view is indicated in the earlier work of Franz on the frontal cerebral lobe of cats and monkeys which was later confirmed by Swift. Franz observed that if parts of the frontal lobes of an animal (cat) that had acquired a habit were extirpated this previously learned habit was lost, but that the animal could re-acquire this habit and learn new ones. While these facts tend to disprove the early strict views of cortical localization, teaching rather that the brain as a whole is more adaptable than we have believed and that each part is tolerant of a varied type of function, it should not be assumed that the cortex is useless or that its functions are not less important than we had hitherto been led to believe: nor is it possible to conclude from such work that the cortex has the same function over the whole cerebral hemisphere or that the whole fabric of cortical localization has been destroyed. We know beyond question that the precentral gyrus is mainly responsible for the cerebral control of motor functions, and that in man at least the cortical representations of the sense organs (sensory areas) cannot be too seriously tampered with without bringing grave trouble to the habits which have previously been formed. Our interest here in the problem centers around the possibility of reëstablishing certain basal habits connected with the care of the person (eating, drinking, talking), and those connected with simple occupations in individuals who have suffered grave cortical lesion. A few years ago the thought of retraining a paralytic of long standing would not have been seriously entertained.

The Determiners of Acts.—In adult life each single object or situation can call out more than one response. The sight of a dog can cause me to run and climb a tree or to whistle for it to come and be petted. Likewise, the sight of this animal may lead me to go and get food for it, or to muzzle it, or to get my gun and go shooting. The more highly educated the man the larger the number of responses any object can call out. When explicit and implicit vocal responses are considered we can gather some idea of the enormous number of reactions that center around each situation and object. It is this possibility of multiple response to a single stimulus that makes man's reactions hard to predict in a particular instance. These habits are flexible in the sense that man is prepared to meet any slight change in the situation or object with an appropriate change in the response. The constant shifting of response is seen to best advantage in the verbal parrying and fencing of two men in argument, in the airy persiflage of a conversational kind that goes on between a witty man and woman, or in the encounters between two wrestlers, fencers, or boxers. So varied is the shading of response that habit seems at first sight to be a poorly chosen term to apply to it. But we neglect the long years of training the individual must go through with before such varied activity can take place. If we could watch the growth of such conduct we should see that its development is gradual and orderly. In view of the fact that there are so many responses possible, the question as to which will appear upon the incidence of a given stimulus becomes one which we must consider. We can answer this only in a general way and in probable terms. (1) The response most likely to appear is the one which was most recently called out by the object. (2) When recency is not pertinent the act which has been most frequently connected with the object is the one most likely to be called out. (3) The act called out is likely to be one which is most closely connected with the general setting of the situation as a whole. For example, one taking an ocean voyage with agreeable men and women companions might begin to hop about and dance at the sight of a man with a violin. But if earlier in the morning several conventional ladies had remarked that "to-day is Sunday, no dancing will be tolerated," the sight of the man with the violin may lead merely to verbal railing against the blue laws enforced beyond the three-mile limit. We are expected to display churchly behavior, funereal behavior and wedding behavior upon certain occasions. The situation as a whole envelops us and each object in that situation can call out for the time being only a narrowly appropriate and conventional type of act. (4) The most important determiners are the situations which the individual has had to come up against during the hours preceding the incidence of the stimulus to which he must now react, and the amount of emotional tension those previous activities have aroused. The usual reactions to a revolver lying on the dresser are possibly to polish and clean it periodi-

cash drawer or safe from day to day you may, on reaching home, pick up the weapon, load it, return to your office and lie in wait for the intruder. (5) Temporary intra-organic factors tremendously influence our reactions. The onset of toothache, headache, or indigestion or the beginning of seasickness may temporarily make out of an ordinarily cheerful individual one from whom normal reactions cannot be obtained. (6) The most important determiner, of course, is the life history of the individual in the sense that his general and special training, illnesses, disappointments, hobbies, family training and the like develop within him definite attitudes, trends, or slants—to the religious man each new discovery in science is a direct evidence of the beneficence of the Creator; to the scientific man it is an evidence of the keenness and assiduity of the research worker; to the down-trodden each new thing is an added burden which will merely serve to overtax him further.

We thus see that although the possibility of varied response is almost unlimited, yet definite factors are always present which rationalize behavior and give it a causal basis. In the normal individual these factors are so powerfully operative that no other line of conduct at the moment is open to him as long as he remains balanced: it is all but impossible for a balanced human being to be so torn by circumstances that he will throw a brick into his neighbor's window, steal his purse or automobile or kidnap his child. It is alike impossible for him to commit suicide or mutilate himself or others. All of these acts are possible to him in the sense that the necessary coördinations used in committing such crimes are in his repertoire. Yet his total systems of responses are so tied together that the moment he starts to perpetrate any one of them a new situation is created which immediately leads to a different act. Psychologically the individual can act only in line with his training and in conformity with his inherited points of weakness and strength. (We would recall here such factors as constitutional inferiority occurring from many causes but seen most frequently in the offspring of alcoholic, syphilitic and feeble-minded parents.)

D. DEFINITION OF "MEMORY" OF EXPLICIT BODILY HABITS.

Introduction.—The term "memory" in psychology, when properly defined, is useful, and can be made to cover a wide series of facts. Take the case of explicit motor habits such as we are now considering. An individual may learn after a short but varying number of hours of practice to write on the typewriter thirty words of ordinary copy per minute; to send ten words by wireless per minute; or to play eighteen holes of golf in eighteen strokes above bogey. The learner then stops practice for a period of time, either for experimental reasons, or because his environment changes. At the end of that time he again begins to practice. The original learning score is kept and compared with the new score now being obtained. It is found that the last score in the original series (or average of the last several scores) is higher than the present initial score (or average of the first several scores). There has been a certain loss in the efficiency of the function. We might divide all such acquisitions which are allowed to lie fallow, and are then re-learned, into three periods: (1) the learning period (original acquisition), (2) the no-practice period (the interval during which the habit was laid aside), and (3) the re-learning period. The learning period we have already discussed. The last two stages (but occasionally also the first or learning stage) are usually discussed under the term memory, although the reason for discussing the second or no-practice period under that heading arises from the misconception that in that stage something mysterious goes on in the nervous system—that there is a process of maturation taking place, expression of which is found in such a popular statement as "we learn to skate in summer and to swim in winter."

What Does Go On in Periods of no Practice?—Apparently two things may happen. (1) The more probable thing is that the various muscular and glandular combinations—the part adjustments in the habit as a whole—begin to function in new habit systems. The adjustment of muscular and glandular elements for specific duties does not stay put like the parts of an inorganic machine. They stay put and function together only so long as the situation allows a reasonable amount of exercise in those specific functions. As soon as the environment changes, so that a given habit cannot be utilized, other habits are put on, and the organism is to a certain extent made over. In the process of making over, certain groups of part activities combined to form the given habit are reincorporated into a new whole. Hence, when the organism is confronted with the old situation the old reaction, while it appears, shows a certain loss in speed and accuracy. In other words, an actual re-learning comparable in all respects to the original acquisition save in that of the total amount of time required, must ensue before the same facility in response can be obtained. (2) Oftentimes it happens that in the latter part of the original learning period the subject becomes "stale" and gives up practice before his physiological limit of skill has been attained. This staleness may be due to one of several things: (a) trying to practice at too fast a rate or under pressure of various kinds: (b) attempting to acquire the habit through a poor distribution of time, that is, the learner practices too long periods and too frequently (page 405); (c) the practice periods utilize so much time that other habit systems have to be thwarted, as happens, for example, when skill is sought rapidly in any particular line: the individual has no time to play, to engage in social functions, to eat and sleep properly, or to adjust his home or business affairs. We may group the results of the effect of all such factors under the term *staleness*. It may be said that staleness is not an idle concept or hypothetical one. It may be seen to perfection in the training for athletic contests. Many a championship game has been lost by staleness. It was such a common phenomenon in the air service during the period of most active training in the recent war that special officers were set aside to cope with the problem.[5] If the learner stops

---

[5] It must be said that the choice of the kind of officers set aside for this purpose was most curious. They were called flight surgeons, and the personnel was composed most largely of otologists. Others composing the group were obstetricians and gynæcologists. Just why this particular assortment of physicians was set aside for this particular purpose must be buried in the archives of the Air Medical Service at Washington. The most reasonable selection of men for this purpose would have been, in our opinion, psychopathologists working in conjunction with psychologists, who understand the laws connected with the formation and functioning of habit.

during a period of staleness and has the opportunity of exercising his normal tendencies it may very well, and sometimes does, happen that the no-practice period proves beneficial, even though the first score in re-learning is not so high as the final score in the original learning (it rarely or never is). Cleveland in his study of chess-playing has brought this out very well. The learner when he begins re-learning has become another individual; he comes back to his task at a higher emotional level, with a reserve strength, with a release from the pressure of thwarted tendencies and set for work. After the first two or three practice periods he may shoot far ahead of any score that he had previously made in the original learning.

Other Connotations of Memory.—Memory as ordinarily used in psychology covers a much larger field than is indicated in our discussion. In the first place it is sometimes used in testing work (page 43) as being co-extensive with organization in general. In testing defective and psychopathic individuals the ability to read is tried out, the ability to repeat or write the salient and important features of a story that is read to them: important dates in history are asked for, as well as the location of important geographical places; their age and date of birth are asked for, the number of children in the family and the like. Such tests while they involve memory in the sense in which we use the term are really random samplings of the patient's general organization. There is no lack of harmony between the use of memory and our own. Memory as we narrowly study it in the laboratory deals usually with a single function in detail and it is presupposed that we have before us the score made in the original learning, the time consumed in learning and the length of time the function was not exercised, and the re-learning score. When we make random sampling tests on an individual's organization we, of course, have no such data at hand nor do we particularly care to have it: our interest in testing patients centers around the location of their defects in organization and equipment. These data give us a picture more or less complete of the general nature of the types of defects, their number and gravity. In other words, it is a part of the diagnosis. Until it is obtained the patient or defective cannot be intelligently looked after.

For some reason the term memory has become tied up closely with the reinstatement of language activities and especially with the implicit word processes. Both psychological and popular language use the terms "recollection," "recall," "recognition" and a host of similar terms to express facts which one can see with such clearness and definiteness in the explicit habits after a period of no practice. Indeed, in the literature of psychology one finds such narrow functions abstracted, set apart and so magnified that the non-technical student begins to feel that the whole of psychology is little more than a discussion of such factors. We should be prepared to see by this time that the isolation and magnification of any particular function is wholly out of keeping with a psychology which deals with the adjustment of man as a whole to his environment.

The Behaviorist's Definition of Memory.—Memory, then, in our sense is a general term to express the fact that after a period of no practice in certain habits—explicit bodily habits, explicit word habits, implicit word habits—the function is not lost but is retained as a part of the individual's organization, although it may, through disuse, have suffered greater or less impairment. After a period of no practice, given the old stimulus or situation (1) the old reaction rises definitely and sharply; or (2) it rises but with undesirable additions (errors); or (3) it rises (if at all) with so great impairment that little organization can be noted— re-learning is as difficult as learning. This formulation of memory fits such explicit habits or functions as hewing a line with an axe or chopping down trees or tennis playing or swimming; such combined explicit and implicit activity as receiving telegraphic messages or typewriting or taking dictation or saying aloud an old poem learned in childhood; such pure implicit habits as are seen in subvocal ("mental") arithmetic or speaking a series of nonsense syllables learned by repeated silent readings twenty-four hours before; or such as those seen finally in naming an object, person, place or date after a long interval of time. In the last case mentioned in order to avoid being misunderstood we hasten to add that memory is not always evidenced by naming or giving expression to a word; often a person confronts us whom we have

not seen for some time; the stimulus of his face and figure is not
sufficient to call out his name, but it does suffice to reinstate our
old attitude toward him and possibly many of our other old reactions. We may walk with him and talk with him for some minutes
before speaking his name. Not until voice, gesture and old situations reinforce one another are all of the old reactions called out.
We become integrated then with respect to this individual, the
final group of activities being the words, "Why, of course, John
Smith! We used to play baseball together at Jonesville High
School." Exactly the same phenomena appear when after a
three-year period of disuse we try to use a complicated camera.
We are stuck for a moment on the use of the trip which releases
the shutter, or the mechanism for changing from time to instan-
taneous work, but two or three minutes of manipulation make
us letter-perfect in the use of the camera. Just so the "forgotten" name, only in that case our manipulation is vocal. We
manipulate vocally by running over the names beginning with
each succeeding letter of the alphabet, or by saying "black hair,"
"blue eyes," "six feet tall," and the like.

   Some Results of Experiments.—Possibly some of the factors
we have been investigating may be better understood if we take
up the results of experiments of laboratory studies upon the
memory of skillful acts. W. F. Book has brought out some interesting and rather startling results. This investigator taught a
number of subjects to typewrite by both the sight and touch
methods. Instead of giving his results in number of words written per minute, he gave them in number of strokes made per
minute, since he had the typewriter connected up with a series
of levers in such a way that he could record such things as
striking the spacer and moving the carriage. The subjects were
brought to a respectable speed, and then were given no practice
for considerable intervals. The record of one subject is given
in some detail below:

   The last regular practice period yielded 1503 strokes in ten
minutes. The machine was not touched again for 135 days. The
first practice in re-learning (memory test) yielded 1365 strokes.
The typewriter was not touched again for approximately a full

year. After this second period of no practice the first re-learning
test yielded 1390 strokes. We see that while there was a slight
loss it was exceedingly small.

Usually in making such tests the daily average of the last
several days in the learning period is compared with the averages of the first several days in the re-learning period. The following table presents these data:

Tests	1	2	3	4	5	6	7	8	9	10	Av.
Last Reg. Prac. Jan. 7–16, 1906	1503	1509	1404	1572	1494	1436	1501	1455	1508	1698	1508
1st Memory Test June 1–10, 1906	1365	1421	1421	1433	1529	1443	1523	1504	1313	1472	1443
2d Memory Test June 1–10, 1907	1390	1344	1345	1537	1681	1694	1634	1845	1761	1850	1611

If one contrasts the average number of strokes during the last
ten practices in learning, 1508, with the average of the ten in
the second memory test, 1611, it would appear that instead of
a loss there has been an actual gain. Indeed, Book has made
this kind of comparison and has advanced the conclusion that,
since there is no memory loss, something must go on in the non-
practice periods in the way of establishing coördinations. We
quote his own conclusions:

The increase in score shown by our second memory series
was due, so far as we could make out, rather *to the disappearance,
with the lapse of time, of numerous psycho-physical difficulties,
interfering associations, bad habits of attention, incidentally acquired in the course of learning, interfering habits and tendencies,
which, as they fade, left the more firmly established typewriting
associations free to act.* (Italics in the text.)

In general, since the so-called "useful" acts in the acquisition of any total act of skill are exercised more frequently as a
rule than the useless, there is no theoretical impossibility in
accepting the conclusions of Book, but he really has no conclusive supporting facts to offer. The curve of the original
learning is not reproduced here, but the fact is that he stopped
practicing on a spurt. Had he taken records for ten more days
his average would probably have been around 1700 strokes per

ten minutes instead of 1503. Furthermore, the practice gained from the ten days in June, 1906, was not without marked effect upon the succeeding and final memory tests. Hence, it seems that we need only to conclude that there is a tremendously great and surprising permanence in the functioning of the typewriting habit, but nothing supernatural in character.

Other investigators find a high degree of permanency, but none that corresponds with that described above. For example, Rejall increased his skill to such a point that he could write at the rate of 25 words per minute with four errors per hundred words copied. After an interval of three and a half years of no practice, he scored in the first five days 18.75 words per minute with eight errors per 100 words, 18.9 with seven and a third errors, 21 with six and two-thirds errors, 22.1 with five errors, and 22.5 with eight and two-thirds errors. In terms of total amount of practice, 30 hours were (originally) required to write 25 words a minute, with 4 errors per 100 words copied. Five hours of re-learning three and a half years later gave him approximately the same degree of skill.

Swift taught his subjects to use one hand in tossing and catching two balls, one ball being caught and thrown while the other was in the air. The number of catches made before a miss occurred gave him a method of scoring, a day's practice consisting in allowing a subject to work until ten misses occurred. Subject "A" began with a score of 4, and in the last six days of 42 days of practice attained average scores of 50, 82, 92, 88, 68 and 105. He was afterwards tested once every thirty days for five months. He attained averages on the five monthly practices respectively of 70, 80, 140, 110, 120. The subject was not retested until the end of 481 days, at which time he attained an average score of 119. He was not again tested until after a period of over four years with no practice. There was a considerable loss. He attained an average score of 5 in ten trials the first day and on successive following days his average scores were 10, 18, 20, 26, 35, 66, 60, 45, 100, 160. "Eleven days were required to regain the skill which had required 42 days of practice."

It is thus seen that the rate of deterioration in habits such as we have considered, while in all cases positive, is very slow indeed. Ordinary observations show that the same is true in regard to swimming, skating, dancing, tennis-playing and skilled mechanical work. We shall see on page 363 that this is in marked contrast to the rapid deterioration observed in habits which belong primarily in the language groups. There the deterioration is so rapid that in some cases, for example, in the learning of a series of nonsense syllables, the organization is lost in from fifteen minutes to half an hour so far as concerns the subject's ability to speak or write the words.

General Summary of Explicit Habits.—The material we have presented in this chapter shows when we consider the formation of first habits in infants (1) that when the infant is put in a situation to which it is not adjusted, it displays its repertoire of instinctive and reflex movements. By a process which we have considered, the groups of movements necessary to bring about the adjustment finally become connected or associated. Each time the situation is presented after this stage is reached only the movements necessary to bring about the adjustment appear. A habit has been formed. We saw further (2) that when we confront the adult with a situation to which he is not adjusted, he displays not the infantile, instinctive movements, but those gained from past habit organization. These larger groups in the case of the adult are combined into a new whole apparently by the same process operative in the combination of the infantile instinctive and reflex movements. We have found (3) that the memory for explicit habits remains fairly accurate over a considerable stretch of time, and what loss there is can be compensated for after a short period of practice.

One cannot overestimate the importance of the system of explicit bodily habits. On account of their definiteness and permanence they become part of man's total organization, and are as essential to him as structural parts. One might contrast our habit systems with the development of a modern factory. A hundred years ago the factory for making shoes consisted largely of an old tanbark mill driven by horses and a series of vats dug in the ground filled with water and ground tanbark for curing the hides. The equipment and personnel consisted further of a few wooden forms, iron lasts, needles, sewing-thread, knives and the shoemaker and his helper. As time went on machines were built for every separate operation in the making of a shoe, so that now the article is hardly touched by hand. The human being cannot develop new hands, muscles, glands and fingers to keep pace with civilization, but each new demand made upon him should find him still plastic and still capable of forming the habits necessary to enable him to meet it.

In the following chapter, as has been mentioned, we shall consider the formation and retention of both explicit and implicit language habits and the memory of these. It should be stated in advance that this separation is made purely in the interests of ease and clearness of presentation. The explicit and implicit language habits are formed along with the explicit bodily habits and are bound up with them and become a part of every total unitary action system that the human organism forms. They are present in the simplest types of adjustment that he makes, but it is obvious that if we desire to make a separation for purposes of presentation we can easily do so. We can see the functioning of language habits only slightly in certain activities, as, for example, in swimming, tapping on the table with a pencil, while in certain other types they form an integral part and seem to be as important as arm and hand movement, for example, in typewriting, sending and receiving telegraphic messages. Finally in certain other functions explicit activity seems to drop out almost entirely, as, for example, in subvocal arithmetic. There the explicit factors show only as excess movements such as wrinkling the brow, closing the eyes and rubbing the forehead, until the final link in the chain is reached and the answer is written down with the hand. This type of implicit (largely word) adjustment culminates in thinking, where an individual may sit for hours with practically no overt movement, finally announcing, ''I have decided to give up university work and enter commercial life.''

CHAPTER IX

THE GENESIS AND RETENTION OF EXPLICIT AND IMPLICIT LANGUAGE HABITS

Introduction.—In many of the preceding chapters we have made reference to explicit and implicit language habits. It remains now to examine these functions separately and with some care. Until language activity has been studied and connected up with the other functions we have by no means given a full account of how the human animal performs its various tasks. Man is a social being and almost from birth language activity becomes a part of his every adjustment even though that adjustment be made to other than a social situation. Our previous study of instinct, emotion and habit cannot be considered complete until we have given language its due place among those activities. The subject of explicit and implicit language processes and of other implicit but non-language processes connected with thinking is so vast and can be approached from so many angles and points of view that we can give only an extremely meagre account of its main features.

The Anatomical Basis of Language.—Throughout the text we have spoken of laryngeal processes as though they were responsible for all language organization. This manner of speaking was chosen for brevity's sake. We hasten to add now that the anatomical basis of language habits involves, of course, the whole body but specifically the neuro-muscular system in the head, neck and chest segments. A little consideration will show that the following parts coöperate in every spoken word: the diaphragm, lungs and muscles of the thorax; the extrinsic and intrinsic muscles of the larynx; the muscles of the pharynx, nose and palate; the cheeks, tongue and lips. The larynx as such when considered merely as a mechanism for controlling the vocal cords is the least important part of the system. It is quite important, of course, as a means of speaking aloud, but relatively unimportant from the standpoint of the functioning of the indi-

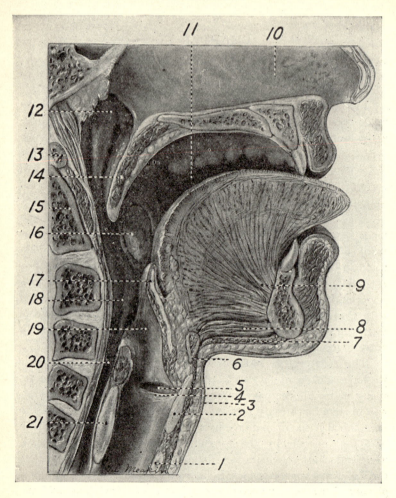

FIG. 59.—Showing pharynx and related structures. 1, Cricoid cartilage (cartilago cricoidea); 2, thyroid cartilage (cartilago thyreoidea); 3, "Adam's apple" (prominentia laryngea); 4, vocal cord (plica vocalis); 5, ventricle (ventriculus laryngis); 6, section of hyoid bone (corpus ossis hyoidei); 7, mylo-hyoid muscle (m. mylohyoideus); 8, genio-hyoid muscle (m. geniohyoideus); 9, genio-glossus muscle (m. genioglossus); 10, nasal septum (septum nasi); 11, mouth cavity; 12, nasal pharynx (pars nasalis pharyngis); 13, anterior arch of atlas; 14, soft palate (palatum molle); 15, body of axis (corpus epistrophei); 16, tonsil (tonsilla palatina); 17, epiglottis; 18, laryngeal pharynx (pars laryngea pharyngis); 19, vestibule (vestibulum laryngis); 20, œsophagus; 21, cricoid cartilage (cartilago cricoidea).

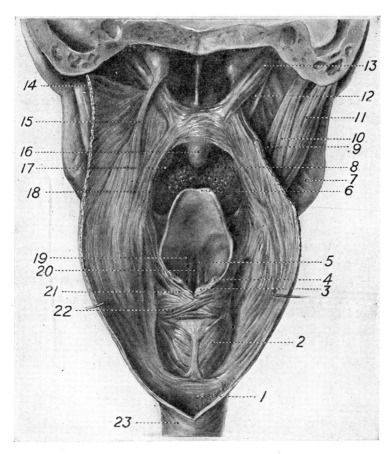

Fig. 60.—Showing the larynx and the muscles of the pharynx, view from behind. As can be inferred, the pharynx has been opened to show the laryngeal mechanism. The mucosa and sub-mucosa have been removed to show the underlying muscular connections. 1, circular muscular fibers of the œsophagus; 2, posterior crico-arytenoid muscle (m. cricoarytænoideus posterior); 4, cuneiform cartilage (tuberculum cuneiforme (Wrisbergi)); 3, corniculate cartilage (tuberculum corniculatum (Santorini)); 5, vocal cord (plica vocalis); 6, epiglottis; 7, m. pterygoideus internus; 8, tongue; 9, m. stylopharyngeus; 10, m. stylohyoideus; 11, m. digastricus; 12, m. tensor veli palatini; 13, m. levator veli palatini; 14, m. constrictor pharyngis superior; 15, m. salpingo-pharyngeus; 16, uvula; 17, tonsil (tonsilla palatina); 18, m. pharyngo palatinus; 19, plica ventricularis; 20, rima glottidis; 21, m. arytænoideus obliquus; 22, m. aryepiglotticus; 23, muscular coating of œsophagus (tunica muscularis œsophagi). (The author is indebted to Mr. Paul Curt Richter for making the dissection for this drawing.)

vidual's word organization. This statement may seem somewhat reactionary since we have seemingly laid so much stress upon the larynx, but we shall soon see that the glottis with its vocal cords may be removed without seriously affecting the subject's ability to use whispered words.

Brief Description of the Larynx and Neighboring Parts.— The anatomy of the neck and upper thorax regions is the most complicated of the whole body. Fig. 59 shows the cavity of the mouth and pharynx with related structures. Attention is called in this figure to the mouth region proper, including the lips, cheeks, tongue, gums, teeth and hard palate; to the pharynx, the nasal portion of which is separated from the mouth region by the overhanging soft palate and uvula. The pharynx extends upward to the base of the skull, receiving the posterior opening of the nasal passages and downward to the œsophagus, at which level one finds the larynx. We can divide the pharynx into three parts, nasal, oral and laryngeal. The larynx itself is easy to locate in the male by the presence of the Adam's apple (Fig. 60). This prominent structure is the thyroid cartilage, consisting of two plates which in the male join at an angle of 90 degrees, in the female at 120 degrees. The larynx is suspended from the tongue and the hyoid bone. Its framework consists of three symmetrical cartilages (thyroid, cricoid and cartilage of the epiglottis) and three paired cartilages (arytenoid, corniculate and cuneiform). Special attention is called to the cartilage of the epiglottis, which is placed in front of the superior opening of the larynx, projecting downward behind the base of the tongue. The epiglottis assists in closing the laryngeal opening during the act of swallowing. Until puberty the larynx is smooth, slight and similar in the male and female. In the female this condition persists, but in the male profound changes occur around the thirteenth year. The larynx becomes prominent, due to the enlargement and thickening of the cartilages. The vocal ligaments likewise become lengthened, thus making a deeper voice possible. The vertical diameter, that is the distance from the upper border of the thyroid cartilage to the lower border of the cricoid, is 4.8 cm. in males, 3.8 cm. in females. The transverse diameter is nearly the same, 4.3 cm. in males and 4.1 cm. in females. The anterior-posterior diameter is 3.6 cm. in males and 2.6 cm. in females. The cavity of the larynx opens upward through the vocal cords into the trachea. The trachea bifurcates into the

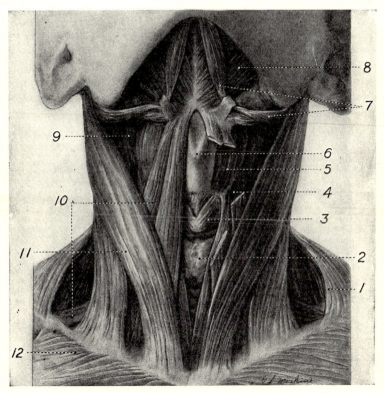

Fig. 61.—Muscles in the region of the larynx. 6, Thyroid cartilage (cartilago thyreoidea): this marks the position of the larynx. In the male the prominent junction of the two plates forming the cartilage is called the Adam's apple (pomum Adami); 1, m. trapezius; 2, thyroid gland (glandular thyreoidea); 3, m. crico thyreoideus; 4, m. sternothyreoideus; 5. m. thyreohyoideus; 7, m. digastricus; 8, m. mylohyoideus; 9, m. longus capitis; 10, m. omohyoideus; 11, m. sternocleidomastoideus; 12, m. pectoralis major.

right and left bronchi, which communicate with the two lungs.

The vocal cords are shown in Fig. 62 stretched across the membranous glottis. Some of the intrinsic and extrinsic muscular connections of the larynx and pharynx are shown in Fig. 61.

It is impossible to enter into the separate action of these muscles by means of which the larynx as a whole is raised or lowered and the vocal cords tightened or relaxed. The whole subject of laryngeal and allied action has developed into the science of phonetics to which anatomy, physiology, medicine, physics and psychology contribute.

The Production of Laryngeal Sounds.—In general it may be said that (1) the membranous glottis with the vocal cords is the exclusive seat of voice production. Removal of the cords renders the production of overt speech impossible; (2) the vibration of the air produced by the vocal cords starts in the glottis and is transmitted to the air lying above and below, to the chest

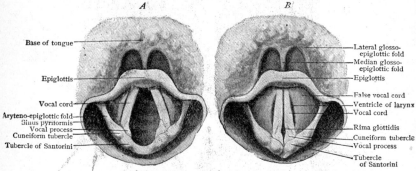

Fig. 62.—Interior of the larynx as seen with laryngoscope. A, with glottis widely open; B, closed. (From Piersol's Human Anatomy.)

cavity on the one hand and to the throat and mouth on the other. These cavities act as resonators. The main source of modification of the sound consists of the parts lying above the vocal cords— the laryngeal vestibule, the pharynx, mouth and nose. In order to produce this resonance there must be a varying tension of the walls and alterations in the length, breadth and shape of this continuous cavity as well as upward and downward movements of the larynx, alterations of the tongue, soft palate, cheeks and lips. The sounds produced by the human voice are comprised in the interval of three and a half octaves. Few individuals ever attain a range of three octaves. The effective range of even a well-developed singer rarely exceeds two octaves.

Effect of the Removal of the Larynx.—Articulate language,

which is limited to man—and which is, as we have elsewhere tried
to bring out, the main behavior difference between man and brute
—consists from the physical standpoint of a series of special
expiratory and inspiratory sounds produced in the resonance
cavity of the mouth, pharynx and nose. It need not be combined
with laryngeal tones. In talking aloud, crying, or singing the
laryngeal tones are combined with pharyngo-buccal sounds, but
in whispering, that is, whispering without voice, there are no
laryngeal tones. Since Czermak in 1858 improved the methods
of laryngeal examination the larynx has been removed many
times. Naturally the immediate effect of the removal of the
larynx is to destroy the ability to speak aloud, since normal speech
requires breath from the lungs acting upon the larynx, but so
long as the air can pass from the lungs to the pharynx and
mouth, faint whispered speech is possible. When the air passage
is entirely closed between lungs and mouth, as happens when the
windpipe is opened below the larynx and the patient has to
breathe through an opening in the neck (tracheal cannula), all
articulate speech even of the whispered *sotto voce* type disappears.
*But such individuals can and do still make all of the movements
necessary for articulate speech.* This is the answer to the criticisms which have been directed against the point of view that has
been advocated throughout the text, namely, that thought is the
action of language mechanisms.[1] In our examination of the
history of the cases where the larynx has been removed we
have found nothing which would seriously discredit the view we
have advocated. To destroy enough of the sensory motor
mechanisms to make language organization and hence thought
impossible would in all probability bring about the death of the
patient. In view of the great importance from a theoretical
standpoint of this subject it would seem worth while to make a
thorough study of such individuals. So far the observation of
these cases has been left to the surgeons who have little theoretical

---

[1] It is aside from our present aims to point out that even those individuals with the breath cut off from the pharynx soon learn to speak by
the formation of new language habits. Scripture and several other authors
have described the process in detail.

22

interest in them and to speech specialists who are interested merely in teaching the patient how to talk again.

A. The Formation of Explicit Language Habits.

Early Reflex and Instinctive Responses.—The birth cry begins the vocal career of the human child. This cry differs markedly in different babies. On the subject of early sounds in infants we quote Mrs. Blanton:

> The crying of one baby can be distinguished with some practice from the cries of another even in a nursery of 25, the overtones varying just as in older people. Subject M., first day, *u* (cut), *nah* (at) accent on last syllable, *wah* (at), *wuh* (cut), *ha* (at). The "hunger cry" has generally a well-marked rhythm, the first syllable of preliminary sound coming on the first part of the first beat, the second or accented syllable on the second part of the first beat and a quick intake of breath as the third beat. This measure is most often repeated in groups of 5 or 6, each slightly more forceful than the preceding ones until the fourth or fifth, the last one being softer. Thus also will the groups be repeated. Each measure is also a trifle higher in pitch than the one preceding.
>
> *Sounds Heard During the First Thirty Days.*—Consonant sounds commonly heard are *m* in conjunction with *a* as *ma* (at), *n* as *nga* (nat), *g* as *gah, h* as in *ha* (at), *w* in *wah* (at), *r* as in *rah* (at), *r* as in *burr,* very slight sound, and *y* as in *yah* (at).
>
> Vowel sounds are *o* as in owl, *e* as in feel, *oo* as in pool, *a* as in and and *a* as in father (relatively rare).

The study which this author made on the vocal acts of infants was purely observational. No very satisfactory laboratory study has yet been made of the early instinctive vocal equipment of the infant. That it is vastly complex is admitted by every one. The extent to which the instinctive equipment varies in the different races is another interesting matter for speculation. The fact that a perfect speaking knowledge of a foreign language can be acquired only in early youth depends probably upon the structural changes going on in the larynx, ossification of those structures beginning about the twentieth year. It is sometimes asserted, of course, that the reason a foreign language is hard to learn is due to the lack of the proper vocal instincts, to differences

in the resonating mechanisms, and the like.   There is probably
little evidence for this.

Whether there are well-marked vocal instincts in the child
corresponding to such instincts in other animals is not known
with sureness.   The popular view gives an affirmative answer
here, namely, that there are distinct hunger cries, colic and pain
cries and various other cries connected with emotional states, as
the gurgle, coo, babble and many others.   A good many of the
articulate sounds that we make under strong emotional excitement may be the direct expression of vocal instincts, that is, they
are not conventional speech words (or were not in origin) but
direct instinctive responses such, for example, as oh! la! ha!
ugh!   Individual variations in vocal sounds are well marked in
infants at the earliest ages.   One learns quickly to name the child
which is crying or performing other vocal acts.

Early Vocal Habits.—Serviceable studies of the formation of
early vocal habits and language habits proper have not yet been
made in the laboratory.   It is well to draw distinction between
a vocal habit and a language habit.   By vocal habit is meant the
mere sounding of words of the non-instinctive type.   The word
has to be learned, but it may be learned as the parrot learns it.
It has not yet been connected up with other vocal action and with
general bodily actions.

Ordinary observation shows that the earliest explicit word
habits are of this type.   These early word habits are formed in
much the same way as are other explicit habits.   The infant starts
with his instinctive repertoire and the various word acts are
fixed in the same way and by the same process that the successful
act is fixed in any other habit.   One additional factor seems to
come in, namely, that of imitation.   Imitation plays a very minor
rôle in the acquisition of manual habits.   In the laboratory we
have tried many times to get children from ten to eighteen months
to imitate simple movements, like putting the hand flat upon the
table, putting the two hands together, but without much success.
The same may be said with reference to putting a child through
various bodily acts.   Apparently imitation of hand and general
body movements cannot take place until the infant has already

learned to make a large group of well-coördinated movements. In other words, imitation is not a process by means of which new (elementary) coördinations may be formed. In the case of vocal acts there seems to be a difference. Imitation seems to be a process directly connected with the establishment of the act. The parents, of course, watch every new instinctive sound that approximates articulate speech and they immediately speak the word that is nearest the child's own vocal efforts (for example, "ma," "pa"— "da"). The imitation here may be more apparent than real. That is, the parents by repeating the sound constantly offer a stimulus for that which the infant's vocal mechanisms are just set to utter.[2] Whether the parent's words can set the mechanism is doubtful. We may be accused here of fighting a straw man. Certainly imitation in the popular sense is the only way a new conventional word can be learned by the child until the elementary laws of word formation are learned through reading and instruction.

Early Language Habits.—Vocal acts or habits, however numerous they may be, do not become language habits until they become associated with arm, hand and leg activities and substitutable for them. This probably accounts in a better way than any hypothetical change in brain structure for the relatively late putting on of language habits. As long as the child remains in its crib or in the arms of its mother, or has the whole household to wait upon it and anticipate its needs, there is no necessity for it to develop language. If we examine the bodily habits of any child just prior to the beginning of true language habits, we find that it can respond appropriately to hundreds of objects and situations, for example, to its doll, bottle, blocks, rattle and many other things. Its environment is becoming complex. Abbreviated and short-circuited actions become a necessity if it is to hold its own in that environment and make progress.

Let us give a partially hypothetical illustration of the way true language habits grow up. We will suppose that for some reason or other a child's toys are laid away and covered up.

---

[2] Conradi has shown that the forms of the cries and songs of young birds brought up by adults of a different species are greatly modified.

What does he do in such a situation? Essentially what the animal does when it is hungry. The child begins general restless movements among which are movements of the language structures as shown by its making "aimless" vocal sounds. His throat formation at that stage of growth is of such a character that a particular sound is uttered frequently (let us say "tata" for illustrative purposes). He begins to utter this sound as he roams about. The attendant, knowing the child's range of toys and the frequency with which he plays with a certain one, predicts that an old rag doll is sought. She finds it, hands it to him and says, "Here's your tata." Repeat this process long enough and "tata" will be always used for rag doll and will always be spoken whenever the doll is sought. This process is, of course, repeated again and again in the course of a day. The word gets tied up with the act of seeking the doll. In this way baby words grow up as the first genuine form of true language organization. A large number of these belong to the vocabulary of every child, such as the grunt or growl as a signal for attention to personal needs. The putting on of conventional speech habits is thus an illustration of conditioned reflex level of functioning (vocal habit) plus later associative connection of the word when learned with the bodily habits connected with the object for which the word stands (true language habits). To further illustrate our point we may give excerpts from an earlier statement:

A stimulus to which a child often responds by opening and closing and putting objects into it is the box in which his toys are kept. The nurse, observing that the child reacts with his hands and fingers to the box begins at a suitable age to say "box" when the child is handed the box, "open box" when the child opens it, and "close box" when he closes it and "put blocks in box" when that act is executed. This is repeated over and over again until the conditioned reflexes are thoroughly established. In the course of time the box in front of him, which originally called out only bodily habits, now begins to call out word habits. He says "box" when it is handed to him, "open box" when he opens it. The sight of the box now becomes a stimulus capable of releasing either the bodily acts or the word acts, or both. A series of functional connections is established between vision and throat and laryngeal muscles which exists alongside of the already earlier established connections which run from the same receptor to the arm and leg muscles. When the box is presented now, which act will take place? Manual action or laryngeal action? It is at this point that the influence of the environment upon the shaping and forcing of language habits comes clearly to the front. There comes an occasion when the box can be seen but not reached. Action in the hand is blocked. He speaks ''box'' and may speak it persistently all over the house. The attendant, hearing the word box, hastens to put it in his hands. In view of the fact that this situation is repeated day in and day out, not only with respect to this object but to hundreds of others, the child learns that the uttered word is a sufficient stimulus to cause the attendant to hand him the objects he names without actually having to execute bodily movements with respect to them. There has been a substitution of the language habit for a bodily habit—now by a word he can cause adults to move—his grunt or growl or infant toy word is law. The tyranny with which the youngster rules this newly acquired kingdom is equaled by that displayed in the reign of but a few crowned heads in history.

This roughly marks what we might call the genesis of a true language habit. It is a very inadequate account, but we are forced to be content with it until the process has been more carefully studied in the laboratory. The formation of simple language habits has often been clothed with a good many high-sounding but rather meaningless phrases. For example, it is said that language is purely social and that words arise only by virtue of the fact that man is a social being. This is perfectly true in one respect, namely, that unless the child is surrounded by individuals who use conventional word forms he would never get the auditory and visual stimuli which would lead to such habit formation. On the other hand, they are no more social so far as the way in which they are acquired is concerned than are the bodily habits described in the last chapter.

Rapidity of Formation of Language Habits.—The growth of the vocabulary of the child is, of course, only a rough measure of the growth of true language habits. It uses many words which belong to the conditioned reflex level of word activity rather than to the highly integrated and associated level of the adult. Children's vocabularies increase with astonishing rapidity. Drever has recently made a study of three children, two boys and one girl. The test was limited to 10 days. Paper and pencil were carried by the observer and every new word was noted. J. at 54 months had a vocabulary of 1712 words (of 2000 if proper names were included); D., 43 months, 824 words; H., 28 months, 354 words. In view of the fact that many words could not be noted, Drever states that it seems fair to put down their respective vocabularies as consisting of 2000, 960, and 400 words. Bateman, working with a larger number of children, states that 9 infants at the age of one year possessed on the average a vocabulary of 9½ words; 23 of them at 24 to 28 months, used on the average 441 words. Fig. 63 plotted from this data (which is not sufficient for a true curve) gives a rough indication of the speed of word habit formation.

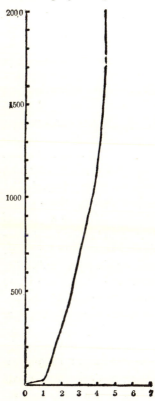

Fig. 63.—Curve showing growth of vocabulary in children. The vertical line gives the number of words; the horizontal, the age of the child in years.

B. Implicit Language Habits.

Gradual Transition from Explicit to Implicit Language.— At what point in their language organization children make the transition from overt to whispered and then to implicit language has been studied only incidentally. Possibly all three forms go on together from the start. The reason why children are so talkative probably is due to the fact that at an early age their environment does not force a rapid shift from explicit to implicit language (they are really thinking aloud. A good many so-called psycho-analytical factors also enter here). The shift is not complete even in the adult. This is clear from the observation of individuals while they are reading and thinking. Many persons never get to the point where they can read without articulating the words sufficiently for the process to become overt —the lips are moved in unison with the eyes (or rather they lag behind the eye as does the voice when reading aloud). A good lip reader can actually gather some of the words read by such an individual. While thinking many use articulate speech or even lip speech much as do the readers just described. Again, certain people who talk to themselves incessantly when alone or when in the presence of one greatly inferior never complete the transition stage. Our view is that overt language develops under social training. It is thus absorbed into and becomes a part of every total integration of the individual. Hence when he is making adjustments in the absence of other like beings language remains as a part of the process. But there is no stimulus for him to talk aloud when alone; as a matter of fact, talking aloud under such circumstances introduces conflicting stimuli, the auditory stimulus breaking in upon the otherwise silent room. Hence, silent talking takes place which rapidly improves by practice since it is exercised during every waking and certainly during many sleeping moments. In the acquisition of general bodily acts of skill we have found by experimentation that every short-cut possible which would abbreviate action and increase speed and skill is finally hit upon by the individual in a trial and error way. Sometimes we note this improvement and phrase it in words, often we neither note nor phrase it until long after it has been learned. The same thing undoubtedly takes place in silent talking or thinking. Even if we could roll out the implicit processes and record them on a sensitive plate or phonograph cylinder it is possible that they would be so abbreviated, short-circuited and economized that they would be unrecognizable unless their formation had been watched from the transition point where they are complete and social in character, to their final stage where they will serve for individual but not for social adjustments.

Non-Language Forms of Thought.—From our standpoint it is not necessary to assume that all thought is laryngeal even if we use "laryngeal" to include the whole mechanism described on page 334. We have learned to write words, sentences and paragraphs, to draw objects and to *trace them with the eyes,* hands and fingers. We have done this so often that the process has become system·atized and substitutive. In other words, they come to serve as stimuli substitutable for the object seen, drawn, written or handled. These implicit processes may bring about a silent word (thought word), a spoken word (name of the object or associated word), or an appropriate bodily act. This form of implicit activity is seen to best advantage in non-speaking individuals such as deaf mutes or blind deaf mutes. The author has carried out some correspondence with the constant companions of such individuals. Those observers who have to communicate constantly with such defectives state that if the mutes are closely watched the sign language corresponding to lip activity in the reading of normal persons can be observed quite often. But of course, even in such cases there is a very rapid transition from overt sign language to implicit sign language. The moment the overt slips into the implicit, instrumentation becomes necessary to bring the process out for observation.

It should be clear now that we would not abstract language, overt or implicit, or other implicit thought processes, from their general setting in bodily integration as a whole. The emphasis that we have placed upon it now and then may have led to that point of view. Our reason for such emphasis is that psychologists as a group have not connected up thought with the rest of the process of integration. They have separated it out and made it something *toto cælo* different from the organization processes with which we are now so familiar. Some writers make a complete mystery of it; something that we can talk about and discuss, something whose manifestations we may observe but whose essence we can never discover. Others have considered thought processes as a correlate of cortical activity (a common assumption). They assume that it is something, no one knows quite what, that can go on in the absence apparently of all muscular activity. If our view is correct, it is a constituent part of every adjustment process. It is not different in essence from tennis-playing, swimming or any other overt activity except that it is hidden from ordinary observation and is more complex and at the same time more abbreviated so far as its parts are concerned than even the bravest of us could dream of.

A More Detailed Analysis of Thinking.—The term thinking ought to be made to cover generally all implicit language activity and other activity substitutable for language activity. [It should be admitted furthermore that under proper stimulation (usually a request is sufficient) the subject can be made to think aloud.] Thinking would comprise then the subvocal use of any language or related material whatever, such as the implicit repetition of poetry, day dreaming, rephrasing word processes in logical terms, running over the day's events verbally, as well as implicit planning for the morrow and the verbal working out of difficult life situations. The term '' verbal '' here must be made broad enough to cover processes substitutable for verbal activity, such as the shrug of the shoulder and the lifting of the brows. It must embrace the implicit movements involved in written words or the implicit movements demanded in the use of the deaf-and-dumb sign manual, which are, in essence, word activity. Thinking then might become our general term to cover all subvocal behavior. It is obvious that this definition can take care of the most mechanical and deeply grounded of our language habits such as those used in the subvocal repetition of childhood verse, the repetition of stanzas of poetry, limericks, etc.; those depending more particularly upon emotional stimuli as day dreaming, as well as those verbal processes not completely habitual such as the working out of a lecture, the planning of a book; and finally those in which new results are brought out. It is clear that if in the interests of systematic psychology we need to sub-divide the whole process of thinking, three lines of cleavage will at once appear.

1. Mere unwinding of vocal habits where the word sequences are invariable: illustrated by rhymes, quotations; by many of the responses in mathematics, as 2 and 2 equal 4, square root of 9 equals 3, and the like. Here there is no new work, no trial movements like those we see in overt manual activity when a new situation capable of solution is presented the first few times. Such thinking corresponds to an extremely simple stimulus and response type of behavior. Similarly day dreaming would fall under this division. We assume that such dreaming takes place in response particularly to deficiency stimuli of one kind or another; such as the absence of sex activity, lack of food and water, lack of habitual surroundings and companions, lack of drugs, or even under the sway of drugs.

2. The solving of problems which are not new, but which are so infrequently met with that trial verbal behavior is demanded; illustrated probably by thinking out of stanzas, partially forgotten; in trying to apply one mathematical formula after another in a particular problem at hand. All of the part processes have been met with by the individual and are part of his organization, but he cannot use these part processes with machine-like facility.

3. Finally we have the extreme extension of 2 above. Here the problem is new and the organism when confronting such a problem is in a grave situation. We will suppose, for example, that a man loses his position and wealth suddenly and must be ready in a few hours to act explicitly in a new undertaking. The problem, it is assumed, is of such a character that it must be worked out verbally before any overt action can take place. Hundreds of examples of this type immediately suggest themselves. Most of the real social and moral problems appearing in one's life are exactly of this type.

These subdivisions are really guesses as to what may go on. No scientific division is as yet possible. It should be expressly stated, furthermore, that thinking in any of the above forms is not an isolated process. A human animal never gets away from his biography; and the varying organic and emotional states the organism is in must exert a tremendous influence upon the course of his thinking. So that once more we would emphasize the fact that thinking, whatever its type, is an integrated bodily process.

Probably not many students would include 1 and 2 under the term "thinking." Thinking has come to be identified with 3 of our division, but for no valid reason. We use the term manual activity when our subject ties his shoe strings in exactly the way we use it when he is *learning* to manipulate (for the first time) the most complicated of machine-gun mechanisms. In our opinion 3 represents a bit of behavior on the part of the human animal which, when stripped of its unessentials, is exactly like that bit of behavior which the rat exhibits when put into a complicated maze for the first time. When it gets to the food the autonomic strivings die down and it goes to sleep. The deficiency stimuli, lack of food, lack of usual surroundings, etc., cease to operate—the adjustment is complete.

Surely a similar thing takes place in man. He is a verbally behaving animal. If he is put into a somewhat similar situation —when for example, his employer says to him: " What would you do about this situation? "—describing to him a certain set of conditions—then trial and error thinking begins if the situation is really new. Ask him to think aloud. Notice how he wanders verbally here and there." No, I wouldn't do that because of X, Y and Z." Past verbal organization keeps guiding and goading him just as culs-de-sac control the rat in the maze. As soon as a point in the thinking progression is reached which causes the nagging impulses to search farther, to cease, then the adjustment is complete. It may take the form of overt action with the arms, hands, legs and trunk; it may be subvocally expressed, or expressed aloud in speech in the form of a " judgment." It may or may not be " right " (logical, moral, etc.). The rat, when he opens the box may be eating indigestible or poisoned food—or food deficient in vitamines—but nevertheless its problem is solved *because the nagging stimuli from the stomach have died away.* So with the man's verbal conclusions and judgments. The adjustment is complete—the problem solved for him—*as soon as he has made a verbal (or other) response which allays,*

*causes to die down, intraorganic stimuli impelling him to fur-
ther verbal activity.*

Illustration of Thinking Made Overt.—Considerable knowledge about thinking behavior can be gained by making the subject
think aloud. Usually a scientific man is quite willing to enter into
such an experiment with zest. If I ask my subject in 1 to
think aloud he overtly responds with his limerick, his day
dreaming or his mathematical answer. Similarly if I ask him
to think aloud in 2, I notice hesitations here and there, false starts
and occasional returns, but in general a fairly ready response
occurs with relatively few errors. It is only when we ask him
to think aloud in 3 above that we begin to grasp how relatively
crude is the process of thinking. Here we see typified all of the
errors made by the rat in the maze; false starts appear; emotional
factors show themselves, such as the hanging of the head and possibly even blushing when a false scent is followed up. The subject
returns again and again to his starting point as shown by his
asking: " You say the given facts are so and so? " The experimenter says " Yes " and again the subject starts off. In conducting an experiment of this kind, one has to be careful to
impose problems upon his subject which are as far as possible
removed from repressed emotional factors. It is never possible
of course completely to do this as the analysts have more than
once pointed out. The following illustration will make clear
some of the points which appear in overt thinking.

A colleague of mine came on a visit to stay in an apartment
in which I had rooms. In a passage leading from the shower
bath was a peculiar piece of apparatus standing near a sink. The
essential features were a curved shallow nickel pan about twelve
inches wide by twenty inches long; at one end the pan had been
bent in in the form of a half circle, while at the other end the side
pieces did not extend for the full width. The pan was mounted on
a stand adjustable in height. Furthermore the pan itself was attached to the stand by a ball and socket joint. My friend had never
seen anything like it and asked me what in the world it was. I told
him I was writing a paper on thinking and pleaded with him to
think his problem out aloud. He entered into the experiment in the
proper spirit. I shall not record all of his false starts and returns

but I will sketch a few of them. " The thing looks a little like an invalid's table, but it is not heavy, the pan is curved, it has side pieces and is attached with a ball and socket joint. It would never hold a tray full of dishes (*cul de sac*). The thing (return to starting point) looks like some of the failures of an inventor. I wonder if the landlord is an inventor. No, you told me he was a porter in one of the big banks down town. The fellow is as big as a house and looks more like a prize-fighter than a mechanician; those paws of his would never do the work demanded of an inventor " (blank wall again). This was as far as we got on the first day. On the second morning we got no nearer the solution. On the second night we talked over the way the porter and his wife lived, and the subject wondered how a man earning not more than $150 per month could live as our landlord did. I told him that the wife was a hair-dresser and earned about eight dollars per day herself. Then I asked him if he did not see the sign " Hair-Dresser " on the door as we entered. The next morning after coming from his bath he said, " I saw that infernal thing again " (original starting point). " It must be something to use in washing or weighing the baby—but they have no baby (*cul de sac* again). The thing is curved at one end so that it would just fit a person's neck. Ah! I have it! The curve does fit the neck. The woman you say is a hair-dresser and the pan goes against the neck and the hair is spread out over it." This was the correct conclusion. Upon reaching it there was a smile, a sigh and an immediate turn to something else (the equivalent of obtaining food after search).

Behaviorist's Right to Assume That a Process of Implicit Thinking Goes on.—Notwithstanding the fact that we can make our subjects think aloud and thereby observe a large part of the process of thinking, Titchener some years ago raised the objection : " How does the behaviorist know there is any such process as thinking since he cannot directly observe it ? " Titchener held the view that the behaviorist—*quâ* behaviorist—doesn't know that there is any such thing as thinking. The introspectionist claims that the behaviorist first uses the method of introspection to find thinking and having once found it shuts his eyes and turns his back upon his original method and begins to externalize the process and to put it in the universal language of science. In other words, he describes it merely as the functioning of laryngeal or other motor processes.

The behaviorist's answer is that he can *at present* arrive at this conclusion only by making use of a logical inference. In those cases where the response to the stimulus is not immediate but where it finally occurs in some form of explicit verbal or manual behavior, it is safe to say that something does go on, and that that something is surely not different in essence from that which goes on when his behavior is explicit. Let us glance for a moment at a manual illustration. I hand a friend a gold cigarette case which can be opened only by pressing a secret spring. I tell him that he can keep the case if he can open it without violence. I watch him for two minutes, noting his rambling trial manipulatory movements. He fails to open it in this period of time. I then place him in a room alone, and tell him to come out when he has opened it. At the end of thirty minutes he emerges smiling and with the case open. Since there are no marks of violence on the case, the behaviorist, utilizing logic, has a right to assume that the subject continued to work at the problem as he had been trained to work at such problems and that his behavior in the empty room was essentially the same as that exhibited by him when he was under direct observation. Merely because observation of his behavior could not take place so long as he was hidden from the observer gives no one the right to assume that any different or unusual process went on. One need not hesitate to call this behavior on the part of our subject manual thinking or non-language thinking. There is no necessity for it, however, since our categories of trial-and-error learning, functioning of habit, etc., are adequate. We suggest manual thinking here to show its complete homology with that type of behavior described below which is more universally called thinking.

Suppose instead of giving him a problem which can be learned by manual trial-and-error manipulation I say: " What would be the result on your social and vocational life if through some accident you suddenly had both arms removed? " Assuming, as would be safe in most instances, that such a problem had not hitherto been faced and formulated, he would be unable to give any adequate statement. Suppose we insisted upon a formulation. At the end of an hour he would probably be able to return a fairly comprehensive reply. Surely the behaviorist has the right to assume, that implicit language activity, sensori-motor in character, has been taking place during the hour on as grand a scale as overt bodily movements would have been taking place had I left him in a room from which there was no obvious exit and suddenly yelled " Fire! " from the outside. We can infer that language activity from infancy onward has been developed just to meet such situations; hence that during the period of his apparent immobility he was using implicit language processes. Such processes are the only available types of organization which we have any objective right to assume can be used in such a situation.[1]

---

[1] In other words, since our assumed explanation is simple and straightforward and adequate to account for all the facts and is in line with what can actually be observed in other activities, the law of parsimony demands that the upholders of " imagery " and " imageless thought " should show the need of such " processes " and demonstrate objectively their presence. In fairness to the behaviorist it should be admitted that words or even objects not usually visually reacted to may through the mechanism of the conditioned reflex arouse muscular reactions in the eyelid, in the muscles of the eye, in the pupil, and *even in the retina itself.* Apparently there is considerable evidence, as we have pointed out elsewhere, that the retina is supplied with centrifugal neural elements. This position is highly speculative but it does give us, theoretically at any rate, a possibility of accounting for a visual stimulus constituent in the absence of actual light. It may be that this intraorganically aroused visual constituent is a much more important element in the total stimulating situation than has been generally admitted. The delicate changes going on in the action currents of the eye lend some support to this view. The long-delayed appearance of after-images now established by Swindel's work also support it as do the phenomena appearing in ordinary after images, phosphenes, electrical stimulation of the eye, hallucinations, dreams and the like.

Whether a similar set of conditions can take place in the case of the ear is more doubtful. The presence of centrifugal neural elements entering the tectorial and basilar membranes of the inner ear has not to our knowledge been discovered.

From the standpoint of theory, this distinction between a *visual reaction* and a " visual image " is important. There is inherent in it the difference between a thoroughgoing monism and a thoroughgoing dualism.

Some unpublished results of experiments of Dr. K. S. Lashley, begin to approach a scientific proof that essentially the same type of responses goes on in implicit thinking as goes on in more explicit types of verbal response.   With a delicate apparatus which recorded the tongue movements in two dimensions he was enabled to show that the overt but whispered repetition of a sentence produced a tracing on the smoked drum which was wholly similar except for amplitude to that obtained when he told the subject to think the same thing without making overt movements. He was enabled to verify this again and again.   On the other hand if he obtained a standard tracing to a whispered sentence and then gave the subject other work to do and later came back and asked him to think the sentence, there was no obvious correspondence in the two tracings (the original motor set had changed). This is not an argument against our point if we recall how varied is the musculature of the larynx and the throat.   We can write the same word by a dozen different combinations in the holding of the pen.   We can speak or think the same word by many different muscular combinations.

The behaviorist need be no more afraid to admit that the subject himself could observe during the apparent immobile period that he used words and sentences (and that for a part of the time he did not know what he was using!) than to admit that the subject can observe that he himself is laying bricks or playing a piano.   We have elsewhere admitted a verbal report method but at the same time insisted upon its untrustworthiness for scientific purposes.   To know anything worth while for science about my brick-laying we must get a Gilbreth or some other observer to record by motion pictures or otherwise my every act while laying bricks.   In other words, scientific conclusions demand instrumentation.   I can observe roughly that I have raised a wall four feet high by my day's work, but I cannot determine how many millions of useless movements I have made or how these useless movements could be eliminated by a change in my method of work.   Apparently the same thing is true of thinking.   The subject can observe that he is using words in thinking.   But how much word material is used, how much his final formulation is influenced by implicit factors which are

23

not put in words and which he cannot himself observe, cannot
be stated by the subject himself.

The point we would emphasize here is that if we are ever
to learn scientifically any more about the intimate nature of
thought other than that which can be obtained by observing
the end results—that is, by observing the overt verbally expressed
behavior or the overt ensuing bodily actions—we shall have to
resort to instrumentation. The time seems far off when such
a thing is possible. While awaiting it the behaviorist has ample
with which to occupy himself. Furthermore he is not in such
bad straits after all. The physiologists in many cases have to be
content with their observations of end results. We know many
factors which affect the functioning of the parotid gland. We
count the drops of saliva which issue from it under varying conditions of stimulation. We analyze the chemical changes occurring, etc. But what goes on in the gland itself we cannot say.
But no one would have the temerity to assume that for this
reason there is no physiology of the gland. We can speculate
about what goes on inside of the gland, what the function of the
unstriped muscular tissue is, why the solution is now thick, now
thin, whether the gland would secrete if this or that were done.
But those speculations to be of any value must be couched in
some kind of terms which will lead not to metaphysical fancies
but to some kind of experimental attack. If they do not lead
to an experimental attack, no physiologist will long entertain
them. The behaviorist feels that we are in exactly this same
position with regard to thinking.

**"Meaning," an Experimental Problem and Not a Problem of
Philosophy or of Speculative Psychology.**—One of the chief
criticisms brought against this conception of thinking is that
" it does not explain meaning." This criticism is urged seriously
notwithstanding the fact that current introspective psychology
has no explanation of meaning to offer. Structural psychology
involves itself everywhere in a sea of words when it tries to
make one " image " mean another " image."

From the behaviorist's point of view the problem of " meaning " is a pure abstraction. It never arises in the scientific
observation of behavior. We watch what the animal or human

being is doing. He " means " what he does. It serves no scientific or practical purpose to interrupt and ask him while he is in action what he is meaning. His action shows his meaning. Hence, exhaust the conception of action—*i.e., experimentally determine all of the organized responses a given object can call forth in a given individual, and you have exhausted all possible " meanings " of that object for that individual.* To answer what the church means to men it is necessary to look upon the church as a stimulus and to find out what reactions are called out by this stimulus in a given race, in a given group or in any given individual. Parallel with this query we can carry out another as to why the church calls out such and such responses. This might take us into folk lore and into the influence of the code upon the individual, into the influence of parents upon children, causing the race to project the father and mother into a heavenly state hereafter; finally into the realms of the incest complex, homosexual tendencies, and so on. In other words, it becomes like all others in psychology, a problem for systematic observation and experimentation. We have emphasized these general statements about meaning in this connection because it is often said that thinking somehow peculiarly reveals meaning. If we look upon thinking as a form of action comparable in all its essential respects to manual action, such speculations concerning meaning in thinking lose their mystery and hence their charm.

Summary of Behaviorist's Conception of Thinking.—Thinking is largely a verbal process; occasionally expressive movements substitutable for word movements (gestures, attitudes, etc.) enter in as a part of the general stream of implicit activity. Thinking in the narrow sense where learning is involved, is a trial-and-error process wholly similar to manual trial and error. Verbal manipulation along one line is checked and stopped and a new line is begun for exactly the same reasons that such processes are checked and begun in manual learning. The thinking adjustment is achieved when the final word-grouping (sentence or judgment) or overt bodily reaction which comes as the end result of the process of thinking makes the initial stimulus to thinking inoperative or inert; that is, the final reaction, verbal or other, so changes the general state of the organism as a whole that the original stimulating factor can no longer act upon the subject. A crude illustration which can properly be carried over to thought is to be found in the hungry hunter's eager search for game. He finds it, captures it, prepares and eats it, lights his pipe and lies down. The hares and quail may peek at him from every corner of the brush, but their driving power for the time is gone.

LABORATORY STUDIES IN LANGUAGE ORGANIZATION[4]
C. Acquisition and Improvement.

Types of Investigations in Language Functions.—Language acquisitions, both explicit and implicit, have been studied only incidentally in the laboratory and usually in their highly organized and total forms such as solving arithmetical problems, committing verse and prose to memory; with later retesting of such activities to obtain a measure of the factor of disuse. A few of the studies deal directly with the learning of a foreign language. Our more immediate concern here is the investigation of word organization. Several studies have been made upon adults. That of Ebbinghaus is best known. In 1885 he made a most careful study of the learning of nonsense syllables. Nonsense words or syllables are made by separating two consonants with a vowel as *ver, gax* and *moc*. Whenever a conventional word is formed by this combination it is discarded. It is possible to construct some two thousand three hundred nonsense words. In this way the attempt is made to get material uniform in difficulty and without wide associative connections. The organism in learning it is made to function on almost an infantile plane. Short or long lists of these nonsense syllables may be made up and presented to the subjects through the eye or the ear. The presenta-

[4] Space limitations deter us from giving any discussion of the acquisition of writing (Judd, Freeman and others) ; of the studies on the associated action of the eyes in reading (Judd, Holt, Huey and others), or of the formation of the various types of language habits in deaf mutes with and without blindness. All of the researches in these fields contribute to our data on language organization in general and of the connection of laryngeal action with manual. The pathological literature on speech defects and the functional cases of stuttering and stammering are also contributive.

tion is repeated again and again until a certain standard proficiency in the habit is obtained. Usually unless the effect of overtraining is being studied the standard is the ability to repeat the whole series in order once without error (Ebbinghaus). Some of the later investigators have demanded the ability to repeat the whole series twice. Concerning such acquisition the following summary of results may be given:

1. *Length of the Series and Time of Learning.*—One of the first things that Ebbinghaus brought out was the fact that it takes a disproportionate amount of time to learn a long series than a short one, for example, he found that with one reading, a series of 7 or 8 syllables could be learned. The table below brings out the relatively greater amount of work required as the number of syllables in the series is increased.

Number of syllables in a series	Number of repetitions necessary for first errorless production
7	1
12	16.6
16	30.0
24	44.0
36	55.0

Later investigations have found that the longer series do not require nearly so disproportionate an amount of time as Ebbinghaus' results would seem to indicate.

2. *Acquisition of Sense Material.*—The same author learned stanzas of Byron's Don Juan. Each stanza required scarcely 8 repetitions in order to enable the learner to recite it correctly. Each of the stanzas contained 80 syllables. Each syllable, however, consisted on the average of less than 3 letters. If we contrast the number of presentations required to learn 80 syllables, the syllables being grouped into ordinary words, with the number of presentations required to learn 80 nonsense syllables, it will be found that the sense material requires relatively few. Ebbinghaus estimated that if a series of 36 nonsense syllables requires 55 repetitions for learning, 80–90 syllables would require at least 80 repetitions; since the sense material required only about 9 repetitions it follows that the learning of sense material requires only about 1/10 as much practice as nonsense material.

3. *Effect of Changing the Order of the Syllables in a Non-sense Series.*—The nonsense material gives us an interesting opportunity of testing some of the fundamental facts about human learning. When any given succession of events or objects is presented serially the parts are learned in the order given. We have discussed this problem to a certain extent already under the heading of the determiners of act (page 319) and we found there that frequency was a most potent factor in determining which act will next be performed. In other words, if acts have been learned in the order A, B, C, D, E, F, and the individual is now performing act E, other things being equal, it is safe to predict that act F will follow next because it has most frequently followed E. The question is whether E is the sole determiner of F. The answer has been conclusively returned from the study of nonsense material. Not only is E a determiner of F, but likewise also in varying measure D, C, B, A. To test this Ebbinghaus learned on any given day several series of nonsense syllables and then made up from this once-learned material several new series. One of the new series was made by skipping one syllable, another by skipping two syllables and so until six syllables were skipped. The following scheme will make this clear. Let the various series once learned be represented by Roman figures and the positions of the various members of this series by the Arabic numerals as follows:

I(1) I(2) I(3) .... I(15) I(16)
II(1) II(2) II(3) .... II(15) II(16)
VI(1) VI(2) VI(3) .... VI(15)VI(16)

The "skipping-one" series would then be made up as follows:

I(1) I(3) I(5) ..... I(15) I(2) I(4) I(6)—I(16)

The other series, of course, can be made up in the same way by skipping two syllables, three, and so on. If the syllables are learned merely in the order in which they are presented and the determiner of each succeeding act is solely the act which has just preceded, then the series made by skipping series ought to be as difficult to learn as the originals. Such is by no means the case. All of the "skip" series are learned more readily than the mean of the six originals from which they were composed. The following table presents the results:

Re-learning in original order—

After 24 hours ....33.3 per cent. saved
Re-learning of skip 1.............10.8 per cent. saved
Re-learning of skip 2............. 7 per cent. saved
Re-learning of skip 3............. 5.8 per cent. saved
Re-learning of skip 7............. 3.3 per cent. saved

If a count is kept of the average number of seconds required for learning the original six series, and then for re-learning each of the various derived series, the saving is as follows: The average for the original learning (6 series) was 1266 seconds; skipping 1, the saving was 110 seconds; skipping 2, 79 seconds; skipping 3, 64 seconds; skipping 6, 40 seconds. Where the series are jumbled together (permutation) there is no saving in time of re-learning. We thus see in learning series of nonsense syllables that every syllable is tied up in a forward direction with every other one. In a similar way it has been shown that they are tied up in a backward direction as well.

The Acquisition of More Complex Material.—Several studies have been made upon material which brings about organization or reorganization of the implicit processes such as the learning of a new language or telegraphy. No experimental studies have been made on learning to compose music. The learner who studied Russian in an experimental way (Swift) had had no previous training in that language. The study began March 30, 1905, and ended June 14 of the same year. It consisted of 30 minutes' study followed immediately by a 15 minutes' test of reading ability. The daily study of 30 minutes was carried on in the ordinary way, the time being divided among the vocabulary, conjugations and declensions. No effort was made to work under any great strain. The score was made on the basis of the number of words read during the daily 15 minutes' test. The learning curve (not shown) shows the same factors at work as in the acquisition of manual skill—a rather rapid rise at first, a severe slip back, then another rapid rise, another severe slip back, then a slower gradual rise with marked fluctuations. The rate of progress even at the beginning was much slower than learning to typewrite. The curve as a whole shows a surprising number of plateaux, at least four well-marked ones appearing, but the lack of material in the day's lesson and the unsatisfactory way in which such scores can be obtained probably keep the curve from being a true picture of such acquisitions. The average score on the first two days was about 20 words read per 15 minutes; the average score on the 65th day was approximately 65. Bryan and Harter have given a somewhat better controlled study in learning to receive telegraphic messages. The curve of receiving rises quite slowly, very much more slowly and irregularly than does the curve for sending messages, since sending is a much less complex habit to form. Furthermore, the curve is marked by several plateaux, each plateau being followed by a period of more or less marked improvement.

Improvement in Subvocal Arithmetic.—It is very difficult, of course, to find examples in the experimental literature of acquisition or improvement in pure implicit laryngeal work. Possibly the best examples of such work and of the types of improvement that occur are found in the working of arithmetic problems without exteroceptive aids. Starch worked with eight subjects and had them multiply a three-place by a one-place number—50 examples per day for 14 days. A table follows (quoted from Thorndike):

Individual	Examples done per 10 minutes on 1st day	Examples done per 10 minutes on 14th day	Gross gain	Percentile gain
S.	25	62.5	37.5	150
D.S.	37.7	81	43.3	115
F.	23.8	45.4	21.6	91
V.	41.7	71.4	29.7	71
W.	14.7	29	14.3	97
H.	37	100	63	170
Si.	25	29.8	4.8	19
B.	23.4	66	42.6	182

It will be seen that the improvement was quite marked, that the small amount of practice done on each day for 14 days enabled the subjects to do nearly twice as many examples on the average as they could do at the beginning of practice. This example, of course, must be looked upon as improvement in a given function and not as the acquisition of a totally new habit. The subjects were adults and hence already possessed a respectable measure of ability in this function. Several other individuals have studied improvement in subvocal arithmetic. In general the results are similar to those obtained by Starch.

It would be extremely instructive to obtain data on the acquisition and improvement in laryngeal organization of other types. For example, we know nothing in a statistical way concerning improvement of ability in subvocal reading or of such total activities as constructing a lecture, organizing a book or planning an invention.

"Transfer" of Practice From One Language Function to Another.—We gave, on page 310, a short statement of the "transfer" of training both in the realm of manual activity and in laryngeal. It seems well to note here again that there is a slight transfer in most cases, but in general this can be accounted for on the basis of the identical elements or identical part processes involved in the two activities under observation.

Summary of Experimental Studies in Laryngeal Learning.—The formation of laryngeal habits is a subject which has been very inadequately studied in psychology largely because of the difficulties involved in getting a measure of improvement and in general in controlling the results. Very many functions which combine laryngeal with manual activity have been studied very carefully in the laboratory, such as the improvement in marking given letters on a page of ordinary print, putting English prose into German script, writing prose in code, and the like. On page 326 we have already considered certain of these habits, such as typewriting.

In general, it may be said that the acquisition of laryngeal habits is similar in most respects to the learning of manual acts. Laryngeal activity has not been studied with sufficient thoroughness for us to give it any detailed discussion.

D. Retention or Memory of Laryngeal Habits.

Effect of No Practice on Laryngeal Habits.—Ebbinghaus and others have tested quite extensively the effect of disuse (forgetting) upon nonsense syllables. One of the things which appeared earliest was the fact that after a series of nonsense syllables had been learned to the point of one errorless reproduction and then put away, it could not be repeated twenty minutes later. The most interesting thing appearing was the fact that any such disused series could be *re-learned* much more rapidly than originally. Hence it became possible to adopt the following method: To learn a large number of nonsense syllables, say 8 series of 13 syllables each, and then re-learn one at the end of 20 minutes, another after an hour, another after one day and so on. A numerical measure of the saving can be obtained by subtracting the number of repetitions required for re-learning from the number of repetitions required in the original learning. The following table from Ebbinghaus gives in percentage the amount of time saved in re-learning the nonsense syllables after varying intervals:

Length of period of disuse	Gain in per cent.
5 minutes	100
63 minutes	44.2
525 minutes	55.8
1 day	33.8
2 days	27.2
6 days	25.2
31 days	21.2

In other words, this table shows that the loss is very rapid at first and very slow thereafter. After the interval of an hour, more than half the original work has to be done before the series can be repeated without error. After 8 hours almost ⅔ of the original work is necessary. After 24 hours the rate of deterioration is very slow indeed. The table is shown graphically in Fig. 64. These experiments have been repeated by Radossawljewitsch, by Bean and by students of nearly every laboratory. In general, Ebbinghaus's work has been confirmed with the possible exception that the loss is less severe at the start than he shows it to be. All investigators agree that the loss is at first extremely rapid. If this rapid deterioration in a language function is contrasted with the hardly perceptible loss in typewriting (page 326) after long periods of no practice the difference in the two types of function, so far as deterioration in the non-practice period is concerned, appears with startling clearness. The curve given below shows the loss during the first 24 hours.

Retention of Sense Material.—Radossawljewitsch and also Magneff studied the effect of disuse on sense material (poetry) learned to the point of two perfect reproductions and then re-learned after a certain interval. The loss after disuse for varying intervals was determined as for nonsense syllables in the above test of Ebbinghaus. The following table presents part of the results:

Length of period of disuse	Gain in per cent.
19 minutes	58.2
20 minutes	95.2
60 minutes	80.9
480 minutes	57.9
1 day	79.2
5 days	56.5
14 days	30
30 days	23.9

It will be seen that the loss is not so rapid at first as in the case of nonsense syllables, but that the loss at the end of thirty days is approximately the same.

It is unfortunate that there are no good studies of this type of forgetting. Radossawljewitsch's work shows so much variation as likewise does Magneff's that too great dependence cannot be placed in them. In apparent contradiction to this rapid forgetting of sense material stand the cases where poems learned in early childhood can be repeated after years of disuse; similarly parts of chapters from the Bible learned in youth, and conversations heard in childhood can be repeated in old age. But these were originally overlearned and in youth were many times taken up and re-learned. Such examples are in no sense a contradiction of the work which has been done in the laboratory.

Effect of Overlearning.—In the above work the series of

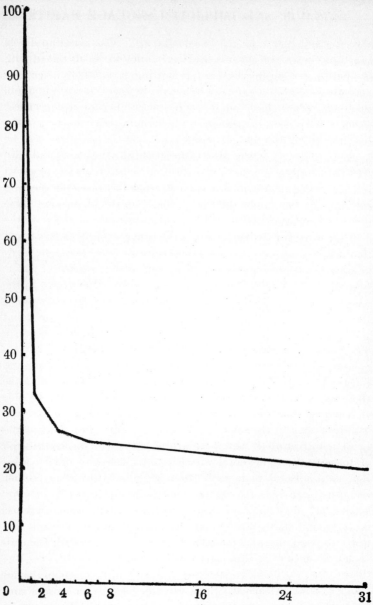

FIG. 64.—The curve of forgetting for nonsense syllables.   Data from Ebbinghaus.
The vertical line shows the percentage of time saved in relearning; the horizontal, the interval
in days between learning and re-learning.   The curve shows in a striking way the tremendous
loss which the first day entails.

nonsense syllables was just barely learned. The question arises next as to what the effect would be in time saved in re-learning if, instead of stopping learning at this point, we continued it for some time. Ebbinghaus found that the effect of reading a series over more often than was necessary to be able to just repeat it was not lost. If it is presented three times more to-day than is required for a first errorless repetition, one presentation will be saved in the re-learning twenty-four hours afterwards; if read six times more than necessary to-day, two repetitions will be saved in re-learning after a similar lapse of time. This saving does not continue in the same ratio when the number of presentations given in learning is increased beyond sixty-four.

Can Memory be Improved?—In order to answer this question it seems necessary to point out that when it is asked, memory is used in a sense somewhat different from that employed in the present text. Memory in this enlarged sense refers really to the whole process of learning and re-learning. Of course, even in the formation of a habit by daily practice retention of what was learned the day before must occur or progress is blocked. The question really at issue can be put concretely: Given homogeneous but different material, for example, several thousand lines of prose to learn verbatim, and assume that I have had some practice in committing (learning) such material, will I be able to learn the last hundred lines any more rapidly than the first hundred lines? Or again, assuming that all ten syllable series of nonsense material are of equal difficulty, will the learning of a thousand series decrease materially the length of time it takes me to commit such material? From the standpoint of acquisition it seems to be true that there is a certain coefficient of commitment for each individual which for that individual remains almost permanent. Undoubtedly there is some slight improvement, but Ebbinghaus, after working some three or four years with nonsense material, found no very great improvement.

The question also refers to the amount of loss after a period of no practice. All of the experiments seem to show, assuming that the material was learned in an associated and connected way in the first place, that there is no way to stop the loss except by greatly overlearning. There are a great many mnemonic devices and special association schemes for "improving" memory. Many of them are exceedingly ingenious and "guaranteed to improve one's memory one hundred per cent. in thirty days." There is nothing new in any of these schemes and they certainly do not "improve the memory" in the sense that psychologists would use the term improvement.

Of prodigies in memory little can be said. That there are enormous individual variations in the ability of different people to carry around with them isolated dates, numbers, whole pages of scientific material, is well known by every one. Little further can be said on the topic. They belong in the same class with the other types of prodigies, for example, the infant mathematical wonder and the child musician and composer.

Concluding Statements.—It would be instructive to take up the study of language in some of its broader aspects; in particular the following points would be of special interest to psychologists: (1) The acquisition of language in blind deaf-mutes. (2) The symbolic and folk-lore side of our own and other languages. (3) Stuttering, stammering and allied defects. (4) The effect of central nervous system lesions upon language mechanisms, as is seen in aphasia and in agraphia. (5) The speech of psychopathic individuals, especially the phenomena seen in the flights of the manic, the disintegration of speech in paretics and the organized language systems of the paranoiac types. (6) The slang and profane words and their connection with emotional states. (7) The language systems in day and night dreaming. Most of these topics are so broad that even a central viewpoint cannot be given without devoting a special chapter to each.

We have attempted in the present chapter merely to trace the similarity in the development and use of explicit and implicit language activities to the development and use of other forms of bodily integration. Language is an intimate and necessary part of the individual's adjustments. While we have singled out language functions for special study, it must be recalled that several times we have mentioned the artificiality of this procedure. The normal human organism functions as a whole always. Through training it becomes organized in all of its parts to make a certain adjustment or perform a certain act, be that act the driving of a nail, flying across the Atlantic Ocean or multiplying silently one four-place number by another four-place number. Each of these complex functions has as its constituent parts emotional, instinctive, and explicit and implicit habit factors. The parts are all tied together and work together when the individual is performing that function. Our illustration in the previous chapter of the behavior of the motor-boat owner in trying to make his engine run properly shows the closely interlocking, integrated activity of the hands, arms and legs, involving also instinctive emotional factors and finally language activity; it is typical of all adjustments.

The present chapter finishes our study of the genesis and functioning of part reactions. In it we have tried to present the data which will enable the student to put the organism back together again and view him as an integrated, biological going concern. This completely integrated organism is a personality or individual. The following chapter takes up the individual at work upon one or another problem.

CHAPTER X

THE ORGANISM AT WORK

A. The Functioning of Established Habit Systems.

What is Meant by Function.—Several times in the text we have had occasion to speak of functions. Now that we have examined most of the phases of an individual's acquisitions both of the explicit and implicit kinds it seems well to get a more exact formulation of what is meant by the term. After an act has been acquired and used for a definite time and is then repeatedly put away and again used, the learning and re-learning phases and periods of no practice become of little consequence. We assume that every normal individual can perform the acts required by a social environment and we do not care particularly whether it took him a long time to learn them or a short time. We are interested, in the discussion which follows, in the question as to the rapidity and accuracy with which those habits work and the factors which influence them. It is convenient to call each organized habit system of an individual which is always ready to act under appropriate stimulation, an acquired function, in contrast to emotional and instinctive functions. (The total assets of an individual are the sum of his hereditary and acquired functions, his retentiveness and his plasticity.) Examples of such acquired functions are, of course, talking, walking, swimming, addition, subtraction, writing and all similar ones discussed in the preceding two chapters. As we use the term, it has no fixed implication and is not a mathematical or even a rigidly scientific one. A function is really, then, a phase of activity that one happens to be studying and measuring; the acquired functions are equivalent really to habits except for the fact that when we use the term function we generally (but not even here always) leave the genetic aspect out of consideration. New habits, if continued, end always by giving us new functions. In studying children (or adults if learning) the term habit is emphasized; in studying adults the term function is most frequently met with, since in the adult the learning and re-learning aspects are not of importance unless we wish to get some index of an individual's plasticity. This distinction between the genetic or acquisition phase of any activity and its later exercise has led to some confusion in psychology.

The efficiency of these organized functional systems never changes very much in the adult. They are not practiced sufficiently at any one time or under the right conditions for any great improvement to occur. On the other hand, they are used so frequently that the memory loss is insignificant after a period of no practice. As adults we are on a permanent plateau with respect to the efficiency of most customary acts: that drugs, lack of oxygen, emotional disturbances and environmental changes in general can produce greater or less fluctuations in efficiency, temporary in character, will now appear.

"Fatigue" Not a Serviceable Conception in Psychology.— Probably the most essential thing for the beginning student to do or for any scientific man planning to do research in the field of human work is to neglect most of the general discussions which have gathered around the subject of fatigue. James somewhere says about emotion: "But as far as 'scientific psychology' of the emotions goes I may have been surfeited by too much reading of classical work on the subject, but I should as lief read verbal descriptions of the shapes of the rocks on a New Hampshire farm as toil through them again." Much the same could be said about fatigue. The literature from the standpoint of discussion is complex and confusing and worthless both because it is not constructive and because it deters men from engaging in the study of the factors influencing the curve of work. Three reasons can be advanced for this condition: (1) and most important, confusion starts the moment the human animal is dissected into a so-called "mental" worker and "physical" worker. This is a most pernicious way of splitting up human activity. No matter what the human animal is doing he works as a whole. What measure of truth is to be found in this division can be better formulated by saying that certain activities, like splitting wood or dragging a cannon over muddy ground, demand the func-

24

tioning mainly of that part of the individual's organization connected with the use of the large muscles of the body. When we need a short phrase we characterize it simply as manual work. To use the term manual in this broad way is, of course, to strip it of its etymological setting. When the individual is multiplying or adding or planning the details of a lecture the process involves mainly that part of his organization connected with the small muscles employed in using words. Short characterizing phrases are subvocal work or vocal work, depending upon whether the work is done silently (thought) or spoken aloud. But neither in manual work nor in implicit laryngeal work does action take place only in the specified parts. The manual worker may be thinking of his family or of the nearness of meal-time, whereas the laryngeal worker may be tearing his hair or walking up and down the room. (2) The attempt is made to literally drag in by the hair pictures of what goes on in the nervous system and the muscles. Thorndike, who in general stays closest to investigatable grounds, defines "mental work" as work done by the animal's connection system. "When, however, such a total activity is examined more critically, it is found desirable to separate off the work and fatigue of the sense organ and of the end plate in the muscle from the work of the connection system and to distinguish sensorial fatigue, intellectual fatigue and muscular fatigue. For the action of a sense organ or of an end plate is only partly, and the action of a muscle fiber is not at all, like that of the connecting neurone." He passes into the realm of classification of fatigue with a vengeance in the following note:

"It will doubtless be better in the long run to subdivide the work of the human animal still further and to replace the terms sensory, mental and muscular work by the work of the accessory apparatus of the sense organs, the work of the peripheral end of the first sensory neurone, the work of conduction along a neurone, the work of conduction across a synapse from neurone to neurone, the work of changing the intimacy of synapses, the work of conduction from the ending of a neurone to a muscle, the work of the muscle fibers." (Italics in text omitted.)

(3) The final factor which has brought the psychology of

fatigue to such a helpless position is the attempt to keep safe the tenets of psycho-physical parallelism. The discussion of this concept belongs to the realm of metaphysics. It can be left safely to the philosophers.

In approaching the problem of the exercise of a function both from the standpoint of research and for collecting data on what has been done it seems safe to assume that no confusion can result and that nothing will be lost to science if psychology will discard the concept of fatigue altogether. All the investigator in this field needs to do is to name the function he is measuring and specify the conditions under which the act is taking place. The function studied may be bricklaying, typewriting, multiplying subvocally or any other function, and we may be as painstaking as we please about the care with which we specify the conditions under which such functions are exercised. For example, we may specify that the individual is multiplying one four-place number by another without being allowed to use pencil or paper or to put the numbers down in any way or to speak aloud or move from his chair or eat or sleep until ten hours of such work has been accomplished. We may still further specify by saying that he performs this work with eyes closed and with ears and nose plugged up and that after he has worked for five hours such and such a drug is administered. In bricklaying, for example, we may be as careful as we please about describing the kind of bricks the mason lays, the kind of mortar he uses, the kind of structure he is building, how far he has to stoop for his brick or mortar, what his family situation is, the wage he receives and similar conditions. When we have described the function being investigated, the conditions surrounding the worker and the method of measuring the function, we would then describe what the standard of efficiency is and how it was obtained and then state the effect the various control factors had upon the quantity and quality of the output.[1]

---

[1] It is quite another problem but again worth while to specify the condition of the worker from time to time. For example, at the end of the fourth hour he may have become dizzy, nauseated or complained of a headache. The position we take here is not at all incompatible with studying the individual's organic condition from moment to moment or even with recording his verbal complaints.

The situation is thus not different in studying human functions from what it would be if we were studying activity in animals.

The point we would make in doing behavior work is to leave out of discussion all of those factors which are not touched or approached by the problem in hand; for example, what possible good does it do when discussing bricklaying or subvocal arithmetic to guess at what goes on in the synapse, in the efferent or afferent leg of the reflex arc or in the muscle itself? These are all worthwhile problems, but they belong in the realm of physiology and this section of physiology has not yet been written. In preceding chapters we have given brief summaries of the few facts on the effect of continuous exercise of the nerve fiber, nerve cell and muscle concerning which there is some agreement. The total known facts are pitifully meagre. For students of behavior to devote hundreds and thousands (literally) of pages to the "physiological aspect" of fatigue problems tends in no way to the advancement of the study. The subject of the effect of continued use of the nervous system should be left to the neuro-physiologists or, better, to the joint work of the psychologists who will do the behavior work and the neuro-physiologists who will examine the nervous and muscular structures.

THE CURVE OF WORK.

General Considerations.—Assuming that a function is any well-established habit like that of typewriting, billiard playing or subvocal arithmetic, the question next arising in measuring the quantity or output of work done and its quality is whether there are well-marked fluctuations or rhythms or bursts of speed during the exercise of the function or whether the only marked change is the slow decrease in the output and possibly increase in errors due to the effect of continuous exercise. There is rather a persistent popular view that there are such fluctuations. In certain laboratories these views have apparently been confirmed. It is stated that there is (1) an initial spurt, (2) an end spurt and (3) a warming up or adaptation period.

In the (1) initial spurt it is assumed that the·worker keyed up for his task assumes an initial rate of speed which cannot be maintained. Thorndike tested this matter by recording the work done by several subjects in subvocal multiplication and in written addition. These subjects were educated adults working continuously for approximately two hours. In general, there was no initial spurt. It was found that the curve of work varied in each individual from day to day and that if any one were interested in proving an initial rise he could pick out occasionally a curve which would show it; but no spurt was characterstic of any of the workers when the several curves gathered from several days' works were examined. In Kraepelin's laboratory the initial spurt was rather a constant occurrence and was supposed to endure for approximately five minutes. A very recent study of Chapman and Nolan tends to confirm the older view of Kraepelin rather than that of Thorndike. Subjects were tested in continuous addition for 16 minutes on 7 successive occasions. They found definite evidence of an initial spurt in beginning the work, with a high percentage of errors. The speed was so great that no system of penalties for errors could cause this spurt to disappear. The spurt was of short duration, the subject always taking on a higher rate than he could possibly maintain. "He very rapidly settles down to a normal rate at which he can work for long periods. It is the rapidity of this decrease in efficiency which has led to the fact that initial spurt has been overlooked and even denied." Thorndike again in his most recent work finds an absence of initial spurt.

In regard to (2) "end spurt," the evidence shows in many cases that there is a slight increase in the output in the last few minutes of work where the subject is working against time and has been informed beforehand that the work is to cease after a specified number of minutes. Book in his study of typewriting where ten-minute periods of work were used shows that the last three minutes are slightly better than any previous three minutes, the output standing in the relation of 100, 101, 102. Arai's last ten minutes of work (twelve hours continuous work) on subvocal arithmetic (page 375) was done at a slightly faster rate than any rate attained in the previous half hour. The end spurt though real under such conditions is not an important factor in the curve of work. There is only very slight evidence to show that spurts occur after interruptions or disturbances or that they occur after momentary periods of decreased efficiency.

The curve illustrating the output of the exercise of any given function is said by some to show a gradual increase in efficiency from the moment of starting (or slightly later, at the end of the decline following after the "initial spurt") up to the end of the first twenty to thirty minutes; to stay at this high level for a definite time and then to show a decline. This is called the (3) "warming-up" period. It is sometimes asserted that there is a slower and more permanent improvement running parallel with the warming-up phase but enduring for a longer time. This is

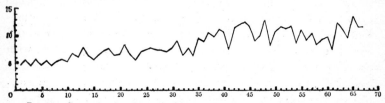

Fig. 65.—Curve showing the gradual increase in time required to multiply (subvocal) one four-place number by another. The work was done continuously from 11 A.M. to 11 P.M. The times of solving the first example on each of the four days are averaged, giving the first point in the curve; the times of solving the second examples on each of the four days are similarly averaged, giving the second point on the curve. This procedure was repeated to the sixty-seventh example, which was the number completed on each day. The curve was constructed by the author from Dr. Arai's tables. It is not corrected for errors. The vertical line gives time in minutes; the horizontal line, the number of examples. Had the time of completing each example not increased—that is, if the function had not decreased in efficiency—the curve would have remained parallel to the base line; as it is, the curve, allowing for slight fluctuations, remains constant for the first ten examples, then declines and remains constant on this higher level to the 34th example, then declines sharply and continuously (with fluctuations) to the 48th example, then improves markedly to the 61st example, then again declines.

called the "adaptation" process. Experimental confirmation for these changes is not at hand. An examination of the curve illustrating Dr. Arai's work (Fig. 65) shows the absence of such asserted improvement. Where there is apparent evidence for it the changes noted seem to be due to a period of improvement by practice in the function (actual learning). Where the function tested is a thoroughly grounded one the phenomenon is lacking.

There is no very satisfactory experimentation upon the curve of work illustrating strictly manual functions. In baseball, track and crew work a process of limbering up or preliminary practice is universally indulged in and is apparently necessary. Probably no manager of a baseball team would risk sending a pitcher in without giving him an opportunity to work up a sweat and to break in his arm. Possibly the main beneficial result comes from increased glandular action: the muscular area in operation in such functions is very great and the consumption of food is large, hence the by-products of activity are enormous. The need of adrenin for breaking up and releasing the stored glycogen and inducing better circulation seems essential. Where the muscular area in operation is small, as in laryngeal work, the warming up period is not essential.

A great deal of speculation has been indulged in in regard to the lack of "fatigue," so-called, in a laryngeal function as contrasted with its very rapid appearance in manual work. Arai continued to work in subvocal arithmetic for a period of twelve hours with a decrease in efficiency possibly of not more than 25 per cent. No crew working as rapidly as possible could continue its rowing beyond a few miles with only a similar loss in efficiency. In view of the difference in the size of the muscular areas involved in the two types of work, the findings are in line with prediction.

Subvocal Arithmetical Functions Continuously Used.— One of the most thorough investigations yet made upon the measurement of a function continuously exercised for a long period of time is that of Dr. Arai in subvocal arithmetic. Having by frequent practice reached the point where practice effects had almost disappeared, she worked on four days from 11 A.M. to 11 P.M. at multiplying four-place numbers by four-place numbers without extraneous aid. During the multiplication, the two four-place numbers (for example, $X \frac{2645}{5784}$) were not in sight but were referred to when necessary. The multiplication took place with eyes closed. The only rest taken was the few seconds required to write down the answer and to learn the next problem. The work involved in making a single such calculation is for most people stupendous or even impossible. Approximately 17 sets, 4 examples in each set, were done during the 12 hours' continuous work. The whole table cannot be reproduced, but we can compare the average time of solving the first set of 4 examples each day with the average of the last set of 4 as follows:

	First day	Second day	Third day	Fourth day
Average time in minutes of solving first 4 examples	23.6	20.7	19.3	16.5
Average time in minutes of solving last 4 examples	62.1	44.4	49.1	32.9

It probably would be fairer to compare the average time of solving the first two sets of four examples (8 examples) with the average time of solving the last two sets of four.

First 8 examples	46.9	45.2	35.8	46.1
Last 8 examples	101.1	96.4	99.1	78.5

An examination of the tables shows that there is a loss in efficiency as measured by the increase in time of solving the last 8 examples. The average increase in time for the last eight examples over the first 8 examples on the 4 days was 119 per cent. While at first sight this loss in efficiency may seem large, a little consideration will convince us that the efficiency of the function even after 12 hours' continuous work was still very high. Dr. Arai thus required a little over twice as long to perform one such example at the end of the 12 hours' work as at the beginning. Even at the end she was performing a feat which could not be equaled probably by two persons out of a thousand engaged in arithmetical work. The second most important point coming from this research was the fact that the normal period of sleep completely restored the function as shown by the fact that the average time of solving the first four examples on each of the four days is about equal. As a matter of fact, there is a decrease in time which looks like a practice effect. The author has taken the figures of Miss Arai and plotted the curve given above, Fig. 65 (without correction for error). She worked four days and did 67 problems on each day. The points on the curve were obtained as follows: The times of solving all first problems (that is, the times of solving the first problems on each of the four days) were averaged; this gives the first point on the curve. Then the times of solving all second problems were similarly averaged to obtain the second point on the curve. This procedure was repeated for all 67 points. The curve shows in the main an increase of time. The first 10 problems show only individual fluctuations; then occurs a slight decline. From that point to the 34th, the function is maintained at fairly uniform efficiency but with upward and downward fluctuations. From the 34th example to the 48th there is a marked decline in efficiency. From the 48th to the 61st a marked improvement occurs, then a fall in efficiency extending to the 65th, and finally a slight rise.

It would take us beyond the limits of this discussion to present all the data which has been collected upon this type of work. Such functions as the following have been tested: Writing sentences from dictation, learning nonsense syllables and digits, translating, marking words containing *a* and *t* and selecting titles for a bibliography. The interesting point about all of the results is that such functions can be exercised continuously for several hours without severe loss in efficiency.

Continuous Exercise of Manual Functions.—No careful measurement of the loss in efficiency in a manual function due to continuous exercise, comparable with Dr. Arai's work, has been made. That the loss is more rapid in manual work every one admits. Furthermore, short periods of rest seem to be advantageous in manual functions, whereas they are certainly not necessary and possibly disadvantageous in subvocal functions. Many of the experiments have been made upon the ergograph where a single group of muscles is singled out and made to work continuously in a way in which no daily task ever employs them. This work we summarized on page 183. It is a most unsatisfactory way to study the curve of work in manual functions.

In the factories loss of efficiency in manual functions as measured in terms of decreased output is being studied with some care. We quote the following, which appeared in *The Iron Age:*

"At these works there was recently constructed a long incline up which heavy loads were to be wheeled in barrows, and premiums were offered to the men who did or exceeded a certain amount of this labor. They attempted it vigorously, but none succeeded in earning any of the extra money; instead, they all fell considerably below the fixed task.

"Prompt investigation by an expert disclosed that the trouble lay in the fact that the men were working without sufficiently frequent periods of rest. Thereupon, a foreman was stationed by a clock, and every twelve minutes he blew a whistle. At the sound every barrowman stopped where he was, sat down on his barrow, and rested for three minutes. The first hour after that was done showed a remarkable change for the better in accomplishment; the second day the men all made the premium allowance by doing more than what had been too much; and on the third day the minimum compensation had risen, on the average, 40 per cent., with no complaints of overdriving from any of the force."

This illustrates the fact that where the task is severe there is a growing tendency to allow a short period of rest after definite intervals of work. The whole question of decrease in the quantity and quality of output is bound up in daily life with a great many emotional factors such as whether the man's pay is sufficient to afford him an outlet for play, marriage and the like; one's personal and family adjustment; political convictions; the sociological theories the worker may have; open- and closed-shop policies; and most important probably, the rate at which the individual works. The heart teaches us a lesson. The heart functions continuously from the beginning of the third month of fœtal life to death but at such a rate and with such a rest period between functions that its efficiency is uniformly maintained. While not very much of value on the problem of efficiency in manual functions has yet come from a psychological laboratory, the solution has to be sought there, since work in the shop and in commercial houses generally cannot be controlled in such a way as to yield very safe results. But the type of work which the laboratory undertakes will have to be considerably broadened in scope. Our own view is that many of the basal laws can be established by using animals. We can force the animal to form very much more complicated habits than would appear from our ordinary laboratory studies. If punishment is used instead of food, the stimulating value of the situation as a whole would probably not decline very much from hour to hour. Given such a set of functions in animals, it would be possible to vary the conditions, such as underfeeding, undersleeping and the administration of drugs, and note the effect of the varying conditions upon the efficiency of the function under observation.

Physiological Aspects of the Continuous Exercise of a Function.—In previous chapters we have discussed certain phases of the physiological findings in regard to the effect of continuous works as follows: Chemical changes occurring in a nerve fiber due to continuous stimulation (page 137); structural and chemical changes in nerve cells (page 137); chemical and form changes in muscle due to work (page 184); effect of adrenin upon the products formed by continuous activity of the muscle (page 243). We briefly summarize these findings again: The question as to whether there are any structural and chemical changes in the nerve fiber due to continued functioning is still in doubt. The question of the changes in the nerve cell is even more problematical; in general, form, size and chemical changes are believed to occur, but the amount of exercise of the function necessary to bring about such changes is tremendously large. The products of muscular activity are slightly better known: there is the elimination of CO_2 in greater amounts when the muscle is active than when inactive; lactic acid is formed and possibly potassium phosphate. These products of activity get into the blood stream, are carried to muscles which have not been active and decrease the amount of work they are capable of doing. In regard to the influence of adrenin, it is stated that due to the increased supply of blood to the muscles such products are rapidly washed out or else neutralized *in situ*.

EFFECT OF DRUGS ON THE FUNCTIONING OF ESTABLISHED HABIT SYSTEMS.

General Considerations.—Several factors should be taken into account in the discussion of experimentation and measurement of any function: (1) only in rare cases has a function been practiced sufficiently in laboratory studies before controlled tests were introduced to gauge the effects of drugs, continuous exercise, loss of sleep and other factors. In other words, the subject improves in skill through practice—this may mask the effects of a drug or the loss of sleep or continuous exercise. Either the function should be practiced to the point where no improvement can be observed before control tests are introduced or else a measurement of the improvement factor should be found. (2) The situation for the worker in such experiments is not normal. He is being tested under unusual conditions, and emotional factors with their reinforcing or inhibiting effects may enter in. This has vitiated many experiments upon alcohol, tobacco and caffeine especially. To eliminate this effect various devices may be used. The subject may be told that he is being given caffeine in a capsule, whereas only flour or meal may be given; or he may be told that he is being given alcohol and some other masked non-alcoholic substance is actually given. On the other hand, he may be told nothing, the experimenter depending upon his own ability to introduce the control substance or condition in such a way that the subject is not able to note whether the drug or control factor has been administered. Rivers first emphasized the importance of the emotional aspect of such experimental conditions, and efficiency experiments may be said to start with his work in 1906. (3) Too narrow functions have been studied—rarely has any of the work been done upon functions used in daily life. As an example, we may mention the fact that in the great mass of experimentation upon manual functions the ergograph has been used. (4) The functions have been followed through for entirely too short periods for wide generalizations to be made.

In the summary of the literature which follows these factors should be taken into consideration and the results cited should be looked upon as being merely provisional.

Alcohol.—On account of various partisans for and against the use of alcohol, it is difficult to obtain unequivocal data upon this subject. The following summary presents the unpartisan view of most scientific men who have taken up the study of alcohol from a psychological and physiological standpoint.

1. There is a wide range of individual variation in the ability of different people to consume alcohol without showing its effect upon their curve of work. The amount may vary from 20 c.c. to 40 c.c. of absolute alcohol (a very much heavier dose than is usually taken for purely social purposes).

2. The effect of alcohol upon all reflexes when any is noted is depressing. This has been confirmed by many investigators working upon the patellar reflex, reflex eye movements and others.

3. The effect of alcohol when taken in large quantities on the amount and quality of muscular work which can be done is deleterious, according to most observers. Some hold that the bad effect upon muscular work can be observed for many hours after the alcohol has been consumed. On the effect of small doses of alcohol Rivers has the following to say:

"I may now sum up the general results which have so far been reached. In the case of muscular work, we have seen that there is definite evidence that small doses, varying from 5 to 20 c.c. of absolute alcohol, have no effect on the amount or nature of the work performed with the ergograph, either immediately or within several hours of their administration, the results previously obtained by other workers being almost certainly due to defects of experimental method. With a larger dose of 40 c.c., there was evidence—in one case, at least—of an increase in the amount of work under the influence of the substance; but the increase was uncertain and inconstant, and the possibility cannot be excluded that it was due to disturbing factors. With larger doses than 40 c.c., we have the work of Hellsten, showing a decided falling off in the amount of work with a dose of 80 grammes."

The effect upon language functions is not clear. They are undoubtedly less affected than are manual habits. Dodge, in his recent study, has shown that the more complex functions, such as memory and thinking, show less effect under the administration of alcohol than do the simple reflexes, although when any effect is noticeable it is one of depression. This seems to contradict the popular view, since it is a matter of common observation that in certain social situations, such as a dinner party, afternoon tea or wedding, conversation becomes accelerated when alcohol is consumed.[2] The situation here is quite complex. The depressive effect seems to be focalized in the cortical centers, thus leaving the segmental speech connections without cortical control. When larger amounts of alcohol are consumed the cord centers become affected and conversation declines, the company becomes dull and depression of all functions can be observed.

4. On the biological side the results are not very clear. Psychopathology shows that many feeble-minded and psychopathic children are born of alcoholic parents. The question here, though, is whether the parents were not psychopathic before becoming alcoholic. Alcoholism may be merely one form in which the neurotic tendencies show themselves. It is questionable whether a sturdy individual free from hereditary stigmata could ever become alcoholic. So many normal interests would come in conflict with the excessive use of alcohol that it is almost unthinkable that a healthy man could sink his cares and worries in that form of oblivion. Experiments upon animals are again not wholly conclusive. Stockard's work on the guinea-pig represents one side, Pearl's experiments on the domestic fowl represent the other. The former found that if guinea-pigs were forced to breathe alcohol fumes for long periods of time the progeny of such individuals was born with a large number of abnormalities, and the tenure of life was shortened. Furthermore, the f_2 generation still showed the evil effects. Pearl, on the other hand, found almost the opposite effect upon domestic fowls. The egg-laying

---

[2] While possibly no good physiological reason can be assigned for it, the different forms of alcohol seem to produce differences in the liveliness of a given company. The consumption of the same amount of grain alcohol at a social gathering will not produce the same effect as will an equal amount of alcohol in the form of champagne or a cocktail. The liveliness which ensues during social functions is not wholly due by any means to the alcohol which is taken. While the dinner as a whole might be a failure without it, the primary effect of the alcohol is probably to bring about an increased glandular activity which raises rapidly the general emotional level of the individuals partaking of it. This is pure speculation, since the author knows of no work which tests the effects of alcohol upon internal secretions. All that we argue for here is that the sight of the wine or cocktail may start conditioned secretion reflexes.

capacity was possibly increased and the fertility of the eggs was
in no way decreased, nor were any evil effects noticed upon
the young.

Certainly no experimental work, either upon humans or
animals, has shown that the consumption of alcohol in small
amounts when taken after the working period of the day is over
produces any evil effect either upon the individual or upon his
progeny. Certain statistics have been advanced by life insurance
companies which would seem to controvert this statement. These
mortality tables seem to show that even the occasional drinker
has a shorter span of life than the total abstainer. These statements have been called into serious question by statisticians of
the highest character who are interested only in the mathematical
side of the problem and not in the good or bad effects of alcohol.

In the opinion of a great many people, the following statements seem to be reasonable: (1) That the only sane thing to do
is to keep alcohol from children during the growing and adolescent periods, not because experiment has shown that small
amounts will injure them but because there may be a risk and
the risk is not worth while since the child is in no need of relaxation from work. (2) That the distribution of alcohol is not
(or rather was not) very wisely handled. The saloon is generally recognized as an unwholesome institution because it pro-
vides a loafing place for individuals out of work, keeps the
working-man from his home, encourages drink during the working hours of the day and because of the fact that undesirable
characters very often frequent it. The more reasonable members of the community feel that if the saloon could be eradicated
and the sale of high-proof liquors stopped, then the lighter wines
and beer could be consumed in small amounts in the evening
after the working period is done with no detriment to the race
as a whole. The advantage they urge from such a handling of
the alcoholic situation is the relaxation which a small amount
of alcohol brings. The concept of relaxation is a growing one
and people realize that when the day's work is done some form
of relaxation is advantageous. No man to-day of any thought-
fulness will tell you that he takes his quota of alcohol to increase

his output of muscular work or to increase his ability to write or think clearly. They frankly admit that when they have a definite and delicate job to do they want to be free from the effects of alcohol. On the other hand, they give as their reason for drinking that when they come home tired, from their work or worn out with business and professional cares they want to be freed from them as rapidly as possible and that alcohol brings the needed relaxation. They state that they can become, through the effects of a cocktail or a glass of wine, a social rather than an unsocial being, that this aids them in putting aside the daily grind and entering into their family life and social relations generally with greater rapidity. They argue further that since no experimental work has ever shown that the amount of alcohol they consume has any detrimental effect upon their character or ability to work on the following day, they see no reason why they should not continue to live as they have in the past.

Regardless of what scientific results may show and what the opinion of the small consumer of alcohol may be, the laws of the country have decided that the manufacture and sale of alcohol must be eliminated. The prediction of the outcome of this experiment is more difficult than most people imagine. Relaxation as we pointed out above, will be obtained in one way or another. Whether the outlet will take place along sane lines, as smoking clubs, coffee houses, greater outside exercise; or along lines far more pernicious than alcohol—for example, in some form of drug consumption or in greater sex freedom—remains to be decided.

If one examines the history of races, the fact appears that the stronger nations have always been the largest consumers of alcohol and have used the most varied forms of it. That alcohol has had any serious effect upon the efficiency of the French, English, Scandinavian, German and Austrian nations cannot be put forth seriously. The argument is often made that Russia's present condition is due to the large consumption of alcoholic drinks. A more reasonable view is that their education is so poor, their outlets for social relaxation so limited and their climate so severe that they have learned to use alcohol as an anæsthetic. With better social conditions alcohol would no longer be used as the only source of relaxation.

Effect of Caffeine.—Caffeine is the active principle in tea, coffee and many soda fountain drinks. Its effects upon various functions have been tested by many investigators. The studies of Rivers and of Hollingworth are most important. The former worked largely with the ergograph and with typewriting. Rivers' general conclusions are as follows:

"The general practical conclusions to be drawn from the experiments which I have recorded, and from those of previous workers, is that caffeine increases the capacity for both muscular and mental work, this stimulating action persisting for a considerable time after the substance has been taken without there being any evidence, with moderate doses, of reaction leading to a diminished capacity for work, the substance thus really diminishing and not merely obscuring the effects of fatigue."

Hollingworth's experiments were made upon a somewhat more pretentious scale. He kept his subjects guarded as to the outside work they did and the amount of food and rest taken. Several subjects were used who worked, except for the drug introduced, under normal conditions. The test lasted forty days. Tests of speed of movement (tapping), motor coördination and steadiness were made. There was an increase in the speed of movement which depended somewhat upon the size of the dose. The amount of caffeine given varied from 2 to 6 grains. The effect was noted usually within the hour after taking the drug (Rivers states that it is often noticeable within 15 minutes) and lasted usually from 1 to 4 hours. No secondary depresssion, as was pointed out by Rivers, occurred within 72 hours. This is unusual, since such depressions usually follow after the exciting phase of a stimulant has worn off. In regard to motor coördination, Hollingworth states that small doses increase efficiency, whereas large doses, from 4 to 6 grains, decrease it. The steadiness test shows that slight tremor occurs with doses of 1 to 4 grains. The tremor appears after several hours. Larger doses increase the tremor and hasten its onset. Other functions were observed under the drug: association tests such as the naming

25

of colors and the giving of opposites of certain words. Caffeine
doses of every size increased efficiency in such functions, the increase lasting from 3 to 7 hours. In such activities as the cancellation of letters and numbers, reacting with the right hand to
a blue paper and with the left hand to a red one, small doses
produced retardation, large doses acceleration.[3] The effect of
caffeine upon typewriting was most carefully studied. The speed
of performance was quickened by small doses and retarded by
large. On the other hand, the quality of performance as measured by the number of errors, both corrected and uncorrected,
was improved by doses of all sizes.

Caffeine also comes under the head of "habit-forming drugs."
Headache and general restlessness ensue if the subject is deprived of its use. No laboratory work touches the influence of
caffeine on daily routine. One needs only to observe the behavior
of the ordinary human being before and after his cup of coffee is
taken in the morning, or of the tired hunter or soldier after the
day's work is over, to gain some idea of the general stimulating
effect of coffee and tea. It is interesting to speculate upon the
number of scientific books and papers that have been written
with the aid and supporting effect of caffeine.

Tobacco.—While experimentation in this field is in its infancy, the results, if taken at their face value, show a deleterious
effect upon efficiency. One of the earliest experiments was made
by Lombard in 1892, who found, measuring the amount of work
done on the ergograph, that one cigar enormously decreased the
output. The effect passed off rapidly after the cigar was finished,
but the function was not completely restored until more than an
hour after the cigar was laid aside. Several others have partly
confirmed the results of Lombard, finding, however, that the
effect was not so marked. Féré found that cigarette smoking
produced an increase in the output of work, if the test was made
five minutes after the cigarette was smoked. A decrease in the
amount of work followed rapidly. If the test was not made until

---

[3] It seems unfortunate that this author with unlimited facilities at his
disposal should have selected so many narrow functions for observation
and functions which mean so little even when accurately measured.

fifteen minutes after smoking, the effect was deleterious on the function from the start. Rivers found a slight decrease in work done (ergograph) on days when cigars were smoked as contrasted with that done on days when cigars were not smoked (2 days with smoking were contrasted in one subject with 3 days without smoking and in another subject 2 days with smoking with 2 days without). The decrease in efficiency was very small.

Bush has recently made an extensive series of tests upon the effect of smoking upon laryngeal functions such as subtraction, free and controlled association and memory. The tests were first given to obtain a standard. The subject then smoked for 15 minutes, after which the tests were repeated. In most cases the effect was deleterious, the average loss being 10.6 per cent. The smoking of non-tobacco material (cubebs) likewise produced a reduction of efficiency of 4.2 per cent., which is rather astonishing in view of the fact that such extra afferent stimulation should, other things being equal, facilitate the output.

The experimental results on tobacco are thus very meagre. If any conclusion can be drawn it is that its effect is depressing upon the function studied. Prohibition of smoking among men undergoing training for athletic contests reflects this.

Tobacco, of course, is another "habit-forming drug." To those addicted to its use no such experiments as the above can be convincing. If deprived of their smoke their efficiency in all functions for the time being, at least, remains at a low ebb (they spend their time in restless roving). The argument of the smoker is that it is his form of relaxation and that no slight loss in efficiency of so temporary a character can be weighed in the scale against the use of tobacco. If the anti-tobacco propagandists had succeeded in prohibiting the use of tobacco in the Army in the recent war it is difficult to tell what the effect would have been upon the morale of the men. Under emotional strain it forms a relatively safe outlet which for the smoker, at any rate, is essential.

Strychnine.—The effect of strychnine on habit functions has not surely been determined. Jones, administering strychnine by the mouth in large (4.2 milligrammes of hydrochloride of strychnine) and in small doses (1.8 milligrammes) found that the drug produced an obvious effect upon the amount of work which could be done on the ergograph. There was with large doses a rise in the amount of work and then a gradual fall. The rise for the smaller doses was less rapid and the decline took place more slowly. There is thus a general increase in efficiency followed by a decrease—the total output being less.

Poffenberger in a recent experiment found no effect from doses ranging from 1/30 to 1/20 grain upon steadiness and accuracy in speed of movement. No effect was observed upon a series of other functions involving largely language organization.

Jones' observations were made under the direction of Rivers; they are, accordingly, probably accurate in so far as ergographic experiments can be made so. The reason for Poffenberger's failure to find any effect was possibly due to the difficulty in administering a suitable dose for the particular subjects tested. Of course, the same functions were not tested, but this hardly accounts for the complete lack of harmony in the two investigations.

Strychnine, of course, is a dangerous drug and should be experimented with only under the direction of a physician.

Cocaine.—There is fairly general agreement obtained from the scattering experimental work done upon this demoralizing and dangerous drug. Its immediate effect is to largely increase the efficiency of the function being tested (usually the ergograph); there is later, of course, a very strongly marked depression. The interesting fact about the drug is that its effect is quickly noticeable in states bordering upon almost complete exhaustion. It is stated that the natives of South America are enabled to perform great feats of endurance owing to its effect, and to withstand severe hunger and thirst under its influence (Rivers). On account of the relaxation it brings and the rapid ensuing temporary improvement in practically all functions it has become a favorite with drug addicts. That there is a marked increase in its use is admitted by every one. One cannot help but see in this drug a possible but unfortunate escape for those who have become really addicted to the use of alcohol.

EFFECT OF CLIMATE AND OTHER FACTORS UPON THE CURVE OF WORK.

Ventilation.—Recent work has upset the older notions concerning the effect of poor ventilation upon the curve of work. The older view was that in crowded, humid, hot rooms the increase of CO_2 in the air, the decrease in the percentage of oxygen and the expired organic matter ("anthropotoxin") were responsible for the ill effects observed. Pure air contains about 21 per cent. of oxygen, 78 per cent. of nitrogen and 0.03 per cent. of carbon-dioxide. In crowded, ill-ventilated factories and schools oxygen may be reduced to 19 per cent. and the carbon-dioxide increased to 0.3 per cent. But these changes in the air's constituents are too slight to produce physiological disturbance. The general changes observed upon subjects sitting or working in poorly ventilated, hot, humid rooms are drowsiness, lassitude, fainting, flushed face, hot skin, sweating, with complaints of headache and various other ills. That these changes are not due to the lack of oxygen and to the increase of CO_2 is proved by the fact that if such individuals while working in the same poorly ventilated rooms are allowed to breathe fresh outside air through a tube they are not restored to normal. The moment, however, the temperature and humidity are lowered, especially at the surface of the body, as can be done by stirring the air with a fan, the disturbances disappear, although no fresh air is introduced. In various ways it has been shown that the optimum conditions for work are 68° F., 50 per cent. relative humidity and 45 cubic feet of outside air per person per minute. Under such an optimum all general bodily disturbances are at a minimum.

These changes in the bodily condition of the subject due to poor ventilation, while they are stimuli that are usually negatively reacted to by most members of the human race, do not necessarily interfere with the possibility of efficient work. The question then arises, suppose we make the work, either through money, social approval, or fear, of high stimulating value, can the subject do as much manual and laryngeal work as under the optimum conditions for work? In manual functions all recent experiments show that there is loss in efficiency in poorly ventilated, crowded rooms. When the temperature and humidity are raised there is a falling off in efficiency in such functions as running a bicycle ergometer which indicates the exact foot-pounds of work accomplished and in the manipulation of dumb-bells. The efficiency at the optimum condition is 37 per cent. greater than at 86° F. and 15 per cent. greater than at 75° F.

In regard to laryngeal work and combined laryngeal and manual work, that is, in all functions where the muscular area involved is small, there seems to be little or no loss in efficiency due to even marked upward variations from the optimum. The following functions have been studied: Cancellation, naming of opposites, color naming, written addition, subvocal multiplication, learning to typewrite, grading of handwriting, and grading of English composition. Thorndike, in summarizing the work done at the laboratory of the New York State Commission on Ventilation, has the following to say:

With the forms of work and lengths of period used, we find that when an individual is urged to do his best he does as much, and does it as well, and improves as rapidly, in a hot, humid, stale, and stagnant air condition (86° F., 80 per cent. relative humidity, with no air or only re-circulated air, and with no movement of the air save what is caused by events in the room and, in the case of re-circulation, by the re-circulating force) as in an optimum condition (68° F., 50 per cent. rel. hum., 45 cu. ft. per person per minute of outside air introduced). This result was obtained when the individuals were subjected to the bad conditions 4 hours a day for five consecutive days. Enough individuals were tested to make the result entirely reliable.

We find further that when an individual is given work to do that is of no interest or value to him and is deprived even of means of telling how well he does do it, and is in other ways tempted to relax standards and do work of a poor quality, he still shows no inferiority in the quality of the product produced in stagnant air at 86°, 80 per cent. r. h., with 30 to 40 parts of CO_2 per 10,000, he being subjected to this condition for 8 hours a day for four successive days, and tested on the second, third, and fourth day. There is some evidence that he spends more time on the work, but even this is not certain.

Finally, we find that when an individual is left to his (or her) own choice as to whether he shall do mental work or read stories, rest, talk, or sleep, he does as much work per hour when the temperature is 75° as when it is 68°. In the experiments on this topic, temperature alone was varied, other air conditions being kept constant. The reason for this limitation was the apparent absence in all experiments to date, of any physiological effect due to staleness of the air as shown by high CO_2 content. The smaller difference was chosen to make the experiments suitable for their main purpose as a test of certain conditions upon appetite, the psychological tests being in this case secondary. It is also the case that the effect of moderate overheating upon the inclination to do mental work is, in practice, more important than the effect of extreme heat. The two conditions (68° and 75°) were maintained each for three successive days of seven hours each.

In a very short experiment wherein the temperature was varied to 86° F., 80 per cent. rel. hum., there did seem to be a diminished inclination to do mental work, but the variability of results in all such experiments with optional work advises us to postpone any conclusions concerning the effect of very high temperatures upon inclination until adequate experiments are made.

Miss Stecher in further work at the laboratory of the New York State Commission on Ventilation has tested several functions under low and high humidity with temperature held at a constant, namely, 75° F. The relative humidity in one case was 50 per cent., in the other 20 per cent. The following functions were tested: Addition, aiming, hand steadiness, tapping, typewriting, arm steadiness, mirror tracing, "industrial fatigue," reflex wink and eyelid tremor. She concludes:

In all these tests the average improvement from the first described above and also the average improvement from the first to the last trial on any particular day, showed no reliable difference. That is, by these tests of nervous and motor control and by the more purely intellectual tests we could detect no influence of excessive dryness during two weeks' exposure or during the working day.

While these results are in sharp contrast to the general view and seem to be opposed even to common-sense, one can but accept them until further tests are made. It is well to remember that in all such tests the stimulating value of the problems even where alternate work is allowed is very much higher than that offered in one's daily routine. Furthermore, the time the tests occupied was extremely short for the advancing of such far-reaching conclusions. The human organism is built to withstand and endure hardships for long periods of time. If lack of food for thirty days will not reduce the efficiency of the biological machine very greatly (page 398) nor the consumption of drugs, nor thirst nor loss of sleep, we should expect some such results as the above during the time these tests were continued. To generalize as many authors have done is at present not warranted.

Thorndike has drawn an extended conclusion from the above work to the effect that fully as efficient work may be carried out in the hot, humid summer months as in the cool of winter. Such an extension is just about as fallacious as would be the generalization that since Agostino Levanzin improved in many functions and showed losses in only a few during a thirty-one day fast, one might safely encourage him to go continuously without food. Such generalizations, however comforting to the summer student, lend themselves to possible abuse by owners of sweatshops, cotton mills and the authorities in control of the schools in cities with corrupt governments. To be on the safe side one would have to carry out experiments upon growing children for long periods of time. In the absence of such experimentation all would agree that the optimum specified is still desirable.

The Effect of Climate.—The experiments showing that the "discomforts" (flushed face, dry skin or sweating, complaints of headache, etc.) and the loss in efficiency were due to a rise in temperature with increase in humidity were made after the observations of Dexter and of Huntington on the effect of climate. Their observations in general are in conformity with and explicable in the terms of the findings of the Ventilation Commission. High winds, cloudy and rainy days seem to have a disturbing effect upon humanity's daily routine. It has been asserted that on days when violent electrical disturbances are present (electric storms) humanity's errors are increased. No trustworthy evidence for this assertion is at hand.

General Effect of Oxygen Deficiency.—The effect of oxygen deficiency has been studied with some degree of care by the psychologists attached to the Medical Research Laboratory at Mineola. It is well known that mountain climbers and pilots flying in high altitudes suffer seriously from lack of oxygen. In order to get a more or less complete picture of these changes and to test the individual variation in the ability to withstand such changes, a large low-pressure chamber was constructed from which the air could be exhausted, thus reducing the oxygen tension until it could be made to correspond to the tension at any barometric level. After oxygen tension has been decreased to a certain point certain habit systems of the human individual begin to decline in efficiency. These effects multiply until complete asphyxiation occurs.. If, during the onset of oxygen hunger, the subject is made to perform certain motor operations somewhat similar to those used in flying the effects will show themselves. In the test devised by Dunlap the subject was seated before a table upon which were placed 14 stimulus lamps arranged in 2 rows of 7 each. Immediately below the lamps were 2 similarly arranged rows of contact buttons, each surrounded by a washer. If the button was touched with a stylus a green check lamp lighted up, but if the surrounding washer was touched a red error light would appear. As soon as any lamp lighted up the subject moved his arm and hand from a position of rest and touched the appropriate contact button with the stylus. The lighting of the small lamps was under the control of the experimenter. The lamps could be made to light in any order. In addition to having him touch the appropriate contact button he had to keep an ammeter reading at a certain point; the amount of current going through the ammeter was under the control of the experimenter. The third thing the subject had to do was to keep a small motor running at low speed by rocking a foot pedal. The speed of the motor, also, was under the control of the experimenter. With the foot pedal in one position the motor would slow down. Without having the subject change his foot the experimenter could again speed the motor up and to slow it the subject would have to rock the pedal to its other position. These acts were all very simple and could be grasped by the subject

after a few minutes of practice. At the same time, they kept
him alert. After touching the light he would have to glance
quickly at the ammeter and then back to the bank of lamps.
The effect of oxygen hunger would show itself in fumbling,
striking too hard or too easily with the stylus; in slowing or speed-
ing of the reactive movements; failure to glance at the light, or
fixating the ammeter and failing to glance at the keys, thus
letting a light go by unreacted to; delaying reaction until he
could not touch the contact with the stylus before the light went
out—the light stayed on only two seconds; touching the contacts
in the wrong row or the wrong column; staring at the light and
making no effort to touch the contact. Finally he would allow
the motor to run continuously at high speed; let the lights go
by without reacting to them; and fail to adjust the ammeter. At
this point complete incapacity had been reached.

The effect upon established habits such as that of handwriting
was studied by the author. A standard psychological vocabulary
test was used in making up the test cards. The one hundred
words of the test were cut up, put in a hat and shuffled. As the
words were drawn from the hat they were typewritten on a
standard library card. By this method three (or any larger
number) test cards of one hundred words each were obtained.
The task of copying the cards offered the same difficulty to the
subject, since the same words were used on each card, only the
order being different. Since the copying of words is an old-
established habit there was little improvement through the practice obtained by the single writing on each of the three cards.
The subject wrote one card at normal barometric pressure (but in
the chamber with the motor running, oxygen tube in the mouth,
etc.). The second card was written 15 minutes after a given "altitude" had been reached. Immediately after writing the (second)
card at this altitude pure oxygen was administered from a tank
through the mouth for two minutes. The third card was then
handed to the subject and he was instructed to copy it. Fig. 66
shows Capt. Davis's normal handwriting, his handwriting at
22,000 feet and his handwriting after breathing oxygen for two
minutes. The records of the men undergoing this test were

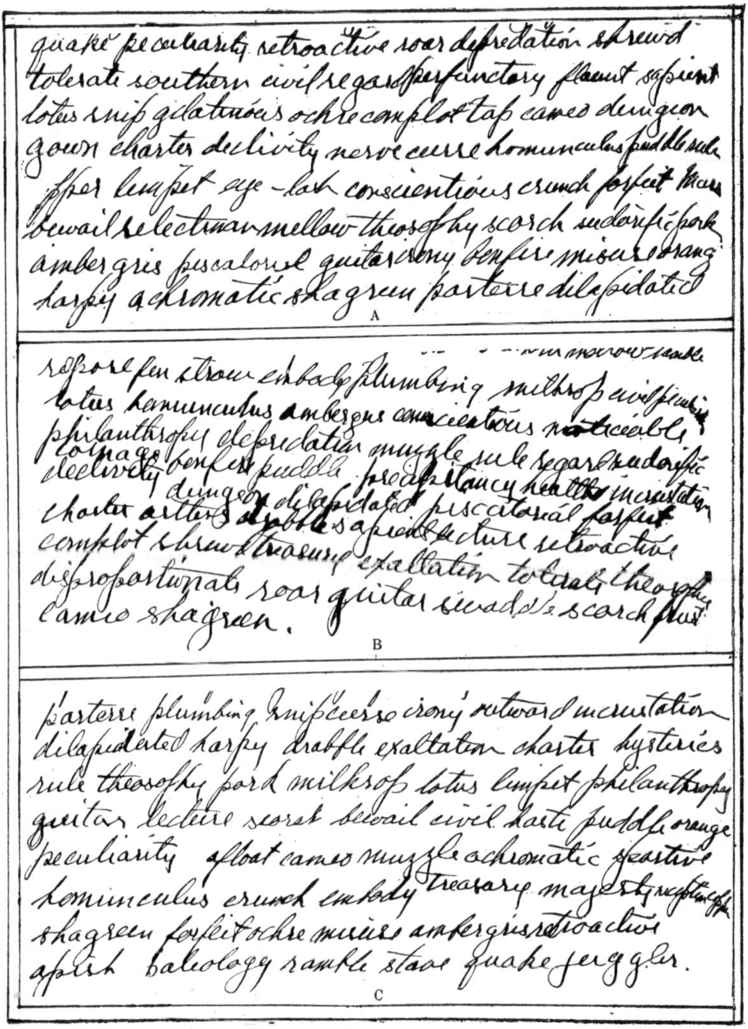

FIG. 66.

examined and evaluated. The legibility was measured on Thorndike's handwriting scale and various penalties were assigned for
errors. The following table will explain the method of rating.
The score was made from the records shown in Fig. 66.

	Normal	Under oxygen hunger	Two minutes after administration of oxygen
Legibility rated on Thorndike scale, last 8 lines only. (Penalty of 20 for each unit lost on Thorndike scale; credit of 20 for each unit gained)	0	— 60	0
Word omitted. (Penalty of 2 each word)	0	0	0
Word misspelled or wrong word used. (Penalty of 2 each word).	0	0	0
Word scratched out and rewritten. (Penalty of 2 each word)	0	0	0
Word careted in. (Penalty of 2 each word)	0	0	0
Word (or any part thereof) written over. (Penalty of 2 each word).	— 3	— 18	— 10
Failure to follow line as well as original. (Penalty of 2 each line on last 8 lines)	0	— 16	0
Time; *penalize* 1 for each 10 seconds increase, or *credit* 1 for each 10 seconds decrease	0	+ 3	0
Total penalties	— 3	— 91	— 10

It will thus be seen that handwriting and the accuracy of copying a list of words is seriously affected by the lack of oxygen, but that the administration of pure oxygen for two minutes almost completely restores this function even though the subject remain at the height of 22,000 feet.

These tables have been made at 14,000 feet, 16,000 feet, 18,000 feet and 22,000 feet. While our records are not complete the results show that at 14,000 feet the effect of a deficient supply of oxygen is very slight. From this point on the various subjects are affected differently. Some individuals are badly affected at 16,000 feet while others are only slightly affected at 18,000 feet. Beyond this point apparently every one shows loss of efficiency. Only one record at 22,000 feet was obtained. Two other subjects tested at 22,000 feet fainted before the last two records could be made. In every case except where fainting occurred the two minutes' administration of oxygen completely restored the handwriting to normal.[4]

---

[4] The author takes this occasion to point out the fact that of the twelve cuts illustrating his work in the Manual of the Medical Research Laboratory at Mineola, twelve either bear wrong titles or else are misplaced; for example, the A in our Fig. 66 is marked in the Manual Capt.

The Diurnal Course of Efficiency.—Several experiments have been carried out for the purpose of determining the relative course of efficiency during the day. Apparently two objects really have been sought: (1) to determine the time of day any given function can be most efficiently exercised and (2) to determine the spread or transfer of "fatigue" (influence of continuous exercise of groups of functions upon some other function).

In regard to (1) there seems to be no reliable conclusion. March states that in manual functions such as aiming, tapping and the like where both accuracy and speed are called for, the maximum of accuracy comes earlier in the day than speed. Hollingworth, on the contrary, finds that mere speed is at a maximum near the end of the day and speed with accuracy near the middle of the day. Gates in a variety of tests finds efficiency increasing in all functions from morning to noon; in the afternoon the efficiency of manual functions continues to increase, whereas the functions involving mainly laryngeal activity show an after-lunch decrease followed by a final increase. Stecher, who has most recently worked upon the problem, obtains still different results. It seems safe to say that until diet, sleep, general activity and certain general organic functions are kept uniform no reliable information can be obtained upon this problem. In the animal world the rhythm of rest and activity can be altered by shifting the feeding periods.

In regard to (2) above we can make the problem more specific: Suppose a student in the grades or in the high school works steadily at a variety of school subjects from 9 to 2:30 (mainly laryngeal functions). Can he perform mathematical computations at well at 9:30 A.M. as at 2 P.M.? Hecht has probably made

Boring's oxygen restoration record, whereas B in our figure is marked Capt. Davis' restoration record. Opportunity was not given the author to read this proof. He had hoped to extend his work to the effect of oxygen hunger upon the accuracy of machine-gun firing which could very easily have been investigated in the tank by means of the machine-gun camera.

In the above report on the effect of oxygen hunger the temperature was not accurately controlled. It ranged from 69° F. at the beginning of the experiment to 72° F. at the close. The tank permitted some circulation of outside air.

the most careful study of this problem in connection with the schools. He tested pupils for 10 minutes at 4 periods in the day and with a careful enough technic to obtain reliable results. The amount and accuracy of the work done practically did not vary. Nearly all other investigators confirm this finding.

Effect of Prolonged Fast Upon Certain Functions.—In the spring of 1912 Langfeld made a study of Agostino Levanzin, a forty-year-old individual, sound and normal in every respect. Before the fast to be described he had gone without food at one other time for 40 days, pleading a case in court on the 26th day of his fast. Before this fast he weighed 180 pounds and after it 140 pounds. On the above date he began his fast at the Nutrition Laboratory of the Carnegie Institute of Washington in Boston. His weight at the beginning of the test was 134 pounds and at the end 106 pounds. The fast endured from the morning of April 14 to May 15, a period of 31 days. During that time 750 c.c. of distilled water was drunk daily, but no food of any kind was taken. The following tests were made at intervals: Rote memory for words, tapping, strength, tactual space threshold, touch threshold, free association, association reaction, cancellation, handwriting, visual acuity, and memory for words after 55 minutes. Unfortunately this subject was not well practiced in many of these functions before the test began, so that the factor of improvement enters in as an offset to the possible loss through fasting. While in one way this is disadvantageous, in another way it is of interest and importance in view of the fact that it shows that lack of food even for long periods does not stop the learning process.

It would take us too far afield to examine separately the various tests upon this fasting individual. In general it may be stated that there was a loss in muscular strength, a gain in sensory acuity and a decided increase in efficiency in those functions not practiced well before the test began. In other words, learning took place much as it would have taken place had the individual not been fasting. Several other tests similar in character have been carried out upon fasting individuals, but not with the same degree of scientific oversight. The most noticeable case is Luciani's test of Succi, who fasted for 30 days. Merlatti is reported to have fasted for 50 days and Dr. Tanner for 40 days. All of these subjects apparently remained in good physical condition during the fast. Luciani states that Succi was at all times very eager to enter into discussions upon abstract subjects. The strength tests on Levanzin and Succi are quite similar. A dynamometer was handed to the subject, who gave it a maximum pressure and returned it to the experimenter. Ten trials were made at intervals of one second with both the right and the left hand. The curve showing the record made by Levanzin is interesting. Langfeld describes it as follows (the subject was probably left-handed):

Both in the right (VII) and left hand (V) curves there is an initial falling off, which is more marked with the former hand. The latter, however, continues to fall to the 11th day, on which day it takes a decided drop, while the former declines more gradually to the ninth day, when it reaches its maximum. Both curves then rise to a maximum, which is reached by the left hand on the 16th day and by the right hand on the 12th day (the record of the first day not being considered in speaking of this maximum). The curves then fall, the left much more than the right, especially in the middle of the series, the former reaching its minimum on the 31st day. Both curves show a slight end spurt. This is, as a glance at the curve will show, merely a rough picture, there being decided rises and falls throughout.

On the day the fast began the dynamometer tests of the left hand averaged about 93 pounds. On the day the fast ended, about 88 pounds.

Other Factors Affecting the Curve of Work.—Efficiency engineers and psychologists are actively engaged in experimentation upon many other factors which may affect the worker and his output. One such form of experimentation is upon the effect of distraction (introduction of conflicting stimuli). In every business office or factory there are, of course, noises of machinery,

typewriters, telephone conversations and the like. Morgan [5] has
shown that where the stimulating value of the problem is kept
high loss in the output from any function through distraction is
very much less than is popularly supposed (although the subject
exerts greater muscular effort, presses down harder upon the
keys, etc.). It is well known that sudden noises and those infrequently met with have a disturbing effect on account of their
tendency to arouse the fear reaction. Where the disturbances
are regular the phenomenon of adaptation enters in and the
worker ceases to be disturbed by extraneous stimuli. One of the
most striking illustrations of this was observed in the Army. In
the Air Personnel office when the force was small typewriters
had to be stopped when long-distance calls were answered. As
the pressure of the work increased and as the office force trebled
and quadrupled, it was no uncommon sight to see a man answering
a long-distance telephone call with fifteen or twenty typewriters
going in his immediate neighborhood and a hundred or more
going in the one large room. Again, while experimentation over
short periods of time may show that such stimuli are without
immediate effect, it still seems safest to have offices and factories
arranged so that the worker is as free as possible from extraneous
disturbances. The wear and tear on the human organism is
probably a positive thing even though temporary laboratory
studies fail to give marked evidence of it.

Recently a large number of experiments have been made
upon the most satisfactory systems of lighting. Indeed, there is

---

[5] Morgan worked with an apparatus in which the subject had to press
a key similar to a typewriter key a certain number of times when a certain
symbol appeared. The activity was thus possibly not very different from
typewriting. As the subject continued to make his adjustments a fire-bell
with an eight-inch gong was sounded directly behind and eight feet away.
Bells of other types were used and various buzzers. Phonographic records
were also played. Some of his conclusions are as follows: The initial or
shock effect of the noise is to retard the speed of the work. After this initial
retardation there is an increase of speed. During distraction extra pressure
is exerted upon the keys and verbal articulation occurs, as is shown by
changes in the breathing. By means of this additional muscular effort put
forth the amount of work done per unit of time is not materially decreased.

now a well-organized society of illuminating engineers. There is general agreement that bright lights are disturbing and that evenness and uniformity in illumination rather than great intensity are the conditions to be striven for except in those cases where the task demands high intensity, as in drafting and the doing of fine work generally.

A General Caution on Efficiency Methods.—It seems that a general caution on all efficiency experimentation is not out of place here. In recent years there has been a constant tendency to turn to the study of the man: the technic and machine sides of industry have been worked up to a point of maximum efficiency. Output if increased must come from a better understanding of man. Psychologists have aided and abetted industry in solving this problem. When the improved output comes from selecting the most suitable man for the task, from eliminating waste effort, improving training methods and allowing recreation and proper periods of rest, such efforts are in the right direction. But the industries are undoubtedly abusing the situation. Every effort is being made, by the bonus system, appeal to loyalty, patriotism and pride, to grind as much out of the organism as possible in the shortest space of time. We would not stay the advance of efficiency engineering for a moment, but we would urge that every new device for getting increased output from the worker should, before being recommended and adopted, be studied from the standpoint of its effect upon the total activity of the worker—in popular terms, its effect upon his happiness and comfort.

THE RELATIVE EFFICIENCY OF THE TWO SEXES.

Sex Differentiation.—Probably no other subject, unless it be that of alcohol, has had so many partisan observations made upon it as that of the relative efficiency of men and women. There are so many variable factors which are not at present under control that everything which may be discovered by putting the two sexes to a test must be looked upon as being purely provisional. The question as to whether there are distinctive differences displaying themselves in the infancy of the two sexes has never been worked out with any degree of sureness. Certain school observations would tend to show that there is a difference from the beginning in the activities of the male and female child; in the things they make with their hands, in the things that they collect, and in the speed with which they acquire certain functions. It has been stated recently that during the first few grades there are as many good writers among boys as among girls, but that after this period is passed the girls are, as a rule, very much better writers than the boys, the handwriting of the boys becoming more or less careless and showing great individual variation. In regard to early differentiation of activities of both the instinctive and habit types it seems safe to say that the conditions from the beginning are different. We do not have common social education for boys and girls: almost immediately the girl is swept into one system and the boy into another—from infancy they are differentiated as to their dress, their general activity and the things that they are allowed to play with. Until the two sexes are brought up side by side and under exactly the same conditions, no reliable conclusions in this division of the problem can be obtained. A good many statements are current with respect to later instinctive and emotional activity. It is stated also that men are more pugnacious than women and that this gives a reason for the greater vocational aggressiveness of the male and also that the male is more variable in tendencies than the female, but there are no reliable data to support these assertions. In the better class of society men are taught to protect women and never to "strike a woman" and where possible to avoid a quarrel with a woman. In the humbler walks of life the police courts show probably more quarrels and fights among women neighbors than among the men in the same locality. On account of having less physical strength women do not engage in actual physical combat with men very often and yet this is not to be generalized in any sense. It is also stated that parental love is stronger in women than in men. Here again we find the influence of the group as a whole at work upon the individual. Men are not less fond of their children than women are, but they cannot nurse them nor are they willing to be bored by looking after their hourly needs and since they are stronger they, in general, have their way. This is made more easily possible by the fact that as society is constructed the man can more readily than the woman win the bread for the family. The divorce courts show that the sticking point in many separations is the child. There would be a great many more separations than at present if the children did not have to go with one or with the other parent. If parental love (which is largely of the associational and non-instinctive type) were not as strong in the man as in the woman there would not be this eternal legal battle for the child. Indeed, an argument may be advanced here for a really stronger attachment for the child in the male than in the female, since by getting the child the amount of alimony coming to the woman is greatly increased and her social position made more secure.

In regard to physical characteristics it is generally admitted that women have a smaller stature and less physical strength and that these differences unquestionably produce some difference in the possibility of certain motor acquisitions: for example, it is all but impossible for a woman to learn to throw a ball or other object with speed and accuracy. Again a comparison of athletic records shows that the speed of women in the 100-yard dash is very much less than that of men. Whether this is due to structural differences or to the lack of an adequate system of coaching does not appear. In certain other manual activities, such as playing tennis, swimming, diving, speed in running a typewriter the women are not so greatly at a disadvantage. Formerly a good deal was made of the asserted difference in brain weight between men and women. Mall has shown that the difference in brain weight is purely a difference in the relative size of the two sexes.

In regard to laboratory tests it has been shown over and over again that the differences if any are very slight. Women are said to excel in such recondite activities as color naming, cancellation tests, spelling and the acquisition of languages; the sexes are said to be equal in retentiveness, speed and accuracy of association, mathematics, differential reactions to color; whereas men are supposed to excel in history (as judged by school marks), ingenuity, accuracy of movement, physics and chemistry (school marks), reaction time and speed of movement.

In so far as life's activities are concerned the accomplishments of women are undoubtedly below those of men. There are few or no great women artists, few who have written enduring literature and few who have obtained great success in instrumental music either as composers or performers. On the other hand, there are and have been as many great women singers as men. It is extremely interesting that the violin, which is an instrument well within the strength and endurance of women, has never been an instrument upon which they excel. There have been few great women scientists. Undoubtedly, the failure of women to achieve greatness in many of these vocational and artistic fields is due to social conditions; for example, it is only within recent years that the universities have encouraged women scientists and even then for them to have a fair show in scientific matters their training in manual dexterity should start at birth, as it does for men. University positions would have to be open to women as they are to men if they are to have the same stimulus for achievement in scientific lines.

The insistent question arises always in discussing these problems as to whether functional periodicity is a serious handicap to women. The common-sense view and the view of commercial houses is that it is a handicap. But if certain recent experimental evidence can be trusted (Hollingworth) there is no difference at such times either in speed or accuracy in the exercise of any given established habit or in the acquisition of habit.

Few or none of these observations touch the really vital question. The fundamental fact is that attractive women do not have to compete in vocational life and nearly every woman has at least one man who passes a favorable judgment upon her. Hence, when business difficulties arise, when hard training periods face them, many women choose the seemingly easier road and allow some man to earn the bread for two. Having once accepted the sheltered position, there is again neither the incentive nor the opportunity to achieve in the field that men achieve in. There are exceptions, of course, to this general statement, but no more than enough to prove the rule, notwithstanding the fact that more and more positions are open to women. The labor turnover among attractive women is greater than among men and probably always will be. Hence, all discussion of and experimentation upon the relative ability of men and women are really academic.

B. FACTORS AFFECTING THE ACQUISITION OF HABITS.

Generalized Statements on Habit Acquisition.—During the past fifteen years there has been a growing body of research on the acquisition of habits both in the field of human psychology and in that of animal behavior. Furthermore, it is an encouraging sign that the general results coming from the two fields agree in most particulars. Without any reference to the feasibility or the advisability of trying to apply these findings as yet in school systems, it seems worth while to present some general formulations on acquisition and then summarize the most characteristic of the researches which support them. The following general statements seem to be justified:

1. The fact of diminishing returns from practice. Within certain limits the less the frequency of practice the more efficient is each practice period.

2. The less the number of habits formed simultaneously the more rapid is the rise of any given habit. 1 is valid here also, apparently, regardless of the number of habits formed simultaneously.

3. Again within certain limits, the younger the organism the more rapidly will the habit be formed. This generalization as yet has not been completely established.

4. Word or other symbolic material which has to be learned to the point of errorless verbal reproduction, regardless of its length, should be learned by the whole rather than by the part method.

5. The higher the incentive to the formation of the habit and the more uniformly this incentive is maintained the more rapidly will the habit be formed.

1. The Fact of Diminishing Returns from Practice.—This

conclusion has now been firmly established for both human and animal acquisitions. Several types of activity have been studied in human learning. Pyle compared the value of practicing 5 hours a day (distributed over the day) with practicing 1 hour per day (distributed over the day). Five of his subjects worked for 10 half-hour periods a day with half-hour rests between practices on learning to use the typewriter. We will call this group the fast group. It worked for 9 successive days, omitting practices on Sunday, putting in a total of 90 half hours of practice. The subjects in this group did nothing else for 9 days. Five other subjects worked for 2 half-hour periods a day, 1 period at 8 A.M. and the other period at 2 P.M. or 3 P.M. We will call this the slow group. This group worked for a period of 45 days, putting in a total of 45 hours, the same as the fast group. The subjects' practice consisted in transcribing fairly homogeneous material on the typewriter. The work of the slow group was better from the start. On the tenth practice the fast group was writing an average of 287 words per half hour, the slow group 370. On the fortieth practice the fast group was writing 351 words, the slow group 557. From the fortieth practice on the difference between the two groups remained nearly constant. The slow group, however, made more errors than the fast group.

A similar study has been made upon the acquisition of skill in archery (Lashley). The subjects were all forced to shoot 500 times, regardless of the number of shots the individual made per day. They were thrown into the following groups: one group shot 5 times per day, another 12 times per day, another 20 times per day and a fourth group 40. These four groups were all carefully selected.[6] None of the individuals had had previous practice in shooting with the English long bow (page 303). The final accuracy of the last 25 shots was chosen as a measure of the amount of improvement which had taken place. The learning

---

[6] A fifth group composed of athletic youths from the Baltimore Polytechnic Institute, shooting 60 shots per day, was also formed. They differed so in their strength and development from the other groups that the results will not be considered here. The records of this group really form exceptions to those of the other four groups.

curve of one of these groups is shown on page 305. The group shooting 5 times per day learned to shoot very much more accurately than the group using the more rapid methods.

Certain other activities have been studied; for example, Dearborn showed in a class experiment in drawing that 10 minutes' practice once a day gives better results than 10 minutes' practice twice a day. Starch contrasted the following four periods: one 120-minute period, three 40-minute periods, six 20-minute periods and twelve 10-minute periods. He thus attempted to answer the question: what is the best distribution of time if you have only 120 minutes to practice? The 10-minute period was found best, the 20-minute nearly as good, the 40-minute next in value and the longest period of least value.

Pyle reports other results bearing upon economy in learning. The subjects were forced to learn new symbols to take the place of the 26 letters of the alphabet and were then practiced in acquiring skill in writing with this new alphabet. The subjects practiced for half an hour, then rested for half an hour and repeated this routine throughout the day. Practice was not continued for a longer period than 1 day—14 half hours of work, 14 half hours of rest. It was found that after 3 or 4 periods of work the remaining practices showed little improvement; nor was the permanent effect from the practice any better for the persons that worked all day than for those who practiced only 4 periods and then stopped.[7]

Although the greater economy and beneficial effects of short infrequent practices are universally established, one cannot argue from this that concentrated practice is worthless. It depends upon the situation the human being is in. Undoubtedly a man could learn to fly better by half an hour's work every other day than by 2 hours' work every day given the same total amount of practice, but with the enemy at the door there is the necessity to train the greatest number of men in the shortest possible time.

---

[7] It seems to be established that the permanence of habits acquired by distributed practice is slightly better than that acquired by concentrated practice.

In such cases the obvious thing to do is to force practice each day to the point where improvement from daily practice ceases. On the other hand, this principle is of very great importance in view of the fact that we can advantageously utilize short periods of time, not otherwise employed, for enormously increasing our repertoire of acts which may later be of economic importance or which may serve us for recreation or relaxation.

2. The Less the Number of Habits Formed Simultaneously the More Rapid is the Rise of Any Given Habit.—So far the only thorough piece of work grounded in experimentation which verifies this formulation comes from the study of animals (Ulrich). If we take three large groups of animals and allow each group to work upon a different problem, thereby establishing reliable norms for the three problems and then take another group and allow it to learn all three problems simultaneously, it will be found that this fourth group will require a larger number of trials to learn each problem than the norm previously established calls for (it will be found also that fact 1 is operative).

Some scattering experimental results would seem to bear out this conclusion for human learning as well, but the results as yet are by no means trustworthy. Even though it be firmly established it has little practical significance, because it runs into conflict with fact 1 in the sense that if we try to instruct the youth by such a method and at the same time give him infrequent practice, he would be idle during the larger part of his time.

3. The Effect of Maturity Upon Learning.—No adequate experiments are at hand upon humans which will enable us to show quantitatively the differences in the speed and accuracy of the acquisition of any given act of skill among a young adult of twenty-one, a man of forty, and a man of sixty-five. In practical life there are a number of taboos, laws and customs relating to age: for example, a man cannot vote until the age of twenty-one is reached. At forty a man is expected to have shown all the originality that is in him and to have accomplished his major piece of work; he is supposed to be content at that age with the habit acquisitions at his command. Again, at from sixty to sixty-five a man's usefulness is supposed to undergo a sharp decline, he is supposed at that age to retire from his university, business and professional duties, to accept a pension and to live thereafter a quiet and retired life. There is hardly any justification, experimental in character, for these age distinctions. The experiments bearing directly upon the problem again come from the study of animals. Although our results from animal learning are not any too secure, we have some evidence to show that a difference exists between the young animal and the old. Miss Hubbert allowed nearly 100 rats differing in age to learn a maze in which the speed of the various trips, the amount of useless running on each trip, and the number of trials necessary to learn the maze could be accurately determined. The two groups of animals beginning work respectively at 25 and 65 days of age learned in about the same number of trials, whereas the 300-day-old animals required nearly a third more trials. This difference in the number of trials between the old and young animals in learning the maze probably needs to be confirmed. However, it was firmly established that the time of the final execution of the act was very much shorter for the young animals than for the old, the young animals traversing the maze in 6 seconds, whereas the old animals required 10 seconds. Probably the most significant thing from the standpoint of middle-aged and old human individuals is that even the oldest animal we could get (500 and 600 days) still had the ability to learn this complicated maze. Thus our former notions about the lack of plasticity in the old are without foundation if such results can be carried over into the human fields, as they doubtless can be. This generalization would seem to be of importance since experiments apparently show that it is possible for a man or woman who has been too busy in youth and in middle-age to form habits of play and recreation to learn to play or even to form vocationally serviceable habits after retiring from active business life. Such a possibility should make old age less of a bugbear and less of an affair of endless reminiscence and total redintegration of earlier experiences.

4. The Whole vs. the Part Method in Learning.—Where prose and poetry in considerable amounts have to be learned to

the point where verbal reproduction is possible, as is the case in
the schools, dramatic work, public speaking and the like, the question arises as to the most economical way of committing this
material.   The schoolboy, if let alone, learns one stanza, and
oftentimes one line, before proceeding to the next; then after the
second stanza is learned he goes back to the first and repeats both
until an errorless reproduction of both is possible. He continues
this routine for the whole poem, regardless of its length.   This
means, of course, that the early stanzas are always over-learned.
With few exceptions the experimental results show that the whole
method of learning is better than the part, that is, that the material, regardless of its length, should be read through again and
again until reproduction as a whole becomes possible.   In addition to the possibility of more rapid acquisition accruing from
the use of the whole method, retentiveness seems to be better
where material is learned in that way than when learned by the
part method (Pyle and Snyder, Lakenan, and others).

5. **The Higher the Incentive and the More Uniform the
Incentive the More Rapid and Steady will be the Improvement.**—There are no separate experimental studies on the effect
of different incentives upon acquisition, but the incidental results
from the study of all recorded learning illustrate this law.   The
industries recognize the law and even during the earliest appren-
ticeship period the attempt is made to give extra monetary reward,
promises of future position, advancement and the like to increase
the speed of acquisition.   As we have already brought out, most
of the plateaux in the recorded learning curves are probably due
to a failure to keep the stimulating value of the task high.   Most
interesting illustrations of the effect of high incentives were
brought out in the recent war.   The number of rivets which could
be driven home in any given day by an individual engaged in
shipbuilding increased by leaps and bounds as soon as the news-
papers began to exploit it and to post the various scores over the
country and as soon as the Government began to offer prizes for
the highest score.   Altitude records in flying and long-distance
flying are equally illustrative of this principle.

One of the greatest difficulties in the ordinary routine of daily life is the fact that the stimulating value of any incentive soon loses its power to arouse emotion. The incentive, then, has to be changed. A good many business houses admit that their devices for offering added stimulation produce only a temporary increase in output. The attempt is now being made with better results to introduce profit-sharing, partial ownership in the business and group insurance (which is lost if the worker leaves). These devices offer permanent and cumulative rewards. In addition to their effect upon keeping the stimulating value of the work high they decrease the labor turnover.

CHAPTER XI

PERSONALITY AND ITS DISTURBANCE

A. The Systematic Study of Personality.

Introduction.—In previous chapters we have dealt largely with the genesis and functioning of individual reaction systems. Psychologists and psychiatrists often have the task of rating the individual as a member of society, passing judgment upon him as a whole from the standpoint of how well or how poorly he functions in his present environment, to form estimates of how smoothly he would react to a new environment and to specify the necessary changes in his equipment which would make for present and future adjustment. Various practical situations force us constantly to examine man in this broader way. In making such estimates or inferences we use the term personality or character[1] as a convenient way of expressing the fact that we are looking at the individual not from the standpoint of how well or how poorly any particular emotion, instinct or group of habits he possesses many function, but from that of how the organism as a whole works or many work under changed conditions.

A Possible Hint from Mechanics.—Several times in the text we have contrasted the reaction of parts with reactions of the individual as a whole. To illustrate this more completely it may be well possibly to turn to the world of mechanics for at least a slight analogy. A marine gas engine is made up of a number of parts, such for example as the carburetor, the pump, the magneto, the valve system, the cylinders with their pistons and

---

[1] As we use these two terms, character is really a subdivision of the broader term personality. Character is generally used when viewing the individual from the standpoint of his reactions to the more conventionalized and standardized situations (conventions, morals, etc.). Personality includes not only these reactions but also the more individual and personal adjustments and capacities as well as their life history. Popularly speaking, we would say that a liar and a profligate had no character, but he may have an exceedingly interesting personality.

rings, connecting rods, etc. Separate tests of each part may show that it functions perfectly when working alone. But in addition to the separate parts there are many interconnecting elements. The parts cannot work well unless the bearing surfaces have just the right amount of play, the magneto must give the spark at the precise instant of greatest compression, the oiling system and pump system must be properly connected with some part moved by the crankshaft. Unless all of the parts are properly interconnected and timed the engine as a whole will not perform its function, that is, *turn the propeller*.

When we speak of the action of the individual as a whole, we mean something of this nature. It must be borne in mind that the human being has not one function to perform but thousands, and the adjustments of the parts must vary in each and every new duty if the work of the whole organism is to be efficient. Only a well constructed biological organism properly trained can meet these requirements. No mechanical contrivance yet hit upon approaches the human organism in its multiplicity of possible functions and in the rapidity with which co-ordinations of separate functions can be so rapidly shifted for each new duty of the machine as a whole.

It is interesting to push our possible analogy one step further. If we know enough about the parts of any mechanical contrivance, the nature of the interlocking systems and the various interdependent functions, we can make safe predictions about how it will work under new conditions or specify the changes which will have to be made if the contrivance must perform some new function. For example, in the case of our engine, we know it is good for high speed and short runs. Such and such changes will have to be made if it is to be used for medium duty or forced to pull heavy loads. We know further that with the oiling and cooling systems as they now are it will not run in a very cold climate; with the fuel system now employed it cannot be used where oxygen tension is low; that heavy fuel such as kerosene or crude oil will not burn in it; that it will run in fresh water indefinitely but that certain parts will have to be made of bronze if it is to run smoothly in sea water for any length of time.

This hint from mechanics should give us a clearer notion of (a) the reaction of the whole and of parts, (b) the possibility of inferring from our data on parts and our records of performance of the apparatus as a whole how the apparatus will work under new conditions and the necessary changes to make in the parts and their interconnections in order to get it to take on a new function.

Practical Use of Personality Inferences.—On a smaller or larger scale we are constantly having to deal with individuals in new situations. Knowing the part reactions of individuals and how they have functioned as a whole in past situations enables us to draw legitimate inferences as to how they will act when the new situation confronts them. Personality study in one form or another is thus essential in every form of social life. All of us face personality problems each day of our lives. We are put face to face with serious problems of personality when we are called upon to pass judgment upon our child's selection of a mate, to select a life associate in business or university work, to begin the study and re-training of some individual whose personality is diseased or distorted. In less serious circumstances we face the problem when we put two people together at a dinner party or make out a list of guests for a bridge party, or even in bringing together two of our intimate friends. Clever hostesses understand the social aspect of the problem very well, but they will tell you that their success is due not to any peculiar intuition on their part but to the fact that they study and keep posted on the intimate details of the lives of their friends.

Confusion in the Concept of Personality.—While everyone would agree that the factors we have discussed are a part of a personality study many would hold that this simple way of looking at personality is not expressive of the whole truth. They would maintain that it includes all these things but also "something" in addition. If one asks what this something is it will be found that no straightforward answer can be given. Instead of a working definition the term will be used with qualifying adjectives: "I mean that his personality overpowers and overawes one," "that there is something magnetic about him," "that he draws or enthralls one," "commands attention or respect," "his personality fills the room." This usage is easily understandable. Two elements predominate. Without going too deeply into them we may briefly state first, that the above type of description is made upon the basis of childhood and adolescent reactions to authority. In infancy and adolescence the father, also the doctor, minister, etc., stand for authority. When they speak, obedience must be rapid and implicit. The child is thrown into an emotional state and jumps to execute commands. This tendency to react to authority is never quite lost and reappears again and again in our reactions to individuals in our business and social circles. Hence in later life those speakers and associates who rearouse the vestiges of reaction to the old authority situation are the individuals who for us would be classed as having a strong personality.

The second element underlying judgments of personality in this popular sense is the sexual or emotional one, sex being used here not in the popular sense but in the modern psychopathological one. When this element is strongest—that is, when the speaker or associate (the stimulus) brings out those positive reaction tendencies, the popular characterization is put in a little different words. The man or woman has a "pleasing," "thrilling" or "engrossing" personality.[2] Friendships are almost instantaneously begun largely upon the basis of this element. It must be recalled that according to modern usage this kind of reaction tendency is aroused not only by members of the opposite sex but also by members of the same sex. The author in making a statistical analysis of the factors entering into the formation of friendship found that the element of truthfulness was ranked first and loyalty second. These are of course conventionally the correct answers and the ranking obtained was the one expected in a mixed crowd. When the questionary asked for other impor-

---

[2] To illustrate, take the following quotation from Arnold Bennett: "I felt that once out of the immediate circle of his tremendous physical influence, I might manage to escape the ordeal which he had suggested. But I could not get away. The silken nets of his personality had been cast, and I was enmeshed."

tant elements, such items as sympathy, congeniality and the like took a prominent place. In general the following question was answered in the affirmative: "Do you decide as soon as you meet a person whether the basis for friendship is present?" The greatest difficulty was experienced by those attempting to make the analysis. They had not hitherto made the effort to phrase that factor in their lives in words. We meet the same difficulty in trying to get an answer as to why men love their wives or women their husbands, or parents love their children. The reasons advanced are conventional ones. The deeper reasons lie below the organized word level; upon unanalyzed (unphrased) emotional instinctive and early habit slants. This is the reason it is so difficult to get people to talk intelligently of what they mean by personality.

The muddled writings we have from the hands of many scientific writers upon self, personality and character give only a slightly better working basis. Nearly every psychologist and medical writer has in the background of his early training certain religious and metaphysical premises. He finds no way to weave these into the straightforward scientific discussion of instinct, emotion and habit. Hence he brings them to the fore in a final discussion of the self and personality where problems are not usually accurately worked out and faced. Again, in the writings of scientists we also see the early reactions to authority. It shows as an unwillingness to admit that the individual has within himself all of the determining factors for action. It is found necessary to bring in to account for self and personality, if not overtly at least covertly, a nucleus, a core, or essence which resists analysis, which cannot be expressed in the plain facts of hereditary and acquired reactions and their integrations. This is illustrated all through the history of philosophy in the "spirit" of Berkley, in the "consciousness" and "self" of modern psychological writers and in the "unconscious" of the Freudian mystics.

Behavioristic and Common-Sense Conception of Personality.—Again we seem to have reached a point in psychology where we can make progress most rapidly by discarding these vague conceptions of personality and starting with premises which will yield useful and practical results capable of being couched in the ordinary language of science. Let us mean by the term personality an individual's total assets (actual and potential) and liabilities (actual and potential) on the reaction side. By assets we mean first the total mass of organized habits; the socialized and regulated instincts; the socialized and tempered emotions; and the combinations and interrelations among these; and secondly, high coefficients both of plasticity (capability of new habit formation or altering of old) and of retention (readiness of implanted habits to function after disuse). Looked at in another way, assets are that part of the individual's equipment which make for his adjustment and balance in his present environment and for readjustment if the environment changes.

By liabilities we mean similarly that part of the individual's equipment which does not work in the present environment and the potential or possible factors which would prevent his rising to meet a changed environment. In more detail, we mean that we can enumerate the reasons for his present lack of adjustment in such terms as insufficiency of habits, lack of social instincts (instinct not modified by habit), violence of emotion or insufficiency or lack of emotion, and that we can infer that with his present equipment and plasticity the individual cannot make a satisfactory adjustment either to his present environment or possibly to any other environment. In case his potential assets are sufficient we can enumerate and begin the inculcation of those factors which will make for his adjustment.

This way of looking at personality seems to call for a standard of adjustment and seems to imply that such a standard is available. Our standard at present is a common-sense and practical one. Practically we do in our daily routine of life take individuals with whom we are acquainted and point out the essential factors which make them occupy the place they do in social and community life. The better trained we are the more accurately we can point these factors out. The question as to whether we shall ever have scientific and accurate standards need not concern us at the present moment.

The Systematic Study of Personality.—At first sight we might be tempted to assume that in order to study personality one should have a microscopic view of an individual's whole life both past and present. Unquestionably the more complete our knowledge is of the present and past of any person the more accurate our analysis of his personality will be. But at best for both practical and scientific purposes we can obtain only a limited amount of data upon each individual. How then shall we proceed in studying personality? It is obvious that we must resort to "sampling." What samples should be taken depends largely upon the purposes for which the study is to be made. The men working in psychiatry were first to recognize the need of a systematic sampling of activity. Through practical experience they have found that if they can gain even limited data upon certain aspects of the individual's past and present life they are in a position to understand his weakness. While there is no absolute agreement among the different workers as to just what data should be gathered the general agreement is fairly close. There are a number of such "guides" to the systematic study of personality (Hoch and Amsden, Adolf Meyer, F. L. Wells, Yerkes, and others). These studies have not been worked out wholly in objective or behavioristic terms, but the results they have yielded are easily interpretable in any objective system. Any modern method should have as its starting point the discarding of all presuppositions and the putting of the individual in front of us for study. In general we study him as we would any other practical or scientific problem. We continue this study until we can answer definite questions about the individual. If we cannot immediately return the answer to an essential question we study him until we can.

The following topics and questions are offered merely as indicatory of some of the more concrete and studiable factors which we should have information about whenever there is practical or scientific need for a personality judgment. The definite questions asked are designed to bring out mainly those factors which common experience in dealing with human individuals from various standpoints has taught us are essential. We are merely

putting in the form of definite questions the basis upon which
so-called intuitive and common-sense judgments about personality
are made.

SUGGESTIONS TOWARD THE STUDY OF PERSONALITY

General Level of Behavior.—(1) If the individual is too
complex to be rated by any of the "intelligence tests" of the
Binet type, what do various special tests show as regards his
range of information, vocabulary, English and literary equipment, mathematical ability, special vocational equipment? (2)
What do actual tests show concerning his learning ability in the
field, both of manual activity and language activity? (3) What
do actual tests show concerning his retentiveness in these fields?
(4) How accurately does he make observations under simple
experimental conditions?

**General Survey of Instinctive and Emotional Equipment
and Attitude.**—Do the number and variety of drives to activity
seem plentiful or deficient? Are there special lines of activity
in which he takes training easily and in which retention is
good? Does he display a normal amount of investigatory
behavior (curiosity) with respect to new situations, systems of
thought, literature? Has he any knack of doing things with his
hands (manipulation)? Does he use or substitute this knack
of doing things for card playing, dancing, golf and other recreation outlets? What particular bents and hobbies has he exhibited
from time to time? What is the history of his early (pre-adoles-
cent) sex enlightenment, sex attachments, and curiosities (see
also under organized sex life, p. 401)? Are there any instinctive
traits especially with regard to eliminative and sex functions yet
unsocialized, such for example as general bodily display, display
of parts, lack of sex fixation, etc?

Are his emotional reactions well balanced or is he over- or
under-emotional; liable to be easily upset, becoming angry or
violent or unduly retiring when certain topics are under discussion or when in the presence of certain situations? If so, what
situations most easily arouse emotional activity both of the
primitive type, such as fears, rages, love, etc., and the more

systematized and adult type which takes the form of attitudes? Have there been strong attachments or antagonisms for any member of the family? Have these been outgrown or have they been carried over into adult life? Would he be classed now, or was he so classed as a boy, as a sissy; was he as a lad ever taunted with being tied to his mother's apron string? How many infantile emotional reactions and attitudes have been carried over into adult life, such as biting the nails, playing with the mouth and face, spitting? What outlets does his more organized emotional life take, *e.g.*, day dreaming, making or writing of fanciful productions? (Consult here chapter on emotions, p. 236, and also the section in the present chapter on personal slants and peculiarities.)

General Habits of Work.—Does he complete work undertaken promptly and neatly or is he a procrastinator, a maker of excuses and in general a temperamental worker? Is he punctual at his tasks and appointments? When stuck on a given task does he give up easily with signs of emotional disturbance or does he as a rule work persistently until the difficulties are overcome? Does he work to his limit or is there a constant tendency to save himself? In leaving his work is he one of the first to drop his task or will he work later than regulations specify? Is he adverse to having extra duties put upon him? Must his duties be laid out for him by rule of thumb or need one give him only general outlines? Would you classify him as being resourceful or merely as a door of chores and routine? Did he as boy or man ever build, design or plan any new object or write an original production? What has been the history of his vocational endeavors and achievements and what have his earnings been (or its equivalent in rank) at different ages? Is he fixed upon his present level of attainment or is he making steady or rapid progress? If not making progress, is his work suited to his attainments? Would he work better in another line, or would he rise from his present level of attainment if his responsibilities were greater and if he had more difficulties to contend with?

Activity Level.—Would you characterize the subject as being lazy, industrious, or active in manual work? Is he talkative or taciturn, slow or active in speech? Is he a story teller or extemporaneous speaker? Are his acts or speech ever violent or rude? Is he given to sudden bursts of loud conversation and frequent laughter? Are his work and talk systematic and logical in character? Are his movements made in good form or is he awkward in gait, work and speech? Would you characterize him as being a man always in a hurry, restless, eager? Is he constantly talking of the many things he has to do or that he has left undone? Can he put his work aside or must he take it with him, conversationally at least, into his social life and moments of recreation?

Social Adaptability.—Does he get along well with his wife, parents or members of his immediate family, with his business associates, with his companions in recreation? What is his history with respect to association with others? How many intimate friends has he among his own and the opposite sex? Of how long standing (carried from infancy or formed in later life)? How easily does he get acquainted with people when in a new environment? How rapidly does he become settled in a new environment? How would you rate him with respect to tactfulness, quarrelsomeness, co-operation, etc.? Apart from any money or social status that he may possess, is his society sought by others? Is he in general loyal to his friends and does he make active efforts to hold them? Has he had any history of leading men? What position of prominence in games, sports or social life has he held?

Recreation and Sports.—What are the main types of his play activities and how successful has he been in them? Is he of the one sport type (*i.e.*, possessing a single hobby, such as golf, poker) or is he an all round sportsman? Does he sacrifice his work and responsibility to exercise his recreation and sporting tendencies? Are there special forms of play, especially of chance such as cards and roulette, which amount to obsessions and toward which he displays a lack of balance?

Organized Sex Life.—Will he talk freely of his sex life when questioned about it for scientific purposes or does he avoid reference to this phase of his life or to certain periods of it? Has he a tendency to talk too freely about his sex experiences and to be boastful of his conquests? Obtain from him as careful a statement as possible of the chief events in his sex life and the effect they have had upon his life history. Include here the adolescent struggle, the transition to heterosexual fixation, his infatuations and the like. Does he attribute his success or lack of success to any of these factors?

If married, what has been the history of the relationship? Is he affectionate and kind or jealous, irritable and fault-finding? Is he domineering or submissive? Does prudishness, frigidity or avoidance mark the relationship? Has there been any tendency towards perversion in any form, cruelty, etc.? Does he show any peculiarities with respect to certain foods and odors? Have children been sought? Has any home life been established? Do husband and wife have the same friends and play the same games or are they held together merely by social pressure or the joint responsibility of children?

Reactions to Conventional Standards.—As judged by ordinary standards (and with special reference to the group in which he lives) is he truthful, faithful to his word, and careful of the rights and reputation of others? Is he frank in his opinions and statements, trustworthy in money matters or the reverse? Put specifically to him such questions as whether under any circumstances it is ever justifiable to tell a lie, to steal, to cheat, to fall in love with an engaged or married woman and tell her about it? To kill another individual or to commit suicide?

Personal Bias and Peculiarities.—Has his early home, school or religious training implanted fixed modes of reacting which are not in line with his present environment—that is, is he easily shocked, for example, at seeing a woman smoke, drink a cocktail or flirt with a man; at card playing; at the fact that many of his associates do not go to church? Have past failures in early home life, married or business life developed a "soured" disposition or attitude? Has he become a woman hater, a rebel against social law and order, and in general a misogamist or does his general restlessness at failure take another form in which he actually attaches himself to each new movement in thought or in philos-

ophy, religion, art, music, politics? Has the early petting or
cruelty he has received at the hands of interested individuals
made him boastful, timid, proud, overbearing; or is he generally
balanced in these respects? Examine him especially with reference to his brooding and sensitiveness. What are his chief lines
of sensitiveness and how does this sensitiveness show itself? In
shutting himself off and putting up a barrier against social
contact or in complaints that every hand is against him? How
in general have his disappointments and successes left him so
far as new undertakings are concerned?

Are there peculiarities in voice, gesture, gait, physical appearance, defects or weaknesses in organs which arouse emotion when
he is forced to face them? Have these been adjusted to and
compensated for to such an extent that he will talk with you freely
about them, or have they developed within him a permanent
inferiority attitude with many peculiarities in behavior developed
to compensate for such weaknesses? Is he over-meticulous with
reference to dirt, money matters and peccadilloes generally?
Would you classify the individual as being foppish and over-
dressed; does he resort to beauty treatments, perfumery, etc.?
Is he lavish in his expenditures, exhibiting a tendency to show
off; or is he miserly and close?

Balancing Factors.—How in general has he reacted to difficulties which could not be overcome? Does renunciation merely
leave him unadjusted or does he attain readjustment by turning to
other activities without loss of time and without serious emotional
breakdown? What has been the history of some specific readjustment, after loss, for example, of position, parent, friend,
sweetheart, wife or child? In general has he found satisfactory
substitutes and balances for things given up and lost and for
weaknesses of training and poor special equipment? For
example, if he never learned to play, what does he substitute
for this? If he has never married, what factors compensate?
If married but with no children, what compensation has been made
(pets, adoption of other children, etc.)? How do his unbalanced
tendencies show: in recklessness, excesses, speed manias, the
seeking of exciting situations, excessive eating, dress, etc.? Can

he resort to games, music, theatre, dancing, and to club life when in trouble or when family relationships bid fair to remain unsatisfactory? Has he engrossing work which serves him as a balance wheel and for compensation when other things go wrong? What verbal account can he give of the things he has substituted for the things he cannot obtain—for example, one man constantly makes a poor score in golf, but he prides himself on having better "form" than any other member belonging to the club. Money suddenly acquired is often a balancing or compensating factor for lack of breeding and social position. A woman lacking beauty of face preens herself over her form, or lacking both, upon her hair, or even upon the size of her feet or the shape of her hand. Lack of special recognition and position of a given family is compensated for by the fact that they are relatives of some person of recognized ability and attainment.

Have religion and church work been for him a balancing factor—one upon which he loads responsibility and from which he receives authority and by means of which he obtains surcease from emotional strain in times of trouble? Would you classify him in general as one who put his responsibilities and troubles upon the Lord or upon himself? [3]

Personality Study Ultimately Belongs to the Laboratory.— In using such outlines as the above in the study of personality we may narrow the questions, make them more specific and then mark the excess of the factor in relations to the average by a $+$ sign and its absence or deficiency by a $-$ sign (Wells). We may obtain our data by living near the individual and observing him systematically under the routine of work and play; by systematically questioning him and examining into his dreams; or we may take him into the laboratory and complete our analysis by experimental methods. Unfortunately the laboratory is not

---

[3] It will be seen that this whole questionary relates principally to the diagnosis and evaluation as we see it in everyday life. It is not planned to be searching enough to throw much light upon the etiology or causation of personality disturbance. This phase of personality, while distinctly psychological in character, at present belongs more particularly to the domain of psychiatry.

yet prepared to enter as extensively into such work as is desirable, but very rapid progress is being made. During the next few years the laboratory should make such further progress that it will be capable of making by actual tests serviceable and comprehensive surveys of personality.

Summary.—When we have faced our individual and have studied his behavior during his ordinary routine of activity by systematic questioning and by experiments where possible, and have received satisfactory answers to such questions as the above, we shall know his personality. We may make the study as complete or as sketchy as the occasion demands. For a guest at a house party all we may care to make sure of is that the person is worth while, decent, attractive, agreeable to others, that he can play and that his personal peculiarities will not unduly protrude. In trying to restore to normal a psychopathic personality the study would have to be made far more complete than we have outlined above.

While we have not emphasized the matter in the above sketch, no examination of a personality would be complete without collateral information coming from a careful study of the individual's heredity, personal illnesses, use of drugs, etc. Meyer, in order to formulate these factors and to keep them in their relation to more detailed personality data, has prepared a life chart upon which the more significant personal data may be put down for each individual. It is undoubtedly advisable for each psychological student to make some such life chart of himself and even a more detailed personality study than we have outlined above. Self and personality under careful scrutiny cease to be mysteries and become problems which can be solved by careful observation.

Rapid Methods of Studying Personality.—That the study of personality must be a genuine research carried out in a systematic manner upon each individual has only recently been recognized. Almost from the earliest history of the race certain rapid methods of arriving at personality judgment have been in use. While these methods with the exception of (1) below are in general all but worthless, the public believes in them and lays itself open to become the victim both of unscrupulous sharpers and misguided enthusiasts. Such judgments are based upon four different sets of asserted data. (1) Voice, gesture, gait, attitude and dress group. (2) Differences in head and skull formation. (3) Differences in biological characteristics, such as eye color, color and type of hair and the shape of the fingers. (4) Differences in handwriting. So-called character experts are supposed to study such differences and to pass judgment upon men and women who are to be employed by business houses. Since time immemorial such prophets have been among us. Banking upon the fact that fifty per cent. of their judgments must by chance be right and that being shrewd observers they can add another fifteen per cent. of correct choices (which any individual who has wide contact with other people can do), they set up as "characterologists" and begin to fleece the public. We shall examine some of the asserted principles involved in these rapid determinations of character.

(1) Personality judgments based upon voice, gesture, gait, etc. A momentary glimpse of an individual reveals very little about his personality. Certain signs, however, have become classic as indicators of character, such as the square chin, the firm mouth, the intellectual brow, erect carriage and the like. It is often asserted that the kind of life the individual has led becomes stamped upon his face and body; that the inferior person shows inferiority in his attitude; that the discontented, complaining, hard-done-by individual has certain lines in his face such as the drooping lip by means of which he can be known. Kempf has recently given more prominence to the view that bodily attitudes reveal the "autonomic strivings" of the individual than most authors are willing to concede. In extreme cases even the static view or the photograph of an individual is sufficient to reveal many factors about personality, such for example that he is a cretin, an idiot or a certain type of schizophrenic (as revealed by the Madonna attitude, etc). But no genuine student of human nature depends much upon what can be gathered from a mere static view of the subject or an examination of his photograph. Any psychologist at the present

time who claims that he can pick out defective individuals from normals by means of photographs or by mere immediate visual inspection would lose the respect of his colleagues: and yet at the present moment there are many "experts" claiming not only to be able to do this, which is the first step in a character study, but also to be able to judge from the photograph or static view whether the individual is fitted for a certain type of vocation. Indeed, they have capital behind them and their advertisements are taken in reputable magazines.

When we pass from the static view to even a cursory observation of *behavior* we are upon a different basis entirely. One can dine once with an individual and place him in a conventional social scale. Often the speaking of two or three sentences or even of a few words enables us to gather volumes about his general social and educational attainments. A ten minutes conversation skilfully conducted will bring out considerable data about a person's range of training and information and show a great deal about his general balance. The militant anti-smoker, anti-drinker, suffragette, the woman or man hater, the religious enthusiast would not let ten minutes go by without revealing the causes in life which they champion. The crank that comes in with his new philosophical theory, the new prophet, the faith healer, and the promoter of forlorn undertakings lose no time in announcing themselves. Again, the silent observation of an individual in action reveals to the well trained observer much concerning his personality, both with reference to his skill and to his emotional balance. We have already developed this aspect to some extent in the chapter on emotions. The signs of, at least, temporary distress, torture, despondency and elation do not long remain hidden. Whether the state is permanent or characteristic is not so easily noticed, but, as we have brought out, the more permanent emotional disturbances are not without distinguishing marks such as the habitual biting of nails, twitching of facial muscles and other tics, stammering, and the inability to sit still.

Since rarely do we have the time or the means for systematically examining into the personality of individuals in practical life, it is obvious that most of our immediate inferences are based upon just such factors as gait, dress, manners, the way the person shakes hands, the changes in his facial expression, bodily attitudes and the like, plus the specific information we gather through chance conversation about his business, sports, taste and general likes and dislikes. There is no particular scientific technique which can be employed in making such inferences and we often have to modify our conclusions. There is no question but that our reactions and attitude towards a new-comer are determined by these somewhat superficial signs. Later modifications of our judgments are often made difficult by reason of these earlier snapshot immediate estimates.

(2) Skull and head markings (phrenology). The history of phrenology is too well known to need discussion. Its adherents assert that the external markings of the skull, the over- and under-development of certain parts are to be correlated with over- and under-development of the brain. Phrenology is based upon two misconceptions: first, that the brain conforms to the various bumps upon the surface of the skull, and, second, that the so-called faculties, such as amativeness, self-assertion, ambition, etc., are to be correlated with any particular part of the brain. Anatomists have constantly brought out the fact that prominences upon the skull may and often are indications not of corresponding development in the underlying brain tissue but often of underlying deficiencies. The brain in general is smooth in its contours, as we learned in our study of the nervous system. The neurophysiologist, as has been pointed out, lays little stress upon localizations of brain function in any detailed sense. Phrenology has thus not one scientific prop to support it. Nevertheless it has had a most interesting and at times flourishing history. The only thing which can be said to the credit of phrenology is that interest in the general subject led to a scientific study of the brain—which in time completely overthrew the doctrine upon which the "theory" was based. It still plays a rôle in the formulæ of the expert characterologist.

(3) Differences in biological characteristics. The most glaring and at the same time the most successful from a financial standpoint of the recently developed non-scientific systems of

character reading is that which purports to read character by means of hair color, skin coloring and texture, shape and set of the eyes, size and shape of the nose, mouth, hands and fingers. To expose the falsity of the extravagant claims of the charlatans who advocate this it needs only to be pointed out that we have several well recognized biological and anthropological laboratories whose research men have patiently recorded both individual traits and biological markings. If there was a correlation between character and such markings it would hardly have escaped their observation. Such correlations may exist, but the scientist who discovers them and actually grounds them will have an enviable place in science for all time.

(4) Handwriting and personality. Since 1662, when Camillo Baldo in Italy published his treatise on the method of determining the character of a person by his handwriting, there has been an increasingly popular belief in the subject. Binet, Preyer and other investigators have made several observations upon correlations between sex and handwriting and between handwriting and general personality. To test whether sex was determinable from handwriting he took 180 envelopes that for the most part had passed through the mail, but from which all seals, headings and the like had been removed, and submitted them to two professional graphologists and to 15 persons ignorant of the art of graphology. Of the envelopes 89 had been addressed either to Binet himself or to members of his family by women, 91 had been addressed by men. There was of course an error here due to the fact that the person could guess at the sex of the writer on account of its being addressed to a female member of the family. The percentage of right judgments in Binet's test made by the unexpert averaged about 70. One of the experts, M. Crépieux-Jamin, had a percentage correct of 78.8. Binet concludes that it is possible with a certain percentage of errors to determine sex from handwriting. Miss Downey improved upon this method by having all the envelopes addressed to a woman. Two hundred were employed, all but 4 passed through the mail, 100 had been addressed by women, 100 by men. These 200 envelopes were submitted to 13 persons each of whom recorded his judgment as to the sex of the writer. The ages

of the judges varied from 15 years to 50. In every case in the present test, as in the French test likewise, the percentage right was over 60. Miss Downey concludes: "From my analysis of my own results I conclude that it is possible to determine sex from handwriting in perhaps 80 cases out of 100." The basis upon which these judgments were made is hard to determine. In general the observers could not phrase the difference. Originality is held to characterize the man's hand, conventionality the woman's; men's writing is said to show a greater range of variability than women's. This leads at times to error. The features are not well analyzed in any of the writings.

Numerous tests, generally popular in nature, have been made upon the determination of character from certain graphological signs. Binet obtained samples of handwriting from 37 individuals of recognized intellectual eminence such as Renan and Bergson. With each of these he paired the writing of a person of similar education and general social level but of very mediocre attainments. The graphologists were asked to state which of each pair of writers was the more intelligent. Crépieux-Jamin came off best with the astonishing score of only 3 errors out of 36 determinations, or nearly 92 per cent. Six other graphologists' scores were 86, 83, 80, 68, 66, 61, all distinctly superior to chance.

Binet also secured specimens of the handwriting of 11 notorious assassins. With each of these he paired the handwriting of an honest citizen in a rather humble walk of life. The expert graphologists were directed to tell which of each pair of writers was superior in general morality. Once more Crépieux-Jamin came off best, with 3 errors out of 11, or 73 per cent. right.

The graphologists assert that they read character by such graphological signs as follows:

Ambition ....lines of writing slope upward
Pride ....lines of writing slope upward
Bashfulness ....writing is traced with fine lines
Force .... (a) ..heavy lines
Force .... (b) ..heavy bars on the t's
Perseverance ....long bars on the t's
Reserve ....closed a's and o's

Hull and Montgomery have recently made a detailed test of some of these asserted correlations. The subjects were 17 students of the University of Wisconsin belonging to the same medical fraternity. Each man was first asked to write in his ordinary manner a paragraph from a popular magazine. The writing was done in each subject's own room at his regular desk with his own pen on uniform unruled paper of good quality. When the writing was finished the subject was given a set of 16 small cards each containing the name of one of the other subjects, his own name not being included. He was directed to arrange the cards in the order of the amount of *ambition* possessed by the persons indicated on each. A ranking was thus obtained. The writing was then subjected to measurement, the m's, n's and t's were especially measured and the ranking for ambition correlated with the pronounced upward slope of the lines of writing or the reverse. A statistical measure showed no tendency whatever for the ambitious person to write in an upward sloping direction. The subjects were also ranked for *pride,* and again the handwriting of each was examined with respect to the sloping character of the lines. There was no evidence of the alleged relation. Bashfulness was ranked and the writing examined for the fineness of the lines at the bend of the upward stroke on the 10 t's in the paragraph. The measurement was made with a microscope with a micrometer in the eye-piece. Statistical data showed that there was no tendency for bashful people to write with fine lines. In a similar way *force* was ranked and the handwriting of each subject was measured. There was no evidence that forceful people cross their t's heavier than anyone else. No correlation could be found with respect to *perseverance* and the length of the bars on the t's. There was no correlation between the closing of the a's and o's and *reserve.*

The tests upon these students thus gave only negative results. When one examines the whole mass of literature bearing upon personality studies of these kinds one is soon convinced that it is a tissue of exaggeration and that the so-called results will not bear critical experimental testing.

B. Habit Disturbance and Its Effect Upon Personality

Introduction.—Within recent years the notion has gained ground that many of the ills that personality is heir to are due rather to failure and inadequacy on the behavior side than to any defect in the organic mechanism. As we pointed out on page 413, the separate organs of the body, heart, lungs and stomach, may all function properly yet the adjustments of the human machine as a whole may be poor and inadequate. The separate anatomical and functional elements are present but integration is bad. We see all the gradations in this lack of integration running from the normal individual who in association tests hesitates upon certain words to the hysterical individual in the clinic who has lost the use of arms, legs or sight.[4]

Without attempting to do more than take a cursory glance at the field of personality disturbance and its causes, which belongs largely to psychiatry, let us consider for a moment some examples taken from laboratory studies where the habit mechanisms are experimentally thrown out of gear and then examine into some of the generalizations which have been made concerning the effects which habit disturbance in daily life has upon personality. Our reason for touching upon the problem of personality disturbance is that no human being, as can be gathered from the preceding part of this chapter, has a perfectly balanced personality. All of us are practical products of our training and heredity. Hence some insight into the factors underlying personality disturbance seems a necessary part of even the most elementary training.

Temporary Disturbance of Habit Experimentally Produced.—Several years ago Stratton made a most interesting series of experiments to test the effect of throwing the visual motor reactions out of gear which was done by wearing lenses, prisms and mirrors in front of the eyes. For example, in one experiment a mirror was worn horizontally over the head and

---

[4] We assume in this discussion of habit disturbance that the organic machine is working properly in the sense that there are no loss of parts, lesions or intoxicants as shown by actual chemical and clinical test.

a small mirror was placed in front of the eye so as to receive the reflected image from the horizontal mirror. The image of the body thus became horizontal instead of vertical. Since two mirrors were used there was no reversal of right and left as when one looks into a glass. "The observer was thus made to watch himself from a point of view apparently above his own head. The field of view included the entire body and a limited region around. . . ."

The experiment continued for three days. When the mirrors were not worn the eyes were blindfolded. The contrivance, of course, threw all of the regular habits out of gear. There was dizziness, loss of balance and marked fumbling of the feet and hands and lack of accurate co-ordination. Objects that were well within range were reached for as though they were at a much greater distance. The process of visual readjustment began almost at once and progressed rapidly. By the end of the third day, although there was occasional fumbling, movements occurred with freedom and precision. In other words, a new habit system had taken the place of the old. The experiment was not continued until the subject became as adept in this new system of visual habits as in the old.

The same phenomenon appeared when lenses were worn in such a way that all visual objects in the field were inverted. Walking and movements of the hands with open eyes were extremely awkward and full of surprises. Naturally, when the subject reacted to objects with eyes closed the old habits reasserted themselves and the reactions were made correctly. "The limb usually started in the opposite direction from the one really desired. When I saw an object near one of my hands and wished to grasp it with that hand the other hand was the one I moved. The mistake was then seen and by trial, observation and correction the desired movement was at last brought about." Again as in the first test new habit systems were established and reactions to the visual objects in the environment became normal. One interesting thing about these experiments is the fact that the moment the lenses or glasses were removed the subject slipped back into his old reaction systems with almost no disturbance. *The disturbing factor had not been present long enough to make the subject react differently from other people after the disturbing environment had been changed.* In a later experiment the tests were continued for a longer time. In this third experiment the right-left relationship of visual objects was again reversed. Stratton discusses his own behavior as follows:

Almost all movements performed under the direct guidance of sight were laborious and embarrassed. Inappropriate movements were constantly made; for instance, in order to move my hand from a place in the visual field to some other place which I had selected, the muscular contractions which would have accomplished this if the normal visual arrangement had existed, now carried my hand to an entirely different place. The movement was then checked off, started off in another direction, and finally, by a series of approximations and corrections, brought to the chosen point. At table the simplest act of serving myself had to be cautiously worked out. The wrong hand was constantly used to seize anything which lay to one side.

By the fifth day at breakfast with the lenses on the inappropriate hand was rarely used to pick up an object lying to one side. The movement itself was easier and less wayward and seldom was it made in an entirely wrong direction. In walking he did not so often run into objects. By the seventh day practically all visual reactions were perfect although some conflict at times appeared. *On removing the glasses on the eighth day there was some disturbance, continuing for that day and into the next morning.* "In walking towards some obstacle on the floor of the room—a chair, for instance—I turned the wrong way in trying to avoid it; so that I frequently either ran into things in the very effort to go around them or else hesitated for a moment, bewildered what I should do. I found myself more than once at a loss which hand I ought to use to grasp the door handle at my side. Of two doors side by side leading to different rooms I was on the point of opening the wrong one. On approaching the stairs I stepped up when nearly a foot too far away, and in writing my notes at this time I continually made a wrong movement of my head in attempting to keep the center of my visual field somewhere near the point where I was writing. I moved my head upward when it should have gone downward; I moved it to the left when it should have gone to the right.'' If one were judging the normality of Stratton's behavior during the first day after the removal of the lenses from the superficial examination of his reactions alone and in ignorance of the causes of the maladjustment, one would draw very wrong conclusions as to his lack of balance and general condition. The visual reactions were undoubtedly sadly ''out of touch with reality'' but the disturbing factors were not present long enough nor under emotional conditions of such a nature as to involve the rest of his organized reactions.

It is of course very difficult in the case of the normal adult whose habit and emotional reactions are highly stabilized to produce any serious and lasting effect upon personality by the introduction of temporary disturbing factors. In the case of the neurotic individual even temporary factors involving the emotions may reduce the total organized reaction system to the level of that of the infant, as is abundantly testified in the cases of shell shock.

It is during infancy and youth that disturbing environmental factors work their most serious and lasting consequences.

The Discarding and Readjusting of Reaction Systems.— During the whole process of human development from infancy to old age, but principally in youth, there goes on not only the process of acquisition of habit and the modification of hereditary reaction but also and equally important that of the elimination of reaction systems which work only up to a certain age. Old situations give way to new and as the situation changes old ways of reacting should be cast off and new ones formed. No normal youngster after a few months of walking slips back to his crawling habits, nor will an older one exhibit his old organized behavior with respect to his blocks and toys after he has learned to use tools. The habits put on in the year gone by simply will not work in the year to come. This is as true with respect to our social activities as to our daily response to objects. The friends of our mature years are as a rule not the friends of our childhood and adolescence. The casting-off process is not an active one but is brought about almost solely by the fact that as age comes on the social and physical environment changes and new habits must be put on if the individual is to remain adjusted to changing conditions. Unquestionably the completeness with which old habits and the emotional factor connected with them which do not work are put away when the new situation is faced, tremendously modifies the type of personality each individual develops into. When the individual is constantly faced by new situations which it can meet, as is normally the case, and when the reaction systems to be outgrown have not been too thoroughly ingrained by bad surroundings, the old order gives way to the new with no scarring and without detrimental factors appearing, but where heredity is bad, where there is sickness in childhood and overindulgence or carelessness in the parents the new orders of habit are put on with the greatest difficulty. The individual then remains hampered by his past. Possibly no one of us escapes unscathed through the childhood and adolescent stages. The early situations when again faced by the adult may not call out the overt infant reactions but they do not wholly lose their power to stir up the old implicit emotional activity. The most convincing evidence for this view comes from psychopathology, but daily life gives us also convincing evidence. A great many individuals have water-tight compartments filled with old reaction systems which resist the storm and stress of adult life. Early religious and social training is modified with difficulty or not at all. Ways of talking and thinking about things learned at the mother's knee remain sometimes unmodified to the bitter end. New situations cannot be reacted to properly until modification occurs—the old habits will not work in the new environment but the old will not give place to the new. The individual thus remains in a permanently unadjusted state. A few illustrations may help in understanding how thwarted tendencies arise and how personality is influenced by them. One individual becomes a psychologist in spite of his strong interest in becoming a medical man because at the time it was easier for him to get the training along psychological lines. Another pursues a business career when if it were possible he would become a writer of plays. Sometimes on account of the care of the mother or of younger brothers and sisters a young man cannot marry even though the mating instinct is normal. Such a course of action necessarily leaves frustrated impulses in its train. Again, a young man will marry and settle down when mature consideration would show that his career would advance much more rapidly if he were not burdened with a family. Another individual marries and without phrasing it in words even to himself that his marriage is a failure he gradually shuts himself off from any emotional expression, protects himself from the married state by substituting for natural domestic ties some kind of engrossing work, but more often hobbies, speed manias and excesses of various kinds. In connection with this it is interesting to note how rapidly women rushed into all kinds of work during the recent war. Women in the present state of society have not the same access to absorbing kinds of work that men have, hence the chances of their outgrowing their adolescence are more limited than in men. If we are right in this analysis these unexercised tendencies to do things other than we are doing are never quite got rid of nor could we get rid of them unless we could build ourselves over again. These maladjustments are exhibited whenever the brakes are off—that is, whenever our adult habits of speech and action are functioning at a low level as in sleep, day-dreaming and in emotional disturbances. For this reason the dream and the slips and accidents of everyday life become of importance in studying personality.

The development of many but not all of these blocked tendencies can be traced to childhood or adolescence, which is a period of strain and excitement. In childhood we often see the boy reacting to his mother in some respects like his father. The girl likewise becomes closely attached to her father and reacts to him as her mother would under certain circumstances. These tendencies from the standpoint of popular morality are perfectly "innocent." But as children grow older they learn from one or another source that such ways of reacting are either "wrong" or unusual; then the process of discarding and replacement is necessary. The replacement or substitution is often very imperfect. The apostle's saying "when we become men we put away childish things" was written before the days of modern psychology. We do not put them away—we replace them but they never for us completely lose their impulsive power. Parents who show excessive emotional reactions toward their children—over much fondling of them—often encourge such reactions and make normal substitution more difficult. Later on in life the old habit systems may show themselves in overt ways. Now and then we find a young man whose mother has long since died who can find little attraction in the girls with whom he associates. He himself can advance no reason for this apathy and would possibly become angry if the true explanation were offered him. In a similar way adults may become too much attached to children. This is often seen in the case of a woman whose husband has died leaving her with an only son. The son becomes substituted for the father and her reactions which she looks upon as those belonging merely to a devoted mother soon take on certain characteristics of those she would show to her husband.

These illustrations have all been chosen from the sphere of normal life. They give us an insight into the character and personality of individuals. They show that in order to understand a person's weaknesses and strength we have to have more than a superficial acquaintance with him. Character and personality are not formed over night nor are they of mushroomlike growth. In summary it seems safe to generalize: *youthful, outgrown and partially discarded habit and instinctive systems of reaction can and possibly always do influence the functioning of our adult systems of reaction and influence to a certain extent even the possibility of our forming the new habit systems which we must reasonably be expected to form.*

Psychopathological Aspects of Habit Distortion.—As psychologists studying normal behavior we shall venture only so far into the realm of psychopathology as to trace the connection between habit distortion discussed above and the psychiatrist's conception of what he calls a "mental disease." As is well known,

there is a growing tendency on the part of modern psychopathologists to break away from the pathologists' conception of disease
in those patients suffering from personality disturbance. When
the pathologist and physiologist visit the psychiatric hospital
they are likely at once to cast around for an adequate explanation of the patient's condition in terms of brain cell lesions,
infections, intoxications and the like. It is as unthinkable to
many of them as it is to the man on the street that an adequate
account of the patient's disease from a causal standpoint can
be given without appeal to pathology, to physiology or to medical chemistry. Many believe that in such cases (the purely
functional cases) the neurological and chemical tests should and
must necessarily show some variation from the normal, and when
no such organic disturbance can be found they insist that the
changes are there but are of so delicate a nature that they
escape observation. Possibly this may be true in some cases,
but the conviction is growing that no organic lesions need be
found to account for the facts and that when found they are not
necessarily the important factors. In other words, we can have a
diseased personality arising through habit distortion—distortion carried to the point where the compensatory factors (serviceable habits) are not sufficient to carry the individual along
in society. He is out of touch with his environment and unless
help is given him he will most certainly go down under
competition. As we have pointed out, the habit distortions may
and do often start in infancy. The indulgent mother favors a certain child, allows it to eat what it wants, to play with what it calls
for, puts no authority upon it, does everything for it and even
anticipates its demands. Under such a regime walking and talking are delayed. Crying, yelling, kicking and screaming are
resorted to when demands are denied. During boyhood he is petted
and spoiled. His side is taken whenever the other boys attempt to
give him the knocks that would straighten him out. His studies
are not enforced, he is not taught to work, to earn extra pennies
or to accept his share of responsibility. Lying and cheating are
not early enough dealt with. Normal burden bearing and responsibility for his own mishaps are not inculcated. As long as the
old favoring environment lasts he floats, but when a crisis occurs,

when he is forced to face the world unaided, he has not the assets with which to do it. His equipment is inadequate. The world is full of such floating wrecks, many of which owing to favorable environment never reach a psychiatric clinic. The war brought some interesting cases. One possibly may be mentioned. The draft caught a man thirty-five years of age of robust constitution. The father had died during the infancy of this individual. The mother was distraught and petitioned Congress and the President direct to get him out of the service on the ground that he was ''her baby'' and that she had had to sleep with him every night since his birth. While the thirty-five-year-old baby was at home the mother kept herself well groomed and was generally alert and cheerful. After his entrance into the service she grew slovenly and despondent. Having some wealth and influence she finally succeeded in getting her son discharged, whereupon the happy relationship was again resumed. Without much question another six months of life without the son would have brought the mother to a clinic. Both of these individuals have diseased personalities as ravaging in their effects as tuberculosis or cancer. But it is futile to hunt for any organic disturbance. They are in the state they are in because of the kinds of adjustment which were never put aside at normal times. The proof that personality disturbances are due to long-continued behavior complications and not to organic disturbances appears from the fact that in many cases, under new and suitable environment the old reactions can be broken down and new ones entrained. The individual is made over from a reaction standpoint and takes his normal place in society. The re-training (''cure''), although more difficult, is neither more nor less mysterious and wonderful than teaching the infant to reach for candy and to withdraw his hand from a candle flame.

Concluding Statements.—Our personality is thus the result of what we start with and what we have lived through. It is the ''reaction mass'' as a whole. The largest component of the mass if we are normal consists of clean-cut and definite habit systems, instincts that have yielded to social control and emotions which have been tempered and modified by the hard knocks received in the school of reality.

INDEX

441